Yvette 6-3-01

May God bless you and keep you.

Ps. 121

Sunnyslope CRC

SPURGEON'S DAILY TREASURY FROM THE PSALMS

SPURGEON'S
DAILY TREASURY
from the
PSALMS

ROBERT BACKHOUSE, EDITOR

CROSSWAY BOOKS

A DIVISION OF
GOOD NEWS PUBLISHERS
WHEATON, ILLINOIS

Spurgeon's Daily Treasury from the Psalms

Adapted from *The Treasury of David* by Charles Haddon Spurgeon

Copyright © 2002 by Good News Publishers / Crossway Books

Published by Crossway Books
        A division of Good News Publishers
        1300 Crescent Street
        Wheaton, Illinois 60187

All rights reserved. No part of this publication may be reproduced, stored in a retrieval system or transmitted in any form by any means, electronic, mechanical, photocopy, recording, or otherwise, without the prior permission of the publisher, except as provided by USA copyright law.

All Scripture quotations are from the King James Version.

Cover design: Cindy Kiple

First printing, 2002

Printed in the United States of America

Library of Congress Cataloging-in-Publication Data
Spurgeon, C. H. (Charles Haddon), 1834-1892/
  Spurgeon's daily treasury from the Psalms : adapted from The treasury of David / by Charles Haddon Spurgeon
    p. cm.
    ISBN 1-58134-361-2
  1. Bible. O.T. Psalms—Meditations. 2. Devotional calendars. I. Title: Daily treasury from the Psalms. II. Spurgeon, C. H. (Charles Haddon), 1834-1892. Treasury of David. III. Title.
BS1430.4 .S67   2002
242'.2—dc21   2002003046

LB		13	12	11	10	09	08	07	06	05	04	03	02
15	14	13	12	11	10	9	8	7	6	5	4	3	2	1

SPURGEON'S
DAILY TREASURY
from the
PSALMS

Publisher's Foreword

Charles Haddon Spurgeon (1834-1892) was England's best-known preacher for most of the second half of the nineteenth century. In 1854, just a few years after his conversion, Spurgeon, only twenty years old, became pastor of London's largest Baptist congregation, the New Park Street Church. He frequently preached to congregations of 10,000 or more. In 1861 the congregation moved permanently to the newly constructed Metropolitan Tabernacle.

Perhaps no Bible book has been more read or loved than the book of Psalms. And Spurgeon's choice comments on the Psalms (*The Treasury of David*, originally seven volumes) have fueled the faith of believers for more than a hundred and thirty years. Few preachers and authors have been more loved and appreciated than Spurgeon.

J. I. Packer in his preface to Spurgeon's *Psalms* in the Crossway Classic Commentaries series has well expressed the many facets of Charles H. Spurgeon: "A perky countryman, a witty depressive, and a self-educated theologian, he was hugely intelligent, massively commonsensical, and totally masterful in utterance. He was a deep, sharp, well-read, high-powered thinker whose easy eloquence, compounded as it was of clarity, simplicity, vividness, and humor, riveted everyone who ever listened to him. And he was a robust saint of the Augustinian and Puritan type, who with unflagging freshness projected the many-sided relationship between God the Creator and the sinners whom he loves and saves through Jesus Christ as the most wonderful and important thing in the world."

Spurgeon wrote hundreds of books, many of which are still in print today. But perhaps his greatest and best-known work was *The Treasury of David*, an unequalled devotional commentary on the Psalms. This work was first published in weekly installments over twenty years in the London Metropolitan Tabernacle's periodical, *The Sword and the Trowel*. Completed sections were published volume by volume until the seventh and final volume was released in 1885.

Like millions of believers before and after him, Spurgeon found his time in the book of Psalms nurturing, challenging, and profitable for spiritual vitality. He wrote in his preface to the *Treasury*, "The delightful study of the Psalms has yielded me boundless profit and ever-growing pleasure; common gratitude constrains me to communicate to others a portion of the benefit, with the prayer that it may induce them to search further for themselves. That I have nothing better of my own to offer upon this peerless book is to me matter of regret; that I have anything whatever to present is subject for devout gratitude to the Lord of grace."

The book of Psalms has indeed been a treasury for God's people through the ages. Strength for the weary, hope for the defeated or despairing, assurance of love for the rejected, forgiveness for the fallen, comfort for the saddened—what a marvelous channel of God's tender grace for all.

Spurgeon's Daily Treasury from the Psalms is a year's worth of daily readings carefully excerpted by Robert Backhouse from the great preacher's *magnum opus*, complete with a reading plan that will take one through the entire book of Psalms in a year. A pilgrimage through the Psalms with this master communicator will draw believers closer to the God they love and adore.

It is with delight and anticipation that we release *Spurgeon's Daily Treasury from the Psalms*, with the hope that many readers will join C. H. Spurgeon and the many saints who have walked in his footsteps in the adventure of meditating upon and living out the book of Psalms. May your journey through the Psalms, when your life is peaceful and when it is difficult, be one of joy and increasing devotion to the Lord who loves and bought you!

The Publisher

JANUARY 1

LIKE A TREE PLANTED

*And he shall be like a tree planted by the rivers of water,
that bringeth forth his fruit in his season;
his leaf also shall not wither; and whatsoever he doeth shall prosper.*

PSALM 1:3

VERSE 1: "Blessed is the man." See how this Book of Psalms opens with a benediction, as did the famous Sermon of our Lord on the Mount! We might read it, "Oh, the blessedness!" and we may well regard this as a joyful acclamation of the gracious person's felicity. May the like blessedness rest on us!

VERSE 2: "But his delight is in the law of the LORD." He is not *under* the law as a curse and condemnation, but he is *in* it, and he delights to be in it as the rule of life. He delights, moreover, to "meditate" in it, to read it by "day" and to think upon it by "night."

VERSE 3: "And he shall be like a tree planted." Not a wild tree, but one "planted," chosen, considered as cultivated and secured from the last terrible uprooting (see Matthew 15:13). "By the rivers of water." Even if one river should fail, he has another. The rivers of pardon and the rivers of grace, the rivers of promise and the rivers of communion with Christ are never-failing sources of supply. "That bringeth forth his fruit in his season." Not unseasonable graces, like untimely figs, which are never full-flavored. Rather the person who delights in God's Word, being taught by it, brings forth patience in the time of suffering, faith in the day of trial, and holy joy in the hour of prosperity. Fruitfulness is an essential quality of a gracious person, and that fruitfulness should be seasonable. "His leaf also shall not wither." His faintest word will be everlasting; his little deeds of love will be remembered. Not only will his fruit be preserved, but "his leaf" also. He will neither lose his beauty nor his fruitfulness. "And whatsoever he doeth shall prosper." Blessed is the man who has such a promise as this.

Verses to meditate upon today: Psalm 1:1-6.

A THOUGHT TO PONDER

Fruitfulness is an essential quality of a gracious person.

JANUARY 2

THE KINGS OF THE EARTH

He that sitteth in the heavens shall laugh: the LORD shall have them in derision.
PSALM 2:4

VERSE 4: Let us now turn our eyes from the wicked counsel-chamber and raging tumult of man (verses 1-3) to the secret place of the majesty of the Most High. What does God say? What will the King do to the men who reject his only-begotten Son, the Heir of all things?

Mark the quiet dignity of the Omnipotent One, and the contempt that he pours upon the princes and their raging people. He has not taken the trouble to rise up and do battle with them—he despises them. He knows how absurd, how irrational, how futile are their attempts against him; he therefore laughs at them.

VERSE 5: After he has laughed he shall "speak." He needs not smite; the breath of his lips is enough. At the moment when their power is at its height and their fury most violent, "then" shall his Word go forth against them. And what is it that he says?—it is a very galling sentence—"yet," says he, despite your malice, despite your tumultuous gatherings, despite the wisdom of your counsels, despite the craft of your lawgivers, "yet have I set my king upon my holy hill of Zion" (verse 6).

Is not that a grand exclamation! He has already done what the enemy seeks to prevent. While they are proposing, he has disposed the matter. Jehovah's will is done, and man's will frets and raves in vain. God's Anointed is appointed and shall not be disappointed.

The first Psalm was a contrast between the righteous man and the sinner; the second Psalm is a contrast between the tumultuous disobedience of the ungodly world and the sure exaltation of the righteous Son of God. In the first Psalm we saw the wicked driven away like chaff; in the second Psalm we see them broken in pieces like a potter's vessel.

Verses to meditate upon today: Psalm 2:1-6.

A THOUGHT TO PONDER
God's Anointed is appointed and shall not be disappointed.

JANUARY 3

BE WISE

Serve the LORD with fear, and rejoice with trembling.
PSALM 2:11

VERSE 10: "Be wise." It is always "wise" to be willing to be instructed, especially when such instruction tends to the salvation of the soul. "Be wise" now therefore; delay no longer, but let good reason weigh with you. Your warfare cannot succeed; therefore desist and yield cheerfully to him who will make you bow if you refuse his yoke.

Oh, how "wise," how infinitely "wise" is obedience to Jesus, and how dreadful is the folly of those who continue to be his enemies!

VERSE 11: "Serve the LORD with fear." Let reverence and humility be mingled with your service. He is a great God, and you are but puny creatures; bend, therefore, in lowly worship, and let a filial fear mingle with all your obedience to the great Father of the Ages.

"Rejoice with trembling." There must ever be a holy fear mixed with the Christian's joy. This is a sacred compound, yielding a sweet smell, and we must see to it that we burn no other upon the altar. Fear without joy is torment; and joy without holy "fear" would be presumption. Mark the solemn argument for reconciliation and obedience.

VERSE 12: It is an awful thing to "perish" in the midst of sin, in the very "way" of rebellion; and yet how easily could "his wrath" destroy us suddenly. This requires not that his anger be heated seven times hotter; let the fuel be "kindled but a little" and we are consumed. O sinner, take heed of the terrors of the Lord, for "our God is a consuming fire."

Note the benediction with which the Psalm closes—"Blessed are all they that put their trust in him." Have we a share in this blessedness? Do we "trust in him"? Our faith may be as slender as a spider's thread; but if it be real, we are in our measure "blessed."

Verses to meditate upon today: Psalm 2:7-12.

A THOUGHT TO PONDER
Fear without joy is torment; and joy without holy "fear" would be presumption.

JANUARY 4

Protected by God

But thou, O Lord, art a shield for me; my glory, and the lifter up of mine head.
PSALM 3:3

Verse 3: Here David avows his confidence in God. "Thou, O Lord, art a shield for me." The word in the original signifies more than a shield; it means a buckler round about, a protection that shall surround a man entirely—a "shield" above, beneath, around, without, and within. Oh, what "a shield" is God for his people! He wards off the fiery darts of Satan from beneath and the storms of trials from above, while at the same instant he speaks peace to the tempest within.

"Thou . . . art . . . my glory." David knew that though he was driven from his capital in contempt and scorn, he would yet return in triumph, and by faith he looks upon God as honoring and glorifying him. Oh, for grace to see our future glory in the middle of present shame! Indeed, there is a present glory in our afflictions, if we could but discern it; for it is no mean thing to have fellowship with Christ in his sufferings. David was honored when he made the ascent of Olivet, weeping, with his head covered, for he was in all this made like unto his Lord. May we learn, in this respect, to glory in tribulations also!

"And the lifter up of mine head"—*you shall yet exalt me. Though I hang my head in sorrow, I shall very soon lift it up in joy and thanksgiving.* What a divine trio of mercies is contained in this verse—defense for the defenseless, glory for the despised, and joy for the comfortless. Verily we may well say, "There is none like the God of Jeshurun."

Verse 4: "I cried unto the Lord with my voice." Why does he say, "with my voice"? Surely, silent prayers are heard. Yes, but good men often find that, even in secret, they pray better aloud than they do when they utter no vocal sound. Perhaps, moreover, David would think thus: *My cruel enemies clamor against me; they lift up their voices, and, behold, I lift up mine, and my cry outsoars them all.*

Verses to meditate upon today: Psalm 3:1-8.

A Thought to Ponder

Defense for the defenseless, glory for the despised, and joy for the comfortless.

JANUARY 5

HELP IN TIMES OF TROUBLE

Hear me when I call, O God of my righteousness: thou hast enlarged me when I was in distress; have mercy upon me, and hear my prayer.

PSALM 4:1

VERSE 1: This is another instance of David's common habit of pleading past mercies as a ground for present favor. Here he reviews his Ebenezers and takes comfort from them. It is not to be imagined that he who has helped us in six troubles will leave us in the seventh. God does nothing by halves, and he will never cease to help us until we cease to need. The manna shall fall every morning until we cross the Jordan.

Observe that David speaks first to God and then to men. Surely we would all speak the more boldly to men if we had more constant conversation with God. He who dares to face his Maker will not tremble before the sons of men.

The name by which the Lord is here addressed, "God of my righteousness," deserves notice, since it is not used in any other part of Scripture. It means, "Thou art the author, the witness, the maintainer, the judge, and the rewarder of my righteousness; to thee I appeal from the calumnies and harsh judgments of men." Herein is wisdom; so let us imitate it and always take our suit not to the petty courts of human opinion, but into the superior court, the King's Bench of heaven.

"Thou hast enlarged me when I was in distress." This figure is taken from an army hard-pressed by the surrounding enemy. *God has dashed down the rocks and given me room; he has broken the barriers and set me in a large place.* Or we may understand it thus: *God has enlarged my heart with joy and comfort, when I was like a man imprisoned by grief and sorrow.* God is a never-failing comforter.

"Have mercy upon me." *Though you may justly permit my enemies to destroy me on account of my many and great sins, yet I flee to your mercy, and I beseech you, "hear my prayer" and bring your servant out of his troubles.*

Verses to meditate upon today: Psalm 4:1-8.

A THOUGHT TO PONDER

God is a never-failing comforter.

JANUARY 6

WORSHIP

But as for me, I will come into thy house in the multitude of thy mercy:
and in thy fear will I worship toward thy holy temple.

PSALM 5:7

VERSE 3: This is not so much a prayer as a resolution: "My voice shalt thou hear." *I will not be dumb, I will not be silent, I will not withhold my speech. I will cry to you, for the fire that dwells within compels me to pray.* We can sooner die than live without prayer. None of God's children are possessed with a dumb devil.

VERSE 7: With this verse the first part of the Psalm ends. The psalmist has bent his knee in prayer; he has described before God, as an argument for his deliverance, the character and the fate of the wicked; and now he contrasts this with the condition of the righteous. "But as for me, I will come into thy house." *I will not stand at a distance. I will come into your sanctuary just as a child comes into his father's house. But I will not come there by my own merits; no, for I have a multitude of sins, and therefore I will come "in the multitude of thy mercy." I will approach you with confidence because of your immeasurable grace.* God's judgments are all numbered, but his mercies are innumerable. "And in thy fear will I worship toward thy holy temple"—toward the temple of his holiness. The temple was not built on earth at that time; it was but a tabernacle. But David was inclined to turn his eyes spiritually to that temple of God's holiness where between the wings of the cherubim Jehovah dwells in light ineffable. Daniel opened his window toward Jerusalem, but we open our hearts toward heaven.

Verses to meditate upon today: Psalm 5:1-7.

A THOUGHT TO PONDER
Daniel opened his window toward Jerusalem,
but we open our hearts toward heaven.

JANUARY 7

GOD'S RIGHTEOUSNESS

*Lead me, O LORD, in thy righteousness because of mine enemies;
make thy way straight before my face.*

PSALM 5:8

VERSE 8: "Lead me, O LORD," as a little child is led by his father, as a blind man is guided by his friend. It is safe and pleasant walking when God leads the way. "In thy righteousness"; *not in my righteousness, for that is imperfect, but in yours, for you are righteousness itself.* "Make thy way," not *my* way, "straight before my face." Brethren, when we have learned to give up our own way and long to walk in God's way, it is a happy sign of grace; and it is no small mercy to see the way of God with clear vision straight before our face. Errors about duty may lead us into a sea of sins before we know where we are.

VERSE 9: This description of depraved man has been copied by the apostle Paul, and, together with some other quotations, he has placed it in the second chapter of Romans as being an accurate description of the whole human race—not of David's enemies only, but of all men by nature. Note that remarkable figure, "their throat is an open sepulchre," a "sepulchre" full of loathsomeness, of pestilence and death. But worse than that, it is an "open" sepulchre, with all its evil gases issuing forth, spreading death and destruction all around. So with the throat of the wicked, it would be a great mercy if it could always be closed. If we could seal the mouth of the wicked in continual silence, it would be like a sepulchre shut up and would not produce much mischief.

But their throat is an "open" sepulchre, and consequently all the wickedness of their heart exhales and comes forth. How dangerous is an "open sepulchre"; men in their journeys might easily stumble therein and find themselves among the dead.

Verses to meditate upon today: Psalm 5:8-12.

A THOUGHT TO PONDER

You are righteousness itself.

JANUARY 8

Healing and Deliverance

*Have mercy upon me, O LORD; for I am weak: O LORD, heal me;
for my bones are vexed.*
Psalm 6:2

Verse 2: "Have mercy upon me, O LORD; for I am weak." *Though I deserve destruction, yet let your mercy pity my frailty.* This is the right way to plead with God if we would prevail. Urge not your goodness or your greatness, but plead your sin and your littleness. Cry, *"I am weak"*; therefore, O Lord, give me strength and crush me not. Send not forth the fury of your tempest against so weak a vessel. Soften the wind for the shorn lamb. Be tender and pitiful to a poor withering flower, and break it not from its stem.

Surely this is the plea that a sick man would make to move the pity of his fellow if he were striving with him: "Deal gently with me, 'for I am weak.'" A sense of sin had so spoiled the psalmist's pride, so taken away his vaunted strength, that he found himself weak to obey the law, weak through the sorrow that was in him, too weak perhaps to lay hold on the promise.

"I am weak." The original may be read, "I am one who droops," withered like a blighted plant. Ah, beloved, we know what this means, for we too have seen our glory stained and our beauty like a faded flower.

"O LORD, heal me; for my bones are vexed." Here he prays for *healing*—not merely the mitigation of the ills he endured, but their entire removal, and the curing of the wounds that had arisen therefrom. His bones were *shaken*, as the Hebrew has it. His terror had become so great that his very bones shook; not only did his flesh quiver, but the bones, the solid pillars of the house of manhood, were made to tremble. My bones are shaken, he says. Ah, when the soul has a sense of sin, it is enough to make the bones shake; it makes a man's hair stand on end when he sees the flames of hell beneath him, an angry God above him, and danger and doubt surrounding him.

Verses to meditate upon today: Psalm 6:1-5.

A Thought to Ponder

Urge not your goodness or your greatness, but plead your sin and your littleness.

JANUARY 9

ACCEPTED PRAYER

The LORD hath heard my supplication; the LORD will receive my prayer.
PSALM 6:9

VERSE 9: "The LORD hath heard my supplication." The Holy Spirit had wrought into the psalmist's mind the confidence that his prayer was heard. This is frequently the privilege of the saints. Praying the prayer of faith, they are often infallibly assured that they have prevailed with God.

We read of Luther that, having on one occasion wrestled hard with God in prayer, he came leaping out of his closet crying, *"Vicimus, vicimus"*; that is, "We have conquered, we have prevailed with God." Assured confidence is no idle dream, for when the Holy Spirit bestows it upon us, we know its reality and could not doubt it, even though all men should deride our boldness.

"The LORD will receive my prayer." Here is past experience used for future encouragement. *He hath, he will.* Note this, O believer, and imitate its reasoning.

VERSE 10: "Let all mine enemies be ashamed and sore vexed." This is a prophecy rather than an imprecation; it may be read in the future: "All my enemies shall be ashamed and sore vexed." They shall "return and be ashamed" instantaneously—in a moment; their doom shall come upon them suddenly. Death's day is doom's day, and both are sure and may be sudden.

The Romans were wont to say, "The feet of the avenging Deity are shod with wool." But with noiseless footsteps vengeance nears its victim, and sudden and overwhelming shall be its destroying stroke. If this were an imprecation, we must remember that the language of the old dispensation is not that of the new. We pray *for* our enemies, not *against* them. May God have mercy on them and bring them into the right way.

Thus this Psalm, like those that precede it, shows the different estates of the godly and the wicked. *O Lord, let us be numbered with your people, both now and forever!*

Verses to meditate upon today: Psalm 6:6-10.

A THOUGHT TO PONDER
Assured confidence is no idle dream, for when the Holy Spirit bestows it upon us, we know its reality.

JANUARY 10

GOD IS MY REFUGE

O LORD my God, in thee do I put my trust:
save me from all them that persecute me, and deliver me.
PSALM 7:1

VERSE 1: David appears before God to plead with him against the accuser, who had charged him with treason and treachery. The case is here opened with an avowal of confidence in God. Whatever may be the emergency of our condition, we shall never find it amiss to retain our reliance upon our God.

"O LORD *my* God," mine by a special covenant, sealed by Jesus' blood, and ratified in my own soul by a sense of union to you; "in thee," and "in thee" only, "do I put my trust," even now in my sore distress. I shake, but my rock moves not. It is never right to distrust God, and never vain to trust him.

And now, with both divine relationship and holy trust to strengthen him, David utters the burden of his desire: "save me from all them that persecute me." His pursuers were very many, and any one of them cruel enough to devour him; he cries, therefore, for salvation from them all. We should never think our prayers complete until we ask for preservation from *all* sin and *all* enemies.

"And deliver me," extricate me from their snares, acquit me of their accusations, give a true and just deliverance in this trial of my injured character. See how clearly his case is stated. Let us see to it that we know what we would have when we come to the throne of mercy. Pause a little while before you pray, that you may not offer the sacrifice of fools. Get a distinct idea of your need, and then you can pray with more fluent fervency.

VERSE 2: "Lest he tear my soul." Here is the plea of fear coworking with the plea of faith. There was one among David's foes mightier than the rest, who had both dignity, strength, and ferocity and was therefore "like a lion." From this foe he urgently seeks deliverance.

Verses to meditate upon today: Psalm 7:1-9.

A THOUGHT TO PONDER
It is never right to distrust God, and never vain to trust him.

JANUARY 11

GOD IS JUDGE

God judgeth the righteous, and God is angry with the wicked every day.
PSALM 7:11

VERSE 11: "God judgeth the righteous." He has not given you up to be condemned by the lips of persecutors. Your enemies cannot sit on God's throne, nor blot your name out of his book. Let them alone, then, for God will find time for his revenge.

"God is angry with the wicked every day." He not only detests sin but is angry with those who continue to indulge in it. We have no unfeeling God to deal with; he can be angry, nay, he *is* angry today and every day with you, you ungodly and impenitent sinners. The best day that ever dawns on a sinner brings a curse with it. Sinners may have many feast days, but no safe days. From the beginning of the year even to its ending, there is not an hour in which God's oven is not hot and burning in readiness for the wicked, who shall be as stubble.

VERSE 12: "If he turn not, he will whet his sword." What blows are those that will be dealt by that long uplifted arm! God's "sword" has been sharpening upon the revolving stone of our daily wickedness, and if we will not repent, it will speedily cut us in pieces. Turn or burn are the sinner's only alternatives. "He hath bent his bow, and made it ready."

VERSE 13: Even now the thirsty arrow longs to wet itself with the blood of the "persecutors." The bow is bent, the aim is taken, the arrow is fitted to the string, and what, O sinner, if the arrow should be let fly at you even now! Remember, God's "arrows" never miss the mark and are, every one of them, "instruments of death." Judgment may tarry, but it will not come too late. The Greek proverb says, "The mill of God grinds late, but grinds to powder."

Verses to meditate upon today: Psalm 7:10-13.

A THOUGHT TO PONDER
"The mill of God grinds late, but grinds to powder."

JANUARY 12

THE SLANDERER

Behold, he travaileth with iniquity, and hath conceived mischief, and brought forth falsehood.

PSALM 7:14

VERSE 14: In three graphic pictures we see the slanderer's history. A woman in travail furnishes the first metaphor. "He travaileth with iniquity." He is full of it, pained until he can carry it out; he longs to work his will; he is full of pangs until his evil intent is executed.

He "hath conceived mischief." This is the beginning of his base design. The devil has had doings with him, and the virus of evil is in him. And now behold the progeny of this unhallowed conception. The child is worthy of its father—his name of old was "the father of lies"; and the birth doth not belie the parent, for he "brought forth falsehood." Thus one figure is carried out to perfection; the psalmist now illustrates his meaning by another, taken from the stratagems of the hunter.

VERSE 15: "He made a pit, and digged it." He was cunning in his plans and industrious in his labors. He stooped to the dirty work of digging. He did not fear to soil his own hands; he was willing to work in a "ditch" if others might fall therein. What mean things men will do to wreak revenge on the godly. They hunt for good men as if they were brute beasts; nay, they will not give them the fair chase afforded to the hare or the fox, but must secretly entrap them because they can neither run them down nor shoot them down. Our enemies will not meet us face to face, for they fear us as much as they pretend to despise us.

But let us look on to the end of the scene. The verse says, he "is fallen into the ditch which he made." Ah! there he is; let us laugh at his disappointment. Lo, he is himself the beast, he has hunted his own soul, and the chase has brought him a victim.

Verses to meditate upon today: Psalm 7:14-17.

A THOUGHT TO PONDER

He is himself the beast, he has hunted his own soul.

JANUARY 13

LOOKING AT THE STARS

O LORD, our Lord, how excellent is thy name in all the earth!
who hast set thy glory above the heavens.
PSALM 8:1

VERSE 1: Unable to express the glory of God, the psalmist utters a note of exclamation. "O Jehovah, our Lord." We need not wonder at this, for no heart can measure, no tongue can utter, the half of the greatness of Jehovah. The whole creation is full of his glory and is radiant with the excellency of his power; his goodness and his wisdom are manifested on every hand.

And not on earth alone is Jehovah extolled, for his brightness shines forth in the firmament above the earth. His glory exceeds the glory of the starry "heavens"; above the region of the stars he has set fast his everlasting throne, and there he dwells in light ineffable.

Let us adore him who "alone spreadeth out the heavens, and treadeth upon the waves of the sea; which maketh Arcturus, Orion, and Pleiades, and the chambers of the south" (Job 9:8-9.) We can scarcely find more fitting words than those of Nehemiah: "Thou, even thou, art LORD alone; thou hast made heaven, the heaven of heavens, with all their host, the earth, and all things that are therein, the seas, and all that is therein, and thou preservest them all; and the host of heaven worshippeth thee" (Nehemiah 9:6).

Returning to the text we are led to observe that this Psalm is addressed to God, because none but the Lord himself can fully know his own glory. The believing heart is ravished with what it sees, but only God knows the glory of God. What a sweetness lies in the little word "our"; how much is God's glory endeared to us when we consider our interest in him as "*our* Lord."

"How excellent is thy name . . . !" No words can express that excellency; and therefore it is proclaimed as a note of exclamation. The very "name" of Jehovah is excellent; so what must his person be. Note the fact that even "the heavens" cannot contain his "glory"; it is set "above the heavens," since it is and ever must be too great for the creature to express.

Verses to meditate upon today: Psalm 8:1-9.

A THOUGHT TO PONDER
The believing heart is ravished with what it sees, but only God knows the glory of God.

JANUARY 14

PRAISING GOD

I will praise thee, O LORD, with my whole heart;
I will show forth all thy marvelous works.

PSALM 9:1

VERSE 1: With a holy resolution the songster begins his hymn: "I will praise thee, O LORD." It sometimes takes all our determination to face the foe and to bless the Lord in the teeth of his enemies, vowing that whoever else may be silent *we* will bless his name. In this Psalm, however, the overthrow of the foe is viewed as complete, and the song flows with sacred fullness of delight.

It is our duty to praise the Lord; let us perform it as a privilege. Observe that David's praise is all given to the Lord. Praise is to be offered to God alone; we may be grateful to the intermediate agent, but our thanks must have long wings and mount aloft to heaven.

"With my whole heart." Half a heart is no heart. "I will show forth." There is true praise in the thankful telling forth to others our heavenly Father's dealings with us. This is one of the themes upon which the godly should speak often to one another, and it will not be casting pearls before swine if we make even the ungodly hear of the loving-kindness of the Lord to us.

"All thy marvelous works." Gratitude for one mercy summons the memory of thousands of others. One silver link in the chain draws up a long series of tender remembrances. Here is eternal work for us, for there can be no end to the showing forth of "all" his deeds of love. If we consider our own sinfulness and nothingness, we must feel that every work of preservation, forgiveness, conversion, deliverance, sanctification, etc., that the Lord has wrought for us or in us is a "marvelous" work. Even in heaven, divine lovingkindness will doubtless be as much a theme of surprise as of rapture.

Verses to meditate upon today: Psalm 9:1-6.

A THOUGHT TO PONDER
It is our duty to praise the Lord; let us perform it as a privilege.

JANUARY 15

A Refuge for the Oppressed

The LORD also will be a refuge for the oppressed, a refuge in times of trouble.
PSALM 9:9

VERSE 9: He who gives no quarter to the wicked in the day of judgment is the defense and refuge of his saints in the day of trouble. There are many forms of oppression; both from man and from Satan oppression comes to us. And for all its forms, "a refuge" is provided in the Lord Jehovah. There were cities of refuge under the law; God is our refuge-city under the Gospel. As the ships when vexed with tempest make for harbor, so do the oppressed hasten to the wings of a just and gracious God. He is a high tower so impregnable that the hosts of hell cannot carry it by storm, and from its lofty heights faith looks down with scorn upon her enemies.

VERSE 10: Ignorance is worst when it amounts to ignorance of God, and knowledge is best when it exercises itself upon the "name" of God. This most excellent knowledge leads to the most excellent grace of faith. Oh, to learn more of the attributes and character of God. Unbelief, that hooting nightbird, cannot live in the light of divine knowledge; it flies away before the sun of God's great and gracious name. The Lord may hide his face for a season from his people, but he never has utterly, finally, really, or angrily "forsaken them that seek" him. Let the poor seekers draw comfort from this fact, and let the finders rejoice yet more exceedingly, for what must be the Lord's faithfulness to those who find if he is so gracious to those who seek.

> *O hope of every contrite heart,*
> *O joy of all the meek,*
> *To those who fall, how kind thou art!*
> *How good to those who seek!*
> *But what to those who find? Ah, this—*
> *Nor tongue nor pen can show*
> *The love of Jesus, what it is*
> *None but his loved ones know.*

Verses to meditate upon today: Psalm 9:7-12.

A Thought to Ponder
Oh, to learn more of the attributes and character of God.

JANUARY 16

A LITTLE PRAYER BOOK

Have mercy upon me, O LORD; consider my trouble which I suffer of them that hate me, thou that liftest me up from the gates of death.

PSALM 9:13

VERSE 13: Memories of the past and confidences concerning the future conducted the man of God to the mercy seat to plead for the needs of the present. Between praising and praying he divided all his time. How could he have spent it more profitably? His first prayer is one suitable for all persons and occasions; it breathes a humble spirit, indicates self-knowledge, and appeals to the proper attributes and to the fitting person. "Have mercy upon me, O LORD."

Just as Luther used to call some texts little Bibles, so we may call this sentence a little prayer book, for it has in it the soul and marrow of prayer. It is *multum in parvo* (much in little) and, like the angelic sword, turns every way. The ladder appears to be short, but it reaches from earth to heaven.

What a noble title is here given to the Most High. "Thou that liftest me up from the gates of death." What a glorious lift! In sickness, in sin, in despair, in temptation, we have been brought very low, and the gloomy portal has seemed as if it would open to imprison us; but underneath us were the everlasting arms, and therefore we have been uplifted even to the gates of heaven. Trapp quaintly says, "He commonly reserveth his hand for a dead lift, and rescueth those who were even talking of their graves."

VERSE 14: We must not overlook David's object in desiring mercy—it is God's glory: "that I may show forth all thy praise." Saints are not so selfish as to look only to self; they desire mercy's diamond that they may let others see it flash and sparkle and may admire him who gives such priceless gems to his beloved. The contrast between "the gates of death" and the gates of the New Jerusalem is very striking; let our songs be excited to the highest and most rapturous pitch.

Verses to meditate upon today: Psalm 9:13-20.

A THOUGHT TO PONDER

Just as Luther used to call some texts little Bibles, so we may call this sentence a little prayer book.

JANUARY 17

IN TIMES OF TROUBLE

Why standest thou afar off, O LORD? Why hidest thou thyself in times of trouble?
PSALM 10:1

VERSE 1: To the tearful eye of the sufferer, the Lord seemed to stand still, as if he calmly looked on and did not sympathize with his afflicted one. Nay, more, the Lord appeared to be "afar off," no longer "a very present help in trouble" (Psalm 46:1) but an inaccessible mountain that no man would be able to climb.

The presence of God is the joy of his people, but any suspicion of his absence is distracting beyond measure. Let us, then, ever remember that the Lord is nigh to us. The refiner is never far from the mouth of the furnace when his gold is in the fire, and the Son of God is always walking in the midst of the flames when his holy children are cast into them. Yet he knows that as frail men and women we easily question when we are sharply exercised, that we find it hard to bear the apparent neglect of the Lord when he forbears to work our deliverance.

"Why hidest thou thyself in times of trouble?" It is not the "trouble" but the hiding of our Father's face that cuts us to the quick. When trial and desertion come together, we are in as perilous a plight as Paul when his ship fell into a place where two seas met (Acts 27:41). It is but little wonder if we are like the vessel that ran aground, and the forepart stuck fast and remained unmovable while the hinder part was broken by the violence of the waves.

When our sun is eclipsed, it is dark indeed. If we need an answer to the question, "Why hidest thou thyself?" it is to be found in the fact that there is a needs-be not only for trial, but for heaviness of heart under trial (1 Peter 1:6); for it is only *felt* affliction that can become *blessed* affliction.

Verses to meditate upon today: Psalm 10:1-12.

A THOUGHT TO PONDER
It is only felt affliction that can become blessed affliction.

JANUARY 18

THE WICKED

Break thou the arm of the wicked and the evil man:
seek out his wickedness till thou find none.

PSALM 10:15

VERSE 15: In this verse we hear again the burden of the psalmist's prayer: "Break thou the arm of the wicked and the evil man." *Let the sinner lose his power to sin; stop the tyrant, arrest the oppressor, weaken the loins of the mighty, dash in pieces the terrible. They deny your justice: let them feel it to the full.*

Indeed, they shall feel it, for God shall hunt the sinner forever; so long as there is a grain of sin in such a man, it shall be sought out and punished. It is not a little worthy of note that very few great persecutors have ever died in their beds. The curse has manifestly pursued them, and their fearful sufferings have made them acknowledge that divine justice at which they could at one time launch defiance.

God permits tyrants to arise as thorn-hedges to protect his church from the intrusion of hypocrites, and that he may teach his backsliding children by them, as Gideon did the men of Succoth with the briers of the wilderness. But he soon cuts up these Herods, like the thorns, and casts them into the fire. Thales, the Milesian, one of the wise men of Greece, being asked what he thought to be the greatest rarity in the world, replied, "To see a tyrant live to be an old man." See how the Lord breaks not only the "arm" but the neck of proud oppressors! To the men who had neither justice nor mercy for the saints, there shall be rendered justice to the full, but not a grain of mercy.

VERSES 16-18: The Psalm ends with a song of thanksgiving to the great and everlasting King, because he granted the desire of his humble and oppressed people, defended the fatherless, and punished the heathen who trampled upon his poor and afflicted children. Let us learn that we are sure to fare well if we carry our complaint to the King of kings.

Verses to meditate upon today: Psalm 10:13-18.

A THOUGHT TO PONDER
Very few great persecutors have ever died in their beds.

JANUARY 19

THE LORD REIGNS

The LORD is in his holy temple, the LORD's throne is in heaven:
his eyes behold, his eyelids try, the children of men.

PSALM 11:4

VERSE 4: David here declares the great source of his unflinching courage. He borrows his light from heaven—from the great central orb of deity. The God of the believer is never far from him; he is not merely the God of the mountain fastnesses, but of the dangerous valleys and battle plains.

Jehovah "is in his holy temple." The heavens are above our heads in all regions of the earth, and the Lord is ever near to us in every state and condition. This is a very strong reason why we should not adopt the vile suggestions of distrust. There is One who pleads his precious blood in our behalf in the temple above, and there is One upon the throne who is never deaf to the intercession of his Son. Why, then, should we fear? What plots can men devise that Jesus will not know? Satan has doubtless desired to have us, that he may sift us as wheat, but Jesus is in the temple praying for us, and how can our faith fail? What attempts can the wicked make that Jehovah shall not behold? And since he is in his holy temple, delighting in the sacrifice of his Son, will he not defeat every device and send us a sure deliverance?

Jehovah's "throne is in heaven"; he reigns supreme. Nothing can be done in heaven, earth, or hell that God does not ordain and overrule. He is the world's great Emperor. Wherefore, then, should we flee? If we trust this King of kings, is not this enough? Cannot he deliver us without our cowardly retreat? Yes! Blessed be the Lord our God, we can salute him as Jehovah-nissi; in his name we set up our banners and, instead of flight, once more raise the shout of war.

Verses to meditate upon today: Psalm 11:1-7.

A THOUGHT TO PONDER
Nothing can be done in heaven, earth, or hell
that God does not ordain and overrule.

JANUARY 20

THE LORD WILL KEEP YOU SAFE

Thou shalt keep them, O LORD, thou shalt preserve them from this generation for ever.
PSALM 12:7

VERSE 7: To fall into the hands of an evil generation, so as to be baited by their cruelty or polluted by their influence, is an evil to be dreaded beyond measure; but it is an evil foreseen and provided for in this text.

In life many a saint has lived a hundred years before his age, as though he had darted his soul into the brighter future and escaped the mists of the beclouded present. He has gone to his grave unreverenced and misunderstood, and lo! as generations come and go, all of a sudden the hero is unearthed and lives in the admiration and love of the excellent of the earth, preserved forever from the generation that stigmatized him as a sower of sedition or burned him as a heretic.

It should be our daily prayer that we may rise above our age as the mountaintops above the clouds and may stand out as heaven-pointing pinnacles high above the mists of ignorance and sin that roll around us. *O Eternal Spirit, fulfill in us the faithful saying of this verse!* Our faith believes those two assuring words and cries, "Thou shalt, thou shalt."

VERSE 8: Here we return to the fount of bitterness that first made the psalmist run to the wells of salvation—namely, the prevalence of wickedness. When those in power are vile, their underlings will be no better. Our turf would not so swarm with abominables if those who are styled honorables did not give their countenance to the craft of evil. Would to God that the glory and triumph of our Lord Jesus would encourage us to walk and work like him on every side; as like acts upon like, since an exalted sinner encourages sinners, our exalted Redeemer must surely excite, cheer, and stimulate his saints. Enheartened by a sight of his reigning power, we shall meet the evils of the times in the spirit of holy resolution and shall the more hopefully pray, "Help, Lord."

Verses to meditate upon today: Psalm 12:1-8.

A THOUGHT TO PONDER
It should be our daily prayer that we may rise above our age.

JANUARY 21

HOW LONG, O LORD?

How long wilt thou forget me, O LORD? for ever?
how long wilt thou hide thy face from me?
PSALM 13:1

VERSE 1: "How long . . . ?" This question is repeated no less than four times. It betokens very intense desire for deliverance and great anguish of heart. And what if there be some impatience mingled therewith; is not this a more true portrait of our own experience? It is not easy to prevent desire from degenerating into impatience. Oh, for grace so that, while we wait on God, we may be kept from indulging a murmuring spirit!

"How long . . . ?" Does not the oft-repeated cry become a howling? And what if grief should find no other means of utterance? Even then, God is not far from the voice of our roaring; for he does not regard the music of our prayers, but his own Spirit's work in them in exciting desire and inflaming the affections.

"How long . . . ?" How long do our days appear when our soul is cast down within us!

Time flies with full-fledged wing in our summer days, but in our winters it flutters painfully. A week within prison walls is longer than a month at liberty. Long sorrow seems to argue abounding corruption. The gold that is long in the fire must have had much dross to be consumed. Hence the question "how long . . . ?" may suggest deep searching of heart.

"How long wilt thou forget me?" Ah, David, how like a fool you are talking! Can God "forget"? Can Omniscience fail in memory? Above all, can Jehovah's heart forget his own beloved child? Ah, brethren, let us drive away the thought and hear the voice of our covenant God by the mouth of the prophet: "But Zion said, The LORD hath forsaken me, and my Lord hath forgotten me. Can a woman forget her sucking child, that she should not have compassion on the son of her womb? yea, they may forget, yet will I not forget thee. Behold, I have graven thee upon the palms of my hands; thy walls are continually before me" (Isa. 49:14-16).

Verses to meditate upon today: Psalm 13:1-6.

A THOUGHT TO PONDER
Can Omniscience fail in memory? Can Jehovah's heart forget his own beloved child?

JANUARY 22

"THERE IS NO GOD"

The fool hath said in his heart, There is no God. They are corrupt, they have done abominable works, there is none that doeth good.

PSALM 14:1

VERSE 1: "The fool." The atheist is *the* fool preeminently, and *a* fool universally.

The atheist would not deny God if he were not a fool by nature, and having denied God it is no marvel that he becomes a fool in practice. Sin is always folly, and as it is the height of sin to attack the very existence of the Most High, so it is also the greatest imaginable folly. To say there is no God is to belie the plainest evidence, which is obstinacy; to oppose the common consent of mankind, which is stupidity; to stifle consciousness, which is madness. If the sinner could by his atheism destroy the God whom he hates, there were some sense, although much wickedness, in his infidelity; but as denying the existence of fire does not prevent its burning a man who is in it, so doubting the existence of God will not stop the Judge of all the earth from destroying the rebel who breaks his laws. Nay, this atheism is a crime that much provokes heaven and will bring down terrible vengeance on the fool who indulges it.

A proverb says, "A fool's tongue cuts his own throat," and in this instance it kills both soul and body forever. Would to God the mischief stopped even there, but alas! one fool makes hundreds, and a noisy blasphemer spreads his horrible doctrines as lepers spread the plague.

Ainsworth, in his "Annotations," tells us that the word here used is *nabal*, which has the signification of fading, dying, or falling away, as a withered leaf or flower; it is a title given to the foolish man as having lost the juice and sap of wisdom, reason, honesty, and godliness.

Trapp hits the mark when he calls him "that sapless fellow, that carcass of a man, that walking sepulchre of himself, in whom all religion and right reason is withered and wasted, dried up and decayed."

Verses to meditate upon today: Psalm 14:1-7.

A THOUGHT TO PONDER

To say there is no God is to belie the plainest evidence, which is obstinacy.

JANUARY 23

ABIDING IN THE LORD

LORD, who shall abide in thy tabernacle? Who shall dwell in thy holy hill?
PSALM 15:1

VERSE 1: *Jehovah, the high and holy One, who shall be permitted to have fellowship with you? The heavens are not pure in your sight, and you charge your angels with folly; who then of mortal mold shall dwell with you, a dread, consuming fire?* A sense of the glory of the Lord and of the holiness that becomes his house, his service, and his attendants excites the humble mind to ask the solemn question before us. If angels bow with veiled faces, how shall man be able to worship at all?

The unthinking many imagine it to be a very easy matter to approach the Most High, and when professedly engaged in his worship they have no questionings of heart as to their fitness for it. But truly humbled souls often shrink under a sense of utter unworthiness and would not dare to approach the throne of the God of holiness if it were not for him, our Lord, our Advocate, who can abide in the heavenly temple because his righteousness endures forever.

"Who shall abide in thy tabernacle?" Who shall be admitted to be a member of the household of God, to sojourn under his roof and enjoy communion with him? "Who shall dwell in thy holy hill?" Who shall be a citizen of Zion, an inhabitant of the heavenly Jerusalem? All men have not this privilege; nay, even among professing believers there are aliens from the commonwealth who have no secret intercourse with God. On the grounds of law no mere man can dwell with God, for there is not one upon earth who answers to the just requirements mentioned in the succeeding verses.

Verses to meditate upon today: Psalm 15:1-5.

A THOUGHT TO PONDER
*The unthinking many imagine it to be a very easy matter
to approach the Most High.*

JANUARY 24

Counsel

I will bless the LORD, who hath given me counsel:
my reins also instruct me in the night seasons.

PSALM 16:7

VERSE 7: "I will bless the LORD, who hath given me counsel." Praise as well as prayer was presented to the Father by our Lord Jesus, and we are not truly his followers unless our resolve be, "I will bless the LORD." Jesus is called Wonderful, Counselor, but as man he spoke not of himself, but as his Father had taught him. Read in confirmation of this John 7:16; 8:28; and 12:49-50 and the prophecy concerning him in Isaiah 11:2-3.

It was our Redeemer's habit to go to his Father for direction; and having received it, he blessed him for giving him "counsel." It would be well for us if we would follow his example of lowliness, cease from trusting in our own understanding, and seek to be guided by the Spirit of God. "My reins also instruct me in the night seasons." By "reins," understand the inner man, the affections and feelings. The communion of the soul with God brings to it an inner spiritual wisdom that in still seasons is revealed to itself. Our Redeemer spent many nights alone upon the mountain, and we may readily conceive that together with his fellowship with heaven, he carried on a profitable commerce with himself—reviewing his experience, forecasting his work, and considering his position.

Great generals fight their battles in their own mind long before the trumpet sounds, and so did our Lord win our battle on his knees before he gained it on the cross. It is a gracious habit after taking counsel from above to take counsel within. Wise men see more with their eyes shut by night than fools can see by day with their eyes open.

He who learns from God and so gets the seed will soon find wisdom within himself growing in the garden of his soul.

Verses to meditate upon today: Psalm 16:1-7.

A THOUGHT TO PONDER
It is a gracious habit after taking counsel from above to take counsel within.

JANUARY 25

REST IN HOPE

Therefore my heart is glad, and my glory rejoiceth: my flesh also shall rest in hope.
PSALM 16:9

VERSE 9: David clearly foresaw that he must die, for he speaks of his flesh resting, and of his soul in the abode of separate spirits. Death was clearly before his face or he would not have mentioned corruption; but such was his devout reliance upon his God that he sang over the tomb and rejoiced in the vision of the sepulchre. He knew that the visit of his soul to Sheol, or the invisible world of disembodied spirits, would be a very short one, and that his body in a very brief space would leave the grave, uninjured by its sojourn there. All this made him say, "my heart is glad" and moved his tongue, the "glory" of his frame, to rejoice in God, the strength of his salvation.

Oh, for such holy faith in the prospect of trial and of death! It is the work of faith not merely to create a peace that passes all understanding, but to fill the heart full of gladness until the tongue, which, as the organ of an intelligent creature, is our "glory," bursts forth in notes of harmonious praise. Faith gives us living joy and bestows dying rest. "My flesh also shall rest in hope."

VERSE 10: Our Lord Jesus was not disappointed in his hope. He declared his Father's faithfulness in the words, "thou wilt not leave my soul in hell," and that faithfulness was proven on resurrection morning. Jesus was not left among the departed and disembodied; he had believed in the resurrection, and he received it on the third day, when his body rose in glorious life, just as he had said in joyous confidence: "neither wilt thou suffer thine Holy One to see corruption." Into the outer prison of the grave his body might go, but into the inner prison of corruption he could not enter.

Verses to meditate upon today: Psalm 16:8-11.

A THOUGHT TO PONDER
Faith gives us living joy and bestows dying rest.

JANUARY 26

AS THE APPLE OF THE EYE

Keep me as the apple of the eye; hide me under the shadow of thy wings.
PSALM 17:8

VERSE 8: "Keep me as the apple of the eye." No part of the body is more precious, more tender, and more carefully guarded than the eye; and of the eye, no portion is more especially to be protected than the central apple, the pupil, or as the Hebrew calls it, "the daughter of the eye."

The all-wise Creator has placed the eye in a well-protected position; it stands surrounded by projecting bones, like Jerusalem encircled by mountains. Moreover, its great Author has surrounded it with many tunics of inward covering, besides the hedge of the eyebrows, the curtain of the eyelids, and the fence of the eyelashes. And in addition to this, he has given to every man so high a value for his eyes, and so quick an apprehension of danger, that no member of the body is more faithfully cared for than the organ of sight.

Thus, Lord, keep me, for I trust I am one with Jesus, and so a member of his mystical body. "Hide me under the shadow of thy wings." *Even as the parent bird completely shields her brood from evil and meanwhile cherishes them with the warmth of her own heart by covering them with her wings, so do with me, most condescending God, for I am your offspring, and you have a parent's love in perfection.*

This last clause is in the Hebrew in the future tense, as if to show that what the writer had asked for but a moment before he was now sure would be granted to him. Confident expectations should keep pace with earnest supplication.

VERSE 9: ". . . from the wicked that oppress me, from my deadly enemies, who compass me about." The foes from whom David sought to be rescued were "wicked" men. It is hopeful for us when our enemies are God's enemies. They were "deadly enemies," whom nothing but David's death would satisfy. The foes of a believer's soul are mortal foes most emphatically.

Verses to meditate upon today: Psalm 17:1-9.

A Thought to Ponder
Confident expectations should keep pace with earnest supplication.

JANUARY 27

I SHALL SEE YOUR FACE

As for me, I will behold thy face in righteousness: I shall be satisfied, when I awake, with thy likeness.

PSALM 17:15

VERSE 14: "They are full of children, and leave the rest of their substance to their babes." They were fat housekeepers and yet left no lean wills. Living and dying they lacked for nothing but grace, but alas! that lack spoils everything. They had a fair portion within the little circle of time, but eternity entered not into their calculations. They were penny-wise but pound-foolish; they remembered the present and forgot the future; they fought for the shell and lost the kernel. How fine a description have we here of many a successful merchant or popular statesman; and it is, at first sight, very showy and tempting. But in contrast with the glories of the world to come, what are these paltry molehill joys. Self, self, self—all these joys begin and end in the basest selfishness. *But oh, our God, how rich are those who begin and end in you!*

VERSE 15: "As for me." I neither envy nor covet these men's happiness but partly have and partly hope for a far better one. To behold God's face and to be changed by that vision into his image, so as to partake in his righteousness—this is my noble ambition; and in the prospect of this I cheerfully waive all my present enjoyments. My satisfaction is to come; I do not look for it as yet. *I shall sleep awhile, but I shall awake at the sound of the trumpet—awake to everlasting joy because I arise in your likeness, O my God and King!* Here below good men have glimpses of glory to stay their sacred hunger, but the full feast awaits them in the upper skies. Compared with this deep, ineffable, eternal fullness of delight, the joys of worldlings are as a glowworm to the sun or the drop of a bucket to the ocean.

Verses to meditate upon today: Psalm 17:10-15.

A THOUGHT TO PONDER
Here below good men have glimpses of glory to stay their sacred hunger, but the full feast awaits them in the upper skies.

JANUARY 28

THE LORD IS MY ROCK

*... my God, my strength, in whom I will trust; my buckler,
and the horn of my salvation, and my high tower.*

PSALM 18:2

VERSE 2: "The LORD is my rock, and my fortress." Dwelling among the crags and mountain fastnesses of Judea, David had escaped the malice of Saul, and here he compares his God to such a place of concealment and security. Believers are often hidden in their God from the strife of tongues and the fury of the storm of trouble. The clefts of the Rock of Ages are safe abodes.

"My deliverer," interposing in my hour of peril. When almost captured, the Lord's people are rescued from the hand of the mighty by him who is mightier still. This title of "deliverer" has many sermons in it and is well worthy of the study of all experienced saints.

"My God"; this is all good things in one. There is a boundless wealth in this expression; it means, my perpetual, unchanging, infinite, eternal good. He who can say truly "my God" may well add, "my heaven, my all."

"My strength"; this word is really "my rock," in the sense of strength and immobility. My sure, unchanging, eternal confidence and support. Thus the word *rock* occurs twice, but it is no tautology, for the first time it is a rock for concealment, but here a rock for firmness and immutability.

"In whom I will trust." Faith must be exercised or the preciousness of God is not truly known; and God must be the object of faith or faith is mere presumption.

"My buckler," warding off the blows of my enemy, shielding me from arrow or sword. The Lord furnishes his warriors with weapons both offensive and defensive. Our armory is completely supplied, so that none need go to battle unarmed.

Verses to meditate upon today: Psalm 18:1-3.

A THOUGHT TO PONDER

Our armory is completely supplied, so that none need go to battle unarmed.

THE SORROWS OF DEATH

The sorrows of death compassed me, and the floods of ungodly men made me afraid.
PSALM 18:4

VERSE 4: "The sorrows of death compassed me." Death, like a cruel conqueror, seemed to twist round about him the cords of pain. He was hemmed in with threatening deaths of the most appalling sort. He was like a mariner broken by the storm and driven upon the rocks by dreadful breakers, white as the teeth of death. A sad plight for the man after God's own heart, but thus it is that Jehovah deals with his sons.

"The floods of ungodly men made me afraid." Torrents of ungodliness threatened to swamp all religion and to hurry away the godly man's hope as a thing to be scorned and despised. So far was this threat fulfilled that even the hero who slew Goliath began to be "afraid." The most seaworthy bark is sometimes hard put when the storm is abroad. The most courageous man, who as a rule hopes for the best, may sometimes fear the worst.

Beloved reader, he who pens these lines has known better than most what this verse means and feels inclined to weep, and yet to sing, while he writes upon a text so descriptive of his own experience. On the night of the lamentable accident at the Surrey Music Hall (when some people were killed in a stampede), the floods of Belial were let loose, and the subsequent remarks of a large portion of the press were exceedingly malicious and wicked. Our soul was afraid as we stood encompassed with the sorrows of death and the blasphemies of the cruel.

But oh, what mercy was there in it all, and what honey of goodness was extracted by our Lord out of this lion of affliction! Surely God has heard me! Are you in an ill plight? Dear friend, learn from our experience to trust in the Lord Jehovah, who forsakes not his chosen.

Verses to meditate upon today: Psalm 18:4-15.

A THOUGHT TO PONDER

What honey of goodness was extracted by our Lord out of this lion of affliction!

January 30

He Reached Down to Me

He sent from above, he took me, he drew me out of many waters.
Psalm 18:16

Verse 16: Now comes the rescue. The Author is divine. "He sent"—the work is heavenly; "from above"—the deliverance is marvelous; "he drew me out of many waters." Here David was like another Moses, drawn from the water; and thus are all believers like their Lord, whose baptism in many waters of agony and in his own blood has redeemed us from the wrath to come. Torrents of evil shall not drown the man whose God sits upon the floods to restrain their fury.

Verse 17: When we have been rescued, we must take care to ascribe all the glory to God by confessing our own weakness and remembering the power of the conquered enemy. God's power derives honor from all the events of the conflict. Our great spiritual adversary is a "strong enemy" indeed, much too strong for poor, weak creatures like ourselves; but we have been delivered hitherto, and shall be even to the end. Our weakness is a reason for divine help; mark the force of the "for" in the text.

Verse 18: It was an ill day, a day of "calamity," of which evil foes took cruel advantage while they used crafty means utterly to ruin David. Yet he could say, "but the Lord was my stay." What a blessed "but" that cuts the Gordian knot and slays the hundred-headed Hydra! There is no doubt of deliverance when our trust is in Jehovah.

Verse 19: "He brought me forth also into a large place." After pining awhile in the prison-house Joseph reached the palace; and from the cave of Adullam David mounted to the throne. Sweet is pleasure after pain. Enlargement is more delightful after a season of oppressive poverty and sorrowful confinement.

Verses to meditate upon today: Psalm 18:16-28.

A Thought to Ponder
Torrents of evil shall not drown the man whose God sits upon the floods to restrain their fury.

JANUARY 31

THE LORD'S PERFECT WAY

*As for God, his way is perfect: the word of the LORD is tried:
he is a buckler to all those that trust in him.*

PSALM 18:30

VERSE 30: "As for God, his way is perfect." Far past all fault and error are God's dealings with his people; all his actions are resplendent with justice, truth, tenderness, mercy, and holiness. Every way of God is complete in itself, and all his ways put together are matchless in harmony and goodness. Is it not very consoling to believe that he who has begun to bless us will perfect his work, for all his ways are perfect?

Nor must the divine "word" be without its song of praise. "The word of the LORD is tried," like silver refined in the furnace. The doctrines are glorious, the precepts are pure, the promises are faithful, and the whole revelation is superlatively full of grace and truth. David had tried it, thousands have tried it, we have tried it, and it has never failed. It was fitting that when way and word had been extolled, the Lord himself should be magnified; hence it is added, "he is a buckler to all those that trust in him." No armor or shield of brass secures the warrior as well as the covenant God of Israel protects his warring people. He himself is the "buckler" of trustful ones. What a thought is this! What peace may every trusting soul enjoy!

VERSE 31: Having mentioned his God, the psalmist's heart burns, and his words sparkle. He challenges heaven and earth to find another being worthy of adoration or trust in comparison with Jehovah. His God, as Matthew Henry says, is a Nonesuch. The idols of the heathen he scorns to mention, snuffing them all out as mere nothings when Deity is spoken of. "Who is God save the LORD?" Who else creates, sustains, foresees, and overrules? Surely in the Lord Jehovah alone can we find rest and refuge.

Verses to meditate upon today: Psalm 18:29-45.

A THOUGHT TO PONDER

*Every way of God is complete in itself, and all his ways put together are
matchless in harmony and goodness.*

FEBRUARY 1

GOD, MY SAVIOR

The LORD liveth; and blessed be my Rock; and let the God of my salvation be exalted.
PSALM 18:46

VERSE 46: "The Lord liveth," possessing underived, essential, independent, and eternal life. We serve no inanimate, imaginary, or dying God. He only has immortality. Like loyal subjects let us cry, "Live on, O God. Long live the King of kings. By your immortality do we dedicate ourselves afresh to you." As the Lord our God lives, so would we live to him.

"And blessed be my Rock." He is the ground of our hope; let him be the subject of our praise. Our hearts bless the Lord, with holy love extolling him.

"Let the God of my salvation be exalted." As our Savior, the Lord should more than ever be glorified. We should publish abroad the story of the covenant and the cross, the Father's election, the Son's redemption, and the Spirit's regeneration. He who rescues us from deserved ruin should be very dear to us. In heaven they sing, "Unto him that loved us and washed us in his blood." Such music should be common in the assemblies of the saints below.

VERSE 47: "It is God that avengeth me, and subdueth the people under me." To rejoice in personal revenge is unhallowed and evil, but David viewed himself as the instrument of vengeance upon the enemies of God and his people. Had he not rejoiced in the success accorded to him, he would have been worthy of censure. That sinners perish is in itself a painful consideration, but that the Lord's law is avenged upon those who break it is to the devout mind a theme for thankfulness. We must, however, always remember that vengeance is never ours. Vengeance belongs to the Lord, and he is so just and long-suffering in the exercise of it that we may safely leave its administration in his hands.

Verses to meditate upon today: Psalm 18:46-50.

A THOUGHT TO PONDER

He is the ground of our hope; let him be the subject of our praise.

FEBRUARY 2

LOOK AT THE HEAVENS

The heavens declare the glory of God; and the firmament showeth his handiwork.
PSALM 19:1

VERSE 1: "The heavens declare the glory of God." The book of nature has three sections—heaven, earth, and sea, of which heaven is the first and the most glorious, and by its aid we are able to see the beauties of the other two. Any book without its first page would be sadly imperfect, and especially the great Natural Bible, since its first pages—the sun, moon, and stars—supply light to the rest of the volume and are thus the keys, without which the writing that follows would be dark and undiscerned. Man, walking erect, was evidently made to scan the skies, and he who begins to read creation by studying the stars begins the book at the right place.

The "heavens" are plural in their variety, comprising the watery heavens with their clouds of countless forms, the aerial heavens with their calms and tempests, the solar heavens with all the glories of the day, and the starry heavens with all the marvels of the night. What the heaven of heavens must be has not entered into the heart of man, but there all things are telling the glory of God. Any part of creation has more instruction in it than the human mind will ever exhaust, but the celestial realm is peculiarly rich in spiritual lore.

The heavens "declare" or "are declaring," for the continuance of their testimony is intended by the participles employed. Every moment God's existence, power, wisdom, and goodness are being sounded abroad by the heavenly heralds that shine upon us from above.

He who would guess at divine sublimity should gaze upward into the starry vault; he who would imagine infinity must peer into the boundless expanse; he who desires to see divine wisdom should consider the balancing of the orbs.

Verses to meditate upon today: Psalm 19:1-6.

A THOUGHT TO PONDER

Every moment God's existence, power, wisdom, and goodness are being sounded abroad by the heavenly heralds that shine upon us from above.

FEBRUARY 3

LOOK AT GOD'S WORD

The law of the LORD is perfect, converting the soul: the testimony of the LORD is sure, making wise the simple.

PSALM 19:7

VERSES 7-9: are brief but instructive, containing six descriptive titles of the Word, six characteristic qualities, and six divine effects. Names, nature, and effect are well set forth.

VERSE 7: "The law of the LORD is perfect," by which the psalmist means not merely the law of Moses but the doctrine of God, the whole run and rule of Sacred Writ. The doctrine revealed by God he declares to be "perfect," and yet David had but a very small part of the Scriptures. If a fragment, and that the darkest and most historical portion, be "perfect," what must the entire volume be? How much more than "perfect" is the book that contains the clearest possible display of divine love and gives us an open vision of redeeming grace.

The Gospel is a complete scheme or law of gracious salvation, presenting to the needy sinner everything that his terrible necessities can possibly demand. There are no redundancies and no omissions in the Word of God and in the plan of grace; why then do men try to paint this lily and gild this refined gold? The Gospel is perfect in all its parts, and perfect as a whole: it is a crime to add to it, treason to alter it, and felony to take from it.

"Converting the soul." The Word makes the man to be returned or restored to the place from which sin had cast him. The practical effect of the Word of God is to turn the man to himself, to his God, and to holiness; and that turn or conversion is not outward alone, for "the soul" is moved and renewed. The great means of the conversion of sinners is the Word of God, and the more closely we keep to it in our ministry, the more likely we are to be successful.

Verses to meditate upon today: Psalm 19:7-14.

A THOUGHT TO PONDER

There are no redundancies and no omissions in the Word of God.

FEBRUARY 4

SUCCESSFUL PLANS

Grant thee according to thine own heart, and fulfil all thy counsel.

PSALM 20:4

VERSE 4: Christ's desire and "counsel" were both set upon the salvation of his people. The church of old desired for him good speed in his design, and the church in these latter days with all her heart desires the complete fulfillment of his purpose. In Christ Jesus sanctified souls may appropriate this verse as a promise; they shall have their desire, and their plans to glorify their Master shall succeed. We are allowed to have our own will when our will is God's will. This was always the case with our Lord, and yet he said, "not as I will, but as thou wilt." What need for submission in our case; if it was necessary to him, how much more for us.

VERSE 5: "We will rejoice in thy salvation." In Jesus there is "salvation"; it is his own, and hence it is called "thy salvation"; but it is ours to receive and ours to "rejoice in." We should fixedly resolve that come what may, we will "rejoice in" the saving arm of the Lord Jesus. The people in this Psalm, before their king went to battle, felt sure of victory and therefore began to rejoice beforehand; how much more ought we to do this who have seen the victory completely won! Buds are beautiful, and promises not yet fulfilled are worthy to be admired. If joy were more general among the Lord's people, God would be more glorified among men; the happiness of the subjects honors the sovereign.

"And in the name of our God we will set up our banners." We lift the standard of defiance in the face of the foe and wave the flag of victory over the fallen adversary. Some proclaim war in the name of one king, and some another, but the faithful go to war in Jesus' name, the name of the incarnate God—Immanuel, God with us.

Verses to meditate upon today: Psalm 20:1-5.

A THOUGHT TO PONDER
The faithful go to war in Jesus' name.

FEBRUARY 5

TRUST IN GOD

Some trust in chariots, and some in horses: but we will remember the name of the LORD our God.

PSALM 20:7

VERSE 7: Contrasts frequently bring out the truth vividly, and here the psalmist sets forth the creaturely confidences of carnal men in contrast with reliance upon the Prince Immanuel and the invisible Jehovah.

"Some trust in chariots, and some in horses." Chariots and horses make an imposing show and with their rattling and dust and fine caparisons make so great a figure that vain man is much taken with them; yet the discerning eye of faith sees more in an invisible God than in all these. The most dreaded war engine of David's day was the war-chariot, armed with scythes, which mowed down men like grass. This was the boast and glory of the neighboring nations, but the saints considered the name of Jehovah to be a far better defense. As the Israelites might not keep horses, it was natural for them to regard the enemy's cavalry with more than usual dread. It is, therefore, all the greater evidence of faith that the bold songster can here disdain even the horses of Egypt in comparison with the Lord of hosts.

Alas, how many in our day who profess to be the Lord's are abjectly dependent upon their fellowmen or upon an arm of flesh in some shape or other as if they had never known the name of Jehovah at all. *Jesus, be alone our rock and refuge, and never may we mar the simplicity of our faith.*

"We will remember the name of the LORD our God." "Our God" in covenant, who has chosen us and whom we have chosen—this God is our God. The name of our God is *Jehovah*, and this should never be forgotten— the self-existent, independent, immutable, ever-present, all-filling I AM. Let us adore that matchless name and never dishonor it by distrust or creaturely confidence. Reader, you must *know* it before you can *"remember"* it. May the blessed Spirit reveal it graciously to your soul!

Verses to meditate upon today: Psalm 20:6-9.

A THOUGHT TO PONDER
Jesus, be alone our rock and refuge.

FEBRUARY 6

ANSWERED PRAYERS

*Thou hast given him his heart's desire, and hast not withholden
the request of his lips. Selah.*

PSALM 21:2

VERSE 2: "Thou hast given him his heart's desire." That desire the Lord Jesus ardently pursued when he was on earth, by his prayer, his actions, and his suffering; he manifested that his heart longed to redeem his people, and now in heaven he has his desire granted him, for he sees his beloved coming to be with him where he is. The desires of the Lord Jesus were from his heart, and God heard them; if our hearts are right with God, he will in our case also fulfill the desires of them who fear him.

"And hast not withholden the request of his lips." What is in the well of the heart is sure to come up in the bucket of the lips, and the only true prayers are those where the heart's desire is first and the lip's request follows after.

Jesus prayed vocally as well as mentally; speech is a great assistance to thought. Some of us feel that even when alone we find it easier to collect our thoughts when we pray aloud. The requests of the Savior were not withheld. He was and still is a prevailing Pleader. Our Advocate on high returns not empty from the throne of grace. He asked for his elect in the eternal council-chamber, he asked for blessings for them here, he asked for glory for them hereafter, and his requests have rushed to the Father. He is ready to ask for us at the mercy seat. Have we not at this hour some desire to send up to his Father by him? Let us not be slack to use our willing, loving, all-prevailing Intercessor.

"Selah." Here a pause is very properly inserted, that we may admire the blessed success of the King's prayers, and that we may prepare our own requests to be presented through him. If we had a few more quiet rests, a few more Selahs in our public worship, it might be profitable.

Verses to meditate upon today: Psalm 21:1-7.

A THOUGHT TO PONDER
Let us not be slack to use our willing, loving, all-prevailing Intercessor.

FEBRUARY 7

THE LORD'S WRATH

Thou shalt make them as a fiery oven in the time of thine anger:
the LORD shall swallow them up in his wrath, and the fire shall devour them.

PSALM 21:9

VERSE 9: "Thou shalt make them as a fiery oven in the time of thine anger." They themselves shall be an "oven" to themselves, and their own tormentors. *Those who burned with anger against you, Lord, shall be burned by your anger.* The fire of sin will be followed by the fire of wrath. Even as the smoke of Sodom and Gomorrah went up to heaven, so shall the enemies of the Lord Jesus be utterly and terribly consumed.

Some read this, "Thou shalt put them as it were into a furnace of fire." Like faggots cast into an oven, they shall burn furiously beneath the anger of the Lord. "They shall be cast into a furnace of fire; there shall be weeping and gnashing of teeth." These are terrible words, and those teachers do not well who endeavor by their sophistical reasonings to weaken their force.

Reader, never tolerate slight thoughts of hell or you will soon have low thoughts of sin. The hell of sinners must be fearful beyond all conception, or such language as the present would not be used. Who would have the Son of God to be his enemy when such an overthrow awaits his foes? The expression "the time of thine anger" reminds us that as now is the time of his grace, so there will be a set time for his wrath. The judge pronounces sentence at an appointed time. There is a day of vengeance of our God; let those who despise the day of grace remember this day of wrath.

"The LORD shall swallow them up in his wrath, and the fire shall devour them." Jehovah will himself visit with his anger the enemies of his Son. The Lord Jesus will, as it were, judge by commission from God, whose solemn assent and cooperation shall be with him in his sentences upon impenitent sinners.

Verses to meditate upon today: Psalm 21:8-13.

A THOUGHT TO PONDER
Let those who despise the day of grace remember this day of wrath.

FEBRUARY 8

FORSAKEN

My God, my God, why hast thou forsaken me? Why art thou so far from helping me, and from the words of my roaring?

PSALM 22:1

VERSE 1: "My God, my God, why hast thou forsaken me?" This was the startling cry of Golgotha: "*Eloi, Eloi, lama sabacthani.*" The Jews mocked, but the angels adored when Jesus cried this exceedingly bitter cry. We behold our great Redeemer in extremities, nailed to the tree, and what do we see?

First, our Lord's faith beams forth and deserves our reverent imitation; he keeps his hold upon his God with both hands and cries twice, "My God, my God!" The spirit of adoption was strong within the suffering Son of man, and he felt no doubt about his interest in his God. Oh, that we would imitate this cleaving to an afflicting God!

What an inquiry is this before us! "Why hast thou forsaken me?" We must lay the emphasis on every word of this saddest of all utterances. "Why?": What is the great cause of such a strange fact as for God to leave his own Son at such a time and in such a plight? There was no cause in him; why then was he deserted? "Hast": it is done, and the Savior is feeling its dread effect as he asks the question; it is surely true, but how mysterious! It was no threatening of forsaking that made the great Surety cry aloud; he endured that forsaking in very deed. "Thou": "I can understand why traitorous Judas and timid Peter would be gone, but *you,* my God, my faithful friend, how can you leave me?" This is worst of all, yea, worse than all put together. Hell itself has for its fiercest flame the separation of the soul from God. "Forsaken": "if you had chastened, I might bear it, for your face would shine. But to forsake me utterly, ah! why is this?" "Me": "your innocent, obedient, suffering Son—why do you leave *me* to perish?" A sight of self seen by penitence and of Jesus on the cross seen by faith will best expound this question. Jesus was forsaken because our sins had separated us from our God.

Verses to meditate upon today: Psalm 22:1-5.

A THOUGHT TO PONDER

Jesus was forsaken because our sins had separated us from our God.

FEBRUARY 9

THEY HURL INSULTS

All they that see me laugh me to scorn: they shoot out the lip, they shake the head.
PSALM 22:7

VERSE 7: "All they that see me laugh me to scorn." Read the Gospel narratives of the ridicule endured by the Crucified One, and then consider, in the light of this expression, how it grieved him. Mockery has for its distinctive description "cruel mockings"; those endured by our Lord were of the most cruel kind. The scornful ridicule of our Lord was universal; all sorts of men were unanimous in the derisive laughter and vied with each other in insulting him. Priests and people, Jews and Gentiles, soldiers and civilians were united in the general scoffing, and that at the time when he was prostrate in weakness and ready to die. Which shall we wonder at the most—the cruelty of man or the love of the bleeding Savior? How can we ever complain of ridicule after this?

"They shoot out the lip, they shake the head." These were gestures of contempt. Pouting, grinning, a shaking of the head, a thrusting out of the tongue, and other modes of derision were endured by our patient Lord. Men made faces at him before whom angels veil their faces, him whom they adore. The basest signs of disgrace that disdain could devise were maliciously cast at him. They ridiculed his prayers; they made his sufferings a matter for laughter and set him utterly at naught. Herbert sings of our Lord as saying:

> *Shame tears my soul, my body many a wound;*
> *Sharp nails pierce this, but sharper that confound;*
> *Reproaches, which are free, while I am bound.*
> *Was ever grief like mine?*

VERSE 8: "He trusted on the LORD that he would deliver him: let him deliver him, seeing he delighted in him." Here the taunt is cruelly aimed at the sufferer's faith in God, which is the tenderest point in a good man's soul, the very apple [pupil] of his eye.

Verses to meditate upon today: Psalm 22:6-11.

A THOUGHT TO PONDER
Which shall we wonder at the most—the cruelty of man or
the love of the bleeding Savior?

THE CRUCIFIED ONE

I may tell all my bones: they look and stare upon me.
PSALM 22:17

VERSE 17: So emaciated was Jesus by his fastings and sufferings that he says, "I may tell all my bones." He could count and recount them. The posture of the body on the cross, Bishop Horne thinks, would so distend the flesh and skin as to make the bones visible, so that they might be numbered. The zeal of Jesus' Father's house had eaten him up; like a good soldier he had endured hardness. Oh, that we cared less for the body's enjoyment and ease and more for our Father's business! It were better to count the bones of an emaciated body than to bring leanness into our souls.

"They look and stare upon me." Unholy eyes gazed insultingly upon the Savior's nakedness and shocked the sacred delicacy of his holy soul. The sight of the agonizing body ought to have elicited sympathy from the throng, but it only increased their savage mirth as they gloated their cruel eyes upon his miseries. Let us blush for human nature and mourn in sympathy with our Redeemer's shame. The first Adam made us all naked, and therefore the second Adam became naked, that he might clothe our naked souls.

VERSE 18: "They part my garments among them, and cast lots upon my vesture." The garments of the executed went to the executioners in most cases, but it was not often that they cast lots at the division of the spoil. This incident shows how clearly David in vision saw the day of Christ, and how surely the Man of Nazareth is he of whom the prophets spake: "These things, *therefore,* the soldiers did." He who gave his blood to cleanse us gave his garments to clothe us. As Ness says, "This precious Lamb of God gave up his golden fleece for us."

Verses to meditate upon today: Psalm 22:12-18.

A THOUGHT TO PONDER

The first Adam made us all naked, and therefore the second Adam became naked, that he might clothe our naked souls.

FEBRUARY 11

PRAISE

For he hath not despised nor abhorred the affliction of the afflicted; neither hath he hid his face from him; but when he cried unto him, he heard.

PSALM 22:24

VERSE 23: "Ye that fear the LORD, praise him." The reader must imagine the Savior as addressing the congregation of the saints. He exhorts the faithful to unite with him in thanksgiving.

The description of fearing the Lord is very frequent and very instructive; it is the beginning of wisdom and is an essential sign of grace. "I am a Hebrew; and I fear the LORD" was Jonah's confession of faith. Humble awe of God is so necessary a preparation for praising him that none are fit to sing to his honor but such as reverence his Word.

"All ye the seed of Jacob, glorify him." The genius of the Gospel is praise. Jew and Gentile saved by sovereign grace should be eager in the blessed work of magnifying the God of their salvation. "All" saints should unite in the song; no tongue may be silent, no heart may be cold. Christ calls us to glorify God; can we refuse?

"And fear him, all ye the seed of Israel." All who are spiritual Israel do this, and we hope the day will come when Israel after the flesh will be brought to the same mind. The more we praise God, the more reverently shall we fear him; and the deeper our reverence, the sweeter our songs. So much does Jesus value praise that we have it here under his dying hand and seal that all the saints must glorify the Lord.

VERSE 24: "For he hath not despised nor abhorred the affliction of the afflicted." Here is good matter and motive for praise. The experience of our covenant Head and Representative should encourage all of us to bless the God of grace. Never was man so afflicted as our Savior in body and soul from friends and foes, by heaven and hell, in life and death; he was the foremost in the ranks of the afflicted. But all those afflictions were sent in love, and not because his Father despised and abhorred him.

Verses to meditate upon today: Psalm 22:19-24

A THOUGHT TO PONDER

Never was man so afflicted as our Savior in body and soul.

FEBRUARY 12

Eternal Satisfaction

The meek shall eat and be satisfied: they shall praise the LORD that seek him: your heart shall live for ever.
Psalm 22:26

Verse 26: "The meek shall eat and be satisfied." Mark how the dying Lover of our souls solaces himself with the result of his death. The spiritually poor find a feast in Jesus; they feed upon him to the satisfaction of their hearts. They were famished until he gave himself for them, but now they are filled with royal dainties. The thought of the joy of his people gave comfort to our expiring Lord.

Note the characters who partake of the benefit of his passion: "the meek," the humble and lowly. *Lord, make us so.* Note also the certainty that gospel provisions shall not be wasted—they "shall eat"—and the sure result of such eating—"and be satisfied."

"They shall praise the LORD that seek him." For a while they may keep a fast, but their thanksgiving days must and shall come. "Your heart shall live for ever." Your spirits shall not fail through trial; you shall not die of grief; immortal joys shall be your portion. Thus Jesus speaks even from the cross to the troubled seeker. If his dying words are so assuring, what consolation may we not find in the truth that he ever lives to make intercession for us! They who eat at Jesus' table receive the fulfillment of the promise, "If any man eat of this bread, he shall live for ever."

Verse 27: In reading this verse one is struck with the Messiah's missionary spirit. It is evidently his grand consolation that Jehovah will be known throughout all places of his dominion. "All the ends of the world shall remember and turn unto the LORD." Out from the inner circle of the present church the blessing is to spread in growing power until the remotest parts of the earth shall be ashamed of their idols, mindful of the true God, penitent for their offenses, and unanimously earnest for reconciliation with Jehovah.

Verses to meditate upon today: Psalm 22:25-31.

A Thought to Ponder
Immortal joys shall be your portion.

FEBRUARY 13

My Shepherd

The LORD is my shepherd; I shall not want.
PSALM 23:1

VERSE 1: "The LORD is my shepherd." What condescension is this, that the infinite Lord assumes toward his people the office and character of a "shepherd"! It should be the subject of grateful admiration that the great God allows himself to be compared to anything that will set forth his great love and care for his own people. David had himself been a keeper of sheep and understood both the needs of the sheep and the many cares of a shepherd. He compares himself to a weak, defenseless, and foolish creature, and he takes God to be his Provider, Preserver, Director, and indeed his everything.

No man has a right to consider himself the Lord's sheep unless his nature has been renewed, for the scriptural description of unconverted men does not picture them as sheep, but as wolves or goats. A sheep is an object of property, not a wild animal; its owner sets great store by it, and frequently it is bought with a great price. It is well to know, as certainly David did, that we belong to the Lord. There is a noble tone of confidence about this sentence. There is no "if" or "but," or even "I hope so." Rather he says, "The LORD *is* my shepherd." We must cultivate the spirit of assured dependence upon our heavenly Father.

The sweetest word of the whole sentence is that monosyllable, "my." He does not say, "The Lord is the shepherd of the world at large and leadeth forth the multitude as his flock," but "The LORD is *my* shepherd." If he is a shepherd to no one else, he is a Shepherd to *me*. He cares for *me*, watches over *me*, and preserves *me*. The words are in the present tense. Whatever the believer's position, he is even now under the pastoral care of Jehovah.

Verses to meditate upon today: Psalm 23:1-6.

A Thought to Ponder
The sweetest word of the whole sentence is that monosyllable, "my."

FEBRUARY 14

PASTURES AND WATERS

He maketh me to lie down in green pastures: he leadeth me beside the still waters.
PSALM 23:2

VERSE 2: The Christian life has two elements in it—the contemplative and the active—and both of these are richly provided for.

First, the contemplative. "He maketh me to lie down in green pastures." What are these "green pastures" but the Scriptures of truth—always fresh, always rich, and never exhausted? There is no fear of biting the bare ground where the grass is long enough for the flock to lie down in it. Sweet and full are the doctrines of the Gospel, fit food for souls, as tender grass is natural nutriment for sheep. When by faith we are enabled to find rest in the promises, we are like the sheep that lie down in the midst of the pasture; we find at the same moment both provender and peace, rest and refreshment, serenity and satisfaction.

But observe: "*He maketh* me to lie down." It is the Lord who graciously enables us to perceive the preciousness of his truth and to feed upon it. How grateful ought we to be for the power to appropriate the promises! There are some distracted souls who would give worlds if they could but do this. They know the blessedness of it, but they cannot say that this blessedness is theirs. They know the "green pastures," but they are not made to "lie down" in them. Those believers who have for years enjoyed a full assurance of faith should greatly bless their gracious God.

The second part of a vigorous Christian's life consists in gracious activity. We not only think, but we act. We are not always lying down to feed, but are journeying onward toward perfection. Hence we read, "he leadeth me beside the still waters." What are these "still waters" but the influences and gracious manifestations of his blessed Spirit? His Spirit attends us in various operations, like waters—in the plural: cleansing, refreshing, fertilizing, cherishing.

Verses to meditate upon today: Psalm 23:1-6.

A THOUGHT TO PONDER
Sweet and full are the doctrines of the Gospel, fit food for souls.

FEBRUARY 15

RESTORATION

He restoreth my soul: he leadeth me in the paths of righteousness for his name's sake.
PSALM 23:3

VERSE 3: "He restoreth my soul." When the soul grows sorrowful, the Lord revives it; when it is sinful, he sanctifies it; when it is weak, he strengthens it. "He" does it. His ministers could not do it if he did not. His Word would not avail by itself.

"He restoreth my soul." Are any of us low in grace? Do we feel that our spirituality is at its lowest ebb? He who turns the ebb into a flood can soon restore our soul. Pray to him, then, for the blessing: *Restore me, Shepherd of my soul!*

"He leadeth me in the paths of righteousness for his name's sake." The Christian delights to be obedient, but it is the obedience of love, to which he is constrained by the example of his Master.

"He *leadeth* me." The Christian is not obedient to some commandments and neglectful of others; he does not pick and choose but yields to all. Observe that the plural is used—"the *paths* of righteousness." Whatever God may give us to do, we will do it, led by his love. Some Christians overlook the blessing of sanctification, and yet to a thoroughly renewed heart this is one of the sweetest gifts of the covenant. If we could be saved from wrath and yet remain unregenerate, impenitent sinners, we would not be saved as we desire, for we mainly and chiefly pant to be saved *from* sin and led in the way of holiness.

All this is done out of pure, free grace: "for his name's sake." It is to the honor of our great Shepherd that we should be a holy people, walking in the narrow way of righteousness. If we would be so led and guided, we must not fail to adore our heavenly Shepherd's care.

Verses to meditate upon today: Psalm 23:1-6.

A THOUGHT TO PONDER
When the soul grows sorrowful, the Lord revives it.

FEBRUARY 16

THE VALLEY OF THE SHADOW OF DEATH

Yea, though I walk through the valley of the shadow of death, I will fear no evil: for thou art with me; thy rod and thy staff they comfort me.
PSALM 23:4

VERSE 4: This unspeakably delightful verse has been sung on many a dying bed and has helped to make the dark valley bright times out of mind. Every word in it has a wealth of meaning.

"Yea, though I *walk*," as if the believer does not quicken his pace when he comes to die but still calmly *walks* with God. To "walk" indicates the steady advance of a soul that knows its road, knows its end, resolves to follow the path, feels quite safe, and is therefore perfectly calm and composed. The dying saint is not in a frenzy; he does not run as though alarmed, nor stand still as though he can go no further; he is neither confounded nor ashamed and therefore keeps to his old pace.

Observe that it is not walking *in* the valley but "through" the valley. We go through the dark tunnel of death and emerge into the light of immortality. We do not die; we do but sleep, to wake in glory. Death is not the house but the porch, not the goal but the passage to it.

The place of dying is called a "valley." The storm breaks on the mountain, but the valley is the place of quietude; and thus often the last days of the Christian are the most peaceful of his whole life. The mountain is bleak and bare, but the valley is rich with golden sheaves, and many a saint has reaped more joy and knowledge when he came to die than he ever knew while he lived. Also, it is not "the valley of death" but "the valley *of the shadow* of death," for death in its substance has been removed, and only the "shadow" of it remains.

Verses to meditate upon today: Psalm 23:1-6.

A THOUGHT TO PONDER
We do not die; we do but sleep, to wake in glory.

FEBRUARY 17

GOODNESS AND MERCY

Surely goodness and mercy shall follow me all the days of my life:
and I will dwell in the house of the LORD for ever.
PSALM 23:6

VERSE 5: "Thou preparest a table before me in the presence of mine enemies." The good man has his "enemies." He would not be like his Lord if he did not. If we were without "enemies," we might fear that we were not the friends of God, for the friendship of the world is enmity to God. Yet see the quietude of the godly man in spite of, and in the sight of, his "enemies." How refreshing is his calm bravery!

"Thou anointest my head with oil." May we live in the daily enjoyment of this blessing, receiving a fresh anointing for every day's duties. Every Christian is a priest, but he cannot execute the priestly office without unction, and hence we must go day by day to God the Holy Spirit, that we may have our heads anointed with oil.

VERSE 6: This statement is a fact as indisputable as it is encouraging, and therefore a heavenly verily or "surely" is set as a seal upon it. This sentence may be read, "*only* goodness and mercy," for there shall be unmingled mercy in our history. These twin guardian angels will always be with me at my back and my beck. Just as when great princes go abroad they must not go unattended, so it is with the believer. "Goodness and mercy" follow him always—"all the days of [his] life"—the dark days as well as the bright days, the days of fasting as well as the days of feasting, the dreary days of winter as well as the bright days of summer. "Goodness" supplies our needs, and "mercy" blots out our sins.

"And I will dwell in the house of the LORD for ever." While I am here on earth, I will be a child at home with my God; the whole world shall be his house to me.

Verses to meditate upon today: Psalm 23:1-6.

A THOUGHT TO PONDER
"Goodness" supplies our needs, and "mercy" blots out our sins.

FEBRUARY 18

CREATOR AND SUSTAINER

The earth is the LORD's, and the fulness thereof; the world, and they that dwell therein.
PSALM 24:1

VERSE 1: How very different is this from the ignorant Jewish notion of God that prevailed in our Savior's day. The Jews said, "The holy land is God's, and the seed of Abraham are his only people." But their great Monarch had long before instructed them, "The earth is the LORD's, and the fulness thereof."

The whole world is claimed for Jehovah, and "they that dwell therein" are declared to be his subjects. When we consider the bigotry of the Jewish people at the time of Christ, and how angry they were with our Lord for saying that many widows were in Israel, but unto none of them was the prophet sent, save only to the widow of Sarepta, and that there were many lepers in Israel, but none of them was healed except Naaman the Syrian, when we recollect, too, how angry they were at the mention of Paul's being sent to the Gentiles, we are amazed that they should have remained in such blindness and yet have sung this psalm, which shows so clearly that God is not the God of the Jews only, but of the Gentiles also.

What a rebuke this is to those wiseacres who speak of the Negro and other despised races as though they were not cared for by the God of heaven! If a man be a man, the Lord claims him, and who dares to brand him as a mere piece of merchandise! The meanest of men is a dweller in the world and therefore belongs to Jehovah.

Jesus Christ has made an end of the exclusiveness of nationalities. There is neither barbarian, Scythian, bond nor free; we all are one in Christ Jesus.

Man lives upon "the earth" and parcels out its soil among his mimic kings and autocrats; but the earth is not man's. He is but a tenant, a leaseholder upon the most precarious tenure, liable to instantaneous ejection. The great Landowner and true Proprietor holds his court above the clouds and laughs at the title deeds of worms of the dust.

Verses to meditate upon today: Psalm 24:1-10.

A THOUGHT TO PONDER
The whole world is claimed for Jehovah.

Looking to God

Unto thee, O Lord, do I lift up my soul.
PSALM 25:1

VERSE 1: "Unto thee, O LORD." See how the holy soul flies to its God like a dove to its cote. When the storm winds are out, the Lord's vessels put about and make for their well remembered harbor of refuge. What a mercy that the Lord will condescend to hear our cries in time of trouble, although we may have almost forgotten him in our hours of fancied prosperity.

"Unto thee, O LORD, do I lift up my soul." It is a mockery to uplift the hands and the eyes unless we also bring our souls into our devotions. True prayer may be described as the soul rising from earth to have fellowship with heaven; it is taking a journey upon Jacob's ladder, leaving our cares and fears at the foot and meeting with a covenant God at the top. Very often the soul cannot rise; she has lost her wings and is heavy and earthbound, more like a burrowing mole than a soaring eagle. At such dull seasons we must not give up prayer but must, by God's assistance, exert all our powers to lift up our hearts. Let faith be the lever and grace the arm, and the dead lump will yet be stirred. But what a lift prayer has sometimes proved! With all our tugging and straining we have been utterly defeated, until the heavenly lodestone of our Savior's love has displayed its omnipotent attractions, and then our hearts have gone up to our Beloved like mounting flames of fire.

VERSE 4: "Show me thy ways, O LORD." Unsanctified natures clamor for their own way, but gracious spirits cry, "Not my will, but yours be done." We cannot at all times discern the path of duty, and at such times it is wise to beseech the Lord himself.

Verses to meditate upon today: Psalm 25:1-7.

A Thought to Ponder
True prayer may be described as the soul rising from earth to have fellowship with heaven.

February 20

The Lord's Provision

Mine eyes are ever toward the LORD; for he shall pluck my feet out of the net.
Psalm 25:15

VERSE 15: "Mine eyes are ever toward the LORD." The writer claims to be fixed in his trust and constant in his expectation; he looks in confidence and waits in hope. We may add to this look of faith and hope the obedient look of service, the humble look of reverence, the admiring look of wonder, the studious look of meditation, and the tender look of affection. Happy are those whose "eyes" are never removed from their God. "The eye," says Solomon, "is not satisfied with seeing," but this sight is the most satisfying in the world.

"For he shall pluck my feet out of the net." Observe the conflicting condition in which a gracious soul may be placed: His eyes are in heaven, and yet his feet are sometimes in a "net"; his nobler nature ceases not to behold the glories of God, while his baser parts are enduring the miseries of the world.

A net is a common metaphor for temptation. The Lord often keeps his people from falling into it, and if they have fallen, he rescues them. The word "pluck" is a rough word, and saints who have fallen into sin find that the means of their restoration are not always easy to the flesh; the Lord plucks at us sharply to let us feel that sin is an exceedingly bitter thing. But what a mercy is here; believer, be very grateful for it. The Lord will deliver us from the cunning devices of our cruel enemy, and even if through infirmity we have fallen into sin, he will not leave us to be utterly destroyed but will "pluck" us out of our dangerous state. Though our feet are in "the net," if our "eyes" are lifted up to God, mercy certainly will interpose.

Verses to meditate upon today: Psalm 25:8-15.

A Thought to Ponder
The Lord will deliver us from the cunning devices of our cruel enemy.

FEBRUARY 21

Alone and Afflicted

Turn thee unto me, and have mercy upon me; for I am desolate and afflicted.
Psalm 25:16

Verse 16: David's eyes were fixed upon God, but he feared that the Lord had averted his face from him in anger. Oftentimes unbelief suggests that God has turned his back upon us. If we know that we turn to God, we need not fear that he will turn from us but may boldly cry, "Turn thee unto me." The ground of our quarrel is always in ourselves, and when that is removed, there is nothing to prevent our full enjoyment of communion with God.

"Have mercy upon me." Saints still must stand upon the footing of "mercy"; notwithstanding all their experience, they cannot get beyond the publican's prayer, "Have mercy upon me."

"For I am desolate and afflicted." The psalmist was lonely and bowed down. Jesus was in the days of his flesh in just such a condition; none could enter into the secret depths of his sorrows. He trod the winepress alone, and hence he is able to succor in the fullest sense those who tread the solitary path.

> *Christ leads me through no darker rooms*
> *Than he went through before;*
> *He that into God's kingdom comes*
> *Must enter by this door.*

Verse 17: "The troubles of my heart are enlarged." When trouble penetrates the heart, it is trouble indeed. In the case before us, the "heart" was swollen with grief like a lake surcharged with water by enormous floods; this is used as an argument for deliverance, and it is a potent one. When the darkest hour of the night arrives, we may expect the dawn; when the sea is at its lowest ebb, the tide must surely turn; and when our troubles are enlarged to the greatest degree, then we may hopefully pray, "O bring thou me out of my distresses."

Verses to meditate upon today: Psalm 25:16-22.

A Thought to Ponder

If we know that we turn to God, we need not fear that he will turn from us.

FEBRUARY 22

TRIALS

Examine me, O LORD, and prove me; try my reins and my heart.
PSALM 26:2

VERSE 2: The psalmist was so clear from the charge laid against him that he submitted himself unconditionally to any form of examination that the Lord might see fit to employ.

"Examine me, O LORD." *Look me over through and through; make a minute survey; put me to the test; cross-examine my evidence.* "And prove me." *Put me to trial; see if I would follow such wicked designs as my enemies impute to me.*

"Try my reins and my heart." *Assay me as metals are assayed in the furnace, and do this to my most secret parts, where my affections hold their court. See, O God, whether or not I love murder and treason and deceit.*

All this is a very bold appeal, and being made by David, who feared the Lord exceedingly, it manifests a most solemn and complete conviction of innocence. The expressions here used should teach us the thoroughness of the divine judgment and the necessity of being in all things profoundly sincere, lest we be found wanting at the last. Our enemies are severe with us with the severity of spite, and this a brave man endures without fear; but God's severity is that of unswerving right. Who shall stand against such a trial? The sweet singer says, "Who can stand before his cold?" and we may well enquire, "Who can stand before the heat of his justice?"

Verse 3: "For thy loving-kindness is before mine eyes." Here is an object of memory and a ground of hope. A sense of mercy received sets a fair prospect before the faithful mind in its gloomiest condition, for it yields visions of mercies yet to come, visions not visionary but real.

Verses to meditate upon today: Psalm 26:1-8.

A THOUGHT TO PONDER
Look me over through and through.

FEBRUARY 23

BRIBERY AND GODLINESS

My foot standeth in an even place: in the congregations will I bless the LORD.
PSALM 26:12

VERSE 10: Bribery, in any form or shape, should be as detestable to a Christian as carrion to a dove or garbage to a lamb. Let those whose dirty hands are fond of bribes remember that neither death nor the devil can be bribed to let them escape their well-earned doom.

VERSE 11: Here is the lover of godliness entering his personal protest against unrighteous gain. He is a nonconformist and is ready to stand alone in his nonconformity. Like a live fish, he swims against the stream. Trusting in God, the psalmist resolves that the plain way of righteousness shall be his choice, and those who so choose prefer this to the tortuous paths of violence and deceit. Yet he is by no means a boaster or a self-righteous vaunter of his own strength, for he cries for redemption and pleads for mercy. Our integrity is not absolute or inherent; it is a work of grace in us and is marred by human infirmity. We must, therefore, resort to the redeeming blood and to the throne of mercy, confessing that though we are saints among men, we must still bow as sinners before God.

VERSE 12: The song began in a minor key, but it has now reached a major key. Saints often sing themselves into happiness. The "even place" upon which our foot stands is the sure covenant faithfulness, eternal promise, and immutable oath of the Lord of Hosts; there is no fear of falling from this solid basis or of its being removed from under us. Established in Christ Jesus, by being vitally united to him, we have nothing left to occupy our thoughts but the praises of our God. Let us not forsake the assembling of ourselves together, and when assembled, let us not be slow to contribute our portion of thanksgiving. Each saint is a witness to divine faithfulness and should be ready with his testimony. As for the slanderers, let them howl outside the door while the children sing within.

Verses to meditate upon today: Psalm 26:9-12.

A THOUGHT TO PONDER
Our integrity is not absolute or inherent; it is a work of grace in us.

FEBRUARY 24

THE LORD IS MY LIGHT

The LORD is my light and my salvation; whom shall I fear?
The LORD is the strength of my life; of whom shall I be afraid?
PSALM 27:1

VERSE 1: "The LORD is my light and my salvation." The psalmist is assured of God's personal interest and therefore declares this boldly.

"My light." Into the soul at the new birth divine "light" is poured as the precursor of salvation; where there is not enough light to see our own darkness and to long for the Lord Jesus, there is no evidence of salvation. Salvation finds us in the dark but does not leave us there. After conversion our God is in every sense our "light." It is not said merely that the Lord gives light, but that he "is" light; not that he gives salvation, but that he "is" salvation. He, then, who by faith has laid hold upon God has all the covenant blessings in his possession.

"The LORD is the strength of my life." Our life derives all its "strength" from him who is the author of it; and if he deigns to make us strong, we cannot be weakened by all the machinations of the adversary.

"Of whom shall I be afraid?" This bold question looks into the future as well as at the present. "If God be for us, who can be against us?" [Romans 8:31].

VERSE 4: "One thing." Divided aims tend to distraction, weakness, disappointment. Let all our affections be bound up in one, set upon heavenly things. "Have I desired." What we cannot at once attain, it is good to desire. God judges us very much by the desire of our hearts. Someone riding a lame horse is not blamed by his master for lack of speed, if he makes all the haste he can. God takes the will for the deed with his children.

Verses to meditate upon today: Psalm 27:1-6.

A THOUGHT TO PONDER
After conversion our God is in every sense our "light."

FEBRUARY 25

SEEKING GOD

*When thou saidst, Seek ye my face; my heart said unto thee,
Thy face, LORD, will I seek.*
PSALM 27:8

VERSE 8: In this verse we are taught that if we would have the Lord hear our voice, we must be careful to respond to *his* voice. The true heart should echo the will of God as the rocks among the Alps repeat in sweetest music the notes of the peasant's horn.

Observe that the command was in the plural, to all the saints—"Seek ye"—but the man of God turned it into the singular by a personal application—"Thy face, LORD, will I seek." The voice of the Lord is very effectual where all other voices fail. "When thou saidst," then my "heart," my inmost nature, was moved to an obedient reply. Note the promptness of the response—no sooner said than done; as soon as God said "seek," the heart said, "thy face will I seek." Oh, for more of this holy readiness! Would to God that we were more alert to the divine hand, more sensitive to the touch of God's Spirit.

VERSE 9: "Hide not thy face far from me." The word "far" is not in the original and is a very superfluous addition of the translators, since even the least hiding of the Lord's face is a great affliction to a believer. The command to seek the Lord's "face" would be a painful one if the Lord, by withdrawing himself, rendered it impossible for the seeker to meet with him. A smile from the Lord is the greatest of comforts, his frown the worst of ills.

"Put not thy servant away in anger." Other servants had been put away when they proved unfaithful, as, for instance, David's predecessor Saul; and this made David, while conscious of many faults, most anxious that divine long-suffering should continue in his favor. This is a most appropriate prayer for us under a similar sense of unworthiness.

Verses to meditate upon today: Psalm 27:7-14.

A THOUGHT TO PONDER
A smile from the Lord is the greatest of comforts.

FEBRUARY 26

LORD, SAVE YOUR CHURCH

Save thy people, and bless thine inheritance: feed them also, and lift them up for ever.
PSALM 28:9

VERSE 8: "The LORD is their strength." The heavenly experience of one believer is a pattern of the life of all. To all the militant church, without exception, Jehovah is the same as he was to his servant David. The least of them shall be as David. They need the same aid, and they shall have it, for they are loved with the same love, are written in the same book of life, and are one with the same anointed Head.

"And he is the saving strength of his anointed." Here behold King David as the type of our Lord Jesus, our covenant Head, our anointed Prince, through whom all blessings come to us. Our Savior has achieved full salvation for us, and we desire saving strength from him; and as we share in the unction that is so largely shed upon him, we expect to partake of his salvation. Glory be unto the God and Father of our Lord Jesus Christ, who has magnified the power of his grace in his only begotten Son, whom he has anointed to be a Prince and a Savior unto his people.

VERSE 9: This is a prayer for the church militant, written in short words but full of weighty meaning. We must pray for the whole church, and not for ourselves alone.

"Save thy people." *Deliver them from their enemies, preserve them from their sins, succor them under their troubles, rescue them from their temptations, and ward off from them every ill.*

There is a plea hidden in the expression, "thy people," for it may be safely concluded that God's interest in the church, as his own portion, will lead him to guard it from destruction. "Bless thine inheritance." *Grant positive blessings, peace, plenty, prosperity, happiness; make all your dearly purchased and precious heritage to be comforted by your Spirit. Revive, refresh, enlarge, and sanctify your church.*

Verses to meditate upon today: Psalm 28:1-9.

A THOUGHT TO PONDER
Our Savior has achieved full salvation for us, and
we desire saving strength from him.

FEBRUARY 27

THE VOICE OF THE LORD

The voice of the LORD maketh the hinds to calve, and discovereth the forests:
and in his temple doth every one speak of his glory.

PSALM 29:9

VERSE 9: "The voice of the LORD maketh the hinds to calve." Those timid creatures, in deadly fear of the tempest, drop their burdens in an untimely manner. Perhaps a better reading is, "the oaks to tremble," especially as this agrees with the next sentence, "and discovereth the forests." The dense shades of the forest are lit up with the lurid glare of lightning, and even the darkest recesses are for a moment laid bare.

> *The gloomy woods*
> *Start at the flash, and from their deep recesses*
> *Wide flaming out, their trembling inmates shake.*

Our first parents sought a refuge among the trees, but the voice of the Lord soon found them out and made their hearts tremble. There is no concealment from the fiery glance of the Almighty; one flash of his angry eye turns midnight into noon. The Gospel has a like revealing power in dark hearts; in a moment it lights up every dark recess of the heart's ungodliness and bids the soul tremble before the Lord.

"In his temple doth every one speak of his glory." Those who were worshiping in the temple were led to speak of the greatness of Jehovah as they heard the repeated thunder claps. The whole world is also a temple for God, and when he rides abroad upon the wings of the wind, all things are vocal in his praise. We too, the redeemed of the Lord, who are living temples for his Spirit, as we see the wonders of his power in creation and feel them in grace, unite to magnify his name. No tongue may be mute in God's temple when his glory is the theme.

The original appears to have the force of, "everyone crieth Glory," as though all things were moved by a sense of God's majesty to shout in ecstasy, "Glory, glory." Here is a good precedent for our Methodist friends and for the zealous Welsh.

Verses to meditate upon today: Psalm 29:1-11.

A THOUGHT TO PONDER

The Gospel bids the soul tremble before the Lord.

February 28

Healing

O LORD my God, I cried unto thee, and thou hast healed me.
Psalm 30:2

Verse 2: David sent up prayers for himself and for his people when visited with pestilence. He went at once to headquarters, and not roundabout to fallible means. God is the best physician, even for our bodily infirmities. We do very wickedly and foolishly when we forget God.

It was a sin in Asa that he trusted to physicians and not to God. If we must have a physician, let it be so, but still let us go to our God first of all. And above all, remember that there can be no power to heal in medicine of itself; the healing energy must flow from the divine hand.

If our watch is out of order, we take it to the watchmaker. If our body or soul be in an evil plight, let us resort to him who created them and has unfailing skill to put them in right condition.

As for our spiritual diseases, nothing can heal these evils but the touch of the Lord Christ. If we do but touch the hem of his garment, we shall be made whole, while if we embrace all other physicians alone in our arms, they can do us no service.

"O LORD my God." Observe the covenant name that faith uses—"my God." Thrice happy is he who can claim the Lord himself to be his portion. Note how David's faith ascends the scale: He sang "O LORD" in the first verse, but it is "O LORD my God" in the second. Heavenly heart music is an ascending thing, like the pillars of smoke that rose from the altar of incense. "I cried unto thee." I could hardly pray, but "I cried." I poured out my soul as a little child pours out its desires. "I cried" to my God. I knew to whom to cry; I did not cry to my friends or to any arm of flesh.

Hence the sure and satisfactory result: "thou hast healed me." *I know it. I am sure of it. I have the evidence of spiritual health within me now: Glory be to your name!* Every humble suppliant with God who seeks release from the disease of sin shall speed to God as well as the psalmist did, but those who will not so much as seek a cure need not wonder if their wounds putrefy and their soul dies.

Verses to meditate upon today: Psalm 30:1-7.

A Thought to Ponder
God is the best physician, even for our bodily infirmities.

FEBRUARY 29

Mourning into Dancing

Thou hast turned for me my mourning into dancing:
thou hast put off my sackcloth, and girded me with gladness.
PSALM 30:11

VERSE 11: Observe the contrast: God takes away the "mourning" of his people, and what does he give them instead of it? Quiet and peace? Aye, and a great deal more than that.

"Thou hast turned for me my mourning into dancing." He makes their hearts dance at the sound of his name. He takes off their "sackcloth." That is good. What a delight to be rid of the trappings of woe! But what then? He clothes us. And how? With some common dress? Nay, but with that royal vestment that is the array of glorified spirits in heaven.

"Thou hast . . . girded me with gladness." This is better than to wear garments of silk or cloth of gold, arrayed with embroidery and bespangled with gems. Many a poor man wears this heavenly apparel wrapped around his heart, though cotton and corduroy are his only outward garb; and such a man needs not envy the emperor in all his pomp. *Glory be to you, O God, if by a sense of full forgiveness and present justification you have enriched my spiritual nature and filled me with all your fullness.*

VERSE 12: "To the end"—namely, with this view and intent—"that my glory"—that is, my tongue or my soul—"may sing praise to thee, and not be silent."

It would be a shameful crime if, after receiving God's mercies, we should forget to praise him. God would not have our tongues lie idle while so many themes for gratitude are spread on every hand. He would have no mute children in the house. They are all to sing in heaven, and therefore they should all sing on earth.

Verses to meditate upon today: Psalm 30:8-12.

A Thought to Ponder

It would be a shameful crime if, after receiving God's mercies,
we should forget to praise him.

MARCH 1

GUIDE ME

For thou art my rock and my fortress; therefore for thy name's sake lead me, and guide me.
PSALM 31:3

VERSE 3: "For thou art my rock and my fortress." Here the tried soul avows yet again its full confidence in God. Faith's repetitions are not vain. The avowal of our reliance upon God in times of adversity is a principal method of glorifying him. Active service is good, but the passive confidence of faith is not one jot less esteemed in the sight of God.

The words before us appear to embrace and fasten upon the Lord with a trusting grip that will not be relaxed. The two personal pronouns ("my" twice), like sure nails, lay hold upon the faithfulness of the Lord. Oh, for grace to have our heart fixed in firm, unstaggering belief in God!

The figure of a "rock" and a "fortress" may be illustrated to us in these times by the vast fortress of Gibraltar, often besieged by our enemies, but never wrested from us. Ancient strongholds, though far from impregnable by our modes of warfare, were equally important in those more remote ages—when in the mountain fastnesses, feeble bands felt themselves to be secure. Note the singular fact that David asked the Lord to be his "rock" (verse 2) because he *was* his "rock" (verse 3); and learn from it that we may pray to enjoy in experience what we grasp by faith. Faith is the foundation of prayer.

"Therefore for thy name's sake lead me, and guide me." The psalmist argues like a logician with his fors and therefores. *Since I do sincerely trust you,* says he, *O my God, be my director.* To "lead" and to "guide" are two things very like each other, but patient thought will detect different shades of meaning, especially as the last may mean *provide for me.* The two words indicate an urgent need: We require double direction, for we are fools, and the way is rough. *Lead me as a soldier; guide me as a traveler!*

Verses to meditate upon today: Psalm 31:1-8.

A THOUGHT TO PONDER
We may pray to enjoy in experience what we grasp by faith.

MARCH 2

HELD IN CONTEMPT

I was a reproach among all mine enemies, but especially among my neighbors, and a fear to mine acquaintance: they that did see me without fled from me.
PSALM 31:11

VERSE 11: "I was a reproach among all mine enemies." They were pleased to have something to throw at me; my mournful estate was music to them, because they maliciously interpreted it to be a judgment from heaven upon me. Reproach is little thought of by those who are not called to endure it, but he who passes under its lash knows how deep it wounds. The best of men may have the bitterest foes and be subject to the most cruel taunts.

"But especially among my neighbors." Those who are nearest can stab the sharpest. We feel most the slights of those who should have shown us sympathy. Perhaps David's friends feared to be identified with his declining fortunes and therefore turned against him in order to win the mercy, if not the favor, of his opponents. Self-interest rules most men; ties the most sacred are soon snapped by its influence, and actions of the utmost meanness are perpetrated without scruple.

"And a fear to mine acquaintance." The more intimate before, the more distant did they become. Our Lord was denied by Peter, betrayed by Judas, and forsaken by all in the hour of his utmost need. All the herd turn against a wounded deer. The milk of human kindness curdles when a despised believer is the victim of slanderous accusations.

"They that did see me without fled from me." Afraid to be seen in the company of a man so thoroughly despised, those who once courted his society hastened from him as though he had been infected with the plague. How villainous a thing is slander, which can make an eminent saint, once the admiration of his people, to become the universal aversion of mankind! To what extremities of dishonor may innocence be reduced!

Verses to meditate upon today: Psalm 31:9-18.

A THOUGHT TO PONDER
The best of men may have the bitterest foes, and be subject to the most cruel taunts.

MARCH 3

THE LORD'S GREAT GOODNESS

Oh how great is thy goodness, which thou hast laid up for them that fear thee; which thou hast wrought for them that trust in thee before the sons of men!

PSALM 31:19

VERSE 19: "Oh how great is thy goodness." Is it not singular to find such a joyful sentence in connection with so much sorrow? Truly the life of faith is a miracle. When faith led David to his God, she set him singing at once. He does not tell us how great was God's "goodness," for he could not; there are no measures that can set forth the immeasurable goodness of Jehovah, who is goodness itself. Holy amazement uses interjections where adjectives utterly fail. Notes of exclamation suit us when words of explanation are of no avail. Though we cannot measure, we can marvel; and though we may not calculate with accuracy, we can adore with fervency.

"Which thou hast laid up for them that fear thee." The psalmist in contemplation divides goodness into two parts—that which is in store and that which is wrought out. The Lord has laid up in reserve for his people supplies beyond all count. In the treasury of the covenant, in the field of redemption, in the chests of the promises, in the granaries of providence, the Lord has provided for all the needs that can possibly occur to his chosen. We ought often to consider the laid-up goodness of God that has not yet been distributed to the chosen but is already provided for them. If we are much in such contemplations, we shall be led to feel devout gratitude, such as glowed in the heart of David.

"Which thou hast wrought for them that trust in thee before the sons of men!" Heavenly mercy is not all hidden in the storehouse; in a thousand ways it has already revealed itself on behalf of those who are bold to avow their confidence in God. Before their fellowmen this goodness of the Lord has been displayed, that a faithless generation might stand rebuked.

Verses to meditate upon today: Psalm 31:19-24.

A THOUGHT TO PONDER

The Lord has provided for all the needs that can possibly occur to his chosen.

MARCH 4

My Hiding Place

Thou art my hiding place; thou shalt preserve me from trouble;
thou shalt compass me about with songs of deliverance. Selah.

PSALM 32:7

VERSE 7: "Thou art my hiding place." Terse, short sentences make up this verse, but they contain a world of meaning. Personal claims upon our God are the joy of spiritual life. To lay our hand upon the Lord with the clasp of a personal "my" is delight at its full. Observe that the same man who in the fourth verse was oppressed by the presence of God here finds a shelter in him. See what honest confession and full forgiveness will do! The Gospel of substitution makes him to be our refuge who otherwise would have been our judge.

"Thou shalt preserve me from trouble." Trouble shall do me no real harm when the Lord is with me; rather it shall bring me much benefit, like the file that clears away the rust but does not destroy the metal. Observe the three tenses: We have noticed the sorrowful past, the last sentence was a joyful present, and this is a cheerful future.

"Thou shalt compass me about with songs of deliverance." What a golden sentence! The man is encircled in song, surrounded by dancing mercies, all of them proclaiming the triumphs of grace. There is no breach in the circle—it completely rings him round; on all sides he hears music. Before him hope sounds the cymbals, and behind him gratitude beats the timbrel. Right and left, above and beneath, the air resounds with joy, and all this for the very man who a few weeks ago was "roaring all the day long." How great a change! What wonders grace has done and still can do!

"Selah." There was need of a pause, for love so amazing needs to be pondered, and joy so great demands quiet contemplation, since language fails to express it.

Verses to meditate upon today: Psalm 32:1-7.

A Thought to Ponder

The Gospel of substitution makes him to be our refuge who otherwise
would have been our judge.

GUIDANCE

*I will instruct thee and teach thee in the way which thou shalt go:
I will guide thee with mine eye.*

Psalm 32:8

VERSE 8: "I will instruct thee." Here the Lord is the speaker and gives the psalmist an answer to his prayer. Our Savior is our instructor. The Lord himself deigns to teach his children to walk in the way of integrity; his holy word and the admonitions of the Holy Spirit are the directors of the believer's daily behavior.

We are not pardoned that we may henceforth live after our own lusts, but that we may be educated in holiness and trained for perfection. A heavenly training is one of the covenant blessings that adoption seals to us: "All thy children shall be taught by the LORD." Practical teaching is the very best of instruction, and they are thrice happy who, although they never sat at the feet of Gamaliel and are ignorant of Aristotle and the ethics of the schools, have nevertheless learned to follow the Lamb whithersoever he goes.

"I will guide thee with mine eye." As servants take their cue from the master's eye, and a nod or a wink is all that they require, so should we obey the slightest hints of our Master, not needing thunderbolts to startle our incorrigible sluggishness, but being controlled by whispers and loving touches. The Lord is the great overseer, whose eye in providence overlooks everything. It is well for us to be the sheep of his pasture, following the guidance of his wisdom.

VERSE 9: "Be ye not as the horse, or as the mule, which have no understanding." "Understanding" separates man from a brute—let us not act as if we were devoid of it. Men should take counsel and advice and be ready to run where wisdom points them the way. Alas, we need to be cautioned against stupidity of heart, for we are very apt to fall into it. We who ought to be as the angels readily become as the beasts.

Verses to meditate upon today: Psalm 32:8-11.

A Thought to Ponder

The Lord himself deigns to teach his children to walk in the way of integrity.

MARCH 6

Music

Praise the LORD with harp: sing unto him with the psaltery and an instrument of ten strings.

PSALM 33:2

VERSE 2: "Praise the LORD with harp." Men need all the help they can get to stir them up to praise. This is the lesson to be gathered from the use of musical instruments under the old dispensation. Israel was at school and used childish things to help her to learn; but in these days, when Jesus gives us spiritual manhood, we can make melody without strings and pipes. However, we who do not believe these things to be expedient in worship, lest they should mar its simplicity, do not affirm them to be unlawful, and if any George Herbert or Martin Luther can worship God better by the aid of well-tuned instruments, who shall gainsay their right? Some of us do not need them, feeling they would hinder rather than help our praise; but if others are otherwise minded, are they not living in gospel liberty?

"Sing unto him." This is the sweetest and best of music. There is no instrument like the human voice.

"With the psaltery and an instrument of ten strings." The Lord must have a full octave, for all notes are his, and all music belongs to him. Where several pieces of music are mentioned, we are taught to praise God with all the powers that we possess.

VERSE 3: "Sing unto him a new song." All songs of praise should be "unto him." Singing for singing's sake is worth nothing; we must carry our tribute to the King, and not cast it to the winds. Do most worshipers mind this? Our faculties should be exercised when we are magnifying the Lord, so as not to run in an old groove without thought; we ought to make every hymn of praise a "new song." To keep the freshness of worship is a great thing, and in private it is indispensable.

Verses to meditate upon today: Psalm 33:1-5.

A THOUGHT TO PONDER

We are taught to praise God with all the powers that we possess.

CREATION

By the word of the LORD were the heavens made; and all the host of them by the breath of his mouth.
PSALM 33:6

VERSE 6: "By the word of the LORD were the heavens made." The angelic heavens, the stellar heavens, and the firmament or terrestrial heavens were all brought into existence by a word; we could say by *the* Word: "And without him was not any thing made that was made" [John 1:3].

It is interesting to note the mention of the Spirit in the next clause, "and all the host of them by the breath of his mouth"; "breath" here is elsewhere rendered "Spirit." The three persons of the Godhead unite in creating all things. How easy for the Lord to make the most ponderous orbs and the most glorious angels! A word, a breath, could do it. It is as easy for God to create the universe as for a man to breathe—nay, far easier, for man breathes not independently but borrows the breath in his nostrils from his Maker. It may be gathered from this verse that the constitution of all things is from the Infinite Wisdom, for his "word" may mean his appointment and determination. A wise and merciful Word has arranged and a living Spirit sustains all the creation of Jehovah.

VERSE 7: "He gathereth the waters of the sea together as a heap." The waters were once scattered like corn strewn upon a threshing floor; they are now collected in their place. Who else could have gathered them but their great Lord, at whose bidding the waters fled away? The miracle of the Red Sea is repeated in nature day by day, for the sea that now invades the shore under the impulse of sun and moon would soon devour the land if bounds were not maintained by the divine decree.

Verses to meditate upon today: Psalm 33:6-11.

A THOUGHT TO PONDER

The three persons of the Godhead unite in creating all things.

MARCH 8

A BLESSED NATION

Blessed is the nation whose God is the LORD; and the people whom he hath chosen for his own inheritance.

PSALM 33:12

VERSE 12: "Blessed is the nation whose God is the LORD." Israel was happy in the worship of the only true God. It was the blessedness of the chosen nation to have received a revelation from Jehovah. While others groveled before their idols, the chosen people were elevated by a spiritual religion that introduced them to the invisible God and led them to trust in him. All who confide in the Lord are blessed in the largest and deepest sense, and none can reverse the blessing.

"And the people whom he hath chosen for his own inheritance." Election is at the bottom of it all. The divine choice rules the day; none take Jehovah to be their God until he takes them to be his people. What an ennobling choice this is! We are selected to no mean estate and for no ignoble purpose; we are made the peculiar domain and delight of the Lord our God. Being so blessed, let us rejoice in our portion and show the world by our lives that we serve a glorious Master.

VERSE 13: "The LORD looketh from heaven." The Lord is represented as dwelling above and looking down below, seeing all things, but especially observing and caring for those who trust in him. It is one of our choicest privileges to be always under our Father's eye, to be never out of sight of our best friend.

"He beholdeth all the sons of men." All Adam's sons are as well watched as was Adam himself, their progenitor in the garden. Ranging from the frozen pole to the scorching equator, dwelling in hills and valleys, in huts and palaces, alike does the divine eye regard all the members of the family of man.

Verses to meditate upon today: Psalm 33:12-22.

A THOUGHT TO PONDER

It is one of our choicest privileges to be always under our Father's eye, to be never out of sight of our best friend.

Being Radiant

They looked unto him, and were lightened: and their faces were not ashamed.
PSALM 34:5

VERSE 5: "They looked unto him, and were lightened." The psalmist avows that his case was not at all peculiar—it was matched in the lives of all the faithful. They too, each one of them, looking to their Lord, were brightened up; their faces began to shine; their spirits were uplifted. What a means of blessing one look at the Lord may be! There is life, light, liberty, love—everything in fact—in a look at the Crucified One. Never did a sore heart look in vain to the Good Physician; never a dying soul turned its darkening eye to the brazen serpent to find its virtue gone.

"And their faces were not ashamed." Their faces were covered with joy but not with blushes. He who trusts in God has no need to be ashamed of his confidence; time and eternity will both justify his reliance.

VERSE 6: "This poor man cried." Here the psalmist returns to his own case. He was "poor" indeed, and so utterly friendless that his life was in great jeopardy; but he "cried" in his heart to the Protector of his people and found relief. His prayer was a cry, with brevity and bitterness, with earnestness and simplicity, with artlessness and grief; it was a poor man's cry, but it was nonetheless powerful with heaven, for "the LORD heard him," and to be heard of God is to be delivered. And so it is added that the Lord "saved him out of all his troubles." At once and altogether David was rid of all his woes. The Lord sweeps our griefs away as men destroy a hive of hornets or as the winds clear away the mists. This verse is the psalmist's own personal testimony, and he being dead yet speaks. Let the afflicted reader take heart and be of good courage.

Verses to meditate upon today: Psalm 34:1-7.

A Thought to Ponder
There is life, light, liberty, love—everything in fact—in a look at the Crucified One.

MARCH 10

TASTE AND SEE

O taste and see that the LORD is good: blessed is the man that trusteth in him.
PSALM 34:8

VERSE 8: "O taste and see." Make a trial—an inward, experimental trial—of the goodness of God. You cannot "see" except by tasting for yourself; but if you "taste" you shall "see."

"That the LORD is good." You can only know this really and personally by experience. There is the banquet with its oxen and fatlings, its fat full of marrow, and wine well refined; but their sweetness will be unknown to you unless you make the blessings of grace your own by a living, inward, vital participation in them.

"Blessed is the man that trusteth in him." Faith is the soul's taste; they who test the Lord by their confidence always find him good, and they are "blessed." The second clause of the verse is an argument in support of the exhortation contained in the first sentence.

VERSE 9: "O fear the LORD, ye his saints." Pay to him humble childlike reverence; walk in his laws; have respect for his will; tremble to offend him; hasten to serve him. Fear not the wrath of men, neither be tempted to sin through the virulence of their threats. Fear God and fear nothing else. "For there is no want to them that fear him." Jehovah will not allow his faithful servants to starve. He may not give luxuries, but the promise binds him to supply necessities, and he will not run back from his word. Many whims and wishes may remain unfulfilled, but real wants the Lord will supply. The fear of the Lord or true piety is not only the duty of those who avow themselves to be saints—that is, persons set apart and consecrated for holy duties—but it is also their path of safety and comfort.

Verses to meditate upon today: Psalm 34:8-14.

A THOUGHT TO PONDER
Jehovah will not allow his faithful servants to starve.

MARCH 11

THE BROKENHEARTED

*The LORD is nigh unto them that are of a broken heart;
and saveth such as be of a contrite spirit.*

PSALM 34:18

VERSE 18: "The LORD is nigh unto them that are of a broken heart." He is near in friendship to accept and console. Broken hearts think God faraway, when he is really most near them; their eyes are blocked so that they see not their best friend. Indeed, he is with them, and in them, but they know it not. They run hither and thither, seeking peace in their own works or in experiences or in proposals and resolutions, whereas the Lord is nigh to them, and the simple act of faith will reveal him.

"And saveth such as be of a contrite spirit." What a blessed token for good is a repentant, mourning heart! Just when the sinner condemns himself, the Lord graciously absolves him. If we chasten our own spirits, the Lord will spare us. He never breaks with the rod of judgment those who are already sore with the rod of conviction. Salvation is linked with contrition.

VERSE 19: "Many are the afflictions of the righteous." Thus are they made like Jesus, their covenant Head. Scripture does not flatter us as do the storybooks with the idea that goodness will secure us from trouble; on the contrary, we are again and again warned to expect tribulation while we are in this body. Our afflictions come from all points of the compass and are as many and as tormenting as the mosquitoes of the Tropics. It is the earthly portion of the elect to find thorns and briars growing in their pathway—yea, to lie down among them, finding their rest broken and disturbed by sorrow.

But, blessed *but,* how the next words take the sting out of the previous sentence! "But the LORD delivereth him out of them all." Through troops of ills Jehovah shall lead his redeemed unharmed and triumphant. There is an end to the believer's affliction, and a joyful end too.

Verses to meditate upon today: Psalm 34:15-22.

A THOUGHT TO PONDER
Broken hearts think God faraway, when he is really most near them.

MARCH 12

THE POOR AND NEEDY

*All my bones shall say, LORD, who is like unto thee,
which deliverest the poor from him that is too strong for him, yea,
the poor and the needy from him that spoileth him?*

PSALM 35:10

VERSE 9: "And my soul shall be joyful in the LORD." Once rescued, David ascribes all the honor to the Judge; to his own valorous arm he offers no boasting. He turns away from his adversaries to his God and finds a deep unbroken joy in Jehovah, and in that joy his spirit revels.

"It shall rejoice in his salvation." We do not triumph in the destruction of others, but in the "salvation" given to us by God. Prayer heard should always suggest praise. It were well if we were more demonstrative in our holy rejoicing. We rob God by suppressing grateful emotions.

VERSE 10: As the tongue is not enough to bless God with, David makes every limb vocal: "All my bones shall say, LORD, who is like unto thee?" His whole anatomy he would make resonant with gratitude. Those "bones" that were to have been broken by my enemies shall now praise God; every one of them shall bring its tribute, ascribing unrivaled excellence to Jehovah, the Savior of his people. Even if worn to skin and bone, yet my very skeleton shall magnify the Lord, "which deliverest the poor from him that is too strong for him, yea, the poor and the needy from him that spoileth him." God is the champion, the true knight-errant of all oppressed ones. Where there is so much justice, kindness, power, and compassion, the loftiest songs should be rendered. Come, dear reader, have you not been delivered from sin, Satan, and death, and will not you bless the Redeemer? You were poor and weak, but in due time Christ sought you and set you free. Oh, magnify the Lord today, and speak well of his name.

Verses to meditate upon today: Psalm 35:1-10.

A THOUGHT TO PONDER

God is the champion, the true knight-errant of all oppressed ones.

MARCH 13

False Accusation

For they speak not peace: but they devise deceitful matters against them that are quiet in the land.

PSALM 35:20

VERSE 20: "For they speak not peace." They love it not; how can they "speak" it? They are such troublers themselves that they cannot judge others to be peaceable. Out of the mouth comes what is in the heart. Riotous men charge others with sedition.

"They devise deceitful matters against them that are quiet in the land." David desired to be an orderly citizen, but they labored to make him a rebel. He could do nothing aright in their eyes; all his dealings were misrepresented. It is an old trick of the enemy to brand good men with S.S. on their cheeks, as sowers of sedition though they have ever been a harmless race, like sheep among wolves. When mischief is meant, mischief is soon made. Unscrupulous partisans even charged Jesus with seeking to overturn Caesar; much more will they accuse his household. At this very hour those who stand up for the crown rights of King Jesus are called enemies of the church, friends of atheists, and it is hard to say what besides.

VERSE 21: "Yea, they opened their mouth wide against me," as if they would swallow him. Uttering great lies that needed wide mouths, they set no bounds to their infamous charges but poured out wholesale abuse, trusting that if all did not stick, some of it would.

"... and said, Aha, aha, our eye hath seen it." They were glad to find a fault or a misfortune, or to swear they had seen evil where there was none. Malice has but one eye; it is blind to all virtue in its enemy. Eyes can generally see what hearts wish. A man with a mote in his eye sees a spot in the sun. How like a man is to a donkey when he brays over another's misfortunes!

Verses to meditate upon today: Psalm 35:11-21.

A Thought to Ponder
Eyes can generally see what hearts wish.

MARCH 14

SHOUT FOR JOY

Let them shout for joy, and be glad, that favor my righteous cause: yea, let them say continually, Let the LORD be magnified, which hath pleasure in the prosperity of his servant.

PSALM 35:27

VERSE 26: Here is the eternal result of all the laborious and crafty devices of the Lord's enemies. God will make little of them, though they magnified themselves; he will shame them for shaming his people, bring them to confusion for making confusion, pull off their fine apparel and give them a beggarly suit of dishonor, and turn all their rejoicing into weeping and wailing and gnashing of teeth. Truly the saints can afford to wait.

VERSE 27: "Let them shout for joy, and be glad, that favor my righteous cause." Even those who could not render him active aid but in their hearts favored him, David would have the Lord reward most abundantly. Men of tender heart set great store by the good wishes and prayers of the Lord's people. Jesus also prizes those whose hearts are with his cause. The day is coming when shouts of victory shall be raised by all who are on Christ's side, for the battle will turn, and the foes of truth shall be routed.

"Yea, let them say continually, Let the LORD be magnified." He desires that their gladness contribute to the divine glory; they are not to shout to David's praise, but for the honor of Jehovah. Such acclamations may fitly be continued throughout time and eternity.

"Which hath pleasure in the prosperity of his servant." They recognized David as the Lord's servant and saw with "pleasure" the Lord's favor to him. We can have no nobler title than "servant of God," and no greater reward than for our Master to delight in our prosperity. What true prosperity may be we are not always best able to judge. We must leave that in Jesus' hand; he will not fail to rule all things for our highest good.

Verses to meditate upon today: Psalm 35:22-28.

A Thought to Ponder
Shouts of victory shall be raised by all who are on Christ's side.

MARCH 15

GOD'S LOVE AND FAITHFULNESS

Thy mercy, O LORD, is in the heavens; and thy faithfulness reacheth unto the clouds.
PSALM 36:5

VERSE 5: "Thy mercy, O LORD, is in the heavens." Like the ethereal blue, God's "mercy" encompasses the whole earth, acting as a canopy for all the creatures of earth, surmounting the loftiest peaks of human provocations, rising high above the mists of mortal transgression. Clear sky is evermore above the earth, and mercy calmly smiles above the din and smoke of this poor world. Darkness and clouds are but of earth's lower atmospheres; the heavens are evermore serene, and bright with innumerable stars. Divine mercy abides in its vastness of expanse and matchless patience, all unaltered by the rebellions of man. When we can measure the heavens, then shall we see the boundaries of the mercy of the Lord. Toward his own servants especially, in the salvation of the Lord Jesus, he has displayed grace higher than the heaven of heavens and wider than the universe. If the atheist could see this, how earnestly would he long to become a servant of Jehovah!

"Thy faithfulness reacheth unto the clouds." Far, far above all comprehension is the truth and faithfulness of God. He never fails, never forgets, never falters, never forfeits his word. Afflictions are like clouds, but the divine truthfulness is all around them. While we are under the cloud, we are in the region of God's faithfulness; when we mount above it, we shall not need such an assurance. To every word of threat, promise, prophecy, or covenant, the Lord has exactly adhered, for he is not a man that he should lie, nor the son of man that he should repent.

VERSE 6: "Thy righteousness is like the great mountains"—firm and unmoved, lofty and sublime. As winds and hurricanes shake not the Alps, so the "righteousness" of God is never in any degree affected by circumstances; he is always just.

Verses to meditate upon today: Psalm 36:1-12.

A THOUGHT TO PONDER
Far, far above all comprehension is the truth and faithfulness of God.

Trust in the Lord

Trust in the LORD, and do good; so shalt thou dwell in the land, and verily thou shalt be fed.

PSALM 37:3

VERSE 3: "Trust in the LORD." Here is the second precept [the first being, "Fret not thyself because of evildoers," verse 1], and one appropriate to the occasion. Faith cures fretting. Sight views things only as they seem, hence her envy; faith beholds things as they really are, hence her peace.

"And do good." True faith is actively obedient. Doing good is a fine remedy for fretting. There is a joy in holy activity that drives away the rust of discontent.

"So shalt thou dwell in the land" that flows with milk and honey, the Canaan of the covenant. You shall not wander in the wilderness of murmuring but will abide in the promised land of content and rest. We who have believed do enter into rest. Very much of our outward life depends upon the inward; where there is heaven in the heart, there will be heaven in the house.

"And verily thou shalt be fed" or shepherded. To integrity and faith, necessities are guaranteed. The Good Shepherd will exercise his pastoral care over all believers. In truth they shall be fed, and fed on truth. The promise of God shall be their perpetual banquet; they shall neither lack spiritually nor temporally. Some read this as an exhortation: "Feed on truth." Certainly this brings good cheer and banishes forever the hungry heart-burnings of envy.

VERSE 4: There is an ascent in this third precept. He who was first bidden not to fret was then commanded actively to trust and now is told with holy desire to delight in God. "Delight thyself also in the LORD." Make Jehovah the joy and rejoicing of your spirit. Bad men delight in carnal objects; do not envy them if they are allowed to take their fill in such vain idols. Look instead to your better delight, and fill yourself to the full with a more sublime portion.

Verses to meditate upon today: Psalm 37:1-6.

A THOUGHT TO PONDER
True faith is actively obedient.

MARCH 17

BE STILL BEFORE THE LORD

Rest in the LORD, and wait patiently for him: fret not thyself because of him who prospereth in his way, because of the man who bringeth wicked devices to pass.

PSALM 37:7

VERSE 7: "Rest in the LORD." This is a most divine precept and requires much grace to carry it out. To hush the spirit, to be silent before the Lord, to wait in holy patience for the time for clearing up the difficulties of providence—that is what every gracious heart should aim at. "Aaron held his peace." "I opened not my mouth; because thou didst it." A silent tongue in many cases not only shows a wise head but a holy heart.

"And wait patiently for him." Time is nothing to God; let it be nothing to you. God is worth waiting for. He is never early; he is never too late. In a story we wait for the end to clear up the plot; we ought not to prejudge the great drama of life but wait until the closing scene and see to what a finish the whole arrives.

"Fret not thyself because of him who prospereth in his way, because of the man who bringeth wicked devices to pass." There is no good but much evil in worrying your heart about the present success of graceless plotters. Be not enticed into premature judgments; they dishonor God, they weary yourself. Determine, let the wicked succeed as they may, that you will treat the matter with indifference and never allow a question to be raised as to the righteousness and goodness of the Lord. What if wicked devices succeed and your own plans are defeated? There is more of the love of God in your defeats than in the successes of the wicked.

VERSE 8: "Cease from anger, and forsake wrath." Especially "anger" against the arrangements of providence and your jealousies of the temporary pleasures of those who are so soon to be banished from all comfort. Since anger will try to keep us company, we must resolvedly forsake it.

Verses to meditate upon today: Psalm 37:7-15.

A THOUGHT TO PONDER

There is more of the love of God in your defeats than in the successes of the wicked.

March 18

In Times of Disaster

They shall not be ashamed in the evil time:
and in the days of famine they shall be satisfied.

PSALM 37:19

VERSE 19: "They shall not be ashamed in the evil time." Calamities will come, but deliverances will come also. As the righteous never reckon upon immunity from trouble, they will not be disappointed when they are called to take their share of it, but rather will cast themselves anew upon their God and prove again his faithfulness and love. God is not a friend in the sunshine only; he is a friend indeed and a friend in need.

"And in the days of famine they shall be satisfied." Their barrel of meal and cruse of oil shall last out the day of distress, and if ravens do not bring them bread and meat, the supply of their needs shall come in some other way, for their bread shall be given them. Our Lord stayed himself upon this when he hungered in the wilderness, and by faith he repelled the tempter. We too may be enabled by the same consideration not to fret ourselves in any wise to do evil. If God's providence is our inheritance, we need not worry about the price of wheat. Unbelief cannot save a single ear of corn from being blasted, but faith, if it does not preserve the crop, can do what is better—namely, preserve our joy in the Lord.

VERSE 20: "But the wicked shall perish." Whatever phantom light may mock their present, their future is dark with substantial night. Judgment has been given against them; they are reserved for execution. Let them flaunt their scarlet and fine linen and fare sumptuously every day; the sword of Damocles is above their heads, and if their wits were a little more awake, their mirth would turn to misery.

Verses to meditate upon today: Psalm 37:16-26.

A Thought to Ponder

If God's providence is our inheritance,
we need not worry about the price of wheat.

MARCH 19

Turn from Evil

Depart from evil, and do good; and dwell for evermore.
PSALM 37:27

VERSE 27: "Depart from evil, and do good." We must not envy the doers of evil, but depart altogether from their spirit and example. As Lot left Sodom without casting a look behind, so must we leave sin. No truce or parley is to be held with sin; we must turn away from it without hesitation and set ourselves practically to work in the opposite direction. He who neglects to do good will soon fall into evil.

"And dwell for evermore." Obtain an abiding and quiet inheritance. Short-lived are the gains and pleasures of evil, but eternal are the rewards of grace.

VERSE 28: "For the LORD loveth judgment." The awarding of honor to whom honor is due is God's delight, especially when the upright man has been maligned by his fellowmen. It must be a divine pleasure to right wrongs and to defeat the machinations of the unjust. The great arbiter of human destinies is sure to deal out righteous measure both to rich and poor, to good and evil, for such "judgment" is his delight.

"And forsaketh not his saints." Such would not be right and therefore shall never be done. God is as faithful to the objects of his love as he is just toward all mankind.

"They are preserved for ever." By covenant engagements their security is fixed, and by suretyship fulfillments that safety is accomplished. Come what may, the saints are preserved in Christ Jesus, and because he lives, they shall live also. A king will not lose his jewels, nor will Jehovah lose his people. As the manna in the golden pot was preserved in the ark of the covenant beneath the mercy seat, so shall the faithful be preserved in the covenant by the power of Jesus, their propitiation.

Verses to meditate upon today: Psalm 37:27-40.

A Thought to Ponder
He who neglects to do good will soon fall into evil.

GUILT

For mine iniquities are gone over mine head:
as a heavy burden they are too heavy for me.
PSALM 38:4

VERSE 4: Like waves of the deep sea, like black mire in which a man utterly sinks, above my hopes, my strength, my life itself, my sin rises in its terror. Unawakened sinners think their sins to be mere shallows; but when conscience is aroused, they see the depths of iniquity.

"As a heavy burden they are too heavy for me." It is well when sin is an intolerable load and when the remembrance of our sins burdens us beyond endurance. This verse is the genuine cry of one who feels himself undone by his transgressions and as yet sees not the great sacrifice.

VERSE 5: "My wounds stink and are corrupt because of my foolishness." Apply this to the body, and it pictures a sad condition of disease; but read it of the soul, and it applies to the life. Conscience lays on stripe after stripe until the swelling becomes a wound and suppurates, and the corruption within grows offensive. What a horrible creature man appears to be in his own consciousness when his depravity and vileness are fully opened up by the law of God, applied by the Holy Spirit! It is true there are diseases that are correctly described in this verse when in the worst stage; but we prefer to receive the expressions as instructively figurative, since the words "because of my foolishness" point rather at a moral than a physical malady. Some of us know what it is to stink in our own nostrils, so as to loathe ourselves. Even the most filthy diseases cannot be as foul as sin. No ulcers, cancers, or putrefying sores can match the unutterable vileness and pollution of iniquity. Our own perceptions have made us feel this. We write what we do know and testify what we have seen; and even now we shudder to think that so much of evil should lie festering deep within our nature.

Verses to meditate upon today: Psalm 38:1-8.

A THOUGHT TO PONDER
It is well when sin is an intolerable load.

MARCH 21

MY SIGHING

Lord, all my desire is before thee; and my groaning is not hid from thee.
PSALM 38:9

VERSE 9: This "groaning" is unuttered, yet perceived. Blessed be God—he reads the longings of our hearts. Nothing can be hidden from him; what we cannot tell him, he perfectly understands. The psalmist is conscious that he has not exaggerated and therefore appeals to heaven for a confirmation of his words. The Good Physician understands the symptoms of our disease and sees the hidden evil that they reveal; hence our case is safe in his hands.

"And my groaning is not hid from thee." Sorrow and anguish hide themselves from the observation of man, but God spies them out. None is more lonely than the brokenhearted sinner; yet he has the Lord for his companion.

VERSE 10: "My heart panteth." Here begins another tale of woe. The psalmist was so dreadfully pained by the unkindness of friends that sharp and quick were the beatings of his heart. He was like a hunted deer, filled with distressing alarms and ready to fly out of itself with fear. The soul seeks sympathy in sorrow, and if it finds none, its sorrowful heart throbs are incessant.

"My strength faileth me." Because of disease and distraction, he was weakened and ready to expire. A sense of sin and a clear perception that none can help him in his distress are enough to bring a man to death's door, especially if there be none to speak a gentle word and point the broken spirit to the beloved Physician.

"As for the light of mine eyes, it also is gone from me." Sweet light departed from his bodily eye, and consolation vanished from his soul. Those who were the very light of his eyes forsook him. Now, as we remember the loving-kindness of the Lord, we see how good it was for us to find our own strength fail us, since it drove us to the strong for strength.

Verses to meditate upon today: Psalm 38:9-12.

A THOUGHT TO PONDER
Blessed be God—he reads the longings of our hearts.

MARCH 22

INIQUITY AND SIN

For I will declare mine iniquity; I will be sorry for my sin.
PSALM 38:18

VERSE 18: "For I will declare mine iniquity." The slander of his enemies David repudiates, but the accusations of his conscience he admits. Open confession is good for the soul. When sorrow leads to hearty and penitent acknowledgment of sin, it is blessed sorrow, a thing to thank God for most devoutly.

"I will be sorry for my sin." My confession will be salted with briny tears. It is well not so much to bewail our sorrows as to denounce the sins that lie at the root of them. To be sorry for sin is no atonement for it, but it is the right spirit in which to go to Jesus, who is our reconciliation and Savior. A man is near the end of his trouble when he comes to an end with his sins.

VERSE 19: "But mine enemies are lively, and they are strong." However weak and dying the righteous man may be, the evils that oppose him are sure to be lively enough. Neither the world, the flesh, nor the devil are ever afflicted with debility or inertness; this trinity of evils labor with mighty unremitting energy to overthrow us. If the devil were sick or our lusts feeble or Madame Bubble [a picture of the world in John Bunyan's *Pilgrim's Progress*] infirm, we might slacken prayer; but with such lively and vigorous enemies we must not cease to cry mightily unto our God.

"And they that hate me wrongfully are multiplied." Here is another misery, that as we are no match for our enemies in strength, so also they outnumber us a hundred to one. Wrong as the cause of evil is, it is a popular one. More and more the kingdom of darkness grows. Oh, misery of miseries, that we see the professed friends of Jesus forsaking him, and the enemies of his cross and his cause mustering in increasing bands!

Verses to meditate upon today: Psalm 38:13-22

A THOUGHT TO PONDER
*With such lively and vigorous enemies we must not cease
to cry mightily unto our God.*

MARCH 23

A FLEETING LIFE

LORD, make me to know mine end, and the measure of my days, what it is; that I may know how frail I am.

PSALM 39:4

VERSE 4: "LORD." It is well that the bent of his soul was toward God and not toward man. *Oh, if my swelling heart must speak, Lord, let it speak with you. Even if there is too much natural heat in what I say, you will be more patient with me than will man, and upon your purity it can cast no stain; whereas if I speak to my fellows, they may harshly rebuke me or else learn evil from my petulance.*

"Make me to know mine end." Did he mean the same as Elijah in his agony: "Take away my life; for I am not better than my fathers"? Perhaps so. Perhaps he rashly and petulantly desired to know the end of his wretched life, that he might begin to reckon the days until death should put a finish to his woe. As if there were no other comfort to be had, unbelief would hide itself in the grave and sleep itself into oblivion.

David was neither the first nor the last who spoke unadvisedly in prayer. Yet there is a better meaning: The psalmist would know more of the shortness of life, that he might better bear its transient ills, and herein we may safely kneel with him, uttering the same petition. That there is no end to its misery is the hell of hell; that there is an end to life's sorrow is the hope of all who have a hope beyond the grave.

God is the best teacher of the divine philosophy that looks for an expected end. They who see death through the Lord's glass see a fair sight that makes them forget the evil of life in foreseeing the end of life.

Verses to meditate upon today: Psalm 39:1-5.

A THOUGHT TO PONDER
That there is an end to life's sorrow is the hope of all who have a hope beyond the grave.

MARCH 24

HEAR MY PRAYER

Hear my prayer, O LORD, and give ear unto my cry; hold not thy peace at my tears: for I am a stranger with thee, and a sojourner, as all my fathers were.

PSALM 39:12

VERSE 12: "Hear my prayer, O LORD." *Drown not my pleadings with the sound of your strokes. You have heard the clamor of my sins, Lord; hear the laments of my prayers.* "And give ear unto my cry." Here is an advance in intensity: A "cry" is more vehement, pathetic, and impassioned than a prayer. The main thing was to have the Lord's ear and heart.

"Hold not thy peace at my tears." This is a yet higher degree of importunate pleading. Who can withstand tears, which are the irresistible weapons of weakness? Tears speak more eloquently than ten thousand tongues; they act as keys in the wards of tender hearts, and mercy denies them nothing, if through them the weeper looks to richer drops, even to the blood of Jesus. When our sorrows draw from the sluices of our eyes, God will ere long interpose and turn our mourning into joy. Long may he be quiet as though he regarded not, but the hour of deliverance will come, and come like the morning when the dewdrops are plentiful.

"For I am a stranger with thee." Not *to* you, but "*with*" you. *Like you, my Lord, I am a "stranger" among the sons of men, an alien from my mother's children.* God made the world, sustains it, and owns it, and yet men treat him as though he were a foreign intruder; and as they treat the Master, so do they deal with his servants. These words may also mean, "I share the hospitality of God," like a stranger entertained by a generous host. Israel was bidden to deal tenderly with the stranger, and the God of Israel has in much compassion treated us poor aliens with unbounded liberality.

Verses to meditate upon today: Psalm 39:6-13.

A THOUGHT TO PONDER

God will ere long interpose and turn our mourning into joy.

MARCH 25

OUT OF THE PIT

He brought me up also out of a horrible pit, out of the miry clay, and set my feet upon a rock, and established my goings.

PSALM 40:2

VERSE 2: "He brought me up also out of a horrible pit." When our Lord bore in his own person the terrible curse that was due to sin, he was so cast down as to be like a prisoner in a deep, dark, fearful dungeon, amid whose horrible glooms the captive heard a noise as of rushing torrents, while overhead resounded the tramp of furious foes. Our Lord in his anguish was like a captive forgotten by all mankind, surrendered with horror, darkness, and desolation. Yet the Lord Jehovah made him to ascend from all his abasement; he retraced his steps from that deep hell of anguish into which he had been cast as our substitute. He who was thus delivered as our surety *in extremis* will not fail to liberate us from our far lighter griefs.

"Out of the miry clay." The sufferer was like one who cannot find a foothold but slips and sinks. The analogy indicates not only positive misery as in the former figure, but the absence of solid comfort by which sorrow might have been rendered supportable. Once give man a good foothold, and a burden is greatly lightened; but to be placed on slimy, slippery clay is to be tried doubly. With humble gratitude adore the dear Redeemer who for your sake was deprived of all consolation while surrounded with every form of misery; mark his gratitude at being borne up amid his arduous labors and sufferings, and if you too have experienced divine help, be sure to join your Lord in this song.

"And set my feet upon a rock, and established my goings." The Redeemer's work is done. He reposes on the firm ground of his accomplished engagements; he can never suffer again; forever does he reign in glory.

Verses to meditate upon today: Psalm 40:1-5.

A THOUGHT TO PONDER

The Redeemer's work is done.

MARCH 26

GOD'S WILL

I delight to do thy will, O my God: yea, thy law is within my heart.
PSALM 40:8

VERSE 8: "I delight to do thy will, O my God." Our blessed Lord alone could completely do the will of God. The law is too broad for such poor creatures as we to hope to fulfill it to the uttermost. But Jesus not only did the Father's will but found a delight therein; from all eternity he had desired the work set before him. Even in Gethsemane itself he chose the Father's will and set aside his own.

Herein is the essence of obedience—namely, in the soul's cheerful devotion to God. And our Lord's obedience, which is our righteousness, is in no measure lacking in this eminent quality. Notwithstanding his measureless griefs, our Lord found delight in his work and "for the joy that was set before him endured the cross, despising the shame."

"Yea, thy law is within my heart." No outward, formal devotion was rendered by Christ; his heart was in his work, holiness was his element, the Father's will his meat and drink. We must each of us be like our Lord in this or we shall lack the evidence of being his disciples. Where there is no heart-work, no pleasure, no delight in God's law, there can be no acceptance. Let the devout reader adore the Savior for the spontaneous and hearty manner in which he undertook the great work of our salvation.

VERSE 9: "I have preached righteousness in the great congregation." The purest morality and the highest holiness were preached by Jesus. Divine righteousness was his theme. Our Lord's whole life was a sermon, eloquent beyond compare, and it is heard each day by myriads. Moreover, he never shunned in his ministry to declare the whole counsel of God; God's great plan of righteousness he plainly set forth.

Verses to meditate upon today: Psalm 40:6-12.

A THOUGHT TO PONDER
Our blessed Lord alone could completely do the will of God.

MARCH 27

SEEKING DELIVERANCE

Be pleased, O LORD, to deliver me: O LORD, make haste to help me.
PSALM 40:13

VERSE 13: How touching! How humble! How plaintive! The words thrill us as we think that after this sort our Lord and Master prayed. His petition is not so much that the cup should pass away undrained, but that he should be sustained while drinking it and set free from its power at the first fitting moment. He seeks deliverance and help; and he entreats that the help may not be slow in coming. This is after the manner of our pleadings, is it not? Note how our Lord was heard in that he feared, for there was after Gethsemane a calm endurance that made the fight as glorious as the victory.

VERSE 14: "Let them be ashamed and confounded together that seek after my soul to destroy it." Whether we read this as a prayer or a prophecy it matters not, for the powers of sin and death and hell may well be ashamed as they see the result of their malice forever turned against themselves. It is to the infinite confusion of Satan that his attempts to destroy the Savior destroyed himself. The diabolical conclave who plotted in council are now all alike put to shame, for the Lord Jesus has met them at all points and turned all their wisdom into foolishness.

"Let them be driven backward and put to shame that wish me evil." The hosts of darkness are utterly put to the rout and made a theme for holy derision forever and ever. How did they gloat over the thought of crushing the seed of the woman! But the Crucified has conquered, the Nazarene has laughed them to scorn, the dying Son of man has become the death of death and hell's destruction. Forever blessed be his name.

Verses to meditate upon today: Psalm 40:13-17.

A THOUGHT TO PONDER
*The dying Son of man has become the death of death
and hell's destruction.*

MARCH 28

IN TIMES OF SICKNESS

The LORD will strengthen him upon the bed of languishing:
thou wilt make all his bed in his sickness.

PSALM 41:3

VERSE 3: "The LORD will strengthen him upon the bed of languishing." The everlasting arms shall support his soul as friendly hands and downy pillows support the body of the sick. How tender and sympathizing is this image; how near it brings our God to our infirmities and sicknesses!

Whoever heard this of the old heathen Jove or of the gods of India or China? This is language peculiar to the God of Israel; he it is who deigns to become nurse and attendant upon good men. If he smites with one hand, he sustains with the other. Oh, it is blessed fainting when one falls upon the Lord's own bosom and is borne up thereby! Grace is the best of restoratives. Divine love is the noblest stimulant for a languishing patient; it makes the soul strong as a giant, even when the aching bones are breaking through the skin. There is no physician like the Lord, no tonic like his promise, no wine like his love.

"Thou wilt make all his bed in his sickness." Does the Lord turn bed maker to his sick children? Herein is love indeed. A bed soon grows hard when the body is weary with tossing to and fro upon it, but grace gives patience, and God's smile gives peace, and the "bed" is made soft because the man's heart is content. The pillows are downy because the head is peaceful.

Note that the Lord will make "*all* his bed," from head to foot. What considerate and indefatigable kindness! Our dear and ever blessed Lord Jesus, though in all respects an inheritor of this promise, for our sakes condescended to forego the blessing and died on a cross and not upon a bed; yet even there he was after a while upheld and cheered by the Lord his God, so that he died in triumph.

Verses to meditate upon today: Psalm 41:1-6.

A THOUGHT TO PONDER

There is no physician like the Lord, no tonic like his promise,
no wine like his love.

MARCH 29

RAISE ME UP

But thou, O LORD, be merciful unto me, and raise me up,
that I may requite them.

PSALM 41:10

VERSE 10: "But thou, O LORD, be merciful unto me." How the hunted and frightened soul turns to God! How such a person seems to take breath with a "but, thou" and clings to the hope of mercy from God when every chance of pity from man is gone!

"And raise me up." *Recover me from my sickness; give me to regain my position.* Jesus was raised up from the grave; his descent was ended by an ascent.

"That I may requite them." This is a truly Old Testament sentence, and quite aside from the spirit of Christianity; yet we must remember that David was a person in magisterial office and might without any personal revengeful desire to punish those who had insulted his authority and libeled his public character.

Our great Apostle and High Priest had no personal animosities, but even he by his resurrection has requited the powers of evil and avenged on death and hell all their base attacks upon his cause and person. Still, the strained application of every sentence of this Psalm to Christ is not to our liking, and we prefer to call attention to the better spirit of the Gospel beyond that of the old dispensation.

VERSE 11: We are all cheered by tokens for good, and the psalmist felt it to be an auspicious omen that after all his deep depression he was not utterly given over to his foe.

"By this I know that thou favorest me." *You have a special regard to me. I have the secret assurance of this in my heart, and therefore your outward dealings do not dismay me, for I know that you love me in them all.*

Verses to meditate upon today: Psalm 41:7-13.

A THOUGHT TO PONDER
Jesus was raised up from the grave; his descent was ended by an ascent.

MARCH 30

Thirsting for God

*My soul thirsteth for God, for the living God:
when shall I come and appear before God?*
PSALM 42:2

VERSE 2: "My soul," that is, all my nature, my inmost self. "Thirsteth." This is more than hungering—hunger you can palliate, but thirst is insatiable, clamorous. Oh, to have the most intense craving after the highest good! This is no questionable mark of grace.

"For God." Not merely for the temple and the ordinances, but for fellowship with God himself. None but spiritual men can sympathize with this thirst.

"For the living God." Because he lives and gives to men the living water, we, with great eagerness, desire him. A dead God is a mere mockery; we loathe such a monstrous deity. But the ever-living God, the perennial fountain of life and light and love, is our soul's desire. What are gold, honor, and pleasure but dead idols? May we never pant for these.

"When shall I come and appear before God?" He who loves the Lord loves also the assemblies wherein his name is adored. Vain are all pretenses to religion where the outward means of grace have no attraction. David was never so much at home as in the house of the Lord. He was not content with private worship; he did not forsake the place where saints assemble, as the manner of some is. See how mournfully he questions the prospect of his again uniting in the joyous gathering! How he repeats and reiterates his desire! Seeking his God, his Elohim (his God to be worshiped, who had entered into covenant with him), he pined even as the drooping flowers for the dew or the moaning turtle for her mate. If all our resortings to public worship were viewed as appearances before God, it would then be a sure mark of grace to delight in them. Alas, how many appear before the minister or their fellowmen and think that enough!

Verses to meditate upon today: Psalm 42:1-4.

A Thought to Ponder
Oh, to have the most intense craving after the highest good!

MARCH 31

DEALING WITH DEPRESSION

Why art thou cast down, O my soul? and why art thou disquieted in me?
Hope thou in God: for I shall yet praise him for the help of his countenance.

PSALM 42:5

VERSE 5: "Why art thou cast down, O my soul?" As though he were two men, the psalmist talks to himself. His faith reasons with his fears; his hope argues with his sorrows. Are these present troubles to last forever? The rejoicings of my foes—are they more than empty talk? My absence from the solemn feasts—is it a perpetual exile? Why this deep depression, this faithless fainting, this chickenhearted melancholy?

As Trapp says, "David chides David out of the dumps"; and herein he is an example for all desponding ones. To search out the cause of our sorrow is often the best surgery for grief. Self-ignorance is not bliss; in this case it is misery. The mist of ignorance magnifies the causes of our alarm; a clearer view will make monsters dwindle into trifles.

"Why art thou disquieted in me?" Why is my quiet gone? If I cannot keep a public Sabbath, yet wherefore do I deny my soul her indoor Sabbath? Why am I agitated like a troubled sea, and why do my thoughts make a noise like a tumultuous multitude? The causes are not enough to justify such utter yielding to despondency. Up, my heart! What aileth you? Play the man, and your castings down shall turn to upliftings, and your disquietudes to calm.

"Hope thou in God." If every evil be let loose from Pandora's box, yet is there hope at the bottom. This is the grace that swims, though the waves roar and be troubled. God is unchangeable, and therefore his grace is the ground for unshaken hope. If everything be dark, yet the day will come, and meanwhile hope carries stars in her eyes. Her lamps are not dependent on oil from without; her light is fed by secret visitations of God, which sustain the spirit.

Verses to meditate upon today: Psalm 42:5-11.

A THOUGHT TO PONDER
His faith reasons with his fears; his hope argues with his sorrows.

APRIL 1

LIGHT AND TRUTH

*O send out thy light and thy truth: let them lead me;
let them bring me unto thy holy hill, and to thy tabernacles.*

PSALM 43:3

VERSE 3: "O send out thy light and thy truth." *The joy of your presence and the faithfulness of your heart—let both of these be manifest to me. Reveal my true character by your light, and reward me according to your truthful promise.* As the sun darts forth his beams, so does the Lord send forth his favor and his faithfulness toward all his people. And as all nature rejoices in the sunshine, even so the saints triumph in the manifestation of the love and fidelity of their God, which, like the golden sunbeam, lights up even the darkest surroundings with delightful splendor.

"Let them lead me." Be these my star to guide me to my rest. Be these my alpine guides to conduct me over mountains and precipices to the abodes of grace.

"Let them bring me unto thy holy hill, and to thy tabernacles." *First in your mercy bring me to your earthly courts and end my weary exile, and then in due time admit me to your celestial palace above.* We seek not "light" to sin by, nor "truth" to be exalted by it, but that they may become our practical guides to the closest communion with God. Only such "light" and "truth" as are sent to us from God will do this. Common light is not strong enough to show the road to heaven, nor will mere moral or physical truths take us to the holy hill. But the "light" of the Holy Spirit and the "truth" as it is in Jesus—these are elevating, sanctifying, and perfecting, and hence their virtue in leading us to the glorious presence of God. It is beautiful to observe how David's longing to be away from the oppression of man always leads him to sigh more intensely for communion with God.

Verses to meditate upon today: Psalm 43:1-5.

A THOUGHT TO PONDER

David's longing to be away from the oppression of man always leads him to sigh more intensely for communion with God.

APRIL 2

GOD'S RIGHT HAND

For they got not the land in possession by their own sword, neither did their own arm save them: but thy right hand, and thine arm, and the light of thy countenance, because thou hadst a favor unto them.

PSALM 44:3

VERSE 3: "For they got not the land in possession by their own sword." Behold how the Lord alone was exalted in bringing his people to the land that flows with milk and honey! He, in his distinguishing grace, had put a difference between Canaan and Israel, and therefore, by his own effectual power, he wrought *for* his chosen and *against* their adversaries. The tribes fought for their allotments, but their success was wholly due to the Lord who wrought with them. The warriors of Israel were not inactive, but their valor was secondary to that mysterious, divine working by which Jericho's walls fell down, and the hearts of the heathen failed them for fear. The efforts of all the men-at-arms were employed, but as these would have been futile without divine succor, all the honor is ascribed unto the Lord.

The passage may be viewed as a beautiful parable of the work of salvation. Men are not saved without prayer, repentance, etc., but none of those save a man. Salvation is altogether of the Lord. Canaan was not conquered without the armies of Israel, but equally true is it that it was not conquered by them. The Lord was the conqueror, and the people were but instruments in his hands.

"Neither did their own arm save them." They could not ascribe their memorable victories to themselves; he who made sun and moon stand still for them was worthy of all their praise. A negative is put both upon their weapons and themselves, as if to show us how ready men are to ascribe success to secondary causes.

"But thy right hand, and thine arm, and the light of thy countenance." The divine "hand" actively fought for them, the divine "arm" powerfully sustained them with more than human energy, and the divine smile inspired them with dauntless courage.

Verses to meditate upon today: Psalm 44:1-3.

A THOUGHT TO PONDER

The Lord was the conqueror, and the people were but instruments in his hands.

APRIL 3

MY KING AND MY GOD

Thou art my King, O God:
command deliverances for Jacob.
PSALM 44:4

VERSE 4: "Thou art my King, O God." *Knowing right well your power and grace, my heart is glad to own you as sovereign prince. Who among the mighty are so illustrious as you are? To whom, then, should I yield my homage or turn for aid? God of my fathers in the olden time, you are my soul's monarch and Lord.*

"Command deliverances for Jacob." To whom should a people look but to their king? He it is who, by virtue of his office, fights their battles for them. In the case of our King, how easy it is for him to scatter all our foes! *O Lord, the King of kings, with what ease can you rescue your people; a word of yours can do it. Give but the command and your persecuted people shall be free.* Jacob's long life was crowded with trials and deliverances, and his descendants are here called by his name, as if to typify the similarity of their experience to that of their great forefather. He who would win the blessings of Israel must share the sorrows of Jacob.

This verse contains a personal declaration and an intercessory prayer. Those can pray best who make most sure of their personal interest in God, and those who have the fullest assurance that the Lord is their God should be the foremost to plead for the rest of the tried family of the faithful.

VERSE 5: "Through thy name will we tread them under that rise up against us." The Lord's "name" served instead of weapons and enabled those who used it to leap on their foes and crush them with jubilant valor. In union and communion with God, saints work wonders. If God be for us, who can be against us?

Verses to meditate upon today: Psalm 44:4-8.

A THOUGHT TO PONDER
The Lord's name served instead of weapons.

APRIL 4

KEEPING ON TRACK

Our heart is not turned back, neither have our steps declined from thy way.
PSALM 44:18

VERSE 17: "All this is come upon us; yet have we not forgotten thee." Here the psalmist insists that Israel had not turned away from her allegiance to Jehovah. When in the midst of many griefs we can still cling to God in loving obedience, it must be well with us. True fidelity can endure rough usage. Those who follow God for what they get will leave him when persecution is stirred up. But not so the sincere believer; he will not forget his God, even though the worst come to him.

"Neither have we dealt falsely in thy covenant." No idol was set up, the ordained worship was not relinquished, and God was still nationally acknowledged. Therefore the psalmist is more earnest that the Lord should interpose. This and the succeeding verses are suitable for the lips of martyrs; indeed the entire psalm might be called the martyr's complaint. Not for sin but for righteousness did the saints suffer, not for falsehood but for truth, not for forsaking the Lord but for following hard after him. Sufferings of such a sort may be very terrible, but they are exceedingly honorable, and the comforts of the Lord shall sustain those who are accounted worthy to suffer for Christ's sake.

VERSE 18: Heart and life were agreed, and both were true to the Lord's way. Neither within nor without had the godly sufferers offended; they were not absolutely perfect, but they were sincerely free from all willful transgression. It was a healthy sign for the nation that her prophet-poet could testify to her uprightness before God, both in heart and act. Far more often the case would have worn quite another color, for the tribes were all too apt to set up other gods and forsake the rock of their salvation.

Verses to meditate upon today: Psalm 44:9-19.

A THOUGHT TO PONDER
Heart and life were agreed, and both were true to the Lord's way.

APRIL 5

SECRETS

Shall not God search this out?
For he knoweth the secrets of the heart.
PSALM 44:21

VERSE 20: An appeal is now made to the omniscience of God; he is himself called in to bear witness that Israel had not set up another God. "If we have forgotten the name of our God." This would be the first step in apostasy; men first forget the true and then adore the false.

"Or stretched out our hands to a strange god." Stretching out the hands was the symbol of adoration or of entreaty in prayer; this they had not offered to any of the idols of the heathens.

VERSE 21: "Shall not God search this out?" Could such idolatry be concealed from him? Would he not with holy indignation have detected unfaithfulness, even had it been hidden in the heart and unrevealed in the life?

"For he knoweth the secrets of the heart." He is acquainted with the inner workings of the mind, and therefore this could not have escaped him. Not the heart only which is secret, but "the secrets of the heart," which are "secrets" of the most secret thing, are as open to God as a book to a reader. The reasoning is that the Lord himself knew the people to be sincerely his followers and therefore was not visiting them for sin; hence, then, affliction evidently came from another cause.

VERSE 22: "Yea [i.e., assuredly, certainly] for thy sake"—that is, not for our offenses but for obeying you. The trials of these suppliants came upon them because they were loyal to their God. "Are we killed all the day long." Persecution never ceased to hound them to the death; they had no respite and found no door of escape—and all in God's behalf, because they would not forsake their covenant God and King.

Verses to meditate upon today: Psalm 44:20-26.

A THOUGHT TO PONDER

The secrets of the heart are as open to God as a book to a reader.

APRIL 6

FROM THE HEART

My heart is inditing a good matter: I speak of the things which I have made touching the king: my tongue is the pen of a ready writer.

PSALM 45:1

VERSE 1: "My heart." There is no writing like that dictated by the heart. Heartless hymns are insults to heaven.

"Is inditing a good matter." A good heart will only be content with good thoughts. Where the fountain is good, good streams will flow forth. The learned tell us that the word "inditing" may be read "overflows," or as others suggest, "boils or bubbles up," denoting the warmth of the writer's love, the fullness of his "heart," and the consequent richness and glow of his utterance, as though it were the exuberant display of his inmost soul when most full of affection.

We have here no single cold expression. The writer is not one who frigidly studies the elegance and proprieties of poetry; his stanzas are the natural outburst of his soul, comparable to the boiling jets of the geysers of Hecla. As the corn offered in sacrifice was parched in the pan, so is this tribute of love hot with sincere devotion. It is a sad thing when the heart is cold with a good matter, and worse when it is warm with a bad matter, but incomparably well when a warm heart and a good matter meet together.

Oh, that we may often offer to God an acceptable and sweet oblation fresh from the pan of hearts warmed with gratitude and admiration. "I speak of the things which I have made touching the king." This song has "the king" for its only subject, and for the King's honor alone was it composed. Well might its writer call it "a good matter." The psalmist did not write carelessly; he calls his poem his works, or things that he had "made." We are not to offer to the Lord that which costs us nothing. Good material deserves good workmanship.

Verses to meditate upon today: Psalm 45:1-6.

A THOUGHT TO PONDER

Oh, that we may often offer to God an acceptable and sweet oblation warmed with gratitude and admiration.

April 7

Anointed with Oil

Thou lovest righteousness, and hatest wickedness: therefore God, thy God, hath anointed thee with the oil of gladness above thy fellows.

Psalm 45:7

Verse 7: "Thou lovest righteousness, and hatest wickedness." Christ Jesus is not neutral in the great contest between right and wrong; as warmly as he loves the one, he abhors the other. What qualifications for a sovereign! What grounds of confidence for a people! The whole of our Lord's life on earth proved the truth of these words. His death to put away sin and bring in the reign of righteousness sealed the fact beyond all question; his providence by which he rules from his mediatorial throne, when rightly understood, reveals the same; and his final rule will proclaim it before all worlds. We should imitate him both in his love and hate; they are both needful to complete a righteous character.

"Therefore God, thy God, hath anointed thee with the oil of gladness above thy fellows." Jesus as Mediator owned God as his God, to whom, being found in fashion as a man, he became obedient. On account of our Lord's perfect life, he is now rewarded with superior joy. Others there are to whom grace has given a sacred fellowship with him; but by their universal consent and his own merit, he is prince among them, the gladdest of all because the cause of all their gladness.

At oriental feasts oil was poured on the heads of distinguished and very welcome guests. God himself anoints the man Christ Jesus as he sits at the heavenly feasts and anoints him as a reward for his work with higher and fuller joy than anyone else can know. Thus is the Son of man honored and rewarded for all his pains. Observe the indisputable testimony to Messiah's deity in verse 6, and to his manhood in the present verse. Of whom could this be written but Jesus of Nazareth? Our Christ is our Elohim. Jesus is God with us.

Verses to meditate upon today: Psalm 45:7-12.

A Thought to Ponder
God himself anoints the man Christ Jesus.

APRIL 8

THE KING'S PALACE

With gladness and rejoicing shall they be brought:
they shall enter into the King's palace.
PSALM 45:15

VERSE 15: "With gladness and rejoicing shall they be brought." Joy becomes a marriage feast. What joy will that be that will be seen at the feasts of paradise when all the redeemed shall be brought home! Gladness in the saints themselves and rejoicing from the angels shall make the halls of the New Jerusalem ring again with shoutings.

"They shall enter into the King's palace." Their peaceful abodes shall be where Jesus the King reigns forever. They shall not be shut out but shut in. Rights of free entrance into the holiest of all shall be accorded them. Bought by grace, they shall enter into glory. If there was joy in the bringing, what in the entering? What in the abiding? The glorified are not field laborers in the plains of heaven, but sons who dwell at home, princes of the blood, residents in the royal palace. Oh, happy hour when we shall enjoy all this and forget the sorrows of time in the triumph of eternity.

VERSE 16: "Instead of thy fathers shall be thy children." The ancient saints who stood as fathers in the service of the great King have all passed away; but a spiritual seed is found to fill their places. The veterans depart, but volunteers fill up the vacant places. The line of grace never becomes extinct. As long as time shall last, the true apostolical succession will be maintained.

"Whom thou mayest make princes in all the earth." Servants of Christ are kings. Where a man has preached successfully and evangelized a tribe or nation, he brings to himself more than regal honors; and his name is like the name of the great men upon the earth. Jesus is the king maker. Ambition of the noblest kind shall win her desire in the army of Christ; immortal crowns are distributed to his faithful soldiers.

Verses to meditate upon today: Psalm 45:13-17.

A THOUGHT TO PONDER
Bought by grace, they shall enter into glory.

APRIL 9

HELP IN TROUBLE

God is our refuge and strength, a very present help in trouble.
PSALM 46:1

VERSE 1: "God is our refuge and strength." Israel's boast is not in armies or fortresses but in Jehovah, the only living and true God. Others vaunt their impregnable castles, placed on inaccessible rocks and secured with gates of iron. But God is a far better refuge from distress than all these. And when the time comes to carry the war into the enemy's territories, the Lord stands his people in better stead than all the valor of legions or the boasted strength of chariots and horses. Soldiers of the cross, remember this, and count yourselves safe, and make yourselves strong in God.

Forget not the personal possessive word "our." Make sure of your portion in God, that you may say, "He is *my* refuge and strength." Neither forget the fact that God is our "refuge" just now, in the immediate present, as truly as when David penned these words. God alone is our all in all. All other refuges are refuges of lies; all other strength is weakness, for power belongs unto God. But as God is all-sufficient, our defense and might are equal to all emergencies.

"A very present help in trouble." In distress he has so been found; he has been tried and proved by his people. He never withdraws himself from his afflicted. He is their help truly, effectually, constantly. He is present or near them, close at their side, and ready for their succor, and this is emphasized by the word "very." He is more present than any friend or relative can be—yea, more nearly present than even the trouble itself. To all this comfortable truth is added the consideration that his assistance comes at the needed time. He is not like the swallows that leave us in the winter; he is a friend in need and a friend indeed.

Verses to meditate upon today: Psalm 46:1-6.

A THOUGHT TO PONDER
God is a friend in need and a friend indeed.

APRIL 10

GOD IS WITH US

The LORD of hosts is with us; the God of Jacob is our refuge. Selah.
PSALM 46:7

VERSE 7: "The LORD of hosts is with us." This is the reason for all Zion's security and for the overthrow of her foes. The Lord rules the angels, the stars, the elements, and all the hosts of heaven; and the heaven of heavens are under his sway. The armies of men, though they know it not, are made to subserve his will. This Generalissimo of the forces of the land and the Lord High Admiral of the seas is on our side—our august ally. Woe unto those who fight against him, for they shall fly like smoke before the wind when he gives the word to scatter them.

"The God of Jacob is our refuge." Immanuel is Jehovah of Hosts, and Jacob's God is our high place of defense. When this glad verse is sung to music worthy of such a joyous song, well may the singers pause and the players wait awhile to tune their instruments again. Here, therefore, fitly stands that solemn, stately, peaceful note of rest, "Selah."

VERSE 8: "Come, behold the works of the LORD." The joyful citizens of Jerusalem are invited to go forth and view the remains of their enemies, that they may mark the prowess of Jehovah and the spoil that his right hand has won for his people. It would be well if we also carefully noted the providential dealings of our covenant God and were quick to perceive his hand in the battles of his church. Whenever we read history, it should be with this verse sounding in our ears. We should read the newspaper in the same spirit, to see how the Head of the church rules the nations for his people's good, as Joseph governed Egypt for the sake of Israel.

"What desolations he hath made in the earth." The destroyers he destroys, and the desolaters he desolates.

Verses to meditate upon today: Psalm 46:7-11.

A THOUGHT TO PONDER

This Generalissimo of the forces of the land and the Lord High Admiral of the seas is on our side.

APRIL 11

SHOUTING FOR JOY

O clap your hands, all ye people; shout unto God with the voice of triumph.
PSALM 47:1

VERSE 1: "O clap your hands." The most natural and most enthusiastic tokens of exultation are to be used in view of the victories of the Lord and his universal reign. Our joy in God may be emotional, and yet he will not censure it.

"All ye people." The joy is to extend to all nations. Israel may lead the vanguard, but all the Gentiles are to follow in the march of "triumph," for they have an equal share in that kingdom where there is neither Greek nor Jew, but Christ is all and in all. Even now if they did but know it, it is the best hope of all nations that Jehovah rules over them. Though they cannot all speak the same tongue, they can all use the symbolic language of the "hands." All people will be ruled by the Lord in the latter days, and all will exult in that rule. Were they wise they would submit to it now, and rejoice to do so; yea, they would "clap [their] hands" in rapture at the thought.

"Shout"; let your voices keep tune with "your hands." "Unto God"; let him have all the honors of the day, and let your praise be loud, joyous, universal, and undivided. "With the voice of triumph"; with happy sounds, consonant with such splendid victories, so great a King, so excellent a rule, and such happy subjects. Many are human languages, and yet the nations may triumph as with one voice. Faith's view of God's government is full of rapture. The prospect of the universal reign of the Prince of Peace is enough to make the tongue of the dumb sing; what will the reality be? Well might the poet of the seasons bid mountains and valleys raise their joyous hymn:

> *For the great Shepherd reigns,*
> *And his unsuffering kingdom yet will come.*

Verses to meditate upon today: Psalm 47:1-5.

A THOUGHT TO PONDER

The prospect of the universal reign of the Prince of Peace
is enough to make the tongue of the dumb sing.

APRIL 12

GOD RULES

For God is the King of all the earth: sing ye praises with understanding.
PSALM 47:7

VERSE 7: "For God is the King of all the earth." The Jews of our Savior's time resented this truth, but had their hearts been right they would have rejoiced in it. They would not have kept their God to themselves, even forbidding the Gentile dogs to eat the crumbs from under his table. Alas, how selfishness turns honey into wormwood! Jehovah is not the God of the Jews only; all the nations of the earth are, through the Messiah, yet to own him Lord. Meanwhile, his providential throne governs all events beneath the sky.

"Sing ye praises with understanding." Sing a didactic Psalm. Sound doctrine praises God. Even under the economy of types and ceremonies, it is clear that the Lord had regard to the spirituality of worship and wants to be praised thoughtfully, intelligently, and with deep appreciation of the reason for song.

It is to be feared from the slovenly way in which some make a noise in singing that they imagine any sound will do. On the other hand, from the great attention paid by some to the mere music, we feel sadly sure that the meaning has no effect upon them. Is it not a sin to be tickling men's ears with sounds when we profess to be adoring the Lord? What has a sensuous delight in organs, anthems, etc., to do with devotion? Do not men mistake physical effects for spiritual impulses? Do they not often offer to God strains far more calculated for human amusement than for divine acceptance? An understanding enlightened of the Holy Spirit is then and then only fully capable of offering worthy praise.

VERSE 8: At this moment, over the most debased idolaters, God holds secret rule; here is work for faith. How we ought to long for the day when this truth shall be changed in its aspect and the rule now unrecognized shall be delighted in!

Verses to meditate upon today: Psalm 47:6-9.

A THOUGHT TO PONDER
God's providential throne governs all events beneath the sky.

APRIL 13

GOD'S GREATNESS

Great is the LORD, and greatly to be praised in the city of our God, in the mountain of his holiness.

PSALM 48:1

VERSE 1: "Great is the LORD." How "great" Jehovah is essentially none can conceive; but we can all see that he is great in the deliverance of his people, great in the esteem of those who are delivered, and great in the hearts of those enemies whom he scatters by their own fears. Instead of the mad cry of Ephesus, "Great is Diana," we bear the reasonable, demonstrable, self-evident testimony, "Great is Jehovah."

There is none great in the church but the Lord. Jesus is "the *great* Shepherd," he is "a saviour, and a great one," our great God and Savior, our great High Priest. His Father has divided him a portion with the great, and his name shall be "great" unto the ends of the earth.

"And greatly to be praised." According to his nature should his worship be; it cannot be too constant, too laudatory, too earnest, too reverential, too sublime.

"In the city of our God." He is "great" there and should be "greatly . . . praised" there. If all the world beside renounced Jehovah's worship, the chosen people in his favored city should continue to adore him, for in their midst and on their behalf his glorious power has been so manifestly revealed. In the church the Lord is to be extolled though all the nations rage against him. Jerusalem was the peculiar abode of the God of Israel, the seat of the theocratic government, and the center of prescribed worship, and even thus is the church the place of divine manifestation.

"In the mountain of his holiness," where his holy temple, his holy priests, and his holy sacrifices might continually be seen. "Zion" (verse 2) was a mount, and as it was the most renowned part of the city, it is mentioned as a synonym for the city itself. The church of God is a mount because of its elevation and conspicuousness, and it should be adorned with holiness, her sons and daughters being partakers of the holiness of God.

Verses to meditate upon today: Psalm 48:1-7.

A THOUGHT TO PONDER

How "great" Jehovah is essentially none can conceive.

April 14

Thoughtful People

We have thought of thy loving-kindness, O God, in the midst of thy temple.
PSALM 48:9

VERSE 9: "We have thought." Holy men are thoughtful men; they do not suffer God's wonders to pass before their eyes and melt into forgetfulness but meditate deeply upon them. "Of thy loving-kindness, O God." What a delightful subject! Devout minds never tire of so divine a theme. It is well to think of past loving-kindness in times of trial, and equally profitable to remember it in seasons of prosperity. Grateful memories sweeten sorrows and sober joys.

"In the midst of thy temple." A fit place for so devout a meditation. Where God is most seen, he is best loved. The assembled saints constitute a living temple, and our deepest musings when so gathered together should have regard to the loving-kindness of the Lord, exhibited in the varied experiences of each of the living stones. Memories of mercy should be associated with continuance of praise. Close to the table of showbread commemorating his bounty should stand the altar of incense denoting our praise.

VERSE 10: "According to thy name, O God, so is thy praise unto the ends of the earth." Great fame is due to his great "name." The glory of Jehovah's exploits overleaps the boundaries of earth; angels behold with wonder, and from every star delighted intelligences proclaim his fame beyond the ends of the earth. If men are silent, the woods, seas, and mountains, with all their countless tribes and all the unseen spirits that walk them, are full of divine praise. As in a shell we listen to the murmurs of the sea, so in the intricacies of creation we hear the praises of God.

"Thy right hand is full of righteousness." *Your scepter and your sword, your government and your vengeance are altogether just. Your hand is never empty, but is full of energy, bounty, and equity.*

Verses to meditate upon today: Psalm 48:8-14.

A Thought to Ponder
Grateful memories sweeten sorrows and sober joys.

APRIL 15

SPEAKING AND MEDITATING

My mouth shall speak of wisdom; and the meditation of my heart shall be of understanding.

PSALM 49:3

VERSE 3: "My mouth shall speak of wisdom." Inspired and therefore lifted beyond himself, the prophet is not praising his own attainments, but is extolling the divine Spirit who spoke in him. He knew that the Spirit of truth and "wisdom" spoke through him. He who is not sure that his matter is good has no right to ask a hearing. "And the meditation of my heart shall be of understanding." The same Spirit who made the ancient seers eloquent also made them thoughtful. The help of the Holy Spirit was never meant to supersede the use of our own mental powers. The Holy Spirit does not make us speak as Balaam's donkey, which merely uttered sounds but never meditated; rather he first leads us to consider and reflect, and then gives us the tongue of fire to speak with power.

VERSE 4: "I will incline mine ear to a parable." He who would have others hear begins by hearing himself. As the minstrel bends his ear to his "harp," so must the preacher give his whole soul to his ministry. The truth came to the psalmist as a parable, and he endeavored to unriddle it for popular use. He would not leave the truth in obscurity but listened to its voice until he understood it well enough to be able to interpret and translate it into the common language of the multitude.

Of necessity it would remain a problem and a dark saying to the unenlightened many, but this would not be the songster's fault, for, says he, "I will open my dark saying upon the harp." The writer was no mystic, delighting in deep and cloudy things; yet he was not afraid of the most profound topics. He tried to open the treasures of darkness and to uplift pearls from the deep.

Verses to meditate upon today: Psalm 49:1-6.

A THOUGHT TO PONDER

The Holy Spirit first leads us to consider and reflect, and then gives us the tongue of fire to speak with power.

APRIL 16

FACING DEATH

None of them can by any means redeem his brother,
nor give to God a ransom for him.
PSALM 49:7

VERSE 7: "None of them can by any means redeem his brother." Some boast of their riches, but the whole of them put together could not rescue a comrade from the chill grasp of death. They boast of what they will do with us—let them see to themselves. Let them weigh their gold in the scales of death, and see how much they can buy therewith from the worm and the grave. The poor are their equals in this respect: Let them love their friend ever so dearly, they cannot "give to God a ransom for him." A king's ransom would be of no avail; a Monte Rosa [a mountain in Switzerland] of rubies, an America of silver, a world of gold, a sun of diamonds would all be utterly condemned. O boasters, think not to terrify us with your worthless wealth; go and intimidate death before you threaten men in whom is immortality and life.

VERSE 8: "For the redemption of their soul is precious, and it ceaseth for ever." Too great is the price—the purchase is hopeless. Forever must the attempt to redeem a soul with money remain a failure. Death comes, and wealth cannot bribe him; hell follows, and no golden key can unlock its dungeon. Vain, then, are your threatenings, you possessors of the yellow clay; your childish toys are despised by men who estimate the value of possessions by the shekel of the sanctuary.

VERSE 9: No price could secure for any man "that he should still live for ever, and not see corruption." Mad are men now after gold; what would they be if it could buy the elixir of immortality? As for the soul, it will not be detained when it hears the divine command to soar through tracks unknown. Never, therefore, will we fear those base nibblers at our heels whose boasted treasure proves to be so powerless to save.

Verses to meditate upon today: Psalm 49:7-14.

A THOUGHT TO PONDER
Forever must the attempt to redeem a soul with money remain a failure.

APRIL 17

REDEMPTION

But God will redeem my soul from the power of the grave:
for he shall receive me. Selah.

PSALM 49:15

VERSE 15: Forth from that temporary resting place we shall come in due time, quickened by divine energy. Like our risen Head, we cannot be held by the bands of "the grave"; redemption has emancipated us from the slavery of death. No redemption can man find in riches, but God has found it in the blood of his dear Son. Our Elder Brother has given to God a ransom, and we are the redeemed of the Lord; because of this redemption by price we shall assuredly be redeemed by power out of the hand of the last enemy.

"For he shall receive me." He shall take me out of the tomb, take me up to heaven. If it is not said of me as of Enoch, "He was not, for God took him," yet shall I reach the same glorious state. My spirit God will receive, and my body shall sleep in Jesus until, being raised in his image, it shall also be received into glory. How infinitely superior is such a hope to anything that our oppressors can boast! Here is something that will bear meditation, and therefore again let us pause at the bidding of the musician, who inserts a "Selah."

VERSE 16: In these last verses the psalmist becomes a preacher and gives admonitory lessons that he has himself gathered from experience. "Be not thou afraid when one is made rich." Let it not give you any concern to see the godless prosper. Raise no questions as to divine justice; allow no foreboding to cloud your mind. Temporal prosperity is too small a matter to be worth fretting about. "When the glory of his house is increased." Though the sinner and his family are in great esteem and stand exceedingly high, never mind; all things will be made right in due time.

Verses to meditate upon today: Psalm 49:15-20.

A THOUGHT TO PONDER

No redemption can man find in riches, but God has found it
in the blood of his dear Son.

APRIL 18

EL, ELOHIM, JEHOVAH

The mighty God, even the LORD, hath spoken, and called the earth from the rising of the sun unto the going down thereof.
PSALM 50:1

VERSE 1: "The mighty God, even the LORD." *El, Elohim,* and *Jehovah* are three glorious names for the God of Israel. To render the address the more impressive, these august titles are mentioned, just as in royal decrees the names and dignities of monarchs are placed in the forefront. Here the true God is described as almighty, as the only and perfect object of adoration, and as the self-existent One.

"Hath spoken, and called the earth from the rising of the sun unto the going down thereof." The dominion of Jehovah extends over the whole earth, and therefore to all mankind is his decree directed. The east and the west are bidden to hear the God who makes his sun rise on every quarter of the globe. Shall the summons of the great King be despised? Will we dare provoke him to anger by slighting his call?

VERSE 2: "Out of Zion, the perfection of beauty, God hath shined." The Lord is represented not only as speaking to the earth, but as coming forth to reveal the glory of his presence to an assembled universe. God of old dwelt in Zion among his chosen people, but here the beams of his splendor are described as shining forth upon all nations. "The sun" was spoken of in the first verse, but here is a far brighter sun. The majesty of God is most conspicuous among his own elect but is not confined to them; the church is not a dark lantern but a candlestick. God shines not only in Zion but out of her. She is made perfect in beauty by his indwelling, and that beauty is seen by all observers when the Lord shines forth from her.

Verse 3: "Our God shall come." The psalmist speaks of himself and his brethren as standing in immediate anticipation of the appearing of the Lord upon the scene.

Verses to meditate upon today: Psalm 50:1-6.

A THOUGHT TO PONDER

The church is made perfect in beauty by the Lord's indwelling, and that beauty is seen by all observers when he shines forth from her.

APRIL 19

LISTENING TO GOD

Hear, O my people, and I will speak; O Israel, and I will testify against thee: I am God, even thy God.

PSALM 50:7

VERSES 7-15: The address that follows is directed to the professed people of God. It is clearly, in the first place, meant for Israel, but is equally applicable to the visible church of God in every age. It declares the futility of external worship when spiritual faith is absent and mere outward ceremonial is rested in.

VERSE 7: "Hear, O my people, and I will speak." Because Jehovah speaks and they are avowedly his own people, they are bound to give earnest heed. "Let me speak," says the great I AM. The heavens and earth are but listeners; the Lord is about both to testify and to judge.

"O Israel, and I will testify against thee." Their covenant name is mentioned to give emphasis to the address; it was a double evil that the chosen nation should become so carnal, so unspiritual, so false, so heartless to their God. God himself, whose eyes sleep not, who is not misled by rumor but sees for himself, enters the scene as witness against his favored nation. Alas for us when God, even our fathers' God, testifies to the hypocrisy of the visible church!

"I am God, even thy God." He had taken them to be his peculiar people above all other nations, and they had in the most solemn manner avowed that he was their God. Hence the special reason for calling them to account. The law began with, "I am the LORD thy God, which have brought thee out of the land of Egypt," and now the session of their judgment opens with the same reminder of their singular position, privilege, and responsibility. It is not only that Jehovah is God, but "*thy* God." O Israel, this is what makes you so answerable to his searching reproofs.

Verses to meditate upon today: Psalm 50:7-15.

A THOUGHT TO PONDER

Alas for us when God, even our fathers' God, testifies to the hypocrisy of the visible church!

APRIL 20

BREAKING GOD'S LAW

*But unto the wicked God saith, What hast thou to do to declare my statutes,
or that thou shouldest take my covenant in thy mouth?*

PSALM 50:16

VERSE 16: "But unto the wicked God saith." He now addresses the breakers of the second table; he had previously spoken to the neglecters of the first. "What hast thou to do to declare my statutes?" "You violate openly my moral law, and yet are great sticklers for my ceremonial commands! What have you to do with them? What interest can you have in them? Do you dare to teach my law to others and profane it yourselves? What impudence, what blasphemy is this! Even if you claim to be sons of Levi, what of that? Your wickedness disqualifies you, disinherits you, puts you out of the succession. It should silence you, and it would if my people were as spiritual as I would have them be, for they would refuse to hear you and to pay you the portion of temporal things that is due to my true servants. You count up your holy days, you contend for rituals, you fight for externals, and yet the weightier matters of the law you despise! You blind guides, you strain out gnats and swallow camels; your hypocrisy is written on your foreheads and is manifest to all."

"Or that thou shouldest take my covenant in thy mouth?" "You talk of being in covenant with me and yet trample my holiness beneath your feet as swine trample upon pearls; do you think I can tolerate this? Your mouths are full of lying and slander, and yet you mouth my words as if they were fit morsels for such as you!" How horrible and evil it is that to this day we see men explaining doctrines who despise precepts! We need the grace of the doctrines as much as the doctrines of grace, and without it an apostle is but a Judas, and a fair-spoken professor is an errant enemy of the cross of Christ.

Verses to meditate upon today: Psalm 50:16-21.

A THOUGHT TO PONDER

We need the grace of the doctrines as much as the doctrines of grace.

APRIL 21

CONSIDER AND REMEMBER

Now consider this, ye that forget God, lest I tear you in pieces, and there be none to deliver.

PSALM 50:22

VERSE 22: "Now" is a word of entreaty, for the Lord is loath even to let the most ungodly run on to destruction. "Consider this"; take these truths to heart, you who trust in ceremonies and you who live in vice, for both of you sin in that you "forget God." Bethink you how unaccepted you are, and turn unto the Lord. See how you have mocked the eternal, and repent of your iniquities.

"Lest I tear you in pieces," as the lion rends his prey, "and there be none to deliver"—no Savior, no refuge, no hope. You reject the Mediator; beware, for you will sorely need one in the day of wrath, and none will be near to plead for you. How terrible, how complete, how painful, how humiliating will be the destruction of the wicked! God uses no soft words or velvet metaphors, nor may his servants do so when they speak of the wrath to come. O reader, consider this.

VERSE 23: "Whoso offereth praise glorifieth me." Praise is the best sacrifice—true, hearty, gracious thanksgiving from a renewed mind. Not the lowing of bullocks bound to the altar, but the songs of redeemed men are the music that the ear of Jehovah delights in. Sacrifice your loving gratitude, and God is honored thereby.

"And to him that ordereth his conversation aright will I show the salvation of God." Holy living is a choice evidence of salvation. He who submits his whole way to divine guidance and is careful to honor God in his life brings an offering that the Lord accepts through his dear Son; and such a one shall be more and more instructed and made experimentally to know the Lord's salvation. He needs salvation, for the best ordering of the life cannot save us, but that salvation he shall have. Not to ceremonies, not to unpurified lips is the blessing promised, but to grateful hearts and holy lives.

Verses to meditate upon today: Psalm 50:22-23.

A THOUGHT TO PONDER

God uses no soft words or velvet metaphors, nor may his servants do so when they speak of the wrath to come.

APRIL 22

WASH ME

Wash me throughly from mine iniquity, and cleanse me from my sin.
PSALM 51:2

VERSE 2: "Wash me throughly." It is not enough to blot out the sin; the psalmist's person is defiled, and he wants to be purified. He would have God himself "cleanse" him, for none but he could do it effectually. The washing must be thorough, it must be repeated, and therefore he cries, "Many times wash me." *The dye is in itself immovable, and I, the sinner, have lain long in it, until the crimson is ingrained; but, Lord, wash, and wash, and wash again, until the last stain is gone, and not a trace of my defilement is left.* The hypocrite is content if his garments are washed, but the true suppliant cries, "Wash *me.*"

The careless soul is content with a nominal cleansing, but the truly awakened conscience desires a real and practical washing, and that of a most complete and efficient kind. "Wash me throughly from mine iniquity." David's sin is viewed as one great pollution, polluting the entire nature, and as all his own, as if nothing were so much his own as his sin. The one sin against Bathsheba served to show the psalmist the whole mountain of his "iniquity," of which that foul deed was but one falling stone. He desires to be rid of the whole mass of his filthiness, which though once so little observed had become a hideous and haunting terror to his mind.

"And cleanse me from my sin." This is a more general expression, as if the psalmist said, "Lord, if washing will not do, try some other process; if water avails not, let fire. Let anything be tried, so that I may but be purified. Rid me of my sin by some means, by any means, by every means; only do purify me completely, and leave no guilt upon my soul." It is not the punishment he cries out against, but the sin.

Verses to meditate upon today: Psalm 51:1-6.

A THOUGHT TO PONDER

*Lord, wash, and wash, and wash again, until the last stain is gone,
and not a trace of my defilement is left.*

April 23

Restore Me

*Restore unto me the joy of thy salvation; and
uphold me with thy free Spirit.*

Psalm 51:12

Verse 11: "Cast me not away from thy presence." *Throw me not away as worthless; banish me not, like Cain, from your face and favor. Permit me to sit among those who share your love, though I only be suffered to keep the door. I deserve to be forever denied admission to your courts; but, O good Lord, permit me still the privilege that is as dear as life itself to me.*

"Take not thy Holy Spirit from me." *Withdraw not his comforts, counsels, assistances, and quickenings; else I am indeed as a dead man. Do not leave me as you did Saul, when neither by Urim, nor by prophet, nor by dream would you answer him. Your Spirit is my wisdom—leave me not to my folly; he is my strength—oh, desert me not to my own weakness. Drive me not away from you, neither go away from me. Keep up the union between us, which is my only hope of salvation. It will be a great wonder if so pure a Spirit deigns to stay in so base a heart as mine; but then, Lord, it is all wonder together. Therefore do this for your mercy's sake, I earnestly entreat you.*

Verse 12: "Restore unto me the joy of thy salvation." "Salvation" he had known, and had known it as the Lord's own; he had also felt the "joy" that arises from being saved in the Lord. But he had lost that "joy" for a while, and therefore he longed for its restoration. None but God can give it back; and he can do it. We may ask for it, and he will do it for his own glory and our benefit. This "joy" comes not first but follows pardon and purity. In such order it is safe; in any other it is vain presumption or idiotic delirium.

Verses to meditate upon today: Psalm 51:7-12.

A Thought to Ponder
*None but God can give this "joy" back; and he can do it,
for his own glory and our benefit.*

APRIL 24

OPEN MY LIPS

*O Lord, open thou my lips; and my mouth
shall show forth thy praise.*
PSALM 51:15

VERSE 15: "O LORD, open thou my lips." The psalmist is so afraid of himself that he commits his whole being to the divine care and fears to speak until the Lord unstops his shame-silenced mouth. How marvelously the Lord can open our lips, and what divine things can we poor simpletons pour forth under his inspiration! This prayer of a penitent is a golden petition for a preacher. *Lord, I offer it for myself and my brethren.* But it may stand in good stead anyone whose shame for sin makes him stammer in his prayers; and when it is fully answered, the tongue of the dumb begins to sing.

"And my mouth shall show forth thy praise." If God opens the mouth, he is sure to have the fruit of it. According to the porter at the gate is the nature of that which comes out of a man's lips. When vanity, anger, falsehood, or lust unbar the door, the foulest villainies troop out. But if the Holy Spirit opens the gate, then grace, mercy, peace, and all the graces come forth in tuneful dances, like the daughters of Israel when they met David returning with the Philistine's head.

VERSE 16: "For thou desirest not sacrifice." This was the subject of the previous Psalm. The psalmist was so illuminated as to see far beyond the symbolic ritual; his eye of faith gazed with delight upon the actual atonement.

"Else would I give it." He would have been glad enough to present tens of thousands of victims if these would have met the need. Indeed, anything that the Lord prescribed he would cheerfully have rendered. We are ready to give up all we have if we may but be cleared of our sins; and when sin is pardoned, our joyful gratitude is prepared for any sacrifice.

Verses to meditate upon today: Psalm 51:13-19.

A THOUGHT TO PONDER
When sin is pardoned, our joyful gratitude is prepared for any sacrifice.

APRIL 25

THE EVIL BOAST

Why boastest thou thyself in mischief, O mighty man?
The goodness of God endureth continually.

PSALM 52:1

VERSE 1: "Why boasteth thyself in mischief, O mighty man?" Doeg had small matter for boasting in having procured the slaughter of a band of defenseless priests. A mighty man indeed to kill men who never touched a sword! He ought to have been ashamed of his cowardice. He had no room for exultation! Honorable titles are but irony where the wearer is mean and cruel. If David alluded to Saul, he meant by these words pityingly to say, "How can one by nature fitted for nobler deeds descend to so low a level as to find a theme for boasting in a slaughter so heartless and mischievous?"

"The goodness of God endureth continually." What a beautiful contrast! The tyrant's fury cannot dry up the perennial stream of divine mercy. If priests be slain, their Master lives. If Doeg for a while triumphs, the Lord will outlive him and will right the wrongs that he has done. This ought to modify the proud exultations of the wicked, for after all, while the Lord lives, iniquity has little cause to exalt itself.

VERSE 2: "Thy tongue deviseth mischiefs." "You speak with an ulterior design." The information given was apparently for Saul's assistance, but in very deed in his heart Doeg the Edomite hated the priests of the God of Jacob. It is a mark of deep depravity when the evil spoken is craftily intended to promote a yet greater evil. "Like a sharp razor, working deceitfully." David represents the false tongue as being effectual for mischief, like a "razor" that, unawares to the person it is being used on, is making him bald. Or he may mean that as with a "razor" a man's throat may be cut very speedily, under the pretense of shaving him, even thus keenly, basely, but effectually Doeg destroyed the band of the priests. Whetted by malice and guided by craft, he did his cruel work with accursed thoroughness.

Verses to meditate upon today: Psalm 52:1-4.

A THOUGHT TO PONDER

The tyrant's fury cannot dry up the perennial stream of divine mercy.

APRIL 26

LIKE AN OLIVE TREE

*But I am like a green olive tree in the house of God:
I trust in the mercy of God for ever and ever.*
PSALM 52:8

VERSE 8: "But I," hunted and persecuted though I am, "am like a green olive tree." I am not plucked up or destroyed but am like a flourishing olive, which out of the rock draws oil, and amid the drought still lives and grows.

"In the house of God." He was one of the divine family and could not be expelled from it; his place was near his God, and there he was safe and happy despite all the machinations of his foes. He was bearing fruit and would continue to do so when all his proud enemies were withered like branches lopped from the tree.

"I trust in the mercy of God for ever and ever." Eternal mercy is my present confidence. David knew God's mercy to be eternal and perpetual, and in that he trusted. What a rock to build on! What a fortress to fly to!

VERSE 9: "I will praise thee for ever." *Like your mercy shall my thankfulness be.* While others boast in their riches, I will boast in my God; and when their glorying is silenced forever in the tomb, my song shall continue to proclaim the loving-kindness of Jehovah.

"Because thou hast done it." *You have vindicated the righteous and punished the wicked.* God's memorable acts of providence, both to saints and sinners, deserve and must have our gratitude. David views his prayer as already answered, the promise of God as already fulfilled, and therefore at once lifts up the sacred Psalm.

"And I will wait on thy name." God shall still be the psalmist's hope; he will not in the future look elsewhere. He whose name has been so gloriously made known in truth and righteousness is justly chosen as our expectation for years to come.

Verses to meditate upon today: Psalm 52:5-9.

A THOUGHT TO PONDER

I am like a flourishing olive, which amid the drought still lives and grows.

APRIL 27

THE ATHEIST

The fool hath said in his heart, There is no God. Corrupt are they, and have done abominable iniquity: there is none that doeth good.

PSALM 53:1

VERSE 1: He does this because he is a "fool." Being a "fool" he speaks according to his nature; being a great "fool" he meddles with a great subject and comes to a wild conclusion. The atheist is, morally as well as mentally, a "fool," a "fool" in the heart as well as in his head, a "fool" in morals as well as in philosophy. With the denial of God as a starting point, we may well conclude that the fool's decline is a rapid, riotous, raving, ruinous one. He who begins at impiety is ready for anything.

"No God," being interpreted, means no law, no order, no restraint to lust, no limit to passion. Who but a "fool" would be of this mind? What a Bedlam [insane asylum in London] would the world become if such lawless principles came to be universal! He who heartily entertains an irreligious spirit and follows it out to its legitimate issues is a son of Belial, dangerous to the commonwealth, irrational, and despicable. Every natural man is more or less a denier of God. Practical atheism is the religion of the race.

"Corrupt are they." They are rotten. It is idle to compliment them as sincere doubters and amiable thinkers—they are putrid. There is too much dainty dealing nowadays with atheism. It is not a harmless error; it is an offensive, putrid sin, and righteous men should look upon it in that light. All men being more or less atheistic in spirit are also in that degree "corrupt"; their heart is foul, their moral nature is decayed.

"And have done abominable iniquity." Bad principles soon lead to bad lives. One does not find virtue promoted by the example of your Voltaires and Tom Paines. Those who talk so abominably as to deny their Maker will act abominably when it serves their turn.

Verses to meditate upon today: Psalm 53:1-6.

A THOUGHT TO PONDER
Every natural man is more or less a denier of God.
Practical atheism is the religion of the race.

APRIL 28

HELP IN ADVERSITY

Behold, God is mine helper: the Lord is with them that uphold my soul.
PSALM 54:4

VERSE 4: "Behold, God is mine helper." The psalmist saw enemies everywhere, and now to his joy as he looks upon the band of his defenders, he sees One whose aid is better than all the help of men. He is overwhelmed with joy at recognizing his divine champion and cries, "Behold." And is not this a theme for pious exultation in all time—that the great God protects us, his own people? What matters the number or violence of our foes when he uplifts the shield of his omnipotence to guard us and the sword of his power to aid us? Little care we for the defiance of the foe while we have the defense of God.

"The Lord is with them that uphold my soul." The reigning Lord, the great *Adonai*, is in the camp of my defenders. Here was a greater champion than any of the three mighties or than all the valiant men who chose David for their captain. The psalmist was very confident; he felt so thoroughly that his heart was on the Lord's side that he was sure God was on *his* side. He asked in the first verse for deliverance, and here he returns thanks for God's upholding; while we are seeking one mercy that we have not, we must not be unmindful of another that we have. It is a great mercy to have some friends left to us, but a greater mercy still to see the Lord among them, for like so many ciphers our friends stand for nothing until the Lord sets himself as a great unit in front of them.

VERSE 5: "He shall reward evil unto mine enemies." They worked for evil, and they shall have their wages. It cannot be that malice should go unavenged. It would be cruelty to the good to be lenient to their persecutors.

Verses to meditate upon today: Psalm 54:1-7.

A THOUGHT TO PONDER
He is overwhelmed with joy at recognizing his divine champion.

THE FEAR OF DEATH

My heart is sore pained within me: and the terrors of death are fallen upon me.
PSALM 55:4

VERSE 4: "My heart is sore pained within me." His spirit writhed in agony, like a poor worm; he was mentally as much in pain as a woman in travail physically. His inmost soul was touched; and a wounded spirit who can bear? If this were written when David was attacked by his own favorite son and ignominiously driven from his capital, he had reason enough for using these expressions.

"And the terrors of death are fallen upon me." Mortal fears seized him; he felt like one suddenly surrounded with the glooms of the shadow of "death," upon whom the eternal night suddenly descends. Within and without he was afflicted, and his chief terror seemed to come from above, for he uses the expression, "fallen upon me." He gave himself up for lost. He felt that he was as good as dead. The inmost center of his nature was moved with dismay.

Think of our Lord in the garden, with his "soul exceeding sorrowful, even unto death," and you have a parallel to the griefs of the psalmist. Perchance, dear reader, if as yet you have not trodden this gloomy way, you will do so soon; then be sure to mark the footprints of your Lord in this miry part of the road.

VERSE 5: "Fearfulness and trembling are come upon me." Like housebreakers these robbers were entering his soul. Like one who feels a fainting fit coming over him, so the oppressed suppliant was falling into a state of terror. His fear was so great as to make him tremble. He did not know what would happen next or how soon the worst should come. The sly, mysterious whisperings of slander often cause a noble mind more fear than open antagonism; we can be brave against an open foe, but cowardly, plotting conspiracies bewilder and distract us.

Verses to meditate upon today: Psalm 55:1-7.

A THOUGHT TO PONDER

Be sure to mark the footprints of your Lord in this miry part of the road.

APRIL 30

TREACHERY

But it was thou, a man mine equal, my guide, and mine acquaintance.
PSALM 55:13

VERSE 13: "But it was thou." The poetic fury is upon him, and he sees the traitor as though he stood before him in flesh and blood. He singles him out, he points his finger at him, he challenges him to his face. "But thou." "*Et tu, Brute?*" And you, Ahithophel, are you here? Judas, do you betray the Son of man?

"A man mine equal." You were treated by me as one of my own rank, never looked upon as an inferior, but as a trusted friend. "My guide," a counselor so sage that I trusted your advice and found it prudent to do so.

"And mine acquaintance," with whom I was on most intimate terms, who knew me even as I knew him by mutual disclosures of heart. You were no stranger occasionally conversed with, but a near and dear friend admitted to my secret fellowship. It was fiendish treason for such a one to prove false-hearted. There was no excuse for such villainy. Judas stood very much in this relation to our Lord. He was treated as an equal, trusted as treasurer, and in that capacity often consulted with. He knew the place where the Master was accustomed to spend his solitude; in fact, he knew all the Master's movements, and yet he betrayed him to his remorseless adversaries. How justly might the Lord have pointed at him and said, "But thou." But his gentler spirit warned the son of perdition in the mildest manner, and had not Iscariot been tenfold a child of hell, he would have relinquished his detestable purpose.

VERSE 14: "We took sweet counsel together." It was not merely the counsel that men take together in public or upon common themes; their fellowship had been tender and confidential.

Verses to meditate upon today: Psalm 55:8-14.

A THOUGHT TO PONDER

And you, Ahithophel, are you here? Judas, do you betray the Son of man?

MAY 1

Prayer from the Heart

As for me, I will call upon God; and the LORD shall save me.
PSALM 55:16

VERSE 16: "As for me, I will call upon God." The psalmist would not endeavor to meet the plots of his adversaries by counterplots or to imitate their incessant violence, but in direct opposition to their godless behavior would continually resort to his God. Thus Jesus did, and it has been the wisdom of all believers to do the same. As this exemplifies the contrast of their character, so it will foretell the contrast of their end—the righteous shall ascend to their God, but the wicked shall sink to ruin.

"And the LORD shall save me." Jehovah will fulfill my desire and glorify himself in my deliverance. The psalmist is quite sure. He knows that he will pray and is equally clear that he will be heard. The covenant name is the pledge of the covenant promise.

VERSE 17: "Evening, and morning, and at noon, will I pray." Often but never too often. Seasons of great need call for frequent seasons of devotion. The three periods chosen are most fitting; to begin, continue, and end the day with God is supreme wisdom. Where time has naturally set up a boundary, there let us set up an altar stone. The psalmist means that he will always pray; he will run a line of prayer right along the day and track the sun with his petitions. Day and night he saw his enemies busy, and therefore he would meet their activity by continuous prayer.

"And cry aloud." He would give a tongue to his complaint; he would be very earnest in his pleas with heaven. Some "cry aloud" who never say a word. It is the bell of the heart that rings loudest in heaven. Some read this, "I will nurse and murmur"; deep heart thoughts should be attended with inarticulate but vehement utterances of grief. Blessed be God—moaning is translatable in heaven. A Father's heart reads a child's heart.

Verses to meditate upon today: Psalm 55:15-19.

A THOUGHT TO PONDER

Day and night he saw his enemies busy, and therefore he would meet their activity by continuous prayer.

MAY 2

Trust God with Your Cares

*Cast thy burden upon the LORD, and he shall sustain thee:
he shall never suffer the righteous to be moved.*

PSALM 55:22

VERSE 22: "Thy burden," or what your God lays upon you, lay it "upon the LORD." His wisdom casts it on you; it is your wisdom to "cast" it on him. He cast your lot for you; cast your lot on him. He gives you your portion of suffering; accept it with cheerful resignation, and then take it back to him by your assured confidence.

"He shall sustain thee." Your bread shall be given to you; your waters shall be sure. Abundant nourishment shall fit you to bear all your labors and trials. As your days, so shall your strength be.

"He shall never suffer the righteous to be moved." The "righteous" man may move like the boughs of a tree in the tempest, but he shall never be moved like a tree torn up by the roots. He stands firm who stands in God. Many would destroy the saints, but God has not allowed it, and never will. Like pillars, the godly stand immovable, to the glory of the Great Architect.

VERSE 23: For the ungodly a sure, terrible, and fatal overthrow is appointed. Climb as they may, "the pit" yawns for them. God himself will cause them to descend into it, and "destruction" there shall be their portion. "Bloody and deceitful men," with double iniquity of cruelty and craft upon them, "shall not live out half their days." They shall be cut off in their quarrels; or being disappointed in their artifices, vexation shall end them. They were in heart murderers of others, and they became in reality self-murderers. Doubt not that virtue lengthens life and that vice tends to shorten it.

"But I will trust in thee." A very wise, practical conclusion. We can have no better ground of confidence. The Lord is all and more than all that faith can need as the foundation of peaceful dependence. *Lord, increase our faith evermore.*

Verses to meditate upon today: Psalm 55:20-23.

A THOUGHT TO PONDER

Abundant nourishment shall fit you to bear all your labors and trials.

MAY 3

WHEN I AM AFRAID

What time I am afraid, I will trust in thee.

PSALM 56:3

VERSE 3: "What time I am afraid." David was no braggart—he does not claim never to be afraid, and he was no brutish stoic free from fear because of the lack of tenderness. David's intelligence deprived him of the stupid heedlessness of ignorance; he saw the imminence of his peril and was "afraid." We are men and therefore liable to overthrow; we are feeble and therefore unable to prevent it; we are sinful men and therefore deserving it—and for all these reasons we are "afraid." But the condition of the psalmist's mind was complex. He feared, but that fear did not fill the whole area of his mind, for he adds, "I will trust in thee."

It is possible, then, for fear and faith to occupy the mind at the same moment. We are strange beings, and our experience in the divine life is stranger still. We are often in a twilight, where light and darkness are both present, and it is hard to tell which predominates. It is a blessed fear that drives us to trust. Unregenerate fear drives *from* God; gracious fear drives *to* him. If I fear man I have only to trust God and I have the best antidote. To trust when there is no cause for fear is but the name of faith, but to be reliant upon God when occasions for alarm are abundant and pressing is the conquering faith of God's elect. Though the verse is in the form of a resolve, it became a fact in David's life; let us make it so in ours. Whether the fear arise from without or within, from past, present, or future, from temporals or spirituals, from men or devils, let us maintain faith, and we shall soon recover courage.

Verses to meditate upon today: Psalm 56:1-6.

A THOUGHT TO PONDER

Whether the fear arise from without or within, from past, present, or future, from temporals or spirituals, from men or devils, let us maintain faith, and we shall soon recover courage.

MAY 4

TRUST VERSUS FEAR

In God have I put my trust: I will not be afraid what man can do unto me.
PSALM 56:11

VERSE 11: "In God have I put my trust." This and the former verse are evidently the chorus of the Psalm. We cannot be too careful of our faith or ensure too diligently that it is grounded on the Lord alone.

"I will not be afraid what man can do unto me." Faith has banished fear. He views his foes in their most forcible character, calling them not *flesh,* but indicating them as "man," and yet he dreads them not. Though the whole race were his enemies, he is not "afraid" now that his "trust' is stayed on God. He is not afraid of what they threaten to do, for much of that they *cannot* do; and even what is in their power, what they *can do,* he defies with holy daring. He speaks for the future—"I will not"—for he is sure that the security of the present will suffice for days to come.

VERSE 12: "Thy vows are upon me, O God." "Vows" made in his trouble he does not lightly forget; nor should we. We voluntarily made them; let us cheerfully keep them. All professed Christians are men under vows, but especially those who in hours of dire distress have rededicated themselves unto the Lord.

"I will render praises unto thee." With heart and voice and gift, we should cheerfully extol the God of our salvation. The practice of making solemn vows in times of trouble is to be commended, when it is followed by the far less common custom of fulfilling them when the trouble is over.

VERSE 13: "For thou hast delivered my soul from death." His enemies were defeated in their attempts upon his life, and therefore he vowed to devote his life to God. "Wilt not thou deliver my feet from falling?" One mercy is a plea for another, for indeed it may happen that the second is the necessary complement of the first.

Verses to meditate upon today: Psalm 56:7-13.

A THOUGHT TO PONDER
Faith has banished fear.

MAY 5

HEAVENLY HELP

He shall send from heaven, and save me from the reproach of him that would swallow me up. Selah. God shall send forth his mercy and his truth.

PSALM 57:3

VERSE 3: "He shall send from heaven." If there be no fit instruments on earth, heaven shall yield up its legions of angels for the succor of the saints. We may in times of great straits expect mercies of a remarkable kind. Like the Israelites in the wilderness, we shall have our bread hot from heaven, new every morning; and for the overthrow of our enemies God shall open his celestial armories and put them to utter confusion. Wherever the battle is more fierce than ordinary, there shall come help from headquarters, for the Commander-in-Chief sees all.

"And save me from the reproach of him that would swallow me up." The Lord will be in time not only to rescue his servants from being swallowed up, but even from being reproached. Not only shall they escape the flames, but not even the smell of fire shall pass upon them. O dog of hell, I am not only delivered from your bite, but even from your bark. Our foes shall not have the power to sneer at us; their cruel jests and taunting gibes shall be ended by the message from heaven, which shall forever save us.

"Selah." Such mercy may well make us pause to meditate and give thanks. Rest, singer, for God has given you rest!

"God shall send forth his mercy and his truth." The psalmist asked for "mercy," and "truth" came with it. Thus evermore does God give us more than we ask or think. His attributes, like angels on the wing, are ever ready to come to the rescue of his chosen.

VERSE 4: "My soul is among lions." He was a Daniel—howled at, hunted, wounded, but not slain. His place was in itself one of extreme peril, and yet faith made him feel secure, so that he could lie down.

Verses to meditate upon today: Psalm 57:1-6.

A THOUGHT TO PONDER

We may in times of great straits expect mercies of a remarkable kind.

MAY 6

ENDLESS LOVE

For thy mercy is great unto the heavens, and thy truth unto the clouds.
PSALM 57:10

VERSE 9: "I will praise thee, O Lord, among the people." Gentiles shall hear my praise. Here is an instance of the way in which the truly devout evangelical spirit overleaps the boundaries that bigotry sets up. The ordinary Jew would never wish the Gentile dogs to hear Jehovah's name, except to tremble at it; but this grace-taught psalmist has a missionary spirit and would spread the praise and fame of his God. "I will sing unto thee among the nations." However far off they may be, I would make them hear of you through my glad psalmody.

VERSE 10: "For thy mercy is great unto the heavens." Right up from man's lowliness to heaven's loftiness mercy reaches. Imagination fails to guess the height of heaven, and the riches of mercy exceed our highest thoughts. The psalmist, as he sits at the cave's mouth and looks up to the firmament, rejoices that God's goodness is more vast and more sublime than even the vaulted skies.

"And thy truth unto the clouds." Upon the cloud God sets the seal of his truth, the rainbow, which ratifies his covenant. In the cloud he hides his rain and snow, which prove his "truth" by bringing to us seedtime and harvest, cold and heat. Creation is great, but the Creator greater far. Heaven cannot contain him; above clouds and stars his goodness far exceeds.

VERSE 11: "Be thou exalted, O God, above the heavens." This is a grand chorus. Take it up, you angels and you spirits made perfect, and join in it, you sons of men below, as you say, "let thy glory be above all the earth." The prophet in the previous verse spoke of "mercy . . . unto the heavens," but here his song flies "above the heavens." Praise rises higher and knows no bound.

Verses to meditate upon today: Psalm 57:7-11.

A THOUGHT TO PONDER
The riches of mercy exceed our highest thoughts.

MAY 7

ENEMIES

Do ye indeed speak righteousness, O congregation?
Do ye judge uprightly, O ye sons of men?
PSALM 58:1

VERSE 1: "Do ye indeed speak righteousness, O congregation?" The enemies of David were a numerous and united band, and because they so unanimously condemned the persecuted one, they were apt to take it for granted that their verdict was a right one. "What everybody says must be true," is a lying proverb. "Have we not all agreed to hound the man to the death," and who dare hint that so many great ones can be mistaken? Yet the persecuted one lays the axe at the root by requiring his judges to answer the question whether or not they were acting according to justice. It were well if men would sometimes pause and candidly consider this. Some of those who surrounded David were rather passive than active persecutors; they held their tongues when the object of royal hate was slandered. In the original this first sentence appears to be addressed to them, and they are asked to justify their silence. Silence gives consent. He who refrains from defending the right is himself an accomplice in the wrong.

"Do ye judge uprightly, O ye sons of men?" You too are only men, though dressed in authority. Your office for men and your relation to men both bind you to rectitude; but have you remembered this? Have you not put aside all truth when you have condemned the godly and united in seeking the overthrow of the innocent? Yet in doing this be not too sure of success, for you are only the "sons of men," and there is a God who can and will reverse your verdicts.

VERSE 2: "Yea, in heart ye work wickedness." Down deep in your very souls you hold a rehearsal of the injustice you intend to practice, and when your opportunity arrives, you wreak vengeance with gusto. Your hearts are in your wicked work, and your hands are therefore ready enough.

Verses to meditate upon today: Psalm 58:1-5.

A THOUGHT TO PONDER
He who refrains from defending the right is himself an accomplice in the wrong.

MAY 8

JUSTICE WILL TRIUMPH

The righteous shall rejoice when he seeth the vengeance:
he shall wash his feet in the blood of the wicked.

PSALM 58:10

VERSE 10: The righteous man will have no hand in meting out, neither will he rejoice in the spirit of revenge, but his righteous soul shall acquiesce in the judgments of God, and he shall rejoice to see justice triumphant. There is nothing in Scripture of that sympathy with God's enemies that modern traitors are so fond of parading as the finest species of benevolence. We shall at the last day say, "Amen" to the condemnation of the wicked and will feel no disposition to question the ways of God with the impenitent. Remember how John, the loving disciple, puts it: "And after these things I heard a great voice of much people in heaven, saying, Alleluia; Salvation, and glory, and honor, and power, unto the Lord our God: for true and righteous are his judgments; for he hath judged the great whore, which did corrupt the earth with her fornication, and hath avenged the blood of his servants at her hand. And again they said, Alleluia. And her smoke rose up for ever and ever."

"He shall wash his feet in the blood of the wicked." He shall triumph over them; they shall be so utterly vanquished that their overthrow shall be final and fatal, and his deliverance complete and crowning. The damnation of sinners shall not mar the happiness of saints.

VERSE 11: "So that a man shall say . . ." Every man, however ignorant, shall be compelled to say, "verily [in very deed, assuredly] there is a reward for the righteous." If nothing else be true, this is. The godly are not after all forsaken and given over to their enemies; the wicked are not to have the best of it; truth and goodness are recompensed in the long run. "Verily he is a God that judgeth in the earth." All men shall be forced by the sight of the final judgment to see that there is a God and that he is the righteous ruler of the universe.

Verses to meditate upon today: Psalm 58:6-11.

A THOUGHT TO PONDER

All men shall be forced by the sight of the final judgment to see that there is a God
and that he is the righteous ruler of the universe.

MAY 9

DELIVERANCE IS FROM GOD

Thou therefore, O LORD God of hosts, the God of Israel, awake to visit all the heathen: be not merciful to any wicked transgressors. Selah.

PSALM 59:5

VERSE 5: *"Thou," you yourself, work for me personally, for the case needs your intervention. I am unjustly assailed and cannot help myself.* "O LORD," ever living "God of hosts," able to rescue me, "the God of Israel," pledged by covenant to redeem your oppressed servant, "awake to visit all the heathen." Arouse your holy mind, bestow your sacred energies, punish the heathen among your Israel, the false-hearted who say they are Jews and are not. And when you are about this business, let all the nations of your enemies and all the heathenish people at home and abroad know that you are judging and punishing.

It is the mark of a thoughtful prayer that the titles that are within it applied to God are appropriate and are, as it were, congruous to the matter and fitted to add force to the argument. Shall Jehovah put up with seeing his people oppressed? Shall the "God of hosts" permit his enemies to exult over his servant? Shall the faithful God of a chosen people leave his chosen to perish? The name of God is, even in a literal sense, a fortress and high tower for all his people. What a forceful petition is contained in the words, "awake to visit." *O God, actively punish, in wisdom judge, with force chastise.*

"Be not merciful to any wicked transgressors." *Be merciful to them as men, but not as transgressors; if they continue hardened in their sin, do not wink at their oppression. To wink at sin in transgressors would be to leave the righteous under their power; therefore do not pass by their offenses but deal out their due reward.* The psalmist feels that the overthrow of oppression that was so needful for himself must be equally desirable for multitudes of the godly placed in like positions, and therefore he prays for the whole company of the faithful, and against the entire confraternity of traitors.

Verses to meditate upon today: Psalm 59:1-5.

A THOUGHT TO PONDER
Shall Jehovah put up with seeing his people oppressed?

God Is Our Strength

Because of his strength will I wait upon thee: for God is my defense.
PSALM 59:9

VERSE 9: "Because of his strength will I wait upon thee." *Is my persecutor strong? Then, my God, for this very reason I will turn to you and leave my matters in your hand.* It is wise to find in the greatness of our difficulties a reason for casting ourselves on the Lord.

> *And when it seems no chance nor change*
> *From grief can set me free,*
> *Hope finds its strength in helplessness,*
> *And, patient, waits on thee.*

"For God is my defense," my high place, my fortress, the place of my refuge in the time of danger. If the foe be too strong for me to cope with him, I will retreat into my castle, where he cannot reach me.

VERSE 10: "The God of my mercy shall prevent [precede] me." God, who is the giver and fountain of all the undeserved goodness I have received, will go before me and lead my way as I march onward. He will meet me in my time of need. Not alone shall I have to confront my foes, but he whose goodness I have long tried and proved will gently clear my way and will be my faithful protector. How frequently have we met with preventing mercy—the supply prepared before the need occurred, the refuge built before the danger arose. Far ahead into the future the foreseeing grace of heaven has projected itself and forestalled every difficulty.

"God shall let me see my desire upon mine enemies." Observe that the words "my desire" are not in the original. From the Hebrew we are taught that David expected to see his "enemies" without fear. God will enable his servant to gaze steadily upon the foe without trepidation; he shall be calm and self-possessed in the hour of peril; and ere long he shall look down on the same foes discomfited, overthrown, destroyed. When Jehovah leads the way, victory follows at his heels.

Verses to meditate upon today: Psalm 59:6-13.

A Thought to Ponder
Far ahead into the future the foreseeing grace of heaven has projected itself and forestalled every difficulty.

MAY 11

A MORNING SONG

But I will sing of thy power; yea, I will sing aloud of thy mercy in the morning:
for thou hast been my defense and refuge in the day of my trouble.

PSALM 59:16

VERSE 16: "But I will sing of thy power." *The wicked howl, but I sing and will sing. Their power is weakness, but yours, O God, is omnipotence; I see them vanquished and your power victorious, and forever and ever will I sing of you.*

"Yea, I will sing aloud of thy mercy in the morning." When those lovers of darkness find their game is up, and their midnight howlings die away, then will I lift up my voice on high and praise the loving-kindness of God without fear of being disturbed. What a blessed morning will soon break for the righteous, and what a song will be theirs! Sons of the morning, you may sigh tonight, but joy will come on the wings of the rising sun. Tune your harps even now, for the signal to commence the eternal music will soon be given; the morning comes, and your sun no more shall go down forever.

"For thou hast been my defense." The song is for God alone, and it is one that none can sing but those who have experienced the loving-kindness of their God. Looking back upon a past all full of mercy, the saints will bless the Lord with their whole hearts and will triumph in him as the high place of their security.

"And refuge in the day of my trouble." The greater our present trials, the louder will our future songs be, and the more intense our joyful gratitude. Had we no day of trouble, where were our season of retrospective thanksgiving? David's besetment by Saul's bloodhounds creates an opportunity for divine interposition and so for triumphant praise.

VERSE 17: "Unto thee, O my strength, will I sing." What transport is here! What a monopolizing of all the psalmist's emotions for the one object of praising God! Strength has been overcome by strength—not by the hero's own prowess, but by the might of God alone.

Verses to meditate upon today: Psalm 59:14-17.

A THOUGHT TO PONDER
Sons of the morning, you may sigh tonight, but joy
will come on the wings of the rising sun.

MAY 12

DELIVERANCE

*That thy beloved may be delivered; save with thy right hand,
and hear me.*

PSALM 60:5

VERSE 5: "That thy beloved may be delivered." David was the Lord's "beloved"; his name signifies "dear or beloved," and there was in Israel a remnant according to the election of grace who were the "beloved" of the Lord; for their sakes the Lord wrought great marvels, and he had his eye upon them in all his mighty acts. God's "beloved" are the inner seed, for whose sake he preserves the entire nation, which acts as a husk to the vital part. This is the main design of providence: "that thy beloved may be delivered." If it were not for their sakes, he would neither give a banner nor send victory.

"Save with thy right hand, and hear me." *Save at once, before the prayer is over; the case is desperate unless there be immediate salvation. Do not wait, O Lord, until I am done pleading: save first and hear afterwards.* The salvation must be a royal and eminent one, such as only the omnipotent hand of God linked with his dexterous wisdom can achieve. Urgent distress brings men to pressing and bold petitions such as this. We may by faith ask for and expect that our extremity will be God's opportunity; special and memorable deliverances will be wrought when dire calamities appear to be imminent.

Here is one suppliant for many, even as in the case of our Lord's intercession for his saints. As the Lord's man, David pleads for the rest of the "beloved," loved and accepted in the Chief Beloved; he seeks salvation as though it were for himself, but his eye is ever upon all those who are one with him in the Father's love. When divine interposition is necessary for the rescue of the elect it must occur, for the first and greatest necessity of providence is the honor of God and the salvation of his chosen.

Verses to meditate upon today: Psalm 60:1-6.

A THOUGHT TO PONDER

*We may by faith ask for and expect that our extremity
will be God's opportunity.*

MAY 13

GILEAD AND MANASSEH

Gilead is mine, and Manasseh is mine; Ephraim also is the strength of mine head; Judah is my lawgiver.

PSALM 60:7

VERSE 7: "Gilead is mine, and Manasseh is mine." David claims the whole land on account of the promise. He mentions two other great divisions of the country, evidently delighting to survey the goodly land that the Lord had given him. All things are ours, whether things present or things to come; no mean portion belongs to the believer, and let him not think meanly of it. No enemy shall withhold from true faith what God has given, for grace makes faith mighty to wrest it from the foe. Life is mine, and death is mine, for Christ is mine.

"Ephraim also is the strength of mine head." All the military power of the valiant tribe was at the command of David, and he praises God for it. God will bow to the accomplishment of his purposes all the valor of men; God will overrule all their achievements for the progress of his cause.

"Judah is my lawgiver." There the civil power was concentrated; the king being of that tribe sent forth his laws out of her midst. We know no lawgiver but the King who came out of Judah. To all the claims of Rome or Oxford or the councils of men, we pay no attention. We are free from all other ecclesiastical rule but that of Christ; but we yield joyful obedience to him: "Judah is my lawgiver." Amid distractions it is a great thing to have good and sound legislation; it was a balm for Israel's wounds, and it is our joy in the church of Christ.

VERSE 8: Having looked at home with satisfaction, the hero king now looks abroad with exultation. "Moab," so injurious to me in former years, "is my washpot," the basin into which the water falls when it is poured from a pitcher upon my feet.

Verses to meditate upon today: Psalm 60:7-12.

A THOUGHT TO PONDER

No enemy shall withhold from true faith what God has given.

MAY 14

Persevering in Prayer

From the end of the earth will I cry unto thee, when my heart is overwhelmed.
Lead me to the rock that is higher than I.

PSALM 61:2

VERSE 2: "From the end of the earth will I cry unto thee." The psalmist was banished from the spot that was the center of his delight, and at the same time his mind was in a depressed and melancholy condition. Both actually and figuratively he was an outcast; yet he does not therefore restrain prayer but rather finds therein a reason for louder and more importunate cries.

To be absent from the place of divine worship was a sore sorrow to saints in olden times; they looked upon the tabernacle as the center of the world, and they counted themselves to be at the far end of the universe when they could no longer resort to the sacred shrine; their heart was heavy as in a strange land when they were banished from its solemnities. Yet even they knew right well that no place is unsuitable for prayer. There may be an end of the earth, but there must not be an end to devotion. On creation's verge we may call upon God, for even there he is within call. No spot is too dreary, no condition too deplorable; whether it be the world's end or life's end, prayer is equally available.

To pray in some circumstances needs resolve, and the psalmist here expresses it: "will I cry." This was a wise resolution, for had he ceased to pray, he would have become the victim of despair; there is an end to a man when he makes an end to prayer. Observe that David never dreamed of seeking any other God; he did not imagine the dominion of Jehovah to be local. He was at the end of the Promised Land, but he knew himself to be still in the territory of the Great King; to him only does he address his petitions.

Verses to meditate upon today: Psalm 61:1-8.

A Thought to Ponder

Whether it be the world's end or life's end, prayer is equally available.

Salvation Is from God Alone

He only is my rock and my salvation; he is my defense;
I shall not be greatly moved.
Psalm 62:2

Verse 2: "He only is my rock and my salvation." Sometimes a metaphor may be more full of meaning and more suggestive than literal speech. Hence the use of the figure of a "rock," the very mention of which would awaken grateful memories in the psalmist's mind. David had often lain concealed in rocky caverns, and here he compares his God to such a secure refuge and indeed declares him to be his only real protection, all-sufficient in himself and never failing. At the same time, as if to show us that what he wrote was not mere poetic sentiment but blessed reality, the literal word "salvation" follows the figurative expression. That our God is our refuge is no fiction; nothing in the world is more a matter of fact.

"He is my defense," my height, my lofty rampart, my high fort. Here we have another and bolder image; the tried believer not only abides in God as in a cavernous rock but dwells in him as a warrior in some bravely defiant tower or lordly castle.

"I shall not be greatly moved." His personal weakness might cause him to be somewhat moved, but his faith would come in to prevent any very great disturbance; not much would he be tossed about. "Moved," but not removed. "Moved" like a ship at anchor that swings with the tide but is not swept away by the tempest. When a man knows assuredly that the Lord is his "salvation," he cannot be very much cast down. It would need more than all the devils in hell greatly to alarm a heart that knows God to be its salvation.

Verse 3: "How long will ye imagine mischief against a man?" It is always best to begin with God, and then we may confront our enemies. Make all sure with heaven; then may you grapple with earth and hell.

Verses to meditate upon today: Psalm 62:1-4.

A Thought to Ponder

It would need more than all the devils in hell greatly to alarm a heart
that knows God to be its salvation.

MAY 16

REST IN GOD ALONE

My soul, wait thou only upon God; for my expectation is from him.
PSALM 62:5

VERSE 5: "My soul, wait thou only upon God." When we have already practiced a virtue, it is yet needful that we bind ourselves to a continuance in it. The soul is apt to be dragged away from its anchorage or is readily tempted to add a second confidence to the one sole and sure ground of reliance. We must, therefore, stir ourselves up to maintain the holy position that we were at first able to assume. Be still silent, O my soul! Submit yourself completely, trust immovably, wait patiently.

Let none of your enemies' imaginings, consultings, flatteries, or maledictions cause you to break the King's peace. Be like the sheep before her shearers, and like your Lord conquer by the passive resistance of victorious patience. You can only achieve this as you shall be inwardly persuaded of God's presence and as you wait solely on him. Unmingled faith is undismayed. Faith with a single eye sees herself secure; but if her eye be darkened by two confidences, she is blind and useless.

"For my expectation is from him." We expect from God because we believe in him. Expectation is the child of prayer and faith and is owned of the Lord as an acceptable grace. We should desire nothing but what would be right for God to give; then our expectation would be all from God. And concerning truly good things we should not look to second causes but to the Lord alone, and so again our expectation would be all from him. The vain expectations of worldly men come not; they promise but there is no performance. Our expectations are on the way and in due season will arrive to satisfy our hopes. Happy is the man who feels that all he has, all he wants, and all he expects are to be found in his God.

Verses to meditate upon today: Psalm 62:5-12.

A THOUGHT TO PONDER
Submit yourself completely, trust immovably, wait patiently.

MAY 17

EAGER FOR GOD

O God, thou art my God; early will I seek thee: my soul thirsteth for thee, my flesh longeth for thee in a dry and thirsty land, where no water is.
PSALM 63:1

VERSE 1: "O God, thou art my God"; or, "O God, thou art my Mighty One." The last Psalm left the echo of power ringing in the ear, and it is here remembered. Strong trust bids the fugitive poet confess his allegiance to the only living God; and firm faith enables him to claim him as his own. He has no doubts about his possession of his God; why should other believers have any? The straightforward, clear language of this opening sentence would be far more becoming in Christians than the timorous and doubtful expressions so usual among those who profess faith. How sweet is such language! Is there any other word comparable to it for delights? Can angels say more?

"Early will I seek thee." Possession breeds desire. Full assurance is no hindrance to diligence but is the mainspring of it. How can I seek another man's God? But it is with ardent desire that I seek after him whom I know to be my own. Observe the eagerness implied in the time mentioned. He will not wait for noon or the cool eventide; he is up as the rooster crows to meet his God. Communion with God is so sweet that the chill of the morning is forgotten and the luxury of the couch is despised. The morning is the time for dew and freshness, and the psalmist consecrates it to prayer and devout fellowship. The best of men have been early on their knees. The word "early" has not only the sense of early in the morning, but that of eagerness, immediateness. He who truly longs for God longs for him now. Holy desires are among the most powerful influences that stir our inner nature; hence the next sentence: "My soul thirsteth for thee." Thirst is an insatiable longing after that which is one of the most essential supports of life; there is no reasoning with it, no forgetting it, no despising it, no overcoming it by stoical indifference.

Verses to meditate upon today: Psalm 63:1-5.

A THOUGHT TO PONDER
It is with ardent desire that I seek after him whom I know to be my own.

Trusting in God at All Times

My soul followeth hard after thee: thy right hand upholdeth me.
Psalm 63:8

Verse 8: "My soul followeth hard after thee" or is glued to you. We follow close at the Lord's heels because we are one with him. Who shall divide us from his love? If we cannot walk with him with equal footsteps, we will at least follow after him with all the strength he lends us, earnestly panting to reach him and abide in his fellowship. When professing believers follow hard after the world, they will fall into the ditch; but none are ever too eager for communion with the Lord.

"Thy right hand upholdeth me." Else he would not have followed the Lord with constancy or even have longed after him. The divine power, which has so often been dwelt upon in this and the preceding Psalms, is here mentioned as the source of man's attachment to God. How strong we are when the Lord works in us by his own right hand, and how utterly helpless if he withholds his aid!

Verse 9: As David earnestly sought for God, so there were men of another order who as eagerly sought after his blood; of these he speaks: "But those that seek my soul, to destroy it." At his life they aimed, at his honor, his best welfare; and this they wished not merely to injure but to utterly ruin. The devil is a destroyer, and all his seed are greedy to do the same mischief; and as he has ruined himself by his crafty devices, so also shall they. But destroyers shall be destroyed. Those who hunt souls shall be themselves the victims.

"Shall go into the lower parts of the earth." Into the pits that they digged for others they shall fall themselves. The slayers shall be slain, and the grave shall cover them. The hell that they in their curse invoked for others shall shut its mouth upon them.

Verses to meditate upon today: Psalm 63:6-11.

A Thought to Ponder
How strong we are when the Lord works in us by his own right hand, and how utterly helpless if he withholds his aid!

Meditating on What God Has Done

And all men shall fear, and shall declare the work of God;
for they shall wisely consider of his doing.
PSALM 64:9

VERSE 9: "And all men shall fear." They shall be filled with awe by the just judgments of God, as the Canaanites were by the overthrow of Pharaoh at the Red Sea. Those who might have been bold in sin shall be made to tremble and to stand in awe of the righteous Judge.

"And shall declare the work of God." It shall become the subject of general conversation. So strange, so pointed, so terrible shall be the Lord's overthrow of the malicious that it shall be spoken of in all companies. They sinned secretly, but their punishment shall be wrought before the face of the sun.

"For they shall wisely consider of his doing." The judgments of God are frequently so clear and manifest that men cannot misread them, and if they have any thought at all, they must extract the true teaching from them. Some of the divine judgments are great deeps, but in the case of malicious persecutors the matter is plain enough, and the most illiterate can understand.

VERSE 10: "The righteous shall be glad in the LORD." Admiring his justice and fully acquiescing in its displays, they shall also rejoice at the rescue of injured innocence; yet their joy shall not be selfish or sensual but altogether in reference to the Lord. "And shall trust in him." Their observation of providence shall increase their faith, since he who fulfills his threatenings will not forget his promises. "And all the upright in heart shall glory." The victory of the oppressed shall be the victory of all upright men; the whole host of the elect shall rejoice in the triumph of virtue. While strangers fear, the children are glad in view of their Father's power and justice. That which alarms the evil cheers the good. *Lord God of mercy, grant to us to be preserved from all our enemies and saved in your Son with an everlasting salvation.*

Verses to meditate upon today: Psalm 64:1-10.

A THOUGHT TO PONDER
Those who might have been bold in sin shall be made to tremble and
to stand in awe of the righteous Judge.

MAY 20

OVERWHELMED BY SIN

*Iniquities prevail against me: as for our transgressions,
thou shalt purge them away.*

PSALM 65:3

VERSE 3: "Iniquities prevail against me." Others accuse and slander me, and in addition my own sins rise up and would beset me to my confusion, were it not for the remembrance of the Atonement, which covers every one of my iniquities. Our sins would, but for grace, prevail against us in the court of divine justice, in the court of conscience, and in the battle of life. Unhappy is the man who despises these enemies, and worse still is he who counts them his friends! He is best instructed who knows their deadly power and flees for refuge to him who pardons iniquity.

"As for our transgressions, thou shalt purge them away." *You cover them all, for you have provided a covering propitiation, a mercy seat that wholly covers your law.* Note the word "our." The faith of the one penitent who speaks for himself in the first clause here embraces all the faithful in Zion; and he is so persuaded of the largeness of forgiving love that he leads all the saints to sing of the blessing.

What a comfort it is that iniquities that prevail against us do not prevail against God. They would keep us away from God, but he sweeps them away from before himself and us. They are too strong for us but not for our Redeemer, who is mighty, yea, and almighty to save. It is worthy of note that as the priest washed in the laver before he sacrificed, so David leads us to obtain purification from sin before we enter upon the service of song. When we have washed our robes and made them white in his blood, then shall we acceptably sing, "Worthy is the Lamb that was slain."

VERSE 4: "Blessed is the man whom thou choosest, and causest to approach unto thee." After cleansing comes benediction, and truly this is a very rich one.

Verses to meditate upon today: Psalm 65:1-4.

A THOUGHT TO PONDER

*What a comfort it is that iniquities that prevail against us
do not prevail against God.*

God's Care in Nature

Thou visitest the earth, and waterest it: thou greatly enrichest it with the river of God, which is full of water: thou preparest them corn, when thou hast so provided for it.

PSALM 65:9

VERSE 9: "Thou visitest the earth, and waterest it." God's visits leave blessings behind; this is more than can be said of every visitor. When the Lord goes on visitations of mercy, he has an abundance of necessary things for all his needy creatures. He is represented here as going around the earth as a gardener surveys his garden and as giving water to every plant that requires it, and that not in small quantities, but until the earth is drenched and soaked with a rich supply of refreshment. "Thou greatly enrichest it." Great amounts of money could not enrich mankind as the showers do. The soil is made rich by the rain and then yields its riches to man; but God is the first giver of all. How truly rich are those who are enriched with grace; they have great riches.

"With the river of God, which is full of water." The brooks of earth are soon dried up, and all human resources, being finite, are liable to failure. But God's provision for the supply of rain is inexhaustible; there is no bottom or shore to his "river." The deluge poured from the clouds of yesterday may be succeeded by another tomorrow, and yet the waters above the firmament shall not fail. How true this is in the realm of grace; there "the river of God . . . is full of water," and "of his fulness have all we received, and grace for grace" [John 1:16].

The ancients in their fables spake of the Pactolus, which flowed over sands of gold. But this "river of God," which flows above and from which the rain is poured, is far more enriching; for after all, the wealth of men lies mainly in the harvest of their fields, without which even gold would be of no value whatever.

Verses to meditate upon today: Psalm 65:5-13.

A THOUGHT TO PONDER
*How truly rich are those who are enriched with grace;
they have great riches.*

MAY 22

LOOK AT WHAT GOD HAS DONE

Come and see the works of God: he is terrible in his doing toward the children of men.

PSALM 66:5

VERSE 5: "Come and see the works of God." Such glorious events as the cleaving of the Red Sea and the overthrow of Pharaoh are standing wonders, and throughout all time a voice sounds forth concerning them: "Come and see." Even until the close of all things, the marvelous works of God at the Red Sea will be the subject of meditation and praise; for, standing on the sea of glass mingled with fire, the triumphal armies of heaven sing the song of the servant of God, Moses, and the song of the Lamb. This has always been the favorite subject of the inspired bards, and their choice was most natural.

"He is terrible in his doing toward the children of men." For the defense of his church and the overthrow of her foes God deals terrific blows and strikes the mighty with fear. O enemy, why do you vaunt yourself? Speak no more so exceedingly proudly, but remember the plagues that bowed the will of Pharaoh, the drowning of Egypt's chariots in the Red Sea, the overthrow of Og and Sihon, the scattering of the Canaanites before the tribes. This same God still lives and is to be worshiped with trembling reverence.

Verse 6: "He turned the sea into dry land." It was no slight miracle to divide a pathway through such a sea and to make it fit for the traffic of a whole nation. He who did this can do anything and must be God, the worthy object of adoration. The Christian's inference is that no obstacle in his journey heavenward need hinder him, for the sea could not hinder Israel, and even death itself shall be as life; the sea shall be dry land when God's presence is felt.

"They went through the flood on foot." Through the river the tribes passed dry shod. Jordan was afraid because of them.

Verses to meditate upon today: Psalm 66:1-7.

A THOUGHT TO PONDER
This same God still lives and is to be worshiped with trembling reverence.

MAY 23

GOD'S PRESERVING POWER

Which holdeth our soul in life, and suffereth not our feet to be moved.
PSALM 66:9

VERSE 9: "Which holdeth our soul in life." At any time the preservation of life, and especially the soul's life, is a great reason for gratitude, but much more when we are called to undergo extreme trials, which of themselves would crush our being. Blessed be God who, having put our souls into possession of life, has been pleased to preserve that heaven-given life from the destroying power of the enemy.

"And suffereth not our feet to be moved." This is another and precious boon. If God has enabled us not only to keep our life but our position, we are bound to give him double praise. Living and standing is the saint's condition through divine grace. Immortal and immovable are those whom God preserves. Satan is put to shame, for instead of being able to slay the saints, as he hoped, he is not even able to trip them. God is able to make the weakest to stand fast, and he will do so.

VERSE 10: "For thou, O God, hast proved us." He proved his Israel with sore trials. David had his temptations. All the saints must go to the proving house; God had one Son without sin, but he never had a son without trial. Why ought we to complain if we are subjected to the rule that is common to all the family and from which so much benefit has flowed to them? The Lord himself proves us. Who then shall raise a question as to the wisdom and the love that are displayed in the operation? The day may come when, as in this case, we shall make hymns out of our griefs and sing all the more sweetly because our mouths have been purified with bitter morsels.

"Thou hast tried us, as silver is tried." Since trial is sanctified to so desirable an end, ought we not to submit to it with abounding resignation?

Verses to meditate upon today: Psalm 66:8-12

A THOUGHT TO PONDER
Immortal and immovable are those whom God preserves.

MAY 24

LISTENING TO GOD

*Come and hear, all ye that fear God, and I will declare
what he hath done for my soul.*
PSALM 66:16

VERSE 16: "Come and hear." Before, they were bidden to "come and see" [verse 5]. Hearing is faith's seeing. Mercy comes to us by way of the ear gate. "Hear, and your soul shall live" [Isaiah 55:3]. They *saw* how terrible God was, but they *heard* how gracious he was.

"All ye that fear God." These are a fit audience when a good man is about to relate his experience; and it is well to select our hearers when inward soul matters are our theme. It is forbidden us to throw pearls before swine. We do not want to furnish wanton minds with subjects for their comedies, and therefore it is wise to speak of personal spiritual matters where they can be understood, and not where they will be mocked. All God-fearing men may hear us, but keep far from us, you profane.

"And I will declare what he hath done for my soul." I will count and recount the mercies of God to me, to my soul, my best part, my most real self. Testimonies ought to be shared by all experienced Christians, in order that the younger and feebler may be encouraged by the recital to put their trust in the Lord. To declare man's doings is needless; they are too trivial, and besides, there are trumpeters enough for man's worthless deeds. But to declare the gracious acts of God is instructive, consoling, inspiring, and beneficial in many respects. Let each man speak for himself, for a personal witness is the surest and most forcible; secondhand experience lacks the flavor of firsthand interest. Let no false modesty restrain the grateful believer from speaking of himself, or rather of God's dealings to himself, for this is justly due to God; neither let him shun the individual use of the first person, which is most correct in detailing the Lord's ways of love.

Verses to meditate upon today: Psalm 66:13-20.

A THOUGHT TO PONDER
They saw how terrible God was, but they heard how gracious he was.

A Missionary Prayer

That thy way may be known upon earth, thy saving health among all nations.
PSALM 67:2

VERSE 2: "That thy way may be known upon earth." As showers that first fall upon the hills afterward run down in streams into the valleys, so the blessing of the Most High comes upon the world through the church. We are blessed for the sake of others as well as ourselves. God deals in a "way" of mercy with his saints, and then they make that "way" known far and wide, and the Lord's name is made famous in the earth. Ignorance of God is the great enemy of mankind, and the testimonies of the saints, experimental and grateful, overcome this deadly foe. God has set a "way" and method of dealing out mercy to men, and it is the duty and privilege of a revived church to make that "way" to be everywhere known.

"Thy saving health among all nations," or "thy salvation." One likes the old words, "saving health"; yet as they are not the words of the Spirit but only of our translators, they must be given up. The word is *salvation,* and nothing else. This all nations need, but many of them do not know it, desire it, or seek it. Our prayer and labor should be that the knowledge of salvation may become as universal as the light of the sun. Despite the gloomy notions of some, we cling to the belief that the kingdom of Christ will embrace the whole habitable globe, and that all flesh shall see the salvation of God; for this glorious consummation we agonize in prayer.

VERSE 3: "Let the people praise thee, O God." *Cause them to own your goodness and thank you with all their hearts. Let nations do this, and do it continually, being instructed in your gracious way.*

"Let all the people praise thee." May every man bring his music, every citizen his canticle, every peasant his praise, every prince his psalm.

Verses to meditate upon today: Psalm 67:1-7.

A Thought to Ponder
The blessing of the Most High comes upon the world through the church.

MAY 26

THE LONELY

God setteth the solitary in families: he bringeth out those which are bound with chains: but the rebellious dwell in a dry land.

PSALM 68:6

VERSE 6: "God setteth the solitary in families." The people had been sundered and scattered over Egypt; family ties had been disregarded, and affections crushed. But when the people escaped from Pharaoh they came together again, and all the fond associations of household life were restored. This was a great joy.

"He bringeth out those which are bound with chains." The most oppressed in Egypt were chained and imprisoned, but the divine Emancipator brought them all forth into perfect liberty. He who did this of old continues his gracious work. The "solitary" heart, convinced of sin and made to pine alone, is admitted into the family of the Firstborn. The fettered spirit is set free, and its prison broken down, when sin is forgiven. And for all this, God is to be greatly extolled, for he has done it and has magnified the glory of his grace.

"But the rebellious dwell in a dry land." If any find the rule of Jehovah to be irksome, it is because their "rebellious" spirits kick against his power. Israel did not find the desert dry, for the smitten rock gave forth its streams. But even in Canaan itself men were consumed with famine because they cast off their allegiance to their covenant God. Even where God is revealed on the mercy seat, some men persist in rebellion, and such need not wonder if they find no peace, no comfort, no joy, even where all these abound. Justice is the rule of the Lord's kingdom, and hence there is no provision for the unjust to indulge their evil lustings. A perfect earth, and even heaven itself, would be a dry land to those who can only drink of the waters of sin. Of the most soul-satisfying of sacred ordinances these witless rebels cry, "What a weariness it is!"

While the self-sufficient faint, the All-Sufficient shall sustain the feeblest believer. "Blessed be God" (verse 35)—a short but sweet conclusion. Let our souls say Amen to it, and yet again, Amen.

Verses to meditate upon today: Psalm 68:1-6.

A THOUGHT TO PONDER
The "solitary" heart, convinced of sin and made to pine alone, is admitted into the family of the Firstborn.

MAY 27

REFRESHMENT FROM GOD

Thou, O God, didst send a plentiful rain, whereby thou didst confirm thine inheritance, when it was weary.

PSALM 68:9

VERSE 9: "Thou, O God, didst send a plentiful rain." The march of God was not shown solely by displays of terror, for goodness and bounty were also made conspicuous. Such rain as never fell before dropped on the desert sand, bread from heaven and winged fowl fell all around the host, good gifts were poured upon them, and rivers leaped forth from rocks. The earth shook with fear, and in reply the Lord, as from a cornucopia, shook out blessings upon it; so the original may be rendered.

"Whereby thou didst confirm thine inheritance, when it was weary." As at the end of each stage, when they halted, "weary" with the march, they found such showers of good things awaiting them that they were speedily refreshed. Their foot did not swell all those forty years. When they were exhausted, God was not. When they were "weary," he was not. They were his chosen heritage, and therefore, although for their good he allowed them to be "weary," yet he watchfully tended them and tenderly considered their distresses. In like manner, to this day the elect of God in this wilderness state are apt to become tired and faint, but their ever-loving Jehovah comes in with timely succor, cheers the faint, strengthens the weak, and refreshes the hungry, so that once again, when the silver trumpets sound, the church militant advances with bold and firm step toward the rest that remains.

By this faithfulness, the faith of God's people is confirmed and their hearts established; if fatigue and want make them waver, the timely supply of grace stays them again upon the eternal foundations.

VERSE 10: "Thy congregation hath dwelt therein." *In the wilderness itself, enclosed as in a wall of fire, your chosen church has found a home; or rather, encircled by the shower of free grace that fell all around the camp, your flock has rested.*

Verses to meditate upon today: Psalm 68:7-14.

A THOUGHT TO PONDER
If fatigue and want make them waver, the timely supply of grace stays them again upon the eternal foundations.

MAY 28

GOD'S CHARIOTS

*The chariots of God are twenty thousand, even thousands of angels:
the Lord is among them, as in Sinai, in the holy place.*

PSALM 68:17

VERSE 17: "The chariots of God are twenty thousand." Other countries, which in the former verse were symbolically referred to as "high hills," gloried in their chariots of war. But Zion, though far more lowly, was stronger than they, for the omnipotence of God was to her as two myriads of chariots. The Lord of Hosts could summon more forces into the field than all the petty lords who boasted in their armies; his horses of fire and chariots of fire would be more than a match for their fiery steeds and flashing carriages. The original is grandly expressive: "the war chariots of Elohim are myriads, a thousand thousands."

The marginal reading of our Bibles, "even many thousands," is far more correct than the rendering, "even thousands of angels." It is not easy to see where our venerable translators found these "angels," for they are not in the text. However, as it is a blessing to entertain them unawares, we are glad to meet with them in English, even though the Hebrew knows them not; and the more so because it cannot be doubted that they constitute a right noble squadron of the myriad hosts of God. We read in Deuteronomy 33:2 of the Lord's coming "with ten thousands of saints" or holy ones, and in Hebrews 12:22 we find upon Mount Zion "an innumerable company of angels," so that our worthy translators, putting the texts together, inferred the angels, and the clause is so truthfully explanatory that we have no fault to find with it.

"The Lord is among them, as in Sinai, in the holy place"; or "it is a Sinai in holiness." God is in Zion as the Commander-in-Chief of his countless hosts, and where he is, there is holiness. The throne of grace on Zion is as holy as the throne of justice on Sinai.

Verses to meditate upon today: Psalm 68:15-20.

A THOUGHT TO PONDER

God is in Zion as the Commander-in-Chief of his countless hosts.

MAY 29

MAKING MUSIC FOR GOD

The singers went before, the players on instruments followed after; among them were the damsels playing with timbrels.

PSALM 68:25

VERSE 25: "The singers went before, the players on instruments followed after." This was the order of the march, and God is to be worshiped evermore with due decorum. First the singers, and lastly the musicians, for the song must lead the music, and not the music drown the singing. In the midst of the vocal and instrumental band, or all around them, were the maidens: "among them were the damsels playing with timbrels." Some have imagined that this order indicates the superiority of vocal to instrumental music; but we need not go so far for arguments when the simplicity and spirituality of the Gospel already teach us that truth. The procession depicted in this sublime song was one of joy, and every means was taken to express the delight of the nation in the Lord their God.

VERSE 26: "Bless ye God in the congregations." Let the assembled company magnify the God whose ark they followed. United praise is like the mingled perfume that Aaron made—it should all be presented unto God. He blesses us; let him be blessed.

"Even the Lord, from the fountain of Israel." This is a parallel passage to that in Deborah's song: "They that are delivered from the noise of archers in the places of drawing water, there shall they rehearse the righteous acts of the LORD" [Judges 5:11]. The seat of the ark would be the fountain of refreshing for all the tribes, and there they were to celebrate his praises. "Drink," says the old inscription, "drink, weary traveler; drink and pray." We may read one word, then drink and praise. If the Lord overflows with grace, we should overflow with gratitude. Ezekiel saw an ever-growing stream flow from under the altar and issue out from under the threshold of the sanctuary, and wherever it flowed it gave life. Let as many as have quaffed this life-giving stream glorify "the fountain of Israel."

Verses to meditate upon today: Psalm 68:21-27.

A THOUGHT TO PONDER

Every means was taken to express the delight of the nation in the Lord their God.

MAY 30

GOD'S STRENGTH

*Thy God hath commanded thy strength: strengthen, O God,
that which thou hast wrought for us.*
PSALM 68:28

The prophet now puts into the mouth of the assembly a song, foretelling the future conquests of Jehovah.

VERSE 28: "Thy God hath commanded thy strength." His decree had ordained the nation strong, and his arm had made them so. As a Commander-in-Chief, the Lord made the valiant men pass in battle array and bade them be strong in the day of conflict. This is a very rich though brief sentence, and whether applied to an individual believer or to the whole church, it is full of consolation.

"Strengthen, O God, that which thou hast wrought for us." As all power comes from God at first, so its continual maintenance is also of him. We who have life should pray to have it "more abundantly"; if we have strength, we should seek to be still more established. We expect God to bless his own work. He has never left any work unfinished yet, and he never will. "When we were yet without strength, in due time Christ died for the ungodly." And now, being reconciled to God, we may look to him to perfect that which concerns us, since he never forsakes the work of his own hands.

VERSE 29: "Because of thy temple at Jerusalem shall kings bring presents unto thee." The palace of God, which towered above Jerusalem, is prophesied as becoming a wonder to all lands, and when it grew from the tabernacle of David to the temple of Solomon, it was so. So splendid was that edifice that the queen of far-off Sheba came with her gifts; and many neighboring princes, overawed by the wealth and power therein displayed, came with tribute to Israel's God. The church of God, when truly spiritual, wins for her God the homage of the nations. In the latter-day glory this truth shall be far more literally and largely verified.

Verses to meditate upon today: Psalm 68:28-31.

A THOUGHT TO PONDER

God's decree had ordained the nation strong, and his arm had made them so.

MAY 31

Proclaim God's Power

*Ascribe ye strength unto God: his excellency is over Israel,
and his strength is in the clouds.*

Psalm 68:34

Verse 34: "Ascribe ye strength unto God." Since even his voice rends the rocks and uproots the cedars, what cannot his hand do? His finger shakes the earth; who can conceive the power of his arm? Let us never by our doubts or daring defiance appear to deny power unto God; on the contrary, by yielding to him and trusting in him, let our hearts acknowledge his might. When we are reconciled to God, his omnipotence is an attribute of which we sing with delight.

"His excellency is over Israel." The favored nation is extended by his majesty; his greatness is to them goodness, and his glory is their defense.

"And his strength is in the clouds." He does not confine his power to the sons of men but makes it like a canopy to cover the skies. Rain, snow, hail, and tempest are his artillery; he rules all nature with awe-inspiring majesty. Praise him, then, in the highest.

Verse 35: "O God, thou art terrible out of thy holy places." *You inspire awe and fear. Your saints obey with fear and trembling, and your enemies flee in dismay. From your threefold courts, and especially from the holy of holies, your majesty flashes forth and makes the sons of men prostrate themselves in awe.*

"The God of Israel is he that giveth strength and power unto his people." *In this you, who are Israel's God by covenant, are terrible to your foes by making your people strong, so that one shall chase a thousand, and two put ten thousand to flight.* All the power of Israel's warriors is derived from the Lord, the fountain of all might. He is strong, and he makes strong. Blessed are they who draw from his resources, for they shall renew their strength.

Verses to meditate upon today: Psalm 68:32-35.

A Thought to Ponder

*When we are reconciled to God, his omnipotence is an attribute
of which we sing with delight.*

June 1

The Waters

Save me, O God; for the waters are come in unto my soul.
PSALM 69:1

VERSE 1: "Save me, O God." "He saved others, himself he cannot save." With strong cries and tears Jesus offered up prayers and supplications "unto him that was able to save him from death, and was heard in that he feared" (Hebrews 5:7). Thus David had prayed, and here his Son and Lord utters the same cry. This is the second Psalm that begins with a "Save me, O God," and the former (Psalm 54) is but a short summary of this more lengthened complaint. It is remarkable that such a scene of woe should be presented to us immediately after the jubilant ascension hymn of the last Psalm, but this only shows how interwoven are the glories and the sorrows of our ever blessed Redeemer. The head that now is crowned with glory is the same that wore the thorns; he to whom we pray, "Save us, O God" is the selfsame person who cried, "Save me, O God."

"For the waters are come in unto my soul." Sorrows—deep, abounding, and deadly—had penetrated his inner nature. Bodily anguish is not his first complaint; he begins not with the gall that embittered his lips, but with the mighty griefs that broke into his heart. All the sea outside a vessel is less to be feared than that which finds its way into the hold. A wounded spirit who can bear? Our Lord in this verse is seen before us as a Jonah, crying, "The waters compassed me about, even to the soul."

He was doing business for us on the great waters at his Father's command; the stormy wind was lifting up the waves thereof, and he went down to the depths until his soul was melted because of trouble. In all this he has sympathy with us and is able to succor us when we, like Peter, beginning to sink, cry to him, "Lord, save us or we perish."

Verses to meditate upon today: Psalm 69:1-4.

A Thought to Ponder
How interwoven are the glories and the sorrows of our ever blessed Redeemer.

JUNE 2

HOPING IN GOD

Let not them that wait on thee, O Lord GOD of hosts, be ashamed for my sake: let not those that seek thee be confounded for my sake, O God of Israel.

PSALM 69:6

VERSE 6: If the psalmist were deserted, others who were walking in the same path of faith would be discouraged and disappointed. Unbelievers are ready enough to grab onto anything that may turn humble faith into ridicule. Therefore, *O God of all the armies of Israel, let not my case cause the enemy to blaspheme*—such is the spirit of this verse.

Our blessed Lord ever had a tender concern for his people and would not have his own oppression of spirit become a source of discouragement to them.

"Let not those that seek thee be confounded for my sake, O God of Israel." He appealed to the Lord of hosts and his power to help him, and now to the God of Israel and his covenant faithfulness to come to the rescue. If the captain of the host fail, how will it fare with the rank and file? If David flee, what will his followers do? If the king of believers shall find his faith unrewarded, how will the feeble ones remain strong on their way?

Our Lord's behavior during his sharpest agonies is no cause of shame to us. He wept, for he was man, but he murmured not, for he was sinless man. He cried, "My Father, if it be possible, let this cup pass from me," for he was human. But he added, "Nevertheless, not as I will, but as thou wilt," for his humanity was without taint of rebellion. In the depths of tribulation no repining word escaped him, for there was no repining in his heart. The Lord of martyrs witnessed a good confession. He was strengthened in the hour of peril and came through more than a conqueror, as we also shall do if we hold fast our confidence even to the end.

Verses to meditate upon today: Psalm 69:5-12.

A THOUGHT TO PONDER

Our Lord wept, for he was man, but he murmured not, for he was sinless man.

JUNE 3

FLOOD WATERS

Let not the waterflood overflow me, neither let the deep swallow me up, and let not the pit shut her mouth upon me.

PSALM 69:15

VERSE 15: "Let not the waterflood overflow me." Our Lord continues to recapitulate the terms of his lament. He is willing to bear suffering but asks for grace, that it may not get the victory over him. He was heard in that he feared.

"Neither let the deep swallow me up." *As Jonah came forth again, so let me also arise from the abyss of woe.* Here also our Lord was heard, and so shall we be. Death itself must disgorge us.

"Let not the pit shut her mouth upon me." When a great stone was rolled over the well or pit, used as a dungeon, the prisoner was altogether enclosed and forgotten like those in the Bastille. This is an apt picture of the state of a man buried alive in grief and left without remedy; against this the great sufferer pleaded and was heard. He was baptized in agony but not drowned in it; the grave enclosed him, but before she could close her mouth he had burst his prison. It is said that truth lies in a well, but it is assuredly an open well, for truth walks abroad in power; and so our great Substitute in the pit of woe and death was yet the conqueror of death and hell. How appropriately may many of us use this prayer. We deserve to be swept away as with a flood, to be drowned in our sins, to be shut up in hell; let us, then, plead the merits of our Savior, lest these things happen unto us.

VERSE 16: "Hear me, O LORD." *Do not refuse your suppliant Son.* It is to the covenant God, the ever-living Jehovah, that he appeals with strong crying.

"For thy loving-kindness is good." *By the greatness of your love, have pity upon your afflicted.* It is always a support to the soul to dwell upon the preeminence and excellence of the Lord's mercy.

Verses to meditate upon today: Psalm 69:13-18.

A THOUGHT TO PONDER

It is always a support to the soul to dwell upon the preeminence and excellence of the Lord's mercy.

JUNE 4

REPROACHES

Reproach hath broken my heart; and I am full of heaviness: and I looked for some to take pity, but there was none; and for comforters, but I found none.

PSALM 69:20

VERSE 20: "Reproach hath broken my heart." There is no hammer like it. Our Lord died of a broken heart, and "reproach" had done the deed. Intense mental suffering arises from slander; and in the case of the sensitive nature of the immaculate Son of man, it sufficed to lacerate the heart until it broke. "Then burst his mighty heart."

"And I am full of heaviness." Defamation and insult bowed him to the dust; he was sick at heart. The heaviness of our Lord in the garden is expressed by many forcible words in the four Gospels, and each term goes to show that the agony was great beyond measure; he was filled with misery, like a vessel that is full to the brim.

"And I looked for some to take pity, but there was none." Deserted in his utmost need by those his former bounty fed. Not one said to him a kindly word or dropped a sympathetic tear. Among ten thousand foes there was not one who was touched by the spectacle of his misery, not one with a heart capable of humane feeling toward him.

"And for comforters, but I found none." His dearest ones had sought their own safety and left their Lord alone. A sick man needs comforters, and a persecuted man needs sympathy; but our blessed Surety found neither on that dark and doleful night when the powers of darkness had their hour. A spirit like that of our Lord acutely feels desertion by beloved and trusted friends and yearns for real sympathy. This may be seen in the story of Gethsemane.

VERSE 21: "They gave me also gall for my meat." This was the sole refreshment cruelty had prepared for him. Others find pleasure in their food, but his taste was made to be an additional path of pain to him.

Verses to meditate upon today: Psalm 69:19-21.

A THOUGHT TO PONDER

A sick man needs comforters, and a persecuted man needs sympathy; but our blessed Surety found neither on that dark and doleful night when the powers of darkness had their hour.

JUNE 5

DARKNESS

Let their table become a snare before them: and that which should have been for their welfare, let it become a trap.

PSALM 69:22

VERSE 22: "Let their table become a snare before them." Where they laid snares, there they shall find them. From their feasts they would provide nothing but wormwood for their innocent victim, and now their banquets shall be their ruin. It is very easy for the daily provisions of mercy to become temptations to sin. As birds and beasts are taken in a trap by means of baits for the appetite, so are men often snared by meats and drinks. Those who despise the upper springs of grace shall find the nether springs of worldly comfort prove their poison. The "table" is used, however, not alone for feeding but for conversations, business, counsel, amusement, and religious observance. To those who are the enemies of the Lord Jesus that "table" may, in all these respects, become "a snare." This first plague is terrible, and the second is like unto it.

"And that which should have been for their welfare, let it become a trap." This, if we follow the original closely, and the version of Paul in Romans, is a repetition of the former phrase; but we shall not err if we say that, to the rejecters of Christ, even those things that are calculated to work their spiritual and eternal good become occasions for yet greater sin. They reject Christ and are condemned for not believing on him; they stumble on this stone and are broken by it. Wretched are those men who not only place a curse upon their common blessings, but also on the spiritual opportunities of salvation.

VERSE 23: "Let their eyes be darkened, that they see not." They shall wander in a darkness that may be felt. They have loved darkness rather than light, and in darkness they shall abide. Judicial blindness fell upon the people of Israel after our Lord's death and their persecution of his apostles; they were blinded by the light that they would not accept.

Verses to meditate upon today: Psalm 69:22-28.

A THOUGHT TO PONDER
They have loved darkness rather than light, and in darkness they shall abide.

A Cry Out of the Depths

But I am poor and sorrowful: let thy salvation, O God, set me up on high.
PSALM 69:29

VERSE 29: "But I am poor and sorrowful." The psalmist was afflicted very much, but his faith was in God. The poor in spirit and mourners are both blessed under the Gospel; so here is a double reason for the Lord to smile on his supplicant. No man was ever poorer or more sorrowful than Jesus of Nazareth; yet his cry out of the depths was heard, and he was uplifted to the highest glory.

"Let thy salvation, O God, set me up on high." How fully has this been answered in our great Master's case, for he not only escaped his foes personally, but he has become the author of eternal salvation to all who obey him, and this continues to glorify him more and more. Oh, you poor and sorrowful ones, lift up your heads, for as with your Lord, so shall it be with you. You are trodden down today as the mire of the streets, but you shall ride upon the high places of the earth ere long; and even now you are raised up together and made to sit together in the heavenlies in Christ Jesus.

VERSE 30: "I will praise the name of God with a song." He who sang after the Passover sings yet more joyously after the Resurrection and Ascension. He is, in very truth, "the sweet singer of Israel." He leads the eternal melodies, and all his saints join in chorus.

"And will magnify him with thanksgiving." How sure was our Redeemer of ultimate victory, since he vowed a song even while yet in the furnace. In us also faith foresees the happy issue of all affliction and makes us even now begin the music of gratitude that shall go on forever increasing in volume, world without end. What clear shining after the rain we have in this and succeeding verses.

Verses to meditate upon today: Psalm 69:29-36.

A Thought to Ponder

No man was ever poorer or more sorrowful than Jesus of Nazareth; yet his cry out of the depths was heard.

JUNE 7

REJOICE IN GOD

Let all those that seek thee rejoice and be glad in thee: and let such as love thy salvation say continually, Let God be magnified.

PSALM 70:4

VERSE 4: Anger against enemies must not make us forget our friends, for it is better to preserve a single citizen of Zion than to kill a thousand enemies. "Let all those that seek thee rejoice and be glad in thee." All true worshipers, though as yet in the humble ranks of seekers, shall have cause for joy. Even though the seeking commence in darkness, their pursuit shall bring light with it.

"And let such as love thy salvation say continually, Let God be magnified." Those who have tasted divine grace and are therefore wedded to it are a somewhat more advanced race, and these shall not only feel joy but shall with holy constancy and perseverance tell abroad their joy and call upon men to glorify God. The doxology "Let the Lord's name be magnified" is infinitely more manly and ennobling than the dog's bark of "Aha, aha."

VERSE 5: "But I am poor and needy." This is the same plea as in the preceding Psalm, verse 29. It seems to be a favorite argument with tried saints; evidently our poverty is our wealth, even as our weakness is our strength. May we learn well this riddle.

"Make haste unto me, O God." This is written instead of "yet the Lord thinketh upon me," as in Psalm 40; and there is a reason for the change, since the keynote of the Psalm frequently dictates its close. Psalm 40 sings of God's thoughts and therefore ends therewith; but the peculiar note of Psalm 70 is "Make haste," and therefore so it concludes.

"Thou art my help and my deliverer"—my help in trouble, my deliverer out of it. "O LORD, make no tarrying." Here is the name of "Jehovah" instead of "my God." We are warranted in using all the various names of God, for each has its own beauty and majesty, and we must reverence each by its holy use as well as by abstaining from taking it in vain.

Verses to meditate upon today: Psalm 70:1-5.

A THOUGHT TO PONDER
All true worshipers shall have cause for joy.

JUNE 8

MY ROCK OF REFUGE

Be thou my strong habitation, whereunto I may continually resort: thou hast given commandment to save me; for thou art my rock and my fortress.

PSALM 71:3

VERSE 3: "Whereunto I may continually resort." Fast shut is this castle against all adversaries. Its gates they cannot burst open; the drawbridge is up, the portcullis is down, the bars are fast in their places. But there is a secret door by which friends of the great Lord can enter at all hours of the day or night, as often as they please. There is never an hour when it is unlawful to pray.

"Thou hast given commandment to save me." Nature is charged to be tender with God's servants, providence is ordered to work their good, and the forces of the invisible world are ordained as their guardians. No stones of the field can throw us down while angels bear us up in their hands; neither can the beasts of the field devour us while David's God delivers us from their ferocity or Daniel's God puts them in awe of us.

"For thou art my rock and my fortress." In God we have all the security that nature, which furnishes the rock, and skill, which builds the fortress, could supply; he is the complete preserver of his people. Immutability may be set forth by "rock" and omnipotence by "fortress." Happy is he who can use the personal pronoun "my"—not only once, but as many times as the many aspects of the Lord may render desirable. Is he a strong "habitation"? I will call him "*my* strong habitation," and he shall be "*my* rock and *my* fortress," "*my* God" (verse 4), "*my* hope," "*my* trust" (verse 5). All mine shall be his; all his shall be mine. This was the reason why the psalmist was persuaded that God had commanded his salvation—namely, because he had enabled him to exercise a calm and appropriating faith.

Verses to meditate upon today: Psalm 71:1-8.

A THOUGHT TO PONDER

There is never an hour when it is unlawful to pray.

JUNE 9

SPEAKING UP FOR GOD

My mouth shall show forth thy righteousness and thy salvation all the day;
for I know not the numbers thereof.
PSALM 71:15

VERSE 15: "My mouth shall show forth thy righteousness and thy salvation all the day." We are to bear testimony as experience enables us, and not withhold from others that which we have tasted and handled. The faithfulness of God in saving us, in delivering us out of the hand of our enemies, and in fulfilling his promises is to be everywhere proclaimed by those who have proved it in their own history. How gloriously conspicuous is righteousness in the divine plan of redemption! It should be the theme of constant discourse.

The devil rages against the substitutionary sacrifice, and false teachers of every form make this the main point of their attack. Be it ours, therefore, to love the doctrine and to spread its glad tidings on every side and at all times. Mouths are never so usefully employed as in recounting the righteousness of God revealed in the salvation of believers in Jesus. The preacher who should be confined to this one theme would never need seek another; it is the very pith and marrow of revealed truth. Has our reader been silent upon this choice subject? Let us, then, press him to tell abroad what he enjoys within; he does not well who keeps such glad tidings to himself.

"For I know not the numbers thereof." He knew the sweetness of it, the sureness, the glory, and the truth of it; but as to the full reckoning of its plenitude, variety, and sufficiency, he felt he could not reach to the height of the great argument. *Lord, where I cannot count I will believe, and when a truth surpasses numeration I will take to admiration.* In the case of the Lord's covenant mercies, David declares, "I know not the numbers" and does not venture upon any sort of comparison. To creatures belong number and limit; to God and his grace there is neither. We may, therefore, continue to tell out his great salvation all day long, for the theme is utterly inexhaustible.

Verses to meditate upon today: Psalm 71:9-18.

A THOUGHT TO PONDER
Mouths are never so usefully employed as in recounting the righteousness of God
revealed in the salvation of believers in Jesus.

June 10

Righteousness Reaching the Skies

Thy righteousness also, O God, is very high, who hast done great things:
O God, who is like unto thee!
Psalm 71:19

Verse 19: "Thy righteousness also, O God, is very high." Very sublime, unsearchable, exalted, and glorious is the holy character of God and his way of making men righteous. His plan of righteousness uplifts men from the gates of hell to the mansions of heaven. It is a high-doctrine gospel; it gives a high experience, leads to high practice, and ends in high felicity.

"Who hast done great things." *The exploits of others are mere child's play compared with yours and are not worthy to be mentioned in the same age.* Creation, providence, redemption are all unique, and nothing can compare with them.

"O God, who is like unto thee!" *As your works are so transcendent, so are you. You are without equal, and such are your works, and such, especially, your plan of justifying sinners by the righteousness that you have provided.* Adoration is a fit frame of mind for the believer. When he draws near to God, he enters into a region where everything is surpassingly sublime; miracles of love abound on every hand, and marvels of mingled justice and grace. A traveler among the high Alps often feels overwhelmed with awe amid their amazing sublimities; much more is this the case when we survey the heights and depths of the mercy and holiness of the Lord. "O God, who is like unto thee!"

Verse 20: "Thou, which hast showed me great and sore troubles, shalt quicken me again." Here is faith's inference from the infinite greatness of the Lord. He has been strong to smite; he will be also strong to save. He has shown me many heavy and severe trials, and he will also show me many and precious mercies. He has almost killed me, he will speedily revive me; and though I have been almost dead and buried, he will give me a resurrection and "bring me up again from the depths of the earth."

Verses to meditate upon today: Psalm 71:19-24.

A Thought to Ponder

Very sublime, unsearchable, exalted, and glorious is the holy character of God.

JUNE 11

LIKE FALLING RAIN

He shall come down like rain upon the mown grass: as showers that water the earth.
PSALM 72:6

VERSE 6: "He shall come down like rain upon the mown grass." Blessings upon his gentle sway! Those great conquerors who have been the scourges of mankind have fallen like the fiery hail of Sodom, transforming fruitful lands into deserts; but he with mild, beneficial influence softly refreshes the weary and wounded among men and makes them spring up in newness of life. Pastures mown with the scythe or shorn by the teeth of cattle present, as it were, so many bleeding stems of grass; but when the rain falls, it is balm to all these wounds, and it renews the verdure and beauty of the field, a fit image of the visits and benedictions of "the consolation of Israel."

My soul, how well it is for you to be brought low, and to be even as the meadows eaten bare and trodden down by cattle, for then to you shall the Lord have respect. He shall remember your misery and with his own most precious love restore you to more than your former glory. *Welcome, Jesus, the Well-beloved; you are far more than the emperor Titus ever was—the Delight of mankind.*

"As showers that water the earth." Each crystal drop of rain tells of heavenly mercy, which forgets not the parched plains. Jesus is all grace; all that he does is love, and his presence among men is joy. We need to preach him more, for no shower can so refresh the nations. Philosophic preaching mocks men as with a dust shower, but the Gospel meets the need of fallen humanity, and happiness flourishes beneath its genial power. *Come down, O Lord, upon my soul, and my heart shall blossom with your praise.*

> *He shall come down as still and light*
> *As scattered drops on genial field;*
> *And in his time who loves the right,*
> *Freely shall bloom, sweet peace her harvest yield.*

Verses to meditate upon today: Psalm 72:1-7.

A THOUGHT TO PONDER

Jesus is all grace; all that he does is love, and his presence among men is joy.

JUNE 12

DELIVERANCE

For he shall deliver the needy when he crieth; the poor also, and him that hath no helper.

PSALM 72:12

VERSE 12: "For he shall deliver the needy." Here is an excellent reason for man's submission to the Lord Christ; it is not because they dread his overwhelming power, but because they are won over by his just and compassionate rule. Who would not fear so good a Prince, who makes the needy his particular care and pledges himself to be their deliverer in times of need?

"When he crieth." He permits them to be so needy as to be driven to cry bitterly for help, but then he hears them and comes to their aid. A child's cry touches a father's heart, and our King is the Father of his people. If we can do no more than cry, it will bring omnipotence to our aid. A cry is the native language of a spiritually needy soul; it is finished with fine phrases and long orations, and it takes to sobs and moans; and so, indeed, it grasps the most potent of all weapons, for heaven always yields to such artillery.

"The poor also, and him that hath no helper." The proverb says, "God helps those that help themselves"; but it is more true that Jesus helps those who cannot help themselves, nor find help in others. All helpless ones are under the special care of Zion's compassionate King. Let them hasten to put themselves in fellowship with him. Let them look to him, for he is looking out for them.

VERSE 13: "He shall spare the poor and needy." His pity shall be manifested to them; he will not allow their trials to overwhelm them. His rod of correction shall fall lightly; he will be sparing of his rebukes, and not sparing in his consolations. "And shall save the souls of the needy." His is the dominion of souls, a spiritual and not a worldly empire.

Verses to meditate upon today: Psalm 72:8-14.

A THOUGHT TO PONDER
A child's cry touches a father's heart, and our King is the Father of his people.

JUNE 13

UNIVERSAL BLESSING

His name shall endure for ever: his name shall be continued as long as the sun: and men shall be blessed in him: all nations shall call him blessed.

PSALM 72:17

VERSE 17: "His name shall endure for ever." In its saving power, as the rallying point of believers, renowned and glorified, our Savior's name shall remain forever the same. "His name shall be continued as long as the sun." As long as time is measured out by days, Jesus shall be glorious among men.

"And men shall be blessed in him." There shall be cause for all this honor, for he shall truly be a benefactor to the race. He himself shall be earth's greatest blessing; when men wish to bless others, they shall bless in his name.

"All nations shall call him blessed." The grateful nations shall echo his benedictions and wish him happy who has made them happy. Not only shall some glorify the Lord, but all. No land shall remain in heathenism; all nations shall delight to do him honor.

VERSES 18-19: As Quesnel well observes, these verses explain themselves. They call rather for profound gratitude and emotion of heart than for an exercise of the understanding; they are rather to be used for adoration than for exposition. It is, and ever will be, the acme of our desires and the climax of our prayers to behold Jesus exalted King of kings and Lord of lords. He has done great wonders such as none else can match, leaving all others so far behind that he remains the sole and only wonder-worker; but equal marvels yet remain future, for which we look with joyful expectation. He is the Blessed God, and his name shall be blessed; his name is glorious, and that glory shall fill the whole earth. For so bright a consummation our heart yearns daily, and we cry "Amen, and Amen."

VERSE 20: "The prayers of David the son of Jesse are ended." What more could he ask? He has climbed the summit of the mount of God; he desires nothing more.

Verses to meditate upon today: Psalm 72:15-20.

A THOUGHT TO PONDER
Jesus Christ himself shall be earth's greatest blessing.

JUNE 14

I NEARLY FELL

But as for me, my feet were almost gone; my steps had well nigh slipped.

PSALM 73:2

VERSE 2: Here begins the narrative of a great soul battle, a spiritual marathon, a hard and well-fought field, in which the half-defeated became in the end wholly victorious.

"But as for me." He contrasts himself with his God who is ever good; he owns his personal want of good, and then also compares himself with the clean in heart, and goes on to confess his defilement. The Lord is good to his saints; "but as for me," am I one of them? Can I expect to share his grace? Yes, I do share it; but I have acted an unworthy part, very unlike one who is truly pure in heart.

"My feet were almost gone." Errors of heart and head soon affect the conduct. There is an intimate connection between the heart and the feet. Asaph could barely stand; his uprightness was going; his knees were bowing like a falling wall. When men doubt the righteousness of God, their own integrity begins to waver.

"My steps had well nigh slipped." Asaph could make no progress in the good road; his feet ran away from under him like those of a man on a sheet of ice. He was weakened for all practical action and in great danger of actual sin, and so of a disgraceful fall. How ought we to watch the inner man, since it has so forcible an effect upon the outward character. The confession in this case is, as it should be, very plain and explicit.

VERSE 3: "For I was envious at the foolish." "The foolish" is the generic title of all the wicked. They are, beyond all others, fools, and he must be a fool who envies fools. Some read this, "the proud," and indeed these, by their ostentation, invite envy, and many a mind that is out of gear spiritually becomes infected with that wasting disease.

Verses to meditate upon today: Psalm 73:1-3.

A THOUGHT TO PONDER

When men doubt the righteousness of God, their own integrity begins to waver.

JUNE 15

THE ARROGANT

They are corrupt, and speak wickedly concerning oppression: they speak loftily.
PSALM 73:8

VERSE 8: "They are corrupt." They rot above ground; their heart and life are depraved.

"And speak wickedly concerning oppression." The reek of the sepulchre rises through their mouths; the nature of the soul is revealed in their speech. They choose "oppression" as their subject, and they not only defend it but advocate it, glory in it, and would fain make it the general rule among all nations.

> "Who are the poor? What are they made for? What, indeed, but to toil and slave that men of education and good family may enjoy themselves? Out on the knaves for prating about their rights! A set of wily demagogues are stirring them up, because they get a living by agitation. Work them like horses, and feed them like dogs; and if they dare complain, send them to the prison or let them die in the workhouse."

There is still too much of this wicked talk abroad, and although the working classes have their faults, and many of them very grave and serious ones, yet there is a race of men who habitually speak of them as if they were an inferior order of animals. God forgive the wretches who thus talk.

"They speak loftily." Their high heads, like tall chimneys, vomit black smoke. Big talk streams from them, their language is colossal, their pompousness ridiculous. They are Sir Oracle in every case; they speak as from the judges' bench and expect all the world to stand in awe of them.

VERSE 9: "They set their mouth against the heavens." Against God himself they aim their blasphemies. One would think, to hear them, that they were demigods themselves and held their heads above the clouds, for they speak down upon other men as from a sublime elevation peculiar to themselves. Yet they should let God alone, for their pride will make them enemies enough without their defying him.

Verses to meditate upon today: Psalm 73:4-11.

A THOUGHT TO PONDER
They should let God alone, for their pride will make them enemies enough without their defying him.

JUNE 16

GOD'S SANCTUARY

Until I went into the sanctuary of God; then understood I their end.
PSALM 73:17

VERSE 17: "Until I went into the sanctuary of God." Asaph's mind entered the eternity where God dwells as in a holy place; he left the things seen for the things invisible; his heart gazed within the veil; he stood where the thrice holy God stands. Thus he shifted his point of view, and apparent disorder resolved itself into harmony. The motions of the planets appear most discordant from this world, which is itself a planet; they appear as "progressive, retrograde, and standing still." But could we fix our observatory in the sun, which is the center of the system, we should perceive all the planets moving in a perfect circle around the head of the great solar family.

"Then understood I their end." He had seen too little to be able to judge; a wider view changed his judgment. He saw with his mind's enlightened eye the future of the wicked, and his soul was in debate no longer as to the happiness of their condition. No envy gnawed now at his heart, but a holy horror both of their impending doom and of their present guilt filled his soul. He recoiled from being dealt with in the same manner as the proud sinners, whom just now he had regarded with admiration.

VERSE 18: The psalmist's sorrow had culminated not in the fact that the ungodly prospered, but that God had arranged it so. Had it happened by mere chance, he would have wondered but could not have complained; but how the arranger of all things could so dispense his temporal favors was the vexatious question. Here he sees that the divine hand purposely placed these men in prosperous and eminent circumstances, not with the intent to bless them but the very reverse.

"Surely thou didst set them in slippery places." Their position was dangerous, and therefore God did not set his friends there but his foes alone. He chose, in infinite love, a rougher but safer standing for his own beloved.

Verses to meditate upon today: Psalm 73:12-20.

A THOUGHT TO PONDER
His mind entered the eternity where God dwells as in a holy place.

JUNE 17

HELD BY GOD'S HAND

Nevertheless I am continually with thee:
thou hast holden me by my right hand.
PSALM 73:23

VERSE 23: "Nevertheless I am continually with thee." The psalmist does not give up his faith, though he confesses his folly. Sin may distress us, and yet we may be in communion with God. It is sin beloved and delighted in that separates us from the Lord, but when we bewail it heartily, the Lord will not withdraw from us. What a contrast is here in this and the former verse! He is as "a beast" and yet "continually with [God]." Our double nature, as it always causes conflict, is a continuous paradox: The flesh allies us with the brutes, and the spirit affiliates us with God.

"Thou hast holden me by my right hand." *With love you embrace me, with honor ennoble me, with power uphold me.* He had almost fallen, and yet was always upheld. He was a riddle to himself, as he had been a wonder unto many. This verse contains the two precious mercies of communion and upholding, and as they were both given to one who confessed himself a fool, we also may hope to enjoy them.

VERSE 24: "Thou shalt guide me with thy counsel." I have done with choosing my own way and trying to pick a path amid the jungle of reason. He yields not only the point in debate, but all intentions of debating, and he puts his hand into that of the great Father, asking to be led and agreeing to follow. Our former mistakes are a blessing when they drive us to this. The end of our own wisdom is the beginning of our being wise. With him is counsel, and when we come to him, we are sure to be led aright.

"And afterward." "Afterward"! Blessed word! We can cheerfully put up with the present when we foresee the future. What is around us just now is of small consequence compared with "afterward."

Verses to meditate upon today: Psalm 73:21-28.

A THOUGHT TO PONDER
He had almost fallen, and yet was always upheld.

JUNE 18

BOUGHT BY GOD

Remember thy congregation, which thou hast purchased of old; the rod of thine inheritance, which thou hast redeemed; this mount Zion, wherein thou hast dwelt.

PSALM 74:2

VERSE 2: "Remember thy congregation, which thou hast purchased of old." What a mighty plea is redemption. *O God, can you see the blood mark on your own sheep and yet allow grievous wolves to devour them?* The church is no new purchase of the Lord; from before the world's foundation the chosen were regarded as redeemed by the Lamb slain. Shall ancient love die out and the eternal purpose be defeated? The Lord would have his people remember the paschal Lamb, the bloodstained lintel, and the overthrow of Egypt; and will he forget all this himself? Let us put him in remembrance; let us plead together. Can he desert his blood-bought and forsake his redeemed? Can election fail and eternal love cease to glow? Impossible. The woes of Calvary, and the covenant of which they are the seal, are the security of the saints.

"The rod of thine inheritance, which thou hast redeemed." So sweet a plea deserved to be repeated and enlarged upon. The Lord's portion is his people; will he lose his "inheritance"? His church is his kingdom, over which he stretches the rod of sovereignty; will he allow his possessions to be torn from him? God's ownership in us is a fact full of comfort. His value of us, his dominion over us, his connection with us are all so many lights to cheer our darkness. No man will willingly lose his inheritance, and no prince will relinquish his dominions; therefore we believe that the King of kings will hold his own and maintain his rights against all comers.

"This mount Zion, wherein thou hast dwelt." The Lord's having made Zion the special center of his worship and the place of his manifestation is yet another plea for the preservation of Jerusalem.

Verses to meditate upon today: Psalm 74:1-23.

A THOUGHT TO PONDER
Can he desert his blood-bought and forsake his redeemed?
Can election fail and eternal love cease to glow? Impossible.

JUNE 19

GOD JUDGES US

But God is the judge: he putteth down one, and setteth up another.
PSALM 75:7

VERSE 7: "But God is the judge." Even now he is actually judging. His seat is not vacant; his authority is not abdicated; the Lord reigns evermore.

"He putteth down one, and setteth up another." Empires rise and fall at his bidding. A dungeon here, and there a throne, his will assigns. Assyria yields to Babylon, and Babylon to the Medes. Kings are but puppets in his hand; they serve his purpose when they rise and when they fall. A certain author (Timbs) has issued a work called *Historic Ninepins*, a fit name of scorn for all the great ones of the earth. Only God is self-existent; all power belongs to him. All else is shadow, coming and going, unsubstantial, misty, dreamlike.

VERSE 8: "For in the hand of the LORD there is a cup." The punishment of the wicked is prepared; God himself holds it in readiness. He has collected and concocted woes most dreadful, and in the chalice of his wrath he holds it. They scoffed at his feast of love; they shall be dragged to his table of justice and made to drink their due deserts.

"And the wine is red." The retribution is terrible. It is blood for blood, foaming vengeance for foaming malice. The very color of divine wrath is terrible; what must the taste be?

"It is full of mixture." Spices of anger, justice, and incensed mercy are there. Their misdeeds, their blasphemies, their persecutions have strengthened the liquor as with potent drugs. Ten thousand woes are burning in the depths of that fiery cup, which to the brim is filled with indignation.

"And he poureth out of the same." The full cup must be quaffed. The wicked cannot refuse the terrible draught, for God himself pours it out for them and into them. Vain are their cries and entreaties. They could once defy him, but that hour is over, and the time to requite them is fully come.

Verses to meditate upon today: Psalm 75:1-10.

A THOUGHT TO PONDER
The punishment of the wicked is prepared; God himself holds it in readiness.

JUNE 20

GOD'S DWELLING PLACE

In Salem also is his tabernacle, and his dwelling place in Zion.
PSALM 76:2

VERSE 2: "In Salem also is his tabernacle." In the peaceful city God dwells, and the peace is perpetuated because there his sacred tent is pitched. The church of God is the place where the Lord abides, and he is to her the Lord and the giver of peace. "And his dwelling place in Zion." Upon the chosen hill was the palace of Israel's Lord. It is the glory of the church that the Redeemer inhabits her by his Holy Spirit. Vain are the assaults of the enemy, for they attack not us alone, but the Lord himself. Immanuel, God with us, finds a home among his people; who then shall work us ill?

VERSE 3: "There brake he the arrows of the bow." Without leaving his tranquil abode, he sent forth his word and snapped "the arrows" of his enemies before they could shoot them. The idea is sublime and marks the ease, completeness, and rapidity of the divine action.

"The shield, and the sword, and the battle." Every weapon, offensive and defensive, the Lord dashed in pieces; death-bearing "arrows" and life-preserving armor were alike of no avail when the Breaker sent forth his word of power. In the spiritual conflicts of this and every age, the like will be seen. No weapon that is formed against the church shall prosper, and every tongue that rises against her in judgment, she shall condemn.

"Selah." It is appropriate that we should dwell on so soul-stirring a theme and give the Lord our grateful adoration; hence a pause is inserted.

VERSE 4: "Thou art more glorious and excellent than the mountains of prey." Far more is Jehovah to be extolled than all the invading powers that sought to oppress his people, though they were in power and greatness comparable to mountains. Assyria had pillaged the nations until it had become rich with mountains of spoil. This was talked of among men as glory, but the psalmist despised such renown and declared that the Lord was far more illustrious.

Verses to meditate upon today: Psalm 76:1-6.

A THOUGHT TO PONDER

Immanuel, God with us, finds a home among his people; who then shall work us ill?

JUNE 21

FEAR GOD ALONE

*Thou, even thou, art to be feared: and who may stand
in thy sight when once thou art angry?*
PSALM 76:7

VERSE 7: "Thou, even thou, art to be feared." Not Sennacherib, nor Nisroch his god, but Jehovah alone, who with a silent rebuke had withered all the monarch's host.

*Fear him, ye saints, and then ye shall
Have nothing else to fear.*

The fear of man is a snare, but the fear of God is a great virtue and has great power for good over the human mind. God is to be feared profoundly, continually, and alone. Let all worship be to him only.

"And who may stand in thy sight when once thou art angry?" Who indeed? The angels fell when their rebellion provoked his justice. Adam lost his place in paradise in the same manner. Pharaoh and other proud monarchs passed away at his frown. Neither is there in earth or hell any who can abide the terror of his wrath. How blessed are they who are sheltered in the atonement of Jesus and hence have no cause to fear the righteous anger of the Judge of all the earth.

VERSE 8: "Thou didst cause judgment to be heard from heaven." So complete an overthrow was evidently a judgment from heaven. Those who saw it not, yet heard the report of it, said, "This is the finger of God." Man will not hear God's voice if he can help it, but God takes care to cause it to be heard. The echoes of that judgment executed on the haughty Assyrians are heard still and will ring on through all the ages, to the praise of divine justice.

"The earth feared, and was still." All nations trembled at the tidings and sat in humbled awe. Repose followed the former turmoils of war, when the oppressor's power was broken, and God was reverenced for having given quiet to the peoples.

Verses to meditate upon today: Psalm 76:7-12.

A THOUGHT TO PONDER
The fear of man is a snare, but the fear of God is a great virtue.

JUNE 22

REMEMBERING GOD

*I remembered God, and was troubled: I complained, and
my spirit was overwhelmed. Selah.*

PSALM 77:3

VERSE 3: "I remembered God, and was troubled." He who is the wellspring of delight to faith becomes an object of dread to the psalmist's distracted heart. The justice, holiness, power, and truth of God all have a dark side, and indeed all the attributes may be made to look darkly upon us if our eye be evil. Even the brightness of divine love blinds us and fills us with a horrible suspicion that we have neither part nor lot in it. He is wretched indeed whose memories of the Ever-Blessed prove distressing to him; yet the best of men know the depth of this abyss.

"I complained, and my spirit was overwhelmed." He mused and mused but only sank deeper. His inward disquietudes did not fall asleep as soon as they were expressed, but rather they returned upon him and leaped over him like raging billows of an angry sea. It was not his body alone that hurt, but his noblest nature writhed in pain, and his life itself seemed crushed into the earth. It is in such a case that death is coveted as a relief, for life becomes an intolerable burden. With no spirit left in us to sustain our infirmity, our case becomes forlorn; like a man in a tangle of briars who is stripped of his clothes, every hook of the thorns becomes a lancet, and we bleed with ten thousand wounds. *Alas, my God, the writer of this exposition well knows what your servant Asaph meant, for his soul is familiar with the way of grief—deep glens and lonely caves of soul depressions. My spirit knows full well your awful glooms!*

"Selah." Let the song go softly; this is no merry dance for the swift feet of the daughters of music. Pause awhile, and let sorrow take breath between her sighs.

Verses to meditate upon today: Psalm 77:1-6.

A THOUGHT TO PONDER

*He is wretched indeed whose memories of the Ever-Blessed prove distressing to him;
yet the best of men know the depth of this abyss.*

JUNE 23

GOD'S UNFAILING LOVE

Is his mercy clean gone for ever? Doth his promise fail for evermore?
PSALM 77:8

VERSE 8: "Is his mercy clean gone for ever?" If God has no love for his elect, has he not still his mercy left? Has that dried up? Has he no pity for the sorrowful?

"Doth his promise fail for evermore?" His word is pledged to those who plead with him; has that become of no effect? Shall it be said that from one generation to another the Lord's word has fallen to the ground, whereas aforetime he kept his covenant to all generations of them that fear him? It is a wise thing thus to put unbelief through the catechism. Each one of the questions is a dart aimed at the very heart of despair. Thus have we also in our days of darkness done battle for life itself.

VERSE 9: "Hath God forgotten to be gracious?" Has El, the Mighty One, become great in everything but grace? Does he know how to afflict but not how to uphold? Can he forget anything? Above all, can he forget to exercise that attribute that lies nearest to his essence, for he is love?

"Hath he in anger shut up his tender mercies?" Are the pipes of goodness choked up so that love can no more flow through them? Do the bowels [today we would say, the heart] of Jehovah no longer yearn toward his own beloved children? Thus with cord after cord unbelief is smitten and driven out of the soul. It raises questions, and we will meet it with questions; it makes us think and act ridiculously, and we will heap scorn upon it. The argument of this passage assumes very much the form of a *reductio ad absurdum*. Strip it naked, and mistrust is a monstrous piece of folly.

"Selah." Here rest awhile, for the battle of questions needs a lull.

Verses to meditate upon today: Psalm 77:7-9.

A THOUGHT TO PONDER
Can he forget to exercise that attribute that lies nearest to his essence, for he is love?

JUNE 24

MEDITATING ON GOD'S DEEDS

I will meditate also of all thy work, and talk of thy doings.
PSALM 77:12

VERSE 12: "I will meditate also of all thy work." It is sweet work to enter into Jehovah's "work" of grace, and there to lie down and ruminate, every thought being absorbed in the one precious subject.

"And talk of thy doings." It is well that the overflow of the mouth should indicate the good matter that fills the heart. Meditation makes rich talking; it is to be lamented that so much of the conversation of professing believers is utterly barren, because they take no time for contemplation. A meditative man should be a talker; otherwise he is a mental miser, a mill that grinds corn only for the miller. The subject of our meditation should be choice, and then our task will be edifying; if we meditate on folly and pretend to speak wisdom, our double-mindedness will soon be known unto all men. Holy talk following upon meditation has a consoling power in it for ourselves as well as for those who listen—hence its value in the connection in which we find it in this passage.

VERSE 13: "Thy way, O God, is in the sanctuary," or "in holiness." In the holy place we understand our God and rest assured that all his ways are just and right. When we cannot trace his way because it is "in the sea," it is a rich consolation that we can trust it, for it is in holiness. We must have fellowship with holiness if we would understand the ways of God to man. He who would be wise must worship. The pure in heart shall see God, and pure worship is the way to the philosophy of providence.

"Who is so great a God as our God?" In him the good and the great are blended. He surpasses in both. None can for a moment be compared with the Mighty One of Israel.

Verses to meditate upon today: Psalm 77:10-15.

A THOUGHT TO PONDER
He who would be wise must worship.

JUNE 25

WATERS AND CLOUDS

The waters saw thee, O God, the waters saw thee; they were afraid:
the depths also were troubled.

PSALM 77:16

VERSE 16: As if conscious of its Maker's presence, the sea was ready to flee from before his face. The conception is highly poetical. The psalmist has the scene before his mind's eye and describes it gloriously. The water saw its God, but man refuses to discern him; it was afraid, but proud sinners are rebellious and fear not the Lord.

"The depths also were troubled." To their heart the floods were made afraid. Quiet caves of the sea, far down in the abyss, were moved with fear, and the lowest channels were left bare as the water rushed away from its place, in terror of the God of Israel.

VERSE 17: "The clouds poured out water." Obedient to the Lord, the lower region of the atmosphere yielded its aid to overthrow the Egyptian host. The cloudy chariots of heaven hurried forward to discharge their floods.

"The skies sent out a sound." From the loftier aerial regions thundered the dread artillery of the Lord of Hosts. Peal on peal, the skies sounded over the heads of the routed enemies, confusing their minds and adding to their horror.

"Thine arrows also went abroad." Lightning flew like bolts from the bow of God. Swiftly hither and thither went the red tongues of flame; on helm and shield they gleamed, with fires revealing the innermost caverns of the hungry sea that waited to swallow up the pride of Mizraim. Behold, how all the creatures wait upon their God and show themselves strong to overthrow his enemies.

VERSE 18: "The voice of thy thunder was in the heaven," or "in the whirlwind." Rushing on with terrific swiftness and bearing all before it, the storm was as a chariot driven furiously, and a voice was heard (*your voice, O Lord!*) out of the fiery chariot, as when a mighty man in battle urges forward his charger and shouts to it aloud.

Verses to meditate upon today: Psalm 77:16-20.

A THOUGHT TO PONDER
The water saw its God, but man refuses to discern him.

JUNE 26

LISTEN TO GOD'S TEACHING

Give ear, O my people, to my law:
incline your ears to the words of my mouth.
PSALM 78:1

VERSE 1: "Give ear, O my people, to my law." The inspired bard calls on his countrymen to give heed to his patriotic teaching. We naturally expect God's chosen nation to be first in hearkening to his voice. When God gives his truth a tongue and sends forth his messengers trained to declare his word with power, it is the least we can do to give them our ears and the earnest obedience of our hearts. Shall God speak, and his children refuse to hear? His teaching has the force of "law"; let us yield both ear and heart to it.

"Incline your ears to the words of my mouth." Give earnest attention; bow your stiff necks; lean forward to catch every syllable. We are at this day, as readers of the sacred records, bound to study them deeply, explore their meaning, and labor to practice their teaching. As the officer of an army commences his drill by calling, "Attention," even so every trained soldier of Christ is called upon to "give ear" to his words. Men lend their ears to music. How much more then should they listen to the harmonies of the Gospel. They sit enthralled in the presence of an orator; how much rather should they yield to the eloquence of heaven.

VERSE 2: "I will open my mouth in a parable." Analogies are not only to be imagined but are intended by God to be traced between the story of Israel and the lives of believers. Israel was ordained to be a type; the tribes and their marchings are living allegories traced by the hand of an all-wise providence. Unspiritual persons may sneer about fancies and mysticisms, but Paul spoke well when he said, "which things are an allegory," and Asaph in the present case spoke to the point when he called his narrative "a parable."

Verses to meditate upon today: Psalm 78:1-5.

A THOUGHT TO PONDER
Shall God speak, and his children refuse to hear?

JUNE 27

THE NEXT GENERATION

That the generation to come might know them, even the children which should be born; who should arise and declare them to their children.

PSALM 78:6

VERSE 6: As far as our brief life allows us to arrange, we must industriously provide for the godly nurture of youth. The narratives, commands, and doctrines of the Word of God are not worn-out; they are calculated to exert an influence as long as our race shall exist.

"Who should arise and declare them to their children." The one object aimed at is transmission; the testimony is only given that it may be passed on to succeeding generations.

VERSE 7: "That they might set their hope in God." "Faith cometh by hearing" [Romans 10:17]. Those who know the name of the Lord will set their hope in him, and that they may be led to do so is the main end of all spiritual teaching.

"And not forget the works of God." Grace cures bad memories. Those who soon forget the merciful works of the Lord have need of teaching; they require to learn the divine art of holy memory.

"But keep his commandments." Those who forget God's works are sure to fail in their own. He who does not keep God's love in memory is not likely to remember his law. The design of teaching is practical; holiness toward God is the end we aim at, and not the filling of the head with speculative notions.

VERSE 8: "And might not be as their fathers, a stubborn and rebellious generation." There was room for improvement. Fathers "stubborn" in their own way and "rebellious" against God's way are sorry examples for their children; and it is earnestly desired that better instruction may bring forth a better race. It is common in some regions for men to count their family custom as the very best rule; but disobedience is not to be excused because it is hereditary.

Verses to meditate upon today: Psalm 78:6-8.

A THOUGHT TO PONDER

We must industriously provide for the godly nurture of youth.

JUNE 28

MIRACLES IN EGYPT

*Marvelous things did he in the sight of their fathers,
in the land of Egypt, in the field of Zoan.*

PSALM 78:12

VERSE 12: "Egypt," here called "the field of Zoan," was the scene of marvelous things that were done in open day "in the sight of" Israel. These were extraordinary, upon a vast scale, astounding, indisputable, and such as ought to have rendered it impossible for an Israelite to be disloyal to Jehovah, Israel's God.

VERSE 13: "He divided the sea, and caused them to pass through." This was a double wonder, for when the waters were divided, the bottom of the sea would naturally be in a very unfit state for the passage of so vast a host as that of Israel. It would in fact have been impassable, had not the Lord made the road for his people. Who else has ever led a nation through a sea? Yet the Lord has done this often for his saints in providential deliverances, making a highway for them where nothing short of an almighty arm could have done so.

"And he made the waters to stand as a heap." He forbade a drop to fall upon his chosen; they felt no spray from the crystal walls on either hand. Fire will descend and water stand upright at the bidding of the Lord of all. The nature of creatures is not their own intrinsically, but is retained or altered at the will of him who first created them. The Lord can cause those evils that threaten to overwhelm us to suspend their ordinary actions and become innocuous to us.

VERSE 14: "In the daytime also he led them with a cloud." *He* did it all. *He* alone. *He* brought them into the wilderness, and *he* led them through it. It is not the Lord's manner to begin a work and then cease from it while it is incomplete. The "cloud" both led and shadowed the tribes. It was by day a vast sunscreen, rendering the fierce heat of the sun and the glare of the desert sand bearable.

Verses to meditate upon today: Psalm 78:9-16.

A THOUGHT TO PONDER
Who else has ever led a nation through a sea?

JUNE 29

They Continued to Sin

*And they sinned yet more against him by provoking
the Most High in the wilderness.*

Psalm 78:17

Verse 17: "And they sinned yet more against him." Outdoing their former sins, they went into greater deeps of evil. The more they had, the more loudly they clamored for more and murmured because they had not every luxury that pampered appetites could desire. It was bad enough to mistrust their God for necessities, but to revolt against him in a greedy rage for luxuries was far worse. Ever is it the nature of the disease of sin to proceed from bad to worse; men never weary of sinning, but rather increase their speed in the race of iniquity. In the case before us, the goodness of God was abused into a reason for greater sin. If he had wrought fewer miracles before, they would not have been so inexcusable in their unbelief, so wanton in their idolatry.

"By provoking the Most High in the wilderness." Although they were in a position of obvious dependence upon God for everything, being in a desert where the soil could yield them no support, yet they were graceless enough to provoke their Benefactor. At one time they provoked his jealousy by hankering after false gods; anon they excited his wrath by their challenges of his power, their slanders against his love, their rebellions against his will. He was all bounty of love, and they all superfluity of naughtiness. They were favored above all nations, and yet none were more offensive. For them the heavens dropped manna, and they returned murmurs; the rocks gave them rivers, and they replied with floods of wickedness. Herein, as in a mirror, we see ourselves. Israel in the wilderness acted out, as in a drama, all the story of man's conduct toward his God.

Verses to meditate upon today: Psalm 78:17-22.

A Thought to Ponder

*The heavens dropped manna, and they returned murmurs;
the rocks gave them rivers, and they replied with floods of wickedness.*

JUNE 30

MANNA FROM HEAVEN

And had rained down manna upon them to eat,
and had given them of the corn of heaven.
PSALM 78:24

VERSE 23: "Though he had commanded the clouds from above." Such a marvel ought to have rendered unbelief impossible. When clouds become granaries, seeing should be believing, and doubts should dissolve.

"And opened the doors of heaven." The great storehouse doors were set wide open, and "the corn of heaven" [verse 24] poured out in heaps. Those who would not believe in such a case were hardened indeed. And yet our own position is very similar, for the Lord has wrought for us great deliverances, quite as memorable and undeniable, and yet suspicions and forebodings haunt us. He might have shut the gates of hell upon us instead of opening the doors of heaven; shall we not both believe in him and magnify him for this?

VERSE 24: "And had rained down manna upon them to eat." There was so much of it that the skies poured with food, the clouds burst with provender. It was fit food, proper not for looking at but for eating; they could eat it as they gathered it. Mysterious though it was, so that they called it manna, or "what is it?" yet it was eminently adapted for human nourishment; and as it was both abundant and adapted, so also was it available. They did not have to go far to fetch it—it was near them, and they had only to gather it up. *O Lord Jesus, blessed manna of heaven, how all this agrees with you! We will even now feed on you as our spiritual meat and will pray you to chase away all wicked unbelief from us. Our fathers ate manna and doubted; we feed upon you and are filled with assurance.*

"And had given them of the corn of heaven." It was all a gift without money and without price. Food that dropped from above and was of the best quality, so as to be called heavenly "corn," was freely granted them.

Verses to meditate upon today: Psalm 78:23-31.

A THOUGHT TO PONDER
When clouds become granaries, seeing should be believing,
and doubts should dissolve.

JULY 1

GOD WAS THEIR ROCK

And they remembered that God was their rock, and the high God their redeemer.
PSALM 78:35

VERSE 35: "And they remembered that God was their rock." Sharp strokes awoke their sleepy memories. Reflection followed infliction. They were led to see that all their dependence must be placed upon their God; for he alone had been their shelter, their foundation, their fountain of supply, and their unchangeable friend. What could have made them forget this? Was it that their stomachs were so full of flesh that they had no space for ruminating upon spiritual things?

"And the high God their redeemer." They had forgotten this also. The high hand and outstretched arm that redeemed them out of bondage had both faded from their mental vision. Alas, poor man, how readily do you forget your God! Shame on you, ungrateful worm, to have no sense of favors a few days after they have been received. Will nothing make you keep in memory the mercy of your God except the utter withdrawal of it?

VERSE 36: "Nevertheless they did flatter him with their mouth." Bad were they at their best—false on their knees, liars in their prayers. Mouth worship must be very detestable to God when dissociated from the heart. Other kings love flattery, but the King of kings abhors it. Since the sharpest afflictions only extort from carnal men a feigned submission to God, there is proof positive that the heart is desperately set on mischief and that sin is ingrained in our very nature. If you beat a tiger with many stripes, you cannot turn him into a sheep. The devil cannot be whipped out of human nature if another devil—namely, hypocrisy—is whipped into it. Piety produced by the dejection of sorrow and the heat of terror is like a mushroom's growth; it is rapid in its springing up—they "inquired early after God"—but it is a mere unsubstantial fungus of unabiding excitement.

Verses to meditate upon today: Psalm 78:32-39.

A THOUGHT TO PONDER

They were led to see that all their dependence must be placed upon their God.

JULY 2

REBELLION IN THE DESERT

How oft did they provoke him in the wilderness, and grieve him in the desert!
PSALM 78:40

VERSE 40: "How oft did they provoke him in the wilderness." Times enough did they rebel; they were as constant in provocation as he was in his patience. In our own case, who can count our errors? In what book could all our perverse rebellions be recorded? "The wilderness" was a place of manifest dependence, where the tribes were helpless without divine supplies; yet they wounded the hand that fed them while it was in the act of feeding them. Is there no likeness between us and them? Does it bring no tears into our eyes when as in a glass we see ourselves?

"And grieve him in the desert!" Their provocations had an effect. God was not unfeeling toward them; he is said to have been grieved. His holiness could not find pleasure in their sin, his justice in their unjust treatment, or his truth in their falsehood. What must it be to grieve the Lord of love! Yet we also have vexed the Holy Spirit, and he would long ago have withdrawn himself from us, were it not that he is God and not man. We are in the desert where we need our God; let us not make it a wilderness of sin by grieving him.

VERSE 41: "Yea, they turned back." Their hearts sighed for Egypt and its fleshpots. They turned to their old ways again and again, after they had been scourged out of them. Preferring many twists and turns, they never kept the straight path.

"And tempted God." As far as in them lay, they "tempted" him. His ways were good, and they in desiring to have them altered "tempted" God. Before they would believe in him they demanded signs, defying the Lord to do this and that, and acting as if he could be cajoled into being the minion of their lusts. What blasphemy was this! Yet let us not tempt Christ lest we also be destroyed by the destroyer.

Verses to meditate upon today: Psalm 78:40-50.

A THOUGHT TO PONDER

Who can count our errors?
In what book could all our perverse rebellions be recorded?

JULY 3

GOD GUIDED THEM

And he led them on safely, so that they feared not:
but the sea overwhelmed their enemies.

PSALM 78:53

VERSE 53: "And he led them on safely, so that they feared not." After the first little alarm, natural enough when they found themselves pursued by their old taskmasters, they plucked up courage and ventured forth boldly into the sea and afterwards into the desert where no man dwelt.

"But the sea overwhelmed their enemies." Their foes were gone forever, never to disturb the fugitives again. That tremendous blow effectually defended the tribes for forty years from any further attempt to drive them back. Egypt found the stone too heavy and was glad to let it alone. Let the Lord be praised who thus effectually freed his elect nation.

What a grand narrative have we been considering. Well might the mightiest master of sacred song select "Israel in Egypt" as a choice theme for his genius; and well may every believing mind linger over every item of the amazing transaction. The marvel is that the favored nation should live as if unmindful of it all, and yet such is human nature. Alas, poor man! Rather, alas, base heart!

We now, after a pause, follow again the chain of events, the narration of which had been interrupted by a retrospect, and we find Israel entering into the Promised Land, there to repeat her follies and enlarge her crimes.

VERSE 54: "And he brought them to the border of his sanctuary." He conducted them to the frontier of the Holy Land, where he intended the tabernacle to become the permanent symbol of his abode among his people. He did not leave them halfway upon their journey to their heritage; his power and wisdom preserved the nation until the palm trees of Jericho were within sight on the other side of the river.

"Even to this mountain, which his right hand had purchased." Nor did he leave them then, but still conducted them until they were in the region round about Zion, which was to be the central seat of his worship.

Verses to meditate upon today: Psalm 78:51-55.

A THOUGHT TO PONDER

They plucked up courage and ventured forth boldly into the sea.

JULY 4

PUTTING GOD TO THE TEST

Yet they tempted and provoked the most high God, and kept not his testimonies.
PSALM 78:56

VERSE 56: "Yet they tempted and provoked the most high God." A change of condition had not altered their manners. They left their nomadic habits, but not their tendencies to wander from their God. Though every divine promise had been fulfilled to the letter, and the land flowing with milk and honey was actually their own, yet they tried the Lord again with unbelief and provoked him with other sins. He is not only high and glorious, but "most high," yea, "*the* most high," the only being who deserves to be so highly held in honor. Yet instead of honoring him, Israel grieved him with rebellion.

"And kept not his testimonies." They were true to nothing but hereditary treachery, steadfast in nothing but falsehood. They knew his truth and forgot it, his will and disobeyed it, his grace and perverted it to an occasion for greater transgression. Reader, do you need a looking glass? Here is one that suits the present expositor well; does it not also reflect your image?

VERSE 57: "But turned back." They turned over the old leaf, repeated the same offenses, went aside like an ill-made bow, were false and faithless to their best promises.

"And dealt unfaithfully like their fathers," manifesting the treachery of their sires. They were a new generation, but not a new nation—another race, yet not another. Evil propensities are transmitted; the birth follows the progenitor. The wild donkey breeds wild donkeys; the children of the raven fly to the carrion. Human nature does not improve; the new editions contain all the errata of the first, and sometimes fresh errors are imported.

"They were turned aside like a deceitful bow," which not only fails to send the arrow toward the mark in a direct line but springs back to the archer's hurt, and perhaps sends the shaft among his friends to their serious jeopardy.

Verses to meditate upon today: Psalm 78:56-64.

A THOUGHT TO PONDER
Though every divine promise had been fulfilled to the letter, yet they tried the Lord again with unbelief and provoked him with other sins.

GOD'S CHOICE

But chose the tribe of Judah, the mount Zion which he loved.
PSALM 78:68

VERSE 68: "But chose the tribe of Judah." To give the nation another trial this tribe was elected to supremacy. This was according to Jacob's dying prophecy. Our Lord sprang out of Judah, and he it is whom his brethren shall praise.

"The mount Zion which he loved." The tabernacle and ark were removed to Zion during the reign of David; no honor was left to the wayward Ephraimites. Hard by this mountain the father of the faithful had offered up his only son, and there in future days the great gatherings of his chosen seed would be, and therefore "Zion" is said to be lovely unto God.

VERSE 69: "And he built his sanctuary like high palaces." The tabernacle was placed on high; literally and spiritually it was a mountain of beauty. True religion was exalted in the land. For sanctity it was a temple; for majesty it was a palace.

"Like the earth which he hath established for ever." Stability as well as stateliness were seen in the temple, and so also in the church of God. The prophets saw both in vision.

VERSE 70: "He chose David also his servant." This was an election of a sovereignly gracious kind, and it operated practically by making the chosen man a willing "servant" of the Lord. He was not chosen because he was a servant, but in order that he might be so. David always esteemed it to be a high honor that he was both elect of God and a "servant" of God.

"And took him from the sheepfolds." A shepherd of sheep he had been, and this was a fit school for a shepherd of men. Lowliness of occupation will debar no man from such honors as the Lord's election confers; the Lord sees not as man sees. He delights to bless those who are of low estate.

Verses to meditate upon today: Psalm 78:65-72.

A THOUGHT TO PONDER
He delights to bless those who are of low estate.

JULY 6

JERUSALEM DEFILED

O God, the heathen are come into thine inheritance;
thy holy temple have they defiled; they have laid Jerusalem on heaps.
PSALM 79:1

VERSE 1: "O God, the heathen are come into thine inheritance." This is a cry of amazement at sacrilegious intrusion, as if the poet were struck with horror. *The stranger pollutes your hallowed courts with his tread. All Canaan is your land, but your foes have ravaged it.*

"Thy holy temple have they defiled." Into the inmost sanctuary they have profanely forced their way and there behaved themselves arrogantly. Thus the holy land, the holy house, and the holy city were all polluted by the uncircumcised. It is an awful thing when wicked men are found in the church and numbered with her ministry. Then are the tares sown with the wheat, and the poisoned gourds cast into the pot.

"They have laid Jerusalem on heaps." After devouring and defiling, they have come to destroying and have done their work with a cruel completeness. Jerusalem, the beloved city, the joy of the nation, the abode of her God, was totally wrecked. Alas, alas, for Israel! It is sad to see the foe in our own house, but worse to meet him in the house of God; they strike hardest who smite at our religion. The psalmist piles up the agony. He was a suppliant, and he knew how to bring out the strong points of his case. We ought to order our case before the Lord with as much care as if our success depended on our pleading. Men in earthly courts use all their powers to obtain their ends, and so also should we state our case with earnestness and bring forth our strong arguments.

VERSE 3: "Their blood have they shed like water round about Jerusalem." The invaders slew men as if "their blood" was of no more value than so much "water"; they poured it forth as lavishly as when the floods deluge the plains. The city of holy peace became a field of blood.

Verses to meditate upon today: Psalm 79:1-4.

A THOUGHT TO PONDER
It is sad to see the foe in our own house, but worse to meet him in the house of God.

JULY 7

How Long, Lord?

How long, LORD? Wilt thou be angry for ever?
Shall thy jealousy burn like fire?
PSALM 79:5

VERSE 5: "How long, LORD?" *Will there be no end to these chastisements? They are most sharp and overwhelming; will you much longer continue them?* "Wilt thou be angry for ever?" *Is your mercy gone so that you will forever smite?*

"Shall thy jealousy burn like fire?" There was great cause for the Lord to be jealous, since idols had been set up, and Israel had gone aside from his worship. But the psalmist begs the Lord not to consume his people utterly as with fire, but to abate their woes.

VERSE 6: "Pour out thy wrath upon the heathen that have not known thee." *If you must smite, look further afield; spare your children and strike your foes. There are lands where you are in no measure acknowledged; be pleased to visit these first with your judgments, and let your erring Israel have a respite.*

"And upon the kingdoms that have not called upon thy name." *Hear us, the prayerful, and avenge yourself upon the prayerless.* Sometimes providence appears to deal much more severely with the righteous than with the wicked, and this verse is a bold appeal founded upon such an appearance. It in effect says, *Lord, if you must empty out the vials of your wrath, begin with those who have no measure of regard for you but are openly up in arms against you; and be pleased to spare your people, who are yours notwithstanding all their sins.*

VERSE 7: "For they have devoured Jacob." The oppressor would eat up the saints if he could. If these lions do not swallow us, it is because the Lord has sent his angel and shut the lions' mouths. "And laid waste his dwelling place," or his pasture. The invader left no food for man or beast but devoured all, like the locusts. The tender mercies of the wicked are cruel.

Verses to meditate upon today: Psalm 79:5-13.

A Thought to Ponder

Sometimes providence appears to deal much more severely with
the righteous than with the wicked.

JULY 8

RESTORE US, O GOD

Turn us again, O God, and cause thy face to shine; and we shall be saved.
PSALM 80:3

VERSE 3: "Turn us again, O God." It is not so much said, "turn our captivity," but "turn *us.*" All will come right if we are right. The best turn is not that of circumstances but of character. When the Lord turns his people, he will soon turn their condition. It needs the Lord himself to do this, for conversion is as divine a work as creation; and those who have been once turned unto God, if they at any time backslide, as much need the Lord to "turn [them] again" as to "turn" them at the first. The word may be read, "restore us"; verily, it is a choice mercy that "he restoreth my soul."

"And cause thy face to shine." *Be favorable to us; smile upon us.* This was the high priest's blessing upon Israel. What the Lord has already given us by our High Priest and Mediator, we may confidently ask of him.

"And we shall be saved." All that is wanted for salvation is the Lord's favor. One glance of his gracious eye would transform Gehenna into paradise. No matter how fierce the foe or dire the captivity, the shining face of God ensures both victory and liberty. This verse is a very useful prayer. Since we too often turn aside, let us often with our lips and heart cry, "Turn us again, O God, and cause thy face to shine, and we shall be saved."

VERSE 4: "O LORD God of hosts, how long wilt thou be angry against the prayer of thy people?" *How long shall the smoke of your wrath drown the smoking incense of our prayers? Prayer wishes to enter your holy place, but your wrath battles with it and prevents its entrance.* That God should be angry with us when sinning seems natural enough, but that he should be angry even with our prayers is a bitter grief.

Verses to meditate upon today: Psalm 80:1-6.

A THOUGHT TO PONDER
Those who have been once turned unto God, if they at any time backslide, as much need the Lord to "turn [them] again" as to "turn" them at the first.

JULY 9

O GOD OF HOSTS

Turn us again, O God of hosts, and cause thy face to shine; and we shall be saved.
PSALM 80:7

VERSE 7: "Turn us again, O God of hosts." The prayer rises in the form of its address to God. He is here the "God of hosts." The more we approach the Lord in prayer and contemplation, the higher will our ideas of him become.

VERSE 8: "Thou hast brought a vine out of Egypt." There it was in unfriendly soil; the waters of the Nile watered it not, but were as death to its shoots, while the inhabitants of the land despised it and trampled it down. Glorious was the right hand of the Lord when with power and great wonders he removed his pleasant plant from the teeth of those who sought its destruction.

"Thou hast cast out the heathen, and planted it." Seven nations were digged out to make space for the vine of the Lord. The old trees, which long had occupied the soil, were torn up root and branch; oaks of Bashan and palm trees of Jericho were displaced for the chosen vine. It was securely placed in its appointed position with divine prudence and wisdom. Small in appearance, very dependent, exceeding weak, and apt to trail on the ground, yet the vine of Israel was chosen of the Lord because he knew that by incessant care and abounding skill he could make of it a goodly fruit-bearing plant.

VERSE 9: "Thou preparedst room before it." The weeds, brambles, and huge stones were cleared; the Amorites and their brethren in iniquity were made to quit the scene. Their forces were routed, their kings slain, their cities captured, and Canaan became like a plot of land made ready for a vineyard.

"And didst cause it to take deep root, and it filled the land." Israel became settled and established as a vine well rooted, and then it began to flourish and to spread to every side. This analogy might be applied to the experience of every believer in Jesus.

Verses to meditate upon today: Psalm 80:7-11.

A THOUGHT TO PONDER

The more we approach the Lord in prayer and contemplation,
the higher will our ideas of him become.

JULY 10

WATCH OVER US

Return, we beseech thee, O God of hosts: look down from heaven, and behold, and visit this vine.

PSALM 80:14

VERSE 14: "Return, we beseech thee, O God of hosts." *Turn yourself to us as well as us to you. You have gone from us because of our sins; come back to us, for we sigh and cry after you. Or if it be too much to ask you to come, then do at least give us some consideration and cast an eye upon our griefs.*

"Look down from heaven, and behold, and visit this vine." *Do not close your eyes. It is your vine; do not utterly turn away from it as though it were quite gone from your mind. Great Husbandman, at least note the mischief that the beasts have done, for then it may be that your heart will pity, and your hand will be outstretched to deliver.*

VERSE 15: "And the vineyard which thy right hand hath planted." *Shall all your care be lost? You have done so much; will you lose your labor? With your power and wisdom you did great things for your people. Will you now utterly give them up and suffer your enemies to exult in the evil that they delight in?*

"And the branch that thou madest strong for thyself." This is a prayer for the leader whom the Lord had raised up, or for the Messiah whom they expected. Though the vine had been left, yet one branch had been regarded of the Lord, as if to furnish a scion for another vine; therefore is the prayer made in this form. Let us pray the Lord, if he will not in the first place look upon his church, to look upon the Lord Jesus and then behold her in mercy for his sake. This is the true art of prayer, to put Christ forward and cry:

> *Him and then the sinner see,*
> *Look through Jesus' wounds on me.*

Verses to meditate upon today: Psalm 80:12-15.

A THOUGHT TO PONDER

Cast an eye upon our griefs.

JULY 11

POWER

Let thy hand be upon the man of thy right hand, upon the son of man whom thou madest strong for thyself.

PSALM 80:17

VERSE 17: "Let thy hand be upon the man of thy right hand." *Let your power rest on your true Benjamin, "son of thy right hand"; give a commission to some chosen man by whom you will deliver. Honor him, save us, and glorify yourself.* There is no doubt here a look ahead to the Messiah, for whom believing Jews had learned to look as the Savior in time of trouble.

"Upon the son of man whom thou madest strong for thyself." *Send forth your power with him whom you shall strengthen to accomplish your purposes of grace.* It pleases God to work for the sons of men by sons of men. "By man came death, by man came also the resurrection of the dead" [1 Corinthians 15:21]. Nations rise or fall largely through the instrumentality of individuals. By a Napoleon the kingdoms are scourged, and by a Wellington nations are saved from the tyrant. It is by the man Christ Jesus that fallen Israel is yet to rise, and indeed through him, who deigns to call himself the Son of man, the world is to be delivered from the dominion of Satan and the curse of sin. *O Lord, fulfill your promise to "the man of thy right hand," who participates in your glory, and give him to see the pleasure of the Lord prospering in his hand.*

VERSE 18: "So will not we go back from thee." Under the leadership of one whom God had chosen, the nation would be kept faithful, and grace would work gratitude and so cement them to their allegiance. It is in Christ that we abide faithful; because he lives, we live also. There is no hope of our perseverance apart from him.

"Quicken us, and we will call upon thy name." If the Lord gives life out of death, his praise is sure to follow. The Lord Jesus is such a leader that in him is life, and that life is the light of men.

Verses to meditate upon today: Psalm 80:16-19.

A THOUGHT TO PONDER
There is no hope of our perseverance apart from him.

JULY 12

SING

Sing aloud unto God our strength: make a joyful noise unto the God of Jacob.
PSALM 81:1

VERSE 1: "Sing," in tune and measure, so that the public praise may be in harmony; sing with joyful notes and melodious sounds.

"Aloud." The heartiest praise is due to our good Lord. His acts of love to us speak more loudly than any of our words of gratitude can do. No dullness should ever stupefy our psalmody or halfheartedness cause us to limp along. "Sing aloud," you debtors to sovereign grace. Your hearts are profoundly grateful; let your voices express your thankfulness.

"Unto God our strength." The Lord was the strength of his people in delivering them out of Egypt with a high hand, and also in sustaining them in the wilderness, placing them in Canaan, preserving them from their foes, and giving them victory. To whom do men give honor but to those upon whom they rely? Therefore let us "sing aloud" unto our God, who is our "strength" and our song.

"Make a joyful noise unto the God of Jacob." The God of the nation, the God of their father Jacob, was extolled in happy music by the Israelite people. Let no Christian be silent or slack in praise, for this God is our God. It is to be regretted that the niceties of modern singing frighten our congregations from joining lustily in the hymns. For our part we delight in full bursts of praise and had rather discover the ruggedness of a want of musical training than miss the heartiness of universal congregational song. The gentility that lisps the tune in well-bred whispers or leaves the singing altogether to the choir is very like a mockery of worship. The gods of Greece and Rome may be worshiped well enough with classical music, but Jehovah can only be adored with the heart, and that music is the best for his service that gives the heart most play.

Verses to meditate upon today: Psalm 81:1-5.

A THOUGHT TO PONDER

Your hearts are profoundly grateful; let your voices express your thankfulness.

JULY 13

BURDENS ARE LIFTED

I removed his shoulder from the burden: his hands were delivered from the pots.
PSALM 81:6

VERSE 6: "I removed his shoulder from the burden." Israel was the drudge and slave of Egypt, but God gave him liberty. It was by God alone that the nation was set free. Other peoples owe their liberties to their own efforts and courage, but Israel received its Magna Carta as a free gift of divine power. Truly may the Lord say of every one of his freed men, "His hands were delivered from the pots." Such a man was no longer compelled to carry earth and mold it and bake it; the earth basket was no more imposed upon the people, nor the tally of bricks exacted, for they came out into the open country where none could exact upon them. How typical all this is of the believer's deliverance from legal bondage when, through faith, the burden of sin glides into the Savior's sepulchre, and the servile labors of self-righteousness come to an end forever.

VERSE 7: "Thou calledst in trouble, and I delivered thee." God heard his people's cries in Egypt and at the Red Sea; this ought to have bound them to him. Since God does not forsake us in our need, we ought never to forsake him at any time. When our hearts wander from God, our answered prayers cry "shame" upon us.

"I answered thee in the secret place of thunder." Out of the cloud the Lord sent forth a tempest upon the foes of his chosen. That cloud was his secret tent. Within it he hung his weapons of war, his javelins of lightning, his trumpet of thunder; forth from that abode he came and overthrew the foe, that his own elect might be secure.

"I proved thee at the waters of Meribah." They had proved him and found him faithful; he afterwards "proved" them in return. Precious things are tested; therefore Israel's loyalty to her King was put to trial, and, alas, it failed lamentably.

Verses to meditate upon today: Psalm 81:6-10.

A THOUGHT TO PONDER
Israel received its Magna Carta as a free gift of divine power.

JULY 14

STUBBORN HEARTS

So I gave them up unto their own hearts' lust: and they walked in their own counsels.
PSALM 81:12

VERSE 12: "So I gave them up unto their own hearts' lust." No punishment is more just or more severe than this. If men will not be checked, but madly take the bit between their teeth and refuse obedience, who shall wonder if the reins are thrown upon their necks and they are let alone to work out their own destruction? It is better to be given up to lions than to our hearts' lusts.

"And they walked in their own counsels." There was no doubt as to what course they would take, for man is everywhere willful and loves his own way, that way being at all times in direct opposition to God's way. Men deserted of restraining grace sin with deliberation; they consult and debate and consider and then elect evil rather than good, with malice aforethought and in cool blood. It is a remarkable obduracy of rebellion when men not only run into sin through passion but calmly "walk in their own counsels" of iniquity.

VERSE 13: "Oh that my people had hearkened unto me, and Israel had walked in my ways!" The condescending love of God expresses itself in painful regrets for Israel's sin and punishment. Such were the laments of Jesus over Jerusalem. Certain men find a stumbling stone in such passages and set themselves to explain them away; but to men in sympathy with the divine nature, the words and the emotions are plain enough. A God of mercy cannot see men heaping up sorrow for themselves through their sins without feeling his compassion excited toward them.

VERSE 14: "I should soon have subdued their enemies." As he in Egypt overthrew Pharaoh, so would he have baffled every enemy. "And turned my hand against their adversaries." He would have smitten them once and then have dealt them a return blow with the back of his hand. See what we lose by sin! Our enemies find the sharpest weapons against us in the armory of our transgressions.

Verses to meditate upon today: Psalm 81:11-16.

A THOUGHT TO PONDER
It is better to be given up to lions than to our hearts' lusts.

JULY 15

GOD PRESIDES

God standeth in the congregation of the mighty; he judgeth among the gods.
PSALM 82:1

VERSE 1: "God standeth in the congregation of the mighty." He is the overlooker who, from his own point of view, sees all that is done by the great ones of the earth. When they sit in state he stands over them, ready to deal with them if they pervert judgment. Judges shall be judged, and to justices justice shall be meted out. Our village squires and country magistrates would do well to remember this. Some of them need to go to the school of Asaph until they have mastered this psalm. Their harsh decisions and strange judgments are made in the presence of him who will surely visit them for every unseemly act, for he has no respect unto the person of any and is the champion of the poor and needy. A higher authority will criticize the decisions of petty sessions, and even the judgments of our most impartial judges will be revised by the High Court of heaven.

"He judgeth among the gods." They are gods to other men, but he is God to them. He lends them his name, and this is their authority for acting as judges; but they must take care that they do not misuse the power entrusted to them, for the Judge of judges is in session among them. Our judges are but puny judges, and their brethren who administer common law will one day be tried by the common law. This great truth is, upon the whole, well regarded among us in these times, but it was not so in the earlier days of English history when Jeffries and such as he were an insult to the name of justice. Oriental judges, even now, are frequently, if not generally, amenable to bribes, and in past ages it was very hard to find a ruler who had any notion of justice apart from his own arbitrary will.

Verses to meditate upon today: Psalm 82:1-8.

A THOUGHT TO PONDER

God has no respect unto the person of any and is the champion of
the poor and needy.

JULY 16

LORD, SPEAK

Keep not thou silence, O God: hold not thy peace, and be not still, O God.

PSALM 83:1

VERSE 1: "Keep not thou silence, O God." *Man is clamorous; Lord, be not speechless. He rails and reviles; will you not reply? One word of yours can deliver your people; therefore, O Lord, break your quiet and let your voice be heard.*

"Hold not thy peace, and be not still, O God." Here the appeal is to El, the Mighty One. He is entreated to act and speak because his nation suffers and is in great jeopardy. How entirely the psalmist looks to God. He asks not for "a leader bold and brave" or for any form of human force but casts his burden upon the Lord, being well assured that God's eternal power and Godhead could meet every difficulty of the case.

VERSE 2: "For, lo, thine enemies make a tumult." They are by no means sparing of their words; they are like a hungry pack of dogs, all giving tongue at once. So sure are they of devouring God's people that they already shout over the feast.

"And they that hate thee have lifted up the head." Confident of conquest, they carry themselves proudly and exalt themselves as if their anticipated victories were already obtained. These enemies of Israel were also God's enemies and are here described as such by way of adding intensity to the argument of the intercession. The adversaries of the church are usually a noisy and a boastful crew. Their pride is a brass that always sounds, a cymbal that is ever tinkling.

VERSE 3: "They have taken crafty counsel against thy people." Whatever we may do, our enemies use their wits and lay their heads together; in united conclave they discourse upon the demands and plans of the campaign, using much treachery and serpentine cunning in arranging their schemes. Malice is cold-blooded enough to plot with deliberation; and pride, though it be never wise, is often allied with craft.

Verses to meditate upon today: Psalm 83:1-4.

A THOUGHT TO PONDER

One word of yours can deliver your people.

JULY 17

EVIL ALLIANCES

For they have consulted together with one consent:
they are confederate against thee.
PSALM 83:5

VERSE 5: "For they have consulted together with one consent." They are hearty and unanimous in their designs. They seem to have but one heart, and that a fierce one, against the chosen people and their God.

"They are confederate against thee." At the Lord himself they aim through the sides of his saints. They make a covenant and ratify it with blood, resolutely banding themselves together to war with the Mighty God.

VERSE 6: "The tabernacles of Edom." Nearest of kin, yet first in enmity. Their sire despised the birthright, and they despise the possessors of it. Leaving their rock-built mansions for the tents of war, the Edomites invaded the land of Israel.

"And the Ishmaelites." A persecuting spirit ran in their blood; they perpetuated the old grudge between the child of the bondwoman and the son of the freewoman. "Of Moab." Born of incest, but yet a near kinsman; the feud of Moab against Israel was very bitter. Little could righteous Lot have dreamed that his unhallowed seed would be such unrelenting enemies of his Uncle Abraham's posterity. "And the Hagarenes"—perhaps descendants of Hagar by a second husband. Whoever they may have been, they cast their power into the wrong pursuit and with all their might sought the ruin of Israel. Children of Hagar, and all others who dwell around Mount Sinai, which is in Arabia, are of the seed that engenders bondage, and hence they hate the seed according to promise.

Verse 7: "Gebal" was probably a near neighbor of Edom, though there was a Gebal in the region of Tyre and Sidon. "And Ammon, and Amalek." Two other hereditary foes of Israel, as fierce and remorseless as ravening wolves. In the roll of infamy let these names remain detestably immortalized. Their name is legion, for they are many.

Verses to meditate upon today: Psalm 83:5-12.

A THOUGHT TO PONDER
At the Lord himself they aim through the sides of his saints.

JULY 18

THE MOST HIGH

That men may know that thou, whose name alone is JEHOVAH,
art the Most High over all the earth.
PSALM 83:18

VERSE 16: "Fill their faces with shame; that they may seek thy name, O LORD." "Shame" has often weaned men from their idols and set them upon seeking the Lord. If this was not the happy result in the present instance with the Lord's enemies, yet it would be so with his people who were so prone to err. They would be humbled by his mercy and ashamed of themselves because of his grace; and then they would with sincerity return to the earnest worship of Jehovah their God, who had delivered them.

VERSE 17: Where no good result followed, and the men remained as fierce and obstinate as ever, justice was invoked to carry out the capital sentence. "Let them be confounded and troubled for ever; yea, let them be put to shame, and perish." What else could be done with them? It was better that they perished than that Israel should be rooted up. What a terrible doom it will be to the enemies of God to be "confounded and troubled for ever," to see all their schemes and hopes defeated, and their bodies and souls full of anguish without end. From such a shameful perishing may our souls be delivered.

Verse 18: Hearing of the Lord's marvelous deeds in defeating such a numerous confederacy, the very heathen would be compelled to acknowledge the greatness of Jehovah. We read in 2 Chronicles 20:29 that the fear of God was on all the neighboring kingdoms when they heard that Jehovah fought against the enemies of Israel. Jehovah is essentially the Most High. He who is self-existent is infinitely above all creatures; all the earth is but his footstool. The godless race of man disregards this, and yet at times the wonderful works of the Lord compel the most unwilling to adore his majesty.

Verses to meditate upon today: Psalm 83:13-18.

A THOUGHT TO PONDER
He who is self-existent is infinitely above all creatures;
all the earth is but his footstool.

GOD'S DWELLING PLACE

How amiable are thy tabernacles, O LORD of hosts!
PSALM 84:1

VERSE 1: "How amiable," or "how lovely." He does not tell us how lovely God's "tabernacles" were, because he could not. His expressions show us that his feelings were inexpressible. Lovely to the memory, to the mind, to the heart, to the eye, to the whole soul are the assemblies of the saints. Earth contains no sight so refreshing to us as the gathering of believers for worship. Those are sorry saints who see nothing "amiable" in the services of the Lord's house.

"Are thy tabernacles." The tabernacle had been pitched in several places and, moreover, was divided into several courts and portions; hence, probably, the plural number is here used. It was all and altogether lovely to the psalmist. Outer court or inner court, he loved every portion of it. Every cord and curtain was dear to him. Even when at a distance, he rejoiced to remember the sacred tent where Jehovah revealed himself, and he cried out with exultation while he pictured in fond imagination its sacred services and solemn rites, as he had seen them in bygone times. *Because they are "thy tabernacles, O LORD of hosts," therefore are they so dear to your people. Your pavilion is the center of the camp, around which all your creatures gather, and toward which their eyes are turned, as armies look to the tent of the king. You rule all the companies of creatures with such goodness that all their hosts rejoice in your dwelling place, and the bands of your saints especially hail you with joyful loyalty as Jehovah of hosts.*

VERSE 2: "My soul longeth"; it longs to meet with the saints in the Lord's house. The desire was deep and insatiable—the very "soul" of the man was yearning for his God. "Yea, even fainteth," as though it could not long hold out but was exhausted with delay.

Verses to meditate upon today: Psalm 84:1-2.

A THOUGHT TO PONDER
*Earth contains no sight so refreshing to us as
the gathering of believers for worship.*

JULY 20

THE SPARROWS AND THE SWALLOWS

Yea, the sparrow hath found a house, and the swallow a nest for herself, where she may lay her young, even thine altars, O LORD of hosts, my King, and my God.

PSALM 84:3

VERSE 3: "Yea, the sparrow hath found a house." The psalmist envied the sparrows that lived around the house of God and picked up the stray crumbs in the courts thereof; he only wished that he, too, could frequent the solemn assemblies and bear away a little of the heavenly food.

"And the swallow a nest for herself, where she may lay her young." He envied also the swallows whose nests were built under the eaves of the priests' houses, who there found a place for their "young" as well as for themselves. We rejoice not only in our personal religious opportunities but in the great blessing of taking our children with us to the sanctuary. The church of God is a house for us and a nest for our little ones.

"Even thine altars, O LORD of hosts." To the very "altars" these free birds drew near; none could restrain them nor would have wished to do so, and the psalmist wished to come and go as freely as they did. Mark how he repeats the blessed name of "Jehovah of hosts"; he found in it a sweetness that helped him to bear his inward hunger. Probably he himself was with the host, and therefore he dwelt with emphasis upon the title that taught him that the Lord was in the tented field as well as within the holy curtains.

"My King, and my God." Here he utters his loyalty from afar. If he may not tread the courts, yet he loves the "King." If an exile, he is not a rebel. When we cannot occupy a seat in God's house, he shall have a seat in our memories and a throne in our hearts. The double "my" is very precious; he lays hold upon his God with both his hands, as one resolved not to let him go until the favor requested be at length accorded.

Verses to meditate upon today: Psalm 84:3-4.

A THOUGHT TO PONDER

We rejoice in the great blessing of taking our children with us to the sanctuary.

JULY 21

SPIRITUAL PILGRIMAGE

Blessed is the man whose strength is in thee; in whose heart are the ways of them.
PSALM 84:5

VERSE 5: "Blessed is the man whose strength is in thee." Having spoken of the blessedness of those who reside in the house of God, the psalmist now speaks of those who are favored to visit it at appointed seasons, going upon pilgrimage with their devout brethren. He is not, however, indiscriminate in his eulogy but speaks only of those who heartily attend the sacred festivals. The blessedness of sacred worship belongs not to halfhearted, listless worshipers, but to those who throw all their energies into it. Neither prayer, nor praise, nor the hearing of the Word will be pleasant or profitable to persons who have left their hearts behind them. A company of pilgrims who had left their hearts at home would be no better than a caravan of carcasses, quite unfit to blend with living saints in adoring the living God.

"In whose heart are the ways of them," or far better, "in whose heart are thy ways." Those who love the "ways" of God are blessed. When we have God's "ways" in our "heart," and our "heart" in his "ways," we are what and where we should be, and hence we shall enjoy the divine approval.

VERSE 6: "Who passing through the valley of Baca make it a well." Traversing joyfully the road to the great assembly, the happy pilgrims found refreshment even in the dreariest part of the road. As around a well men meet and converse cheerfully, being refreshed after their journey, so even in the vale of tears, or any other dreary glen, the pilgrims to the skies find sweet solace in brotherly communion and in anticipation of the general assembly above, with its joys unspeakable. Probably there is here a local allusion, which will never now be deciphered, but the general meaning is clear enough. There are joys of pilgrimage that make men forget the discomforts of the road.

Verses to meditate upon today: Psalm 84:5-9.

A THOUGHT TO PONDER
The pilgrims to the skies find sweet solace in brotherly communion and in anticipation of the general assembly above, with its joys unspeakable.

JULY 22

ONE DAY WITH GOD

For a day in thy courts is better than a thousand. I had rather be a doorkeeper in the house of my God, than to dwell in the tents of wickedness.

PSALM 84:10

VERSE 10: "For a day in thy courts is better than a thousand." Of course the psalmist means "a thousand" days spent elsewhere. The most favorable circumstances in which earth's pleasures can be enjoyed are not comparable by so much as one in a thousand to the delights of the service of God. To feel his love, to rejoice in the person of the anointed Savior, to survey the promises and feel the power of the Holy Spirit in applying precious truth to the soul is a joy that worldlings cannot understand, but that true believers are ravished with. Even a glimpse of the love of God is better than ages spent in the pleasures of sense.

"I had rather be a doorkeeper in the house of my God, than to dwell in the tents of wickedness." The lowest station in connection with the Lord's "house" is better than the highest position among the godless. Only to wait at his threshold and peep within, so as to see Jesus, is bliss. To bear burdens and open doors for the Lord is a greater honor than to reign among the wicked. Every man has his choice, and this is ours. God's worst is better than the devil's best. God's doorstep is a happier rest than downy couches within the pavilions of royal sinners, though we might lie there for a lifetime of luxury. Note how he calls the tabernacle "the house of *my* God"; there's where the sweetness lies. If Jehovah be our God, his "house," his altars, his doorstep all become precious to us. We know by experience that where Jesus is within, the outside of the house is better than the noblest chambers where the Son of God is not to be found.

Verses to meditate upon today: Psalm 84:10-12.

A THOUGHT TO PONDER

God's worst is better than the devil's best. God's doorstep is a happier rest than downy couches within the pavilions of royal sinners, though we might lie there for a lifetime of luxury.

July 23

Sin Forgiven

*Thou hast forgiven the iniquity of thy people;
thou hast covered all their sin. Selah.*

Psalm 85:2

Verse 2: "Thou hast forgiven the iniquity of thy people." Often had God done this, pausing to pardon even when his sword was bared to punish. *Who is a pardoning God like you, O Jehovah? Who is so slow to anger, so ready to forgive?* Every believer in Jesus enjoys the blessing of pardoned sin, and he should regard this priceless boon as the pledge of all other needful mercies. He should plead with God: *Lord, have you pardoned me, and will you let me perish for lack of grace or fall into my enemies' hands for want of help? You will not thus leave your work unfinished.*

"Thou hast covered all their sin." All of it, every spot and wrinkle—the veil of love has covered it all. Sin has been divinely put out of sight. Hiding it beneath the propitiation, covering it with the sea of the atonement, blotting it out, making it to cease to be, the Lord has put it so completely away that even his omniscient eye sees it no more. What a miracle is this! To cover up the sun would be easy work compared with the covering up of sin. Not without a covering atonement is sin removed, but by means of the great sacrifice of our Lord Jesus; it is most effectually put away by one act forever. What a covering does his blood afford!

Verse 3: "Thou hast taken away all thy wrath." Having removed the sin, the anger is removed also. How often did the long-suffering of God take away from Israel the punishments that had been justly laid upon them! How often also has the Lord's chastising hand been removed from us when our waywardness called for heavier strokes!

"Thou hast turned thyself from the fierceness of thine anger." Even when judgments had been most severe, the Lord had in mercy stayed his hand.

Verses to meditate upon today: Psalm 85:1-7.

A Thought to Ponder

Every believer in Jesus enjoys the blessing of pardoned sin.

JULY 24

MERCY AND TRUTH

Mercy and truth are met together; righteousness and peace have kissed each other.
PSALM 85:10

VERSE 10: "Mercy and truth are met together." In answer to prayer, the exulting psalmist sees the attributes of God banding together to bless the once afflicted nation. "Mercy" comes hand in hand with "truth" to fulfill the faithful promise of their gracious God. The people recognize at once the grace and the veracity of Jehovah; he is to them neither a tyrant nor a deceiver.

"Righteousness and peace have kissed each other." The Lord, whose just severity inflicted the pain, now in pity sends "peace" to bind up the wound. The people, now made willing to forsake their sins and to follow after "righteousness," find "peace" granted to them at once. "The war drum throbbed no longer, and the battle flags were furled," for idolatry was forsaken, and Jehovah was adored. This appears to be the immediate and primary meaning of these verses; but the inner sense is Christ Jesus, the reconciling Word. In him the attributes of God unite in glad unanimity in the salvation of guilty men; they meet and embrace in a manner that is otherwise inconceivable either to our just fears or to our enlightened hopes. God is as true as if he had fulfilled every letter of his threatenings, as righteous as if he had never spoken peace to a sinner's conscience; his love in undiminished splendor shines forth, but no other of his ever-blessed characteristics is eclipsed thereby.

It is the custom of modern thinkers to make sport of this representation of the result of our Lord's substitutionary atonement. But had they ever been themselves made to feel the weight of sin upon a spiritually awakened conscience, they would cease from their vain ridicule. We cannot expect animals to set much store by the discoveries of science; neither can we hope to see unspiritual men rightly estimate the solution of spiritual problems—they are far above and out of their sight. Meanwhile, it remains for those who rejoice in the great reconciliation to continue both to wonder and adore.

Verses to meditate upon today: Psalm 85:8-13.

A THOUGHT TO PONDER

*The exulting psalmist sees the attributes of God banding together
to bless the once afflicted nation.*

JULY 25

GUARD MY LIFE

Preserve my soul; for I am holy: O thou my God,
save thy servant that trusteth in thee.

PSALM 86:2

VERSE 2: "Preserve my soul." *Let my life be safe from my enemies, and my spiritual nature secure from their temptations.* He feels himself unsafe unless he is covered by the divine protection.

"For I am holy." *I am set apart for holy uses; therefore do not let your enemies commit a sacrilege by injuring or defiling me. I am clear of the crimes laid to my charge, and in that sense innocent; therefore, I beseech you, do not allow me to suffer from unjust charges. And I am inoffensive, meek, and gentle toward others; therefore deal mercifully with me as I have dealt with my fellowmen.* Any of these renderings may explain the text; perhaps all together will expound it best.

It is not self-righteous in good men to plead their innocence as a reason for escaping from the results of sins wrongfully ascribed to them. Penitents do not bedaub themselves with mire for the love of it or make themselves out to be worse as a compliment to heaven. No, the humblest saint is not a fool, and he is as well aware of the matters wherein he is clear as of those wherein he must cry *"peccavi"* ["I have sinned"]. To plead guilty to offenses we have never committed is as great a lie as the denial of our real faults.

"O thou my God, save thy servant that trusteth in thee." Lest any man should suppose that David trusted in his own holiness, he immediately declared his trust in the Lord and begged to be saved as one who was not holy in the sense of being perfect, but was even yet in need of the very clemency of salvation. How sweet is that title "my God" when joined to the other, "thy servant"; and how sweet is the hope that on this ground we shall be saved.

Verses to meditate upon today: Psalm 86:1-4.

A THOUGHT TO PONDER

He feels himself unsafe unless he is covered by the divine protection.

JULY 26

COME AND WORSHIP

All nations whom thou hast made shall come and worship before thee,
O Lord; and shall glorify thy name.

PSALM 86:9

VERSE 9: "All nations whom thou hast made." *These include all mankind, since they all come from the first Adam, and their lives are all distinct creations of your omnipotence. All these "shall come" with penitent hearts, in your own way, to your own self, "and worship before thee, O Lord." Because you are thus above all gods, the people who have been so long deceived shall at last discover your greatness and shall render you the worship which is your due. You have created them all, and unto you shall they all yield homage.*

This was David's reason for resorting to the Lord in trouble, for he felt that one day all men would acknowledge the Lord to be the only God. It makes us content to be in the minority today when we are sure that the majority will be with us tomorrow; aye, and that the truth will one day be carried unanimously and heartily. David was not a believer in the theory that the world will grow worse and worse, and that the dispensation will wind up with general darkness and idolatry. Earth's sun is to go down amid tenfold night, if some of our prophetic brethren are to be believed.

Not so do we expect; rather we look for the day when the dwellers in all lands shall learn righteousness, shall trust in the Savior, shall worship you alone, O God, "and shall glorify thy name." The modern notion has greatly dampened the zeal of the church for missions, and the sooner this is shown to be unscriptural, the better for the cause of God. It neither consorts with prophecy, honors God, nor inspires the church with ardor. Far hence may it be driven.

VERSE 10: "For thou art great." He had before said, "thou art good"; it is a grand thing when greatness and goodness are united. It is only in the Divine Being that either of them exists absolutely and essentially.

Verses to meditate upon today: Psalm 86:5-10.

A THOUGHT TO PONDER

You have created them all, and unto you shall they all yield homage.

JULY 27

TEACH ME YOUR WAY

*Teach me thy way, O Lord; I will walk in thy truth:
unite my heart to fear thy name.*
PSALM 86:11

VERSE 11: "Teach me thy way, O LORD." *Instruct me thus at all times. Let me live in your school; but "teach" me especially now since I am in trouble and perplexity. Be pleased to show me the "way" that your wisdom and mercy have prepared for my escape. Behold, I lay aside all willfulness and only desire to be informed as to your holy and gracious mind. Not my way give me, but "thy way teach me." I would follow you and not be willful.*

"I will walk in thy truth." When taught, I will practice what I know. "Truth" shall not be a mere doctrine or sentiment to me, but a matter of daily life. The true servant of God regulates his "walk" by his Master's will, and hence he never walks deceitfully, for God's way is ever "truth." Providence has a way for us, and it is our wisdom to keep in it. We must not be as the bullock that needs to be driven and urged forward because it likes not the road, but as men who voluntarily go where their trusted friend and helper appoints their path.

"Unite my heart to fear thy name." *Having taught me one way, give me one "heart" to walk therein, for too often I feel a heart and a heart, two natures contending, two principles struggling for sovereignty.* Our minds are apt to be divided between a variety of objects, like trickling streamlets that waste their force in a hundred runnels; our great desire should be to have all our life floods poured into one channel and to have that channel directed toward the Lord alone. A man with a divided heart is weak. God who created the bands of our nature can draw them together, tighten, strengthen, and fasten them; and so braced and inwardly knit by his uniting grace, we shall be powerful for good—but not otherwise.

Verses to meditate upon today: Psalm 86:11-17.

A THOUGHT TO PONDER
A man with a divided heart is weak.

JULY 28

JERUSALEM

His foundation is in the holy mountains.

PSALM 87:1

VERSE 1: The Psalm begins abruptly. The poet's heart was full, and it gained vent suddenly.

> *God's foundation stands forever*
> *On the holy mountain towers;*
> *Sion's gates Jehovah favors*
> *More than Jacob's thousand bowers.*

Sudden passion is evil, but bursts of holy joy are most precious. God has chosen to found his earthly temple upon the "mountains"; he might have selected other spots, but it was his pleasure to have his chosen abode upon Zion. His election made the "mountains" "holy"; they were by his determination ordained and set apart for the Lord's use.

The foundation of the church, which is the mystical Jerusalem, is laid in the eternal, immutable, and invincible decrees of Jehovah. He wills that the church shall be; he settles all arrangements for her calling, salvation, maintenance, and perfection; and all his attributes, like the mountains round about Jerusalem, lend their strength for her support. Not on the sand of carnal policy, nor in the morass of human kingdoms has the Lord founded his church, but on his own power and Godhead, which are pledged for the establishment of his beloved church, which is to him the chief of all his works.

What a theme for meditation is the founding of the church of God in the ancient covenant engagements of eternity. The abrupt character of this first verse indicates long consideration on the part of the writer, leading up to his bursting forth in wonder and adoration. Well might such a theme cause his heart to glow. Rome stands on her seven hills and has never lacked a poet's tongue to sing her glories. But more glorious far are you, O Zion, among the eternal mountains of God; while pen can write or mouth can speak, your praises shall never lie buried in inglorious silence.

Verses to meditate upon today: Psalm 87:1-7.

The foundation of the church is laid in the eternal, immutable,
and invincible decrees of Jehovah.

JULY 29

Prayers Day and Night

*O Lord God of my salvation, I have cried day and
night before thee.*
Psalm 88:1

Verse 1: "O Lord God of my salvation." This is a hopeful title by which to address the Lord, and it has about it the only ray of comfortable light that shines throughout this Psalm. The writer has "salvation," he is sure of that, and God is the sole author of it. When a man can see God as his Savior, it is not altogether midnight with him. When the living God can be spoken of as the life of our salvation, our hope will not quite expire. It is one of the characteristics of true faith that she turns to Jehovah, the saving God, when all other confidences have proved liars unto her.

"I have cried day and night before thee." The psalmist's distress had not blown out the sparks of his prayer but thickened them into a greater ardency, until they burned perpetually like a furnace at full blast. His prayer was personal—whoever had not prayed, he had done so; it was intensely earnest, so that it was correctly described as a cry, such as children utter to move the pity of their parents; and it was unceasing—neither the business of the "day" nor the weariness of the "night" had silenced it. Surely such entreaties could not be in vain.

If Heman's pain had not been incessant, his supplications might have been intermittent; it is a good thing that sickness will not let us rest if we spend our restlessness in prayer.

"Day and night" are both suitable to prayer. It is no work of darkness; therefore let us go with Daniel and pray when men can see us. Yet since supplication needs no light, let us accompany Jacob and wrestle at Jabbok until the day breaks. Evil is transformed to good when it drives us to prayer.

Verses to meditate upon today: Psalm 88:1-5.

A Thought to Ponder

Evil is transformed to good when it drives us to prayer.

JULY 30

IN THE DARKEST DEPTHS

Thou hast laid me in the lowest pit, in darkness, in the deeps.
PSALM 88:6

VERSE 6: What a collection of forcible metaphors, each one expressive of the utmost grief. Heman compared his forlorn condition to an imprisonment in a subterranean dungeon, to confinement in the realms of the dead, and to a plunge into the abyss. None of the similes are strained.

The mind can descend far lower than the body, for in it there are bottomless pits. The flesh can bear only a certain number of wounds and no more, but the soul can bleed in ten thousand ways and die over and over again each hour. It is grievous to the good man to see the Lord whom he loves laying him in the sepulchre of despondency, putting out all his candles and heaping over him solid masses of sorrow. Evil from so good a hand seems evil indeed, and yet if faith could but be allowed to speak, she would remind the depressed spirit that it is better to fall into the hand of the Lord than into the hands of man. Moreover, she would tell the despondent heart that God never placed a Joseph in a pit without drawing him up again to fill a throne, never caused a horror of great darkness to fall upon an Abraham without revealing his covenant to him, and never cast even a Jonah into the deeps without preparing the means to land him safely on dry land.

Alas when under deep depression the mind forgets all this and is only conscious of its unutterable misery. The man sees the lion but not the honey in its carcass; he feels the thorns but cannot smell the roses that adorn them. He who now feebly expounds these words knows within himself more than he would care or dare to tell of the abysses of inward anguish.

Verses to meditate upon today: Psalm 88:6-10.

A THOUGHT TO PONDER

God never caused a horror of great darkness to fall upon an Abraham without revealing his covenant to him.

JULY 31

THE GRAVE

Shall thy loving-kindness be declared in the grave?
or thy faithfulness in destruction?
PSALM 88:11

VERSE 11: "Shall thy loving-kindness be declared in the grave?" *Your tender goodness—who shall testify concerning it in that cold abode where the worm and corruption hold their riot?* The living may compose "meditations among the Tombs," but the dead know nothing and therefore can declare nothing.

"Or thy faithfulness in destruction?" If the Lord suffered his servant to die before the divine promise was fulfilled, it would be quite impossible for his faithfulness to be proclaimed. The poet is dealing with this life only and is looking at the matter from the point of view afforded by time and the present race of men. If a believer were deserted and permitted to die in despair, there could come no voice from his grave to inform mankind that the Lord had rectified his wrongs and relieved him of his trials; no songs would leap up from the cold sod to sing the truth and goodness of the Lord. As far as men are concerned, a voice that loved to magnify the grace of God would be silenced, and a loving witness for the Lord removed from the sphere of testimony.

VERSE 12: "Shall thy wonders be known in the dark?" If not here permitted to prove the goodness of Jehovah, how could the singer do so in the land of darkness and death shade? Could his tongue, when turned into a clod, alarm the dull, cold ear of death? Is not a living dog better than a dead lion, and a living believer of more value to the cause of God on earth than all the departed put together?

"And thy righteousness in the land of forgetfulness?" What shall be told concerning you in the regions of oblivion? Where memory and love are lost, and men are alike unknowing and unknown, forgetful and forgotten, what witness to the divine holiness can be borne? The whole argument amounts to this: If the believer dies unblessed, how will God's honor be preserved?

Verses to meditate upon today: Psalm 88:11-14.

A THOUGHT TO PONDER
The dead know nothing and therefore can declare nothing.

AUGUST 1

I AM AFFLICTED

I am afflicted and ready to die from my youth up:
while I suffer thy terrors I am distracted.
PSALM 88:15

VERSE 15: "I am afflicted and ready to die from my youth up." His affliction had now lasted so long that he could hardly remember when it commenced; it seemed to him as if he had been at death's door ever since he was a child. This was no doubt an exaggeration of a depressed spirit, and yet perhaps Heman may have been all his days afflicted with some chronic disease or bodily infirmity. There are holy men and women whose lives are a long apprenticeship to patience, and these deserve both our sympathy and our reverence—our reverence, we venture to say, for since the Savior became acquainted with grief, sorrow has become honorable in believers' eyes. A lifelong sickness may by divine grace prove to be a lifelong blessing. Better to suffer from childhood to old age than to be let alone to find pleasure in sin.

"While I suffer thy terrors I am distracted." Long use had not blunted the edge of sorrow; God's "terrors" had not lost their terror. Rather had they become more overwhelming and had driven the man to despair. He was unable to collect his thoughts; he was so tossed about that he could not judge and weigh his own condition in a calm and rational manner. Sickness alone will thus distract the mind; and when a sense of divine anger is added thereto, it is not to be wondered at if reason finds it hard to hold the reins. How near akin to madness soul-depression sometimes may be, it is not our province to decide. But we speak what we do know when we say that a feather's weight might be sufficient to turn the scale at times. Thank God, O you tempted ones who yet retain your reason!

Verses to meditate upon today: Psalm 88:15-18.

A THOUGHT TO PONDER

A lifelong sickness may by divine grace prove to be a lifelong blessing.
Better to suffer from childhood to old age than to be let alone to find pleasure in sin.

AUGUST 2

GOD'S FAITHFULNESS

I will sing of the mercies of the LORD for ever: with my mouth will I make known thy faithfulness to all generations.

PSALM 89:1

VERSE 1: "I will sing of the mercies of the Lord for ever." A devout resolve, and very commendable when a man is exercised with great trouble on account of an apparent departure of the Lord from his covenant and promise. Whatever we may observe abroad or experience in our own persons, we ought still to praise God for his mercies, since they most certainly remain the same, whether we can perceive them or not. Sense sings but now and then, but faith is an eternal songster.

Whether others "sing" or not, believers must never give up; in them should be constancy of praise, since God's love to them cannot by any possibility have changed, however providence may seem to frown. We are not only to believe the Lord's goodness but to rejoice in it evermore. It is the source of all our joy, and as it cannot be dried up, so the stream ought never to fail to flow or cease to flash in sparkling crystal of song.

We have not one but many "mercies" to rejoice in and should therefore multiply the expressions of our thankfulness. It is Jehovah who deigns to deal out to us our daily benefits, and he is the all-sufficient and immutable God; therefore our rejoicing in him must never suffer diminution. By no means let his treasury of glory be deprived of the continual revenue that we owe to it. Even time itself must not limit our praises—they must leap into eternity. He blesses us with eternal mercies—let us sing unto him "for ever."

"With my mouth will I make known thy faithfulness to all generations." The utterances of the present will instruct future "generations." What Ethan sang is now a textbook for Christians and will be so as long as this dispensation shall last. We ought to have an eye to posterity in all that we say and write, for we are the schoolmasters of succeeding ages.

Verses to meditate upon today: Psalm 89:1-4.

A THOUGHT TO PONDER

Sense sings but now and then, but faith is an eternal songster.

AUGUST 3

THE HEAVENS PRAISE GOD

And the heavens shall praise thy wonders, O LORD: thy faithfulness also in the congregation of the saints.
PSALM 89:5

VERSE 5: Looking down upon what God had done and was about to do in connection with his covenant of grace, all heaven would be filled with adoring wonder. The sun and moon, which had been made tokens of the covenant, would praise God for such an extraordinary display of mercy, and the angels and redeemed spirits would sing "as it were a new song" [Revelation 14:3].

"Thy faithfulness also in the congregation of the saints." By this is probably intended the holy ones on earth, so that "the whole family in heaven and earth" [Ephesians 3:14] would join in the praise. Earth and heaven are one in admiring and adoring the covenant God. Saints above see most clearly into the heights and depths of divine love; therefore they praise its wonders. And saints below, being conscious of their many sins and multiplied provocations of the Lord, admire his "faithfulness." The heavens broke forth with music at the wonders of mercy contained in the glad tidings concerning Bethlehem, and the saints who came together in the temple magnified the "faithfulness" of God at the birth of the Son of David. Since that auspicious day, the general assembly on high and the sacred congregation below have not ceased to sing unto Jehovah, the Lord who keeps his covenant with his elect.

VERSE 6: "For who in the heaven can be compared unto the LORD?" Therefore all heaven worships him, seeing none can equal him. "Who among the sons of the mighty can be likened unto the LORD?" Therefore the assemblies of the saints on earth adore him, seeing none can rival him. Until we can find one equally worthy to be praised, we will give unto the Lord alone all the homage of our praise. Neither among the sons of the morning nor the sons of the mighty can any peer be found for Jehovah; therefore he is rightly praised.

Verses to meditate upon today: Psalm 89:5-8.

A THOUGHT TO PONDER
*Looking down upon what God had done,
all heaven would be filled with adoring wonder.*

AUGUST 4

HEAVEN AND EARTH BELONG TO GOD

The heavens are thine, the earth also is thine: as for the world and the fulness thereof, thou hast founded them.

PSALM 89:11

VERSE 11: "The heavens are thine, the earth also is thine." All things are alike God's—rebellious earth as well as adoring heaven. Let us not despair of the kingdom of truth; the Lord has not abdicated the throne of earth or handed it over to the sway of Satan. "As for the world and the fulness thereof, thou hast founded them." The habitable and cultivated earth, with all its produce, owns the Lord to be both its Creator and Sustainer, builder and upholder.

VERSE 12: "The north and the south thou hast created them." "North" and "south," opposite poles, agree in this—that Jehovah fashioned them.

"Tabor and Hermon shall rejoice in thy name." *East and west are equally formed by you and therefore give you praise.* Turn to all points of the compass, and behold the Lord is there. The regions of snow and the gardens of the sun are his dominions; both the land of the dawning and the home of the setting sun rejoice to own his sway. Tabor was on the west of Jordan and Hermon on the east, and it seems natural to consider these two mountains as representatives of the east and west. Keble paraphrases the passage thus:

> *Both Heman moist, and Tabor lone,*
> *They wait on thee with glad acclaim.*

VERSE 13: "Thou hast a mighty arm"—*omnipotence is yours in smiting or uplifting*; "strong is thy hand"—*your power to create and grasp is beyond conception great*; "and high is thy right hand"—*your skill is incomparable, your favor ennobling, your working glorious.* The power of God so impressed the psalmist that in many ways he repeated the same thought; and indeed the truth of God's omnipotence is so full of refreshment to gracious hearts that it cannot be too much dwelt upon, especially when viewed in connection with his mercy and truth, as in the following verse.

Verses to meditate upon today: Psalm 89:9-13.

A THOUGHT TO PONDER
All things are alike God's—rebellious earth as well as adoring heaven.

AUGUST 5

THE JOYFUL SOUND

Blessed is the people that know the joyful sound: they shall walk, O LORD, in the light of thy countenance.

PSALM 89:15

VERSE 14: "Justice and judgment are the habitation of thy throne." They are the basis of the divine government, the sphere within which God's sovereignty moves. God as a sovereign is never unjust or unwise. He is too holy to be unrighteous, too wise to be mistaken; this is constant matter for joy to the upright in heart.

"Mercy and truth shall go before thy face." They are the harbingers and heralds of the Lord. He calls these to the front to deal with guilty and changing man; he makes them, in the person of the Lord Jesus, to be his ambassadors, and so poor, guilty man is enabled to endure the presence of his righteous Lord. If "mercy" had not paved the way, the coming of God to any man would have been swift destruction.

Thus has the poet sung the glories of the covenant God. It was appropriate that before he poured forth his lament, he should record his praise, lest his sorrow should seem to have withered his faith. Before we argue our case before the Lord, it is most becoming to acknowledge that we know him to be supremely great and good, whatever may be the appearance of his providence. This is a course every wise man will take who desires to have an answer of peace in the day of trouble.

VERSE 15: "Blessed is the people that know the joyful sound." It is a blessed God of whom the psalmist has been singing, and therefore they are a "blessed . . . people" who partake of his bounty and know how to exult in his favor. Praise is a peculiarly joyful sound, and blessed are those who are familiar with its strains. The covenant promises have also a sound precious beyond measure, and they are highly favored who understand their meaning and recognize their own personal interest in them.

Verses to meditate upon today: Psalm 89:14-18.

A THOUGHT TO PONDER
Praise is a peculiarly joyful sound, and blessed are those who are familiar with its strains.

AUGUST 6

YOU ARE MY FATHER

He shall cry unto me, Thou art my father, my God, and the rock of my salvation.

PSALM 89:26

VERSE 26: "He shall cry unto me, Thou art my father." David's seed would be a praying race, and so in the main they were; and when they were not, they suffered for it. The Lord Jesus was often in prayer, and his favorite mode of address was "Father." Never was there a son more filial in his cries than "the firstborn among many brethren" [Romans 8:29]. God had one Son without sin, but he never had a Son who lived without prayer.

"My God." So our Lord called his Father when upon the cross.

"And the rock of my salvation." It was to his Father that Jesus turned for help when in sore anguish in Gethsemane, and to him he committed his spirit in the moment of death. In this filial crying the true sons should imitate him. This is the common language of the elect family; adoption, reverence, trust must all speak in their turns and will do so if we are heirs according to promise. To say to God, "Thou art my father" is more than learning and talent can teach us; the new birth is essential to this. Reader, do you have the nature of a child and the spirit of one who can cry, "Abba, Father"?

VERSE 27: "Also I will make him my firstborn." Among kings those who were the seed of David were to be most favored and indulged with most love and paternal regard from God. But in Jesus we see this verified in the highest degree, for he has preeminence in all things, inasmuch as by inheritance he has a more glorious name than any other and is "higher than the kings of the earth." Who can rival heaven's Firstborn? The double portion and the government belong to him. "Kings" are honored when they honor him, and those who honor him are kings!

Verses to meditate upon today: Psalm 89:19-29.

A THOUGHT TO PONDER

The Lord Jesus was often in prayer, and his favorite mode of address was "Father."

AUGUST 7

GOD'S HOLINESS

Once have I sworn by my holiness that I will not lie unto David.
PSALM 89:35

VERSE 35: Because God could swear by no greater, he swore by himself, and by that peculiar attribute that is his highest glory, being the subject of threefold adoration by all the hosts of heaven ["Holy, holy, holy"]. God here pledges the crown of his kingdom, the excellent beauty of his person, the essence of his nature. It is as if he says that if he ceases to be true to his covenant, he will have forfeited his holy character. What more can he say? In what stronger language can he express his unalterable adherence to the truth of his promise? An oath is the end of all strife; it ought to be the end of all doubt on our part.

VERSE 36: "His seed shall endure for ever." David's line in the person of Jesus is an endless one, and the race of Jesus, as represented in successive generations of believers, shows no sign of failure. No power, human or satanic, can break the Christian succession. As saints die, others shall rise up to fill their places, so that until the last day, the day of doom, Jesus shall have a seed to serve him.

"And his throne as the sun before me." In our Lord Jesus the dynasty of David remains upon the "throne." Jesus has never abdicated, nor gone into banishment. He reigns, and must reign so long as "the sun" continues to shine upon the earth. A "seed" and a "throne" are the two great promises of the covenant, and they are as important to us as to our Lord Jesus himself; for we are the "seed" who must "endure for ever," and we are protected and ennobled by that King whose royalties are to last forever.

Verses to meditate upon today: Psalm 89:30-37.

A THOUGHT TO PONDER
*God here pledges the crown of his kingdom, the excellent beauty
of his person, the essence of his nature.*

AUGUST 8

GOD'S ACTIONS

But thou hast cast off and abhorred, thou hast been wroth with thine anointed.
PSALM 89:38

VERSE 38: "But thou hast cast off and abhorred." The Lord had promised not to cast off the seed of David, and yet it looked as if he had done so, and that too in the most angry manner, as if he loathed the person of the king. God's actions may appear to us to be the reverse of his promises, and then our best course is to come before him in prayer and put the matter before him just as it strikes our apprehension. We are allowed to do this, for this holy and inspired man did so unrebuked; but we must do it humbly and in faith.

"Thou hast been wroth with thine anointed." He deserved the wrath, doubtless, but the psalmist's point is that this appeared to him to conflict with the gracious covenant. He puts the matter plainly and makes bold with the Lord, and the Lord loves to have his servants so do; it shows that they believe his engagements to be matters of fact.

VERSE 39: "Thou hast made void the covenant of thy servant." The dispensations of providence looked as if there had been a disannulling of the sacred compact, though indeed it was not so.

"Thou hast profaned his crown by casting it to the ground." The king had been subject to such sorrow and shame that his diadem had been as it were taken from his head, dashed on the earth, and rolled in the mire. He was a theocratic monarch, and the Lord, who gave him his "crown," took it from him and treated it with contempt—at least so it seemed. In these sad days we may utter the same complaint, for Jesus is not acknowledged in many of the churches, and usurpers have profaned his crown.

Verses to meditate upon today: Psalm 89:38-45.

A THOUGHT TO PONDER

God's actions may appear to us to be the reverse of his promises, and then our best course is to come before him in prayer.

AUGUST 9

REMEMBER ME, LORD

Remember, Lord, the reproach of thy servants; how I do bear in my bosom the reproach of all the mighty people.
PSALM 89:50

VERSE 50: "Remember, Lord, the reproach of thy servants." By reason of their great troubles they were made a mock of by ungodly men, and hence the Lord's pity is entreated. Will a father stand by and see his children insulted? The psalmist entreats the Lord on account of the wretchedness brought upon his servants by the taunts of their adversaries, who jested at them on account of their sufferings.

"How I do bear in my bosom the reproach of all the mighty people." The psalmist himself laid the scorn of the great and the proud to heart. He felt as if all the reproaches that vexed his nation were centered in himself, and therefore in sacred sympathy with the people he poured out his heart. We ought to weep with those that weep; "reproach" brought upon the saints and their cause ought to burden us. If we can hear Christ blasphemed and see his servants insulted and remain unmoved, we have not the true Israelite spirit. Our grief at the griefs of the Lord's people may be pleaded in prayer, and it will be acceptable argument.

There is one interpretation of this verse that must not be passed over. The original is, "Remember my bearing in my bosom all the many nations," and this may be understood as a pleading of the church that the Lord would remember her because she was yet to be the mother of many nations, according to the prophecy of Psalm 77:1-20. She was as it were ready to give birth to nations. But how could they be born if she herself died in the meanwhile? The church is the hope of the world; should she expire, the nations would never come to the birth of regeneration but must abide in death.

Verses to meditate upon today: Psalm 89:46-52.

A THOUGHT TO PONDER
We ought to weep with those that weep; reproach brought upon the saints and their cause ought to burden us.

AUGUST 10

ONE THOUSAND YEARS AND ONE DAY

For a thousand years in thy sight are but as yesterday when it is past, and as a watch in the night.
PSALM 90:4

VERSE 4: "For a thousand years in thy sight are but as yesterday when it is past." "A thousand years"! This is a long stretch of time. How much may be crowded into it—the rise and fall of empires, the glory and obliteration of dynasties, the beginning and the end of elaborate systems of human philosophy, and countless events, all important to household and individual, which elude the pens of historians. Yet this period, which might even be called the limit of modern history and is in human language almost identical with an indefinite length of time, is to the Lord as nothing, even as time already gone. A moment yet to come is longer than "yesterday when it is past," for that no longer exists at all; yet such is a millennium in the light of the eternal. In comparison with eternity, the most lengthened reaches of time are mere points; there is in fact no possible comparison between them.

"And as a watch in the night," a time that is no sooner come than gone. There is scarce time enough in "a thousand years" for the angels to change watches; when their millennium of service is almost over, it seems as though the "watch" was newly set. We are dreaming through the long "night" of time, but God is ever keeping watch, and "a thousand years" are as nothing to him. A host of days and nights must be combined to make up "a thousand years" to us, but to God that space of time does not make up a whole night but only a brief portion of it. If a thousand years be to God as a single night "watch," what must be the lifetime of the eternal!

VERSE 5: "Thou carriest them away as with a flood." As when a torrent rushes down the riverbed and bears all before it, so does the Lord bear away by death the succeeding generations of men.

Verses to meditate upon today: Psalm 90:1-6.

A THOUGHT TO PONDER
If a thousand years be to God as a single night "watch," what must be the lifetime of the eternal!

AUGUST 11

OUR SECRET SINS

*Thou hast set our iniquities before thee, our secret sins
in the light of thy countenance.*
PSALM 90:8

VERSE 8: "Thou hast set our iniquities before thee." Hence our tears! Sin seen by God must work death; it is only by the covering blood of atonement that life comes to any of us. When God was overthrowing the tribes in the wilderness, he had their "iniquities" before him and therefore dealt with them in severity. He could not have their "iniquities" before him and not smite them.

"Our secret sins in the light of thy countenance." There are no secrets before God; he unearths man's hidden things and exposes them to the "light." There can be no more powerful luminary than the face of God, and yet in that strong "light" the Lord set the hidden sins of Israel. Sunlight can never be compared with the "light" of him who made the sun, of whom it is written, "God is light, and in him is no darkness at all" [1 John 1:5]. If by his "countenance" is here meant his love and favor, it is not possible for the heinousness of sin to be more clearly manifested than when it is seen to involve ingratitude to one so infinitely good and kind.

Rebellion in the "light" of justice is wrong, but in the "light" of love it is devilish. How can we grieve so good a God? The children of Israel had been brought out of Egypt with a high hand, fed in the wilderness with a liberal hand, and guided with a tender hand, and their sins were peculiarly atrocious. We, too, having been redeemed by the blood of Jesus and saved by abounding grace, will be exceedingly guilty if we forsake the Lord. What manner of persons ought we to be? How ought we to pray for cleansing from secret faults!

It is to us a wellspring of delights to remember that our sins as believers are now cast behind the Lord's back and shall never be brought to light again. Therefore we live because, the guilt being removed, the death penalty is removed also.

Verses to meditate upon today: Psalm 90:7-12.

A THOUGHT TO PONDER
God unearths man's hidden things and exposes them to the "light."

AUGUST 12

GOD'S UNFAILING LOVE

O satisfy us early with thy mercy; that we may
rejoice and be glad all our days.
PSALM 90:14

VERSE 14: "O satisfy us early with thy mercy." Since they must die, and die so soon, the psalmist pleads for speedy mercy upon himself and his brethren. Good men know how to turn the darkest trials into arguments at the throne of grace. He who has but the heart to pray need never be without pleas in prayer. The only satisfying food for the Lord's people is the favor of God. This Moses earnestly seeks, and as the manna fell in the morning he beseeches the Lord to send at once his satisfying favor, that all through the little day of life they might be filled therewith. *Are we so soon to die? Then, Lord, do not starve us while we live. Satisfy us at once, we pray you. Our day is short, and the night hastens on. Oh, help us in the early morning of our days to be satisfied with your favor, that all through our little day we may be happy.*

"That we may rejoice and be glad all our days." Being filled with divine love, their brief life on earth would become a joyful festival, which would continue as long as life lasted. When the Lord refreshes us with his presence, our joy is such that no man can take it from us. Fears of speedy death are not able to distress those who enjoy the present favor of God. Though they know that the night comes, they see nothing to fear in it, triumphing in the present favor of God and leaving the future in his loving hands. Since the whole generation that came out of Egypt had been doomed to die in the wilderness, they would naturally feel despondent, and therefore their great leader seeks for them that blessing that, beyond all others, consoles the heart—namely, the presence and favor of the Lord.

Verses to meditate upon today: Psalm 90:13-17.

A THOUGHT TO PONDER
Though they know that the night comes, they see nothing to fear in it,
triumphing in the present favor of God and leaving
the future in his loving hands.

AUGUST 13

THE SECRET PLACE

He that dwelleth in the secret place of the Most High shall abide under the shadow of the Almighty.

PSALM 91:1

VERSE 1: "He that dwelleth in the secret place of the Most High." The blessings here promised are not for all believers, but for those who live in close fellowship with God. Every child of God looks toward the inner sanctuary and the mercy seat, yet all do not dwell in the most holy place; they run to it at times and enjoy occasional approaches, but they do not habitually reside in the mysterious presence. Those who through rich grace obtain unusual and continuous communion with God, so as to abide in Christ and Christ in them, become possessors of rare and special benefits, which are missed by those who follow afar off and grieve the Holy Spirit of God.

Into "the secret place" come only those who know the love of God in Christ Jesus; those only dwell there to whom to live is Christ. To them the veil is rent, the mercy seat is revealed, the covering cherubs are manifest, and the awesome glory of "the Most High" is apparent. These, like Simeon, have the Holy Spirit upon them, and like Anna they depart not from the temple; they are the courtiers of the Great King, the valiant men who keep watch around the bed of Solomon, the virgin souls who follow the Lamb whithersoever he goes.

Elect out of the elect, they shall walk with their Lord in white, for they are worthy. Sitting in the august presence chamber where shines the mystic light of the *Shekinah*, they know what it is to be raised up together and to be made to sit together with Christ in the heavenlies, and of them it is truly said that their life is in heaven.

Verses to meditate upon today: Psalm 91:1-8.

A THOUGHT TO PONDER

Into "the secret place" come only those who know the love of God in Christ Jesus; those only dwell there to whom to live is Christ.

AUGUST 14

GUARDIAN ANGELS

For he shall give his angels charge over thee,
to keep thee in all thy ways.

PSALM 91:11

VERSE 11: "For he shall give his angels charge over thee." Not one guardian angel, as some fondly dream, but all the "angels" are alluded to here. They are the bodyguards of the princes of heaven, and they have received commission from their Lord and ours to watch carefully over all the interests of the faithful. When men have a charge they become doubly careful, and the angels are represented as bidden by God himself to see to it that the elect are secured. It is written in the marching orders of the hosts of heaven that they take special note of the people who dwell in God. It is not to be wondered at that the servants are bidden to be careful of the comfort of their Master's guests; and we may be quite sure that being specially charged by the Lord himself, they will carefully discharge the duty imposed upon them.

"To keep thee in all thy ways." They are to be bodyguards, garrisons to the body, soul, and spirit of the saints. The limit of this protection ("in all thy ways") is no limit to the heart that is right with God. It is not the way of the believer to go out of God's way. He keeps in God's way, and then the angels "keep" him. The protection here promised is exceedingly broad as to place, for it refers to *"all"* our ways, and what do we wish for more? How angels thus "keep" us we cannot tell. Whether they repel demons, counteract spiritual plots, or even ward off the more subtle physical forces of disease, we do not know. Perhaps we shall one day stand amazed at the multiplied services that the unseen bands have rendered to us.

Verses to meditate upon today: Psalm 91:9-13.

A THOUGHT TO PONDER
Perhaps we shall one day stand amazed at the multiplied services
that the unseen bands have rendered to us.

AUGUST 15

GOD'S PROTECTION

*Because he hath set his love upon me, therefore will I deliver him:
I will set him on high, because he hath known my name.*

PSALM 91:14

VERSE 14: Here we have the Lord himself speaking of his own chosen one. "Because he hath set his love upon me, therefore will I deliver him." Not because he deserves to be thus kept, but because with all his imperfections he does love his God. Therefore not the angels of God only, but the God of angels will himself come to his rescue in all perilous times and will effectually "deliver him." When the heart is enamored of the Lord, taken up with him and intensely attached to him, the Lord will recognize the sacred flame and preserve the man who bears it in his bosom. Love set upon God is the distinguishing mark of those whom the Lord secures from ill.

"I will set him on high, because he hath known my name." The man has known the attributes of God so as to trust in him and then by experience has arrived at a yet deeper knowledge. This shall be regarded by the Lord as a pledge of his grace, and he will set the owner of it above danger or fear, where he shall dwell in peace and joy. None abide in intimate fellowship with God unless they possess a warm affection toward God and an intelligent trust in him; these gifts of grace are precious in Jehovah's eyes, and wherever he sees them, he smiles upon them. How elevated is the standing that the Lord gives to the believer. We ought to covet it earnestly. If we climb on high it may be dangerous, but if God sets us there it is glorious.

VERSE 15: "He shall call upon me, and I will answer him." He will have need to pray, he will be led to pray aright, and the answer shall surely come. Saints are first called *of* God, and then they call *upon* God; and such calls as theirs always obtain answers.

Verses to meditate upon today: Psalm 91:14-16.

A THOUGHT TO PONDER

Not the angels of God only, but the God of angels will himself come to the believer's rescue in all perilous times and will effectually "deliver him."

AUGUST 16

GOD'S DEEDS AND THOUGHTS

For thou, LORD, hast made me glad through thy work:
I will triumph in the works of thy hands.
PSALM 92:4

VERSE 4: "For thou, LORD, hast made me glad through thy work." It was natural for the psalmist to sing because he was "glad," and to sing unto the Lord because his gladness was caused by a contemplation of the divine "work." If we consider either creation or providence, we shall find overflowing reasons for joy; but when we come to review the "work" of redemption, gladness knows no bounds but feels she must praise the Lord with all her might. There are times when in the contemplation of redeeming love we feel that if we did not sing we must die; silence would be as horrible to us as if we were gagged by inquisitors or stifled by murderers.

"I will triumph in the works of thy hands." I cannot help it—I must and I will rejoice in the Lord, even as one who has won the victory and has divided great spoil. In the first sentence of this verse the psalmist expresses the unity of God's "work," and in the second the variety of his "works"; in both there is reason for gladness and "triumph." When God reveals his "work" to a man and performs a "work" in his soul, he makes his heart "glad" most effectually, and then the natural consequence is continual praise.

VERSE 5: "O LORD, how great are thy works!" He is lost in wonder. He utters an exclamation of amazement. How vast, how stupendous are the doings of Jehovah! Great in number, extent, glory, and design are all the creations of the Infinite One.

"And thy thoughts are very deep." The Lord's plans are as marvelous as his acts; his designs are as profound as his doings are vast. Creation is immeasurable, and the wisdom displayed in it unsearchable. Some men think but cannot work, and others are mere drudges working without thought; in the Eternal the conception and the execution go together.

Verses to meditate upon today: Psalm 92:1-7.

A THOUGHT TO PONDER

The Lord's plans are as marvelous as his acts; his designs are as profound
as his doings are vast.

AUGUST 17

A Flourishing Palm Tree

The righteous shall flourish like the palm tree: he shall grow like a cedar in Lebanon.
PSALM 92:12

VERSE 12: The song now contrasts the condition of "the righteous" with that of the graceless. The wicked "spring as the grass" (verse 7), but "the righteous shall flourish like the palm tree," whose growth may not be so rapid, but whose endurance for centuries is in fine contrast with the transitory verdure of the meadow. When we see a noble palm standing erect, sending all its strength upward in one bold column, growing amid the dearth and drought of the desert, we have a fine picture of the godly man, who in his uprightness aims alone at the glory of God and, independent of outward circumstances, is made by divine grace to live and thrive where all things else perish. The text tells us not only what "the righteous" is, but what he shall be; come what may, the good man shall "flourish," and "flourish" after the noblest manner.

"He shall grow like a cedar in Lebanon." This is another noble and long-lived tree. "As the days of a tree are the days of my people" [Isaiah 65:22], says the Lord. On the summit of the mountain, unsheltered from the blast, the "cedar" waves its mighty branches in perpetual verdure; and the truly godly man under all adversities retains the joy of his soul and continues to make progress in the divine life. Grass, which makes hay for oxen, is a good enough emblem of the unregenerate; but cedars, which build the temple of the Lord, are none too excellent to set forth the heirs of heaven.

VERSE 13: "Those that be planted in the house of the LORD shall flourish in the courts of our God." In the courtyards of oriental houses, trees were planted; and being thoroughly screened, they would be likely to bring forth their fruit to perfection in trying seasons. Even so, those who by grace are brought into communion with the Lord shall be likened to trees "planted" in the Lord's house and shall find it good to their souls.

Verses to meditate upon today: Psalm 92:8-15.

A THOUGHT TO PONDER
The truly godly man under all adversities retains the joy of his soul and continues to make progress in the divine life.

AUGUST 18

God's Eternal Throne

Thy throne is established of old: thou art from everlasting.
PSALM 93:2

VERSE 2: "Thy throne is established of old." *Though you may now appear in more conspicuous sovereignty, yet yours is no upstart sovereignty. In the most ancient times your dominion was secure; yes, before time was, your throne was set up.* We often hear of ancient dynasties, but what are they when compared with the Lord? Are they not as the bubble on the breaking wave, born an instant ago and gone as soon as seen?

"Thou art from everlasting." The Lord is eternal. Let the believer rejoice that the government under which he dwells has an immortal Ruler at its head, has existed from all eternity, and will flourish when all created things have forever passed away. Vain are the rebellions of mortals; the kingdom of God is not shaken.

VERSE 3: "The floods have lifted up, O LORD." Men have raged like angry waves of the sea, but vain has been their tumult. Observe that the psalmist turns to the Lord when he sees the billows foam and hears the breakers roar. He does not waste his breath by talking to the waves or to violent men; but like Hezekiah he spreads the blasphemies of the wicked before the Lord.

"The floods have lifted up their voice; the floods lift up their waves." These repetitions are needed for the sake both of the poetry and the music; but they also suggest the frequency and the violence of wicked assaults upon the government of God, and the repeated defeats that they sustain. Sometimes men are furious in words—they "lift up their voice," and at other times they rise to acts of violence—they "lift up their waves"; but the Lord has control over them in either case. The ungodly are all foam and fury, noise and bluster during their little hour, and then the tide turns or the storm is hushed, and we hear no more of them; while the kingdom of the Eternal abides in the grandeur of its power.

Verses to meditate upon today: Psalm 93:1-5.

A THOUGHT TO PONDER
The kingdom of the Eternal abides in the grandeur of its power.

AUGUST 19

ARROGANT WORDS

How long shall they utter and speak hard things? and all the workers of iniquity boast themselves?

PSALM 94:4

VERSE 4: "How long shall they utter and speak hard things?" The ungodly are not content with deeds of injustice, but they add "hard" speeches, boasting, threatening, and insulting over the saints. Will the Lord forever endure this? Will he leave his own children much longer to be the prey of their enemies? Will not the insolent speeches of his adversaries and theirs at last provoke his justice to interfere? Words often wound more than swords; they are as hard to the heart as stones to the flesh. And these are poured forth by the ungodly in redundance, for such is the force of the word translated "utter"; and they use them so commonly that they become their common speech (they "utter" and "speak" them). Will this always be endured?

"And all the workers of iniquity boast themselves?" They even soliloquize and talk to "themselves," and of "themselves," in arrogance of spirit, as if they are doing some good deed when they crush the poor and needy and spit their spite on gracious men. It is the nature of "workers of iniquity" to "boast," just as it is a characteristic of good men to be humble. Will their boasts always be suffered by the great Judge, whose ear hears all that they say? Long, very long, have they had the platform to themselves, and loud, very loud, have been their blasphemies of God and their railings at his saints. Will not the day soon come when the threatened heritage of shame and everlasting contempt shall be meted out to them?

Thus the oppressed plead with their Lord, and shall not God avenge his own elect? Will he not speak out of heaven to the enemy and say, "Why persecutest thou me"?

Verses to meditate upon today: Psalm 94:1-7.

A THOUGHT TO PONDER

Will their boasts always be suffered by the great Judge, whose ear hears all that they say?

AUGUST 20

LEARNING FROM GOD'S DISCIPLINE

Blessed is the man whom thou chastenest, O LORD,
and teachest him out of thy law.
PSALM 94:12

VERSE 12: "Blessed is the man whom thou chastenest, O LORD." The psalmist's mind is growing quiet. He no longer complains to God or argues with men but tunes his harp to softer melodies, for his faith perceives that with the most afflicted believer all is well. Though he may not feel blessed while hurting under the rod of chastisement, yet blessed he is. He is precious in God's sight or the Lord would not take the trouble to correct him, and right happy will the results of his correction be. The psalmist calls the chastened one a "man" in the best sense, using the Hebrew word that implies strength. He is a "man" indeed who is under the teaching and training of the Lord.

"And teachest him out of thy law." The book and the rod, the "law" and the chastening, go together and are made doubly useful by being found in connection. Affliction without the Word is a furnace for the metal, but there is no flux to aid the purifying. The Word of God supplies that need and makes the fiery trial effectual. After all, the blessing of God belongs far rather to those who suffer under the divine hand than to those who make others suffer. Better far to cry out as a "man" under the hand of our heavenly Father than to roar and rave as a brute and to bring down upon oneself a deathblow from the destroyer of evil.

The afflicted believer is under private instruction; he is in training for something higher and better, and all that he meets with is working out his highest good. Therefore is he a blessed man, however much his outward circumstances may argue the reverse.

Verses to meditate upon today: Psalm 94:8-15.

A THOUGHT TO PONDER
He is precious in God's sight or the Lord would not take the trouble to correct him,
and right happy will the results of his correction be.

AUGUST 21

Unless the Lord Had Helped Me

Unless the LORD had been my help, my soul had almost dwelt in silence.
PSALM 94:17

VERSE 17: Without Jehovah's help, the psalmist declares that he would have died outright and gone into the silent land, where no more testimonies can be borne for the living God. Or he may mean that he would not have had a word to speak against his enemies but would have been wrapped in speechless shame. Blessed be God, we are not left to that condition yet, for the Almighty Lord is still the helper of all those who look to him. Our inmost soul is bowed down when we see the victories of the Lord's enemies. We cannot tolerate it; we cover our mouths in confusion. But he will yet arise and avenge his own cause; therefore have we hope.

VERSE 18: "When I said, My foot slippeth," is slipping even now, I perceived my danger and cried out in horror, and then, at the very moment of my extremity, came the needed help—"thy mercy, O LORD, held me up." Often enough this is the case; we feel our weakness and see our danger, and in fear and trembling we cry out. At such times nothing can help us but "mercy"; we can make no appeal to any fancied merit, for we feel that it is our inbred sin that makes our feet so ready to fail us. Our joy is that "mercy" endures forever and is always at hand to pluck us out of the danger and hold us up, else we should fall to our destruction. Ten thousand times has this verse been true in relation to some of us, and especially to the writer of this comment. The danger was imminent, it was upon us, we were going down; the peril was apparent, we saw it and were aghast at the sight; our own heart was failing, and we concluded that it was all over with us. But then came the almighty interposition.

Verses to meditate upon today: Psalm 94:16-23.

A Thought to Ponder

The Almighty Lord is still the helper of all those who look to him.

AUGUST 22

EXTOL GOD WITH MUSIC

Let us come before his presence with thanksgiving, and
make a joyful noise unto him with psalms.

PSALM 95:2

VERSE 2: "Let us come before his presence with thanksgiving." Here is probably a reference to the peculiar presence of God in the Holy of Holies above the mercy seat, and also to the glory that shone forth out of the cloud that rested above the tabernacle. Everywhere God is present, but there is a peculiar presence of grace and glory into which men should never come without the profoundest reverence. We may make bold to come before the immediate presence of the Lord, for the voice of the Holy Spirit in this Psalm invites us; and when we do draw near to him, we should remember his great goodness to us and cheerfully confess it. Our worship should have reference to the past as well as to the future; if we do not bless the Lord for what we have already received, how can we reasonably look for more. We are permitted to bring our petitions, and therefore we are in honor bound to bring our thanksgivings.

"And make a joyful noise unto him with psalms." We should shout as exultingly as those do who triumph in war, and as solemnly as those whose utterance is a psalm. It is not always easy to unite enthusiasm with reverence, and it is a frequent fault to destroy one of these qualities while straining after the other. The perfection of singing is that which unites joy with gravity, exultation with humility, fervency with sobriety. The invitation given in the first verse is thus repeated in the second, with the addition of directions that indicate more fully the intent of the writer. One can imagine David in earnest tones persuading his people to go up with him to the worship of Jehovah with sound of harp and hymn and with holy delight. The happiness of his exhortation is noteworthy—the noise is to be *joyful*; this quality he insists upon twice.

Verses to meditate upon today: Psalm 95:1-5.

A THOUGHT TO PONDER
We should shout as exultingly as those do who triumph in war, and
as solemnly as those whose utterance is a psalm.

AUGUST 23

KNEELING BEFORE OUR MAKER

*O come, let us worship and bow down: let us kneel
before the LORD our maker.*

PSALM 95:6

VERSE 6: Here the exhortation to worship is renewed and backed with a motive that, to Israel of old and to Christians now, is especially powerful; for both the Israel after the flesh and the Israel of faith may be described as the people of his pasture, and by both he is called "our God" [verse 7].

"O come, let us worship and bow down." The adoration is to be humble. The "joyful noise" (verse 1) is to be accompanied with lowliest reverence. We are to worship in such style that the bowing down shall indicate that we count ourselves to be as nothing in the presence of the all-glorious Lord.

"Let us kneel before the LORD our maker." As suppliants must we come; joyful, but not presumptuous; familiar as children before a father, yet reverential as creatures before their Maker. Posture is not everything, yet it is something. Prayer is heard when knees cannot bend, but it is seemly that an adoring heart should show its awe by prostrating the body and bending the knee.

VERSE 7: "For he is our God." Here is the master reason for worship. Jehovah has entered into covenant with us and from all the world beside has chosen us to be his own elect. If others refuse him homage, we at least will render it cheerfully. He is ours, and "our God"; ours, therefore will we love him; "our God," therefore we will worship him. Happy is that man who can sincerely believe that this sentence is true in reference to himself.

"And we are the people of his pasture, and the sheep of his hand." As he belongs to us, so do we belong to him. "My beloved is mine, and I am his" [Song of Solomon 2:16]. We are his as the people whom he daily feeds and protects. Our pastures are not ours, but his; we draw all our supplies from his stores.

Verses to meditate upon today: Psalm 95:6-11.

A THOUGHT TO PONDER
*Prayer is heard when knees cannot bend, but an adoring heart should show
its awe by prostrating the body and bending the knee.*

AUGUST 24

DECLARE GOD'S GLORY

*Declare his glory among the heathen,
his wonders among all people.*
PSALM 96:3

VERSE 3: "Declare his glory among the heathen." His salvation is "his glory"; the word of the Gospel glorifies him; and this should be published far and wide, until the remotest nations of the earth have known it. England has spent much blood and treasure to keep up her own prestige among barbarians; when will she be equally anxious to maintain the honor of her religion, the glory of her Lord? It is to be feared that too often the name of the Lord Jesus has been dishonored among the heathen by the vices and cruelties of those who call themselves Christians. May this fact excite true believers to greater diligence in causing the Gospel to be proclaimed as with a trumpet in all quarters of the habitable globe.

"His wonders among all people." The Gospel is a mass of "wonders," its history is full of "wonders," and it is in itself far more marvelous than miracles themselves. In the person of his Son the Lord has displayed "wonders" of love, wisdom, grace, and power. All "glory" be unto his name. Who can refuse to tell the story of redeeming grace and love unto death? All the nations need to hear of God's marvelous works; and a really living, self-denying church would solemnly resolve that speedily they shall hear thereof. The tribes that are dying out are not to be excluded from gospel teaching any more than the great growing families that, like the fat cows of Pharaoh, are eating up other races. Red Indians as well as Anglo-Saxons are to hear of the "wonders" of redeeming love. None are too degraded, none too cultured, none too savage, and none too refined.

Verses to meditate upon today: Psalm 96:1-6.

A THOUGHT TO PONDER
*In the person of his Son the Lord has displayed "wonders" of love,
wisdom, grace, and power. All "glory" be unto his name.*

AUGUST 25

TREMBLE BEFORE GOD

O worship the LORD in the beauty of holiness:
fear before him, all the earth.
PSALM 96:9

VERSE 9: "O worship the LORD in the beauty of holiness." This is the only beauty that he cares about in our public services, and it is one for which no other can compensate. Beauty of architecture and apparel he does not regard; moral and spiritual beauty is that in which his soul delights. Worship must not be rendered to God in a slovenly, sinful, superficial manner; we must be reverent, sincere, earnest, and pure in heart both in our prayers and praises. Purity is the white linen of the Lord's choristers, righteousness the comely garment of his priests, "holiness" the royal apparel of his servants.

"Fear before him, all the earth." "Tremble" is the word in the original, and it expresses the profoundest awe, just as the word "worship" does, which would be more accurately translated "bow down." Even the bodily frame would be moved to trembling and prostration if men were thoroughly conscious of the power and glory of Jehovah. Men of the world ridiculed the Quakers for trembling when under the power of the Holy Spirit. Had they been able to discern the majesty of the Eternal, they would have quaked also. There is a sacred trembling that is quite consistent with joy; the heart may even quiver with an awe-inspired excess of delight. The sight of the King in his beauty caused no alarm to John in Patmos, and yet it made him fall at his feet as dead. Oh, to behold the Lord and worship him with prostrate awe and sacred fear!

VERSE 10: "Say among the heathen that the LORD reigneth." This is the gladdest news that can be carried to them: The Lord Jehovah, in the person of his Son, has assumed the throne and has great power. Tell this among "the heathen," and let the heathen themselves, being converted, repeat the same rejoicing.

Verses to meditate upon today: Psalm 96:7-13.

A THOUGHT TO PONDER

There is a sacred trembling that is quite consistent with joy.

AUGUST 26

RIGHTEOUSNESS AND JUSTICE

Clouds and darkness are round about him: righteousness and judgment are the habitation of his throne.
PSALM 97:2

VERSE 2: "Clouds and darkness are round about him." The Lord revealed himself at Sinai; he must ever surround his essential deity when he shows himself to the sons of men, or his excessive glory would destroy them. In every revelation of God there must be a veiling of his infinite splendor if anything is to be seen by finite beings. It is often thus with the Lord in providence; when working out designs of unmingled love he conceals the purpose of his grace, that it may be the more clearly discovered at the end. "It is the glory of God to conceal a thing" [Proverbs 25:2]. Around the history of his church dark clouds of persecution hover, and an awful gloom at times settles down, but the Lord is there; and though men for a while see not the bright light in the clouds, it bursts forth in due season, to the confusion of the adversaries of the Gospel.

This passage should teach us the impertinence of attempting to pry into the essence of the Godhead, the vanity of all endeavors to understand the mystery of the Trinity in Unity, the arrogance of arraigning the Most High before the bar of human reason, the folly of dictating to the Eternal One the manner in which he should proceed. Wisdom veils her face and adores the mercy that conceals the divine purpose; folly rushes in and perishes, blinded first and by and by consumed by the blaze of glory.

"Righteousness and judgment are the habitation of his throne." There he abides; he never departs from strict justice and right. "His throne" is fixed upon the rock of eternal holiness. "Righteousness" is his immutable attribute, and "judgment" marks his every act.

Verses to meditate upon today: Psalm 97:1-12.

A THOUGHT TO PONDER
*Righteousness is his immutable attribute,
and judgment marks his every act.*

AUGUST 27

MERCY AND TRUTH

He hath remembered his mercy and his truth toward the house of Israel:
all the ends of the earth have seen the salvation of our God.
PSALM 98:3

VERSE 3: "He hath remembered his mercy and his truth toward the house of Israel." To them Jesus came in the flesh, and to them was the Gospel first preached; and though they counted themselves unworthy of eternal life, yet the covenant was not broken, for those who are the true Israel were called into fellowship and still remain so. The "mercy" that endures forever and the fidelity that cannot forget a promise secure to the chosen seed the salvation long ago guaranteed by the covenant of grace.

"All the ends of the earth have seen the salvation of our God." Not to Abraham's seed alone after the flesh, but to the elect among all nations has grace been given. Therefore, let the whole church of God sing unto him a new song. It was no small blessing or little miracle that throughout all lands the Gospel should be published in so short a time, with such singular success and such abiding results. Pentecost deserves a new song as well as the Passion and the Resurrection; let out hearts exult as we remember it. "Our God," our own forever blessed God, has been honored by those who once bowed down before dumb idols. His "salvation" has not only been heard of but seen among all people; it has been experienced as well as explained. His Son is the actual Redeemer of a multitude out of all nations. In these three verses we are taught how to praise the Lord.

VERSE 4: "Make a joyful noise unto the LORD, all the earth." Every tongue must applaud, and that with the rigor that joy of heart alone can arouse to action. As men shout when they welcome a king, so must we. Loud hosannas, full of happiness, must be lifted up. If ever men shout for joy, it should be when the Lord comes among them in the proclamation of his gospel reign.

Verses to meditate upon today: Psalm 98:1-9.

A THOUGHT TO PONDER
The mercy that endures forever and the fidelity that
cannot forget a promise secure salvation to the chosen seed.

August 28

Our God Is Holy

Exalt ye the LORD our God, and worship
at his footstool; for he is holy.
Psalm 99:5

Verse 5: "Exalt ye the LORD our God." If no others adore him, let his own people render to him the most ardent worship. Infinite condescension makes him stoop to be called our God, and truth and faithfulness bind him to maintain that covenant relationship; and surely we, to whom by grace he so lovingly gives himself, should exalt him with all our hearts. He shines upon us from under the veiled wings of cherubim and above the seat of mercy; therefore let us come and "worship at his footstool." When he reveals himself in Christ Jesus, as our reconciled God who allows us even to approach his throne, it becomes us to unite earnestness and humility, joy and adoration and, while we exalt him, prostrate ourselves in the dust before him. It ought to be our daily delight to magnify so good and great a God.

"For he is holy." A second time this note rings out, and as the ark, which was the divine "footstool," has just been mentioned, the voice seems to sound forth from the cherubim [see verse 1] where the Lord sits, who continually cry, "Holy, Holy, Holy. Lord God of Sabaoth!" Holiness is the harmony of all the virtues. The Lord has not one glorious attribute alone or in excess, but all glories are in him as a whole; this is the crown of his honor and the honor of his crown. His power is not his choicest jewel, nor his sovereignty, but his holiness. In this all-comprehensive moral excellence he would have his creatures take delight; and when they do so, their delight is evidence that their hearts have been renewed and they themselves have been made partakers of his holiness.

Verses to meditate upon today: Psalm 99:1-9.

A Thought to Ponder
Holiness is the harmony of all the virtues.

AUGUST 29

KNOWING GOD

Know ye that the LORD *he is God: it is he that hath made us, and not we ourselves; we are his people, and the sheep of his pasture.*

PSALM 100:3

VERSE 3: "Know ye that the LORD he is God." Our worship must be intelligent. We ought to know whom we worship and why. "Man, know thyself" is a wise aphorism; yet to know our God is truer wisdom. And it is very questionable whether a man can know himself until he knows his God. Jehovah is God in the fullest, most absolute, and most exclusive sense; he is God alone. To know him in that character and prove our knowledge by obedience, trust, submission, zeal, and love is an attainment that only grace can bestow. Only those who practically recognize his Godhead are at all likely to offer acceptable praise.

"It is he that hath made us, and not we ourselves." Shall not the creature reverence its Maker? Some men live as if they made themselves; they call themselves "self-made men," and they adore their supposed creators. But Christians recognize the origin of their being and their well-being and take no honor to themselves, either for being or for being what they are. Neither in our first or second creation dare we put so much as a finger upon the glory, for it is the sole right and property of the Almighty.

To disclaim honor for ourselves is as necessary a part of true reverence as to ascribe glory to the Lord. *"Non nobis, domine!"* ["not to us, O Lord"] will forever remain the true believer's confession. Of late philosophy has labored hard to prove that all things have been developed from atoms, or have, in other words, made themselves. The amount of credence necessary to accept this dogma of skepticism is a thousandfold greater than that which is required even by an absurd belief in winking Madonnas and smiling Bambinos.

Verses to meditate upon today: Psalm 100:1-5.

A THOUGHT TO PONDER
It is very questionable whether a man can know himself until he knows his God.

AUGUST 30

A BLAMELESS LIFE

I will behave myself wisely in a perfect way. O when wilt thou come unto me? I will walk within my house with a perfect heart.

PSALM 101:2

VERSE 2: "I will behave myself wisely in a perfect way." To be holy is to be wise; a "perfect" way is a wise way. David's resolve was excellent, but his practice did not fully tally with it. Alas! he was not always wise or perfect, but it was well that it was so in his heart. A king must be both sage and pure; and if he be not so in intent when he comes to the throne, his later conduct will be a sad example to his people. He who does not even resolve to do well is likely to do very ill. Householders, employers, and especially ministers should pray for both wisdom and holiness, for they will need them both.

"O when wilt thou come unto me?" This is an ejaculation, not an interruption. He feels the need not merely of divine help, but also of the divine presence, so he may be instructed and sanctified and made fit for the discharge of his high vocation. David longed for a more special and effectual visitation from the Lord before he began his reign. If God be with us, we shall neither err in judgment nor transgress in character; his presence brings us both wisdom and holiness. Away from God we are away from safety. Good men are so aware of infirmity that they cry for help from God, so full of prayer that they cry at all seasons, so intense in their desires that they cry with sighs and groanings that cannot be uttered, saying, "O when wilt thou come unto me?"

"I will walk within my house with a perfect heart." Piety must begin at home. Our first duties are those within our own abode. We must have "a perfect heart" at home or we cannot keep a perfect way abroad. Notice that these words are part of a song and that there is no music like the harmony of a gracious life, no psalm so sweet as the daily practice of holiness.

Verses to meditate upon today: Psalm 101:1-8.

A THOUGHT TO PONDER

Piety must begin at home.

AUGUST 31

ANSWER ME QUICKLY

Hide not thy face from me in the day when I am in trouble; incline thine ear unto me: in the day when I call answer me speedily.

PSALM 102:2

VERSE 2: "Hide not thy face from me in the day when I am in trouble." *Do not seem as if you did not see me or would not own me. Smile now at any rate. Reserve your frowns for other times when I can bear them better, if indeed I can ever bear them; but now in my heavy distress, favor me with looks of compassion.*

"Incline thine ear unto me." *Bow your greatness to my weakness. If because of sin your face is turned away, at least let me have a side view of you. Lend me your ear if I may not see your eye. Turn yourself to me again if my sin has turned you away; give to your ear an inclination to my prayers.*

"In the day when I call answer me speedily." *The case is urgent, and my soul is little able to wait.* We may ask to have answers to prayer as soon as possible, but we may not complain to the Lord if he should think it more wise to delay. We have permission to request and to use importunity, but no right to dictate or to be petulant. If it is important that the deliverance arrive at once, we are quite right in making an early time a point of our entreaty, for God is as willing to grant us a favor now as tomorrow, and he is not slack concerning his promise. It is a proverb concerning favors from human hands that "he gives twice who gives quickly," because a gift is enhanced in value by arriving in a time of urgent necessity; and we may be sure that our Heavenly Patron will grant us the best gifts in the best manner, granting us grace to help in time of need. When answers come upon the heels of our prayers, they are all the more striking, more consoling, and more encouraging.

Verses to meditate upon today: Psalm 102:1-11.

A THOUGHT TO PONDER

We may ask to have answers to prayer as soon as possible, but we may not complain to the Lord if he should think it more wise to delay.

SEPTEMBER 1

GOD IS KING

But thou, O LORD, shalt endure for ever;
and thy remembrance unto all generations.

PSALM 102:12

VERSE 12: Now the writer's mind is turned away from his personal and relative troubles to the true source of all consolation—namely, the Lord himself—and his gracious purposes toward his own people.

"*But thou, O LORD, shalt endure for ever.*" *I perish, but you will not; my nation has become almost extinct, but you are altogether unchanged.* The original has the word "sit": "thou, Jehovah, to eternity shalt sit." That is to say, *you reign on; your throne is still secure even when your chosen city lies in ruins and your people are carried into captivity.* The sovereignty of God in all things is an unfailing ground for consolation; he rules and reigns whatever happens, and therefore all is well.

"*And thy remembrance unto all generations.*" *Men will forget me, but as for you, O God, the constant tokens of your presence will keep the race of man in mind of you from age to age.* What God is now, he always will be; that which our forefathers told us of the Lord, we find to be true at this present time, and what our experience enables us to record will be confirmed by our children and their children's children. All things else are vanishing like smoke and withering like grass, but over all the one eternal, immutable light shines on and will shine on when all these shadows have declined into nothingness.

VERSE 13: "*Thou shalt arise, and have mercy upon Zion.*" He firmly believed and boldly prophesied that apparent inaction on God's part would turn to effective working. Others might remain sluggish in the matter, but the Lord would most surely bestir himself. "Zion" had been chosen of old and was highly favored, gloriously inhabited, and wondrously preserved; and therefore by the memory of her past mercies it was certain that mercy would again be shown to her.

Verses to meditate upon today: Psalm 102:12-17.

A THOUGHT TO PONDER

The sovereignty of God in all things is an unfailing ground for consolation;
he rules and reigns whatever happens, and therefore all is well.

SEPTEMBER 2

GOD HEARS

... to hear the groaning of the prisoner; to loose those that are appointed to death.

PSALM 102:20

VERSE 19: "For he hath looked down from the heights of his sanctuary [or, leaned from the high place of his holiness]; from heaven did the LORD behold the earth," looking out like a watcher from his tower. What was the object of this leaning from the battlements of heaven? Why this intent gaze upon the race of men? The answer is full of astounding mercy. The Lord does not look upon mankind to note their great ones and observe the doings of their nobles, but, verse 20, "to hear the groaning of the prisoner; to loose those that are appointed to death." The groans of those in prison are horrible to hear; yet God bends to hear them. And those who are bound for "death" are usually ill company; yet Jehovah deigns to stoop from his greatness to relieve their extreme distress and break their chains. This he does by his providential care, by restoring health to the dying, and by finding food for the famishing. Spiritually this deed is accomplished by sovereign grace, which delivers us by pardon from the sentence of sin; the sweetness of the promise rescues us from the deadly despair that a sense of sin had created within us.

Well may those of us praise the Lord who were once the children of "death" but are now brought into the glorious liberty of the children of God. The Jews in captivity were in Haman's time appointed to death, but their God found a way of escape for them, and they joyfully kept the feast of Purim in memorial thereof. May souls that have been set free from the crafty malice of the old dragon but are now filled with great gratitude magnify the Lord of infinite compassion.

Verses to meditate upon today: Psalm 102:18-22.

A THOUGHT TO PONDER

Those who are bound for "death" are usually ill company; yet Jehovah deigns to stoop from his greatness to relieve their extreme distress and break their chains.

SEPTEMBER 3

OUR NEVER-CHANGING GOD

But thou art the same, and thy years shall have no end.
PSALM 102:27

VERSE 27: "But thou art the same." As a man remains the same when he has changed his clothing, so is the Lord evermore the unchanging One, though his works in creation may be changed, and the operations of his providence may vary. When heaven and earth shall flee away from the dread presence of the great Judge, he will be unaltered by the terrible confusion, and the world in conflagration will effect no change in him. Even so, the psalmist remembered that when Israel was vanquished, her capital destroyed, and her temple leveled, her God remained the same self-existent, all-sufficient being and would restore his people, even as he will restore the heavens and the earth, bestowing at the same time a new glory never known before. The doctrine of the immutability of God should be more considered than it is, for the neglect of it tinges the theology of many religious teachers and makes them utter many things of which they would have seen the absurdity long ago if they had remembered the divine declaration, "I am God, I change not; therefore you sons of Jacob are not consumed."

"And thy years shall have no end." God lives on; no decay can happen to him or destruction overtake him. What a joy is this! We may lose our dearest earthly friends, but not our heavenly Friend. Men's days are often suddenly cut short, and at the longest they are but few; but the "years" of the Most High cannot be counted, for they have neither first nor last, beginning nor end. O my soul, rejoice in the Lord always, since he is always the same.

VERSE 28: "The children of thy servants shall continue." The psalmist had early in the psalm looked forward to a future generation, and here he speaks with confidence that such a race would arise and be preserved and blessed of God.

Verses to meditate upon today: Psalm 102:23-28.

A THOUGHT TO PONDER
When Israel was vanquished, her capital destroyed, and her temple leveled, her God remained the same self-existent, all-sufficient being.

SEPTEMBER 4

FORGIVENESS AND HEALING

Who forgiveth all thine iniquities; who healeth all thy diseases.
PSALM 103:3

VERSE 3: "Who forgiveth all thine iniquities." Here David begins his list of blessings received, which he rehearses as themes and arguments for praise. He selects a few of the choicest pearls from the jewelry box of divine love, threads them on the string of memory, and hangs them about the neck of gratitude. Pardoned sin is, in our experience, one of the choicest boons of grace, one of the earliest gifts of mercy—in fact, the needful preparation for enjoying all that follows it. Until iniquity is forgiven, healing, redemption, and satisfaction are unknown blessings. Forgiveness is first in the order of our spiritual experience, and in some respects first in value.

The pardon granted is a present one—"forgiveth." It is continual, for he still "forgiveth." It is divine, for God gives it. It is far-reaching, for it removes all our sins. It takes in omissions as well as commissions, for both these are "iniquities." And it is most effectual, for it is as real as the healing and the rest of the mercies with which it is placed.

"Who healeth all thy diseases." When the cause is gone—namely, iniquity—the effect ceases. Sicknesses of body and soul came into the world by sin, and as sin is eradicated, bodily, mental, and spiritual diseases will vanish, until "the inhabitant shall not say, I am sick" [Isaiah 33:24]. Many-sided is the character of our heavenly Father, for having forgiven as a judge, he then cures as a physician. He is all things to us, as our needs call for him; and our infirmities do but reveal him in new ways.

> *In him is only good,*
> *In me is only ill.*
> *My ill but draws his goodness forth,*
> *And me he loveth still.*

God gives efficacy to medicine for the body, and his grace sanctifies the soul.

Verses to meditate upon today: Psalm 103:1-4.

A THOUGHT TO PONDER
Forgiveness is first in the order of our spiritual experience, and in some respects first in value.

An Eagle's Strength

Who satisfieth thy mouth with good things; so that thy youth is renewed like the eagle's.

PSALM 103:5

VERSE 5: "Who satisfieth thy mouth with good things," or rather "filling thy soul with good." No one is ever filled to satisfaction except a believer, and only God himself can satisfy even him. Many a worldling is satiated, but not one is satisfied. God satisfies the very soul of man, his noblest part, his ornament and glory; and in consequence he satisfies his "mouth," however hungry and craving it might otherwise be. Soul satisfaction loudly calls for soul praise, and when the "mouth" is filled with good, it is bound to speak good of him who filled it. Our good Lord bestows really "*good* things," not vain toys and idle pleasures; and these he is always giving, so that from moment to moment he is satisfying our soul with "good." Shall we not be ever praising him? If we never cease to bless him till he ceases to bless us, our employment will be eternal.

"So that thy youth is renewed like the eagle's." Renewal of strength, amounting to a grant of a new lease of life, was granted to the psalmist. He was so restored to his former self that he grew young again and looked as vigorous as an eagle, whose eye can gaze upon the sun and whose wing can mount above the storm. Our version [KJV] refers to the annual molting of the eagle, after which it looks fresh and young; but the original does not appear to allude to any such fact of natural history, but simply to describe the diseased one as so healed and strengthened that he became as full of energy as the bird that is strongest among the feathered race, most fearless, most majestic, and most soaring. He who sat moping with the owl in the previous Psalm [102:6] here flies on high with the eagle. The Lord works marvelous changes in us, and we learn by such experiences to bless his holy name.

Verses to meditate upon today: Psalm 103:5-12.

A THOUGHT TO PONDER

He who sat moping with the owl in the previous Psalm here flies on high with the eagle.

SEPTEMBER 6

Everlasting Love

But the mercy of the LORD is from everlasting to everlasting upon them that fear him, and his righteousness unto children's children.

PSALM 103:17

VERSE 17: Blessed "but"! How vast the contrast between the fading flower [v. 15] and the everlasting God! How wonderful that his mercy should link our frailty with his eternity and make us everlasting too! From eternity the Lord viewed his people as objects of "mercy," and as such chose them to become partakers of his grace. The doctrine of eternal election is most delightful to those who have light to see it and love wherewith to accept it. It is a theme for deepest thought and highest joy.

The "to everlasting" is equally precious. Jehovah changes not; he has "mercy" without end as well as without beginning. Never will those who "fear him" find that either their sins or their needs have exhausted the great depths of his grace. The main question is, do we "fear him"? If we are lifting up to heaven the eye of filial fear, the gaze of paternal love is never removed from us, and it never will be, world without end.

"And his righteousness unto children's children." Mercy to those with whom the Lord makes a covenant is guaranteed by "righteousness"; it is because he is just that he never revokes a promise or fails to fulfill it. Our believing sons and their seed forever will find the word of the Lord the same: To them will he display his grace and bless them even as he has blessed us. Let us sing, then, for posterity. The past commands our praise, and the future invites it. For our descendants let us sing as well as pray. If Abraham rejoiced concerning his seed, so also may the godly, for as the last Psalm told us in its concluding verse, "the children of thy servants shall continue, and their seed shall be established before thee."

Verses to meditate upon today: Psalm 103:13-22.

A THOUGHT TO PONDER

From eternity the Lord viewed his people as objects of mercy.

SEPTEMBER 7

GOD'S MESSENGERS

Who maketh his angels spirits; his ministers a flaming fire.
PSALM 104:4

VERSE 4: "Who maketh his angels spirits," or "winds," for the word means either. "Angels" are pure "spirits," though they are permitted to assume a visible form when God desires us to see them. God is a spirit, and he is waited upon by "spirits" in his royal courts. "Angels" are like winds in terms of mystery, force, and invisibility, and no doubt the winds themselves are often the "angels" or messengers of God. God who makes his "angels" to be as winds can also make winds to be his "angels," and they are constantly so in the economy of nature.

"His ministers a flaming fire." Here, too, we may choose which we will of two meanings: God's "ministers" or servants he makes to be as swift, potent, and terrible as fire, and on the other hand he makes fire, that devouring element, to be his minister flaming forth upon his errands. That the passage refers to angels is clear from Hebrews 1:7; and it was most proper to mention them here in connection with light and the heavens and immediately after the robes of the Great King. Should not the retinue of the Lord of Hosts be mentioned as well as his chariot? It would have been a flaw in the description of the universe had the angels not been alluded to, and this is the most appropriate place for their introduction.

When we think of the extraordinary powers entrusted to angelic beings, and the mysterious glory of the seraphim and the four living creatures, we are led to reflect upon the glory of the Master whom they serve, and again we cry out with the psalmist, "O LORD, my God, thou art very great" [v. 1].

VERSE 5: "Who laid the foundations of the earth." Thus the commencement of creation is described in almost the very words employed by the Lord himself in Job 38:4.

Verses to meditate upon today: Psalm 104:1-9.

A THOUGHT TO PONDER
When we think of the extraordinary powers entrusted to angelic beings, we are led to reflect upon the glory of the Master whom they serve.

SEPTEMBER 8

GOD'S BOUNTY

He causeth the grass to grow for the cattle, and herb for the service of man: that he may bring forth food out of the earth.

PSALM 104:14

VERSE 14: "He causeth the grass to grow for the cattle, and herb for the service of man." "Grass" grows as well as herbs, for "cattle" must be fed as well as men. God appoints to the lowliest creature its portion and takes care that it has it. Divine power is as truly and as worthily put forth in the feeding of beasts as in the nurturing of man; watch a blade of "grass" with a devout eye, and you may see God at work within it. The "herb" is for "man," and he must till the soil or it will not be produced; yet it is God who causes it to grow in the garden, even the same God who makes "the grass . . . grow" in the unenclosed pastures of the wilderness. Man forgets this and talks of his produce, but in truth without God he would plow and sow in vain. The Lord causes each green blade to spring and each ear to ripen; watch with opened eye and you shall see the Lord walking through the cornfields.

"That he may bring forth food out of the earth." Both grass for cattle and corn for man are "food" brought forth "out of the earth," and they are signs that it was God's design that the very dust beneath our feet, which seems better adapted to bury us than to sustain us, should actually be transformed into the staff of life. The more we think of this, the more wonderful it will appear. How great is that God who from among the sepulchres finds the support of life, and out of the ground that was cursed brings forth the blessings of corn and wine and oil.

VERSE 15: "And wine that maketh glad the heart of man." By the aid of genial showers the earth produces not merely necessities but luxuries, that which furnishes a feast as well as that which makes a meal.

Verses to meditate upon today: Psalm 104:10-18.

A THOUGHT TO PONDER
Watch with opened eye and you shall see the Lord walking through the cornfields.

SEPTEMBER 9

GOD'S MANY WORKS

*O LORD, how manifold are thy works! In wisdom hast thou
made them all: the earth is full of thy riches.*

PSALM 104:24

VERSE 24: "O LORD, how manifold are thy works." They are not only many in number but "manifold" in variety. Mineral, vegetable, animal—what a range of "works" is suggested by these three names! No two even of the same class are exactly alike, and the classes are more numerous than science can number. "Works" in the heavens above and in the earth beneath and in the waters under the earth, "works" that abide through the ages, "works" that come to perfection and pass away in a year, "works" that with all their beauty do not outlive a day, "works" within "works," and "works" within these—God is the great worker and ordainer of variety. It is ours to study his "works," for they are great. The kingdom of grace contains as "manifold" and as great "works" as that of nature, but the chosen of the Lord alone discern them.

"In wisdom hast thou made them all," or *wrought* them all. They are all his "works," wrought by his own power, and they all display his "wisdom." It was wise to make them—none could be spared. Every link is essential to the chain of nature—wild beasts as much as men, poisons as truly as herbs. They are wisely made—each one fits its place, fills it, and is happy in so doing. As a whole, the "all" of creation is a wise achievement, and however it may be checkered with mysteries and clouded with terrors, it all works together for good; as one complete harmonious piece of workmanship it answers the great Worker's end.

"The earth is full of thy riches." It is not a poor house but a palace; not a hungry ruin but a well-filled storehouse. The Creator has filled the earth with food, and not with bare necessities only, but with luxuries and treasures.

Verses to meditate upon today: Psalm 104:19-26.

A THOUGHT TO PONDER

*The kingdom of grace contains as manifold and as great works
as that of nature.*

SEPTEMBER 10

GOD'S PROVISION

*That thou givest them they gather: thou openest thine hand,
they are filled with good.*
PSALM 104:28

VERSE 28: "That thou givest them they gather." God gives it, but they must "gather" it, and they are glad that he does so, for otherwise their gathering would be in vain. We often forget that animals and birds in their free life have to work to obtain food even as we do; and yet it is true with them as with us that our heavenly Father feeds all. When we see the chickens picking up the corn that the housewife scatters from her lap, we have an apt illustration of the manner in which the Lord supplies the needs of all living things—he gives, and "they gather."

"Thou openest thine hand, they are filled with good." Here is divine liberality with its open "hand" filling needy creatures till they want no more; and here is divine omnipotence feeding a world by simply opening its "hand." What should we do if that "hand" were closed? There would be no need to strike a blow; the mere closing of it would produce death by famine. Let us praise the openhanded Lord, whose providence and grace satisfy our mouths with "good" things.

VERSE 29: "Thou hidest thy face, they are troubled." So dependent are all living things upon God's smile that a divine frown fills them with terror, as though convulsed with anguish. This is so in the natural world, and certainly not less so in the spiritual: When the Lord hides his face, saints are in terrible perplexity.

"Thou takest away their breath, they die, and return to their dust." "Breath" appears to be a trifling matter, and the air an impalpable substance of but small importance; yet once withdrawn, the body loses all vitality and crumbles back to the earth from which it was originally taken. All animals come under this law, and even the dwellers in the sea are not exempt from it. Thus dependent is all nature upon the will of the Eternal.

Verses to meditate upon today: Psalm 104:27-30.

A THOUGHT TO PONDER
Our heavenly Father feeds all.

SEPTEMBER 11

MY MEDITATION

My meditation of him shall be sweet: I will be glad in the LORD.
PSALM 104:34

VERSE 34: "My meditation of him shall be sweet." "Sweet" both to him and to me. I shall be delighted thus to survey his works and think of his person, and he will graciously accept my notes of praise. "Meditation" is the soul of religion. It is the tree of life in the midst of the garden of piety, and very refreshing is its fruit to the soul that feeds thereon. And as it is good toward man, so is it toward God. As the fat of the sacrifice was the Lord's portion, so are our best meditations due to the Most High and are most acceptable to him. We ought to therefore, both for our own good and for the Lord's honor, be much occupied with "meditation," and that "meditation" should chiefly dwell upon the Lord himself; it should be "meditation of him." For want of it much communion is lost, and much happiness is missed.

"I will be glad in the LORD." To the meditative mind every thought of God is full of joy. Each one of the divine attributes is a wellspring of delight now that in Christ Jesus we are reconciled unto God.

VERSE 35: "Let the sinners be consumed out of the earth, and let the wicked be no more." They are the only blot upon creation. In holy indignation the psalmist would fain rid the world of beings so base as not to love their gracious Creator, so blind as to rebel against their Benefactor. He does but ask for that which just men look forward to as the end of history, for the day is eminently to be desired when in all God's kingdom there shall not remain a single traitor or rebel. The Christian way of putting it will be to ask that grace may turn sinners into saints and win the wicked to the ways of truth.

Verses to meditate upon today: Psalm 104:31-35.

A THOUGHT TO PONDER

I shall be delighted to survey his works and think of his person, and he will graciously accept my notes of praise.

SEEKING GOD'S FACE

Seek the LORD, and his strength: seek his face evermore.
PSALM 105:4

VERSE 4: "Seek the LORD, and his strength." Put yourselves under his protection. Regard him not as a puny God, but look unto his omnipotence, and seek to know the power of his grace. We all need "strength"; let us look to the Strong One for it. We need infinite power to bear us safely to our eternal resting-place; let us look to the Almighty Jehovah for it.

"Seek his face evermore." Seek, seek, seek—the word is implied three times, and though the words differ in the Hebrew, the sense is the same. It must be a blessed thing to "seek," or we should not be thus stirred up to do so. To "seek his face" is to desire his presence, his smile, his favor consciously enjoyed. First we "seek" him, then his "strength," and then his "face." From the personal reverence, we pass on to the imparted power, and then to the conscious favor. This seeking must never cease; the more we know, the more we must seek to know. Finding him, we must "our minds inflame to seek him more and more." He seeks spiritual worshipers, and spiritual worshipers seek him; they are therefore sure to meet face to face ere long.

VERSE 5: "Remember his marvelous works that he hath done." Memory is never better employed than upon such topics. Alas, we are far more ready to recollect foolish and evil things than to retain in our minds the glorious deeds of Jehovah. If we would keep these in remembrance, our faith would be stronger, our gratitude warmer, our devotion more fervent, and our love more intense. Shame upon us that we should let slip what it would seem impossible to forget. We ought to need no exhortation to remember such wonders, especially as he has wrought them all on behalf of his people.

Verses to meditate upon today: Psalm 105:1-6.

A THOUGHT TO PONDER

*To "seek his face" is to desire his presence, his smile,
his favor consciously enjoyed.*

SEPTEMBER 13

GOD'S COVENANT

Which covenant he made with Abraham, and his oath unto Isaac.
PSALM 105:9

VERSE 9: "Which covenant he made with Abraham." When the victims were divided and the burning lamp passed between the pieces (Genesis 15), the Lord made, or ratified, the covenant with the patriarch. This was a solemn deed, performed not without blood and the cutting in pieces of the sacrifice; it points us to the greater covenant that in Christ Jesus is signed, sealed, and ratified, that it may stand fast forever and ever.

"And his oath unto Isaac." Isaac did not in a vision see the solemn making of the covenant, but the Lord renewed unto him his oath (Genesis 26:2-5). This was enough for him and must have established his faith in the Most High. We have the privilege of seeing in our Lord Jesus both the sacrificial seal and the eternal oath of God, by which every promise of the covenant is made yea and amen to all the chosen seed.

VERSE 10: "And confirmed the same unto Jacob for a law." Jacob in his wondrous dream (Genesis 28:10-15) received a pledge that the Lord's mode of procedure with him would be in accordance with covenant relations. Jehovah said, "I will not leave thee till I have done that which I have spoken to thee of." Thus, if we may so speak with all reverence, the covenant became a law unto the Lord himself by which he bound himself to act. Oh, matchless condescension, that the most free and sovereign Lord should put himself under covenant bonds to his chosen and make a law for himself, though he is above all law.

"And to Israel for an everlasting covenant." When God changed Jacob's name, he did not change his covenant, for it is written, "he blessed him there" (Genesis 32:29), and it was with the old blessing, according to the unchangeable word of abiding grace.

Verses to meditate upon today: Psalm 105:7-15.

A THOUGHT TO PONDER
*We have the privilege of seeing in our Lord Jesus both
the sacrificial seal and the eternal oath of God.*

SEPTEMBER 14

JOSEPH

He sent a man before them, even Joseph, who was sold for a servant.
PSALM 105:17

VERSE 17: "He sent a man before them, even Joseph." Joseph was the advance guard and pioneer for the whole clan. His brethren sold him, but God "sent" him. Where the hand of the wicked is visible, God's hand may be invisibly at work, overruling their malice. No one was more of a man or more fit to lead than Joseph. An interpreter of dreams was wanted, and his brethren had said of him, "Behold, this dreamer cometh."

"Who was sold for a servant," or rather as a slave. Joseph's journey into Egypt was not as costly as Jonah's voyage when he paid his own fare. Joseph's free passage was provided by the Midianites, who also secured his introduction to a great officer of state by handing him over as a slave. His way to a position in which he could feed his family lay through the pit, the slaver's caravan, the slave market, and the prison, and who shall deny that it was the right way, the surest way, the wisest way, and perhaps the shortest way. Yet assuredly it seemed not so.

Were we to send a man on such an errand we would furnish him with money—Joseph went as a pauper; we would clothe him with authority—Joseph went as a slave; we would leave him at full liberty—Joseph was a bondman. Yet money would have been of little use when corn was so dear, authority would have been irritating rather than influential with Pharaoh, and freedom might not have thrown Joseph into connection with Pharaoh's captain and his other servants, and so the knowledge of his skill in interpretation might not have reached the monarch's ear. God's way is the best way. Our Lord's path to his mediatorial throne ran by the cross of Calvary; our road to glory runs by the rivers of grief.

Verses to meditate upon today: Psalm 105:16-22.

A THOUGHT TO PONDER
Joseph's brethren sold him, but God "sent" him.

MOSES

He sent Moses his servant; and Aaron whom he had chosen.
PSALM 105:26

VERSE 26: "He sent Moses his servant; and Aaron whom he had chosen." When the oppression was at the worst, Moses came. For the second time we have here the expression, "he sent." He who sent Joseph sent also Moses and his eloquent brother. The Lord had the men in readiness, and all he had to do was commission them and thrust them forward. They were two, for mutual comfort and strength, even as the apostles and the seventy in our Lord's day were sent forth two by two. The men differed, and so the one became the supplement of the other, and together they were able to accomplish far more than if they had been exactly alike. The main point is that they were both "sent" and hence both clothed with divine might.

VERSE 27: "They showed his signs among them, and wonders in the land of Ham." The miracles that were wrought by Moses were the Lord's, not his own. These "signs," being the marks of Jehovah's presence, are here called "his." The plagues were words of his "signs"; that is to say, they were marvels that testified more plainly than words to the omnipotence of Jehovah, to his determination to be obeyed, to his anger at the obstinacy of Pharaoh.

Never were discourses more plain, pointed, personal, or powerful, and yet it took ten of them to accomplish the designed end. In the preaching of the Gospel there are words, signs, and wonders, and these leave men without excuse for their impenitence. To have the kingdom of God come nigh unto them, and yet to remain rebellious is the unhappy sin of obstinate spirits. Those are wonders of sin who see wonders of grace and yet are unaffected by them. Bad as he was, Pharaoh had not this guilt, for the prodigies that he beheld were marvels of judgment and not of mercy.

Verses to meditate upon today: Psalm 105:23-36.

A THOUGHT TO PONDER
When the oppression was at the worst, Moses came.

SEPTEMBER 16

ABRAHAM

For he remembered his holy promise, and Abraham his servant.
PSALM 105:42

VERSE 42: "For he remembered his holy promise, and Abraham his servant." Here is the secret reason for all this grace. The covenant and he for whose sake it was made are ever on the heart of the Most High. He remembered his people because he "remembered" his covenant. He could not violate that gracious compact, for it was sacred to him—"his holy promise." A holy God must keep his promise "holy." In our case the Lord's eye is upon his beloved Son and his engagements with him on our behalf. This is the source and well of those innumerable favors that enrich us in all our wanderings through this life's wilderness.

VERSE 43: "And he brought forth his people with joy, and his chosen with gladness." Up from the wilderness he led them, rejoicing over them himself and making them rejoice too. They were his people, his chosen, and hence in them he rejoiced, and upon them he showered his favors, that they might rejoice in him as their God and their portion.

VERSE 44: "And gave them the lands of the heathen." He drove out the Canaanites and allotted the lands to the tribes. They were called on to fight, but the Lord wrought so wonderfully that the conquest was not effected by their bow or spear—the Lord "gave" them the land.

"And they inherited the labor of the people." They dwelt in houses they had not built and gathered fruit from vines and olives they had not planted. They were not settled in a desert that needed to be reclaimed, but in a fertile land cultivated carefully by its inhabitants. Like Adam, they were placed in a garden. This entrance into the goodly land was fitly celebrated when the ark was being moved to Zion.

VERSE 45: "That they might observe his statutes, and keep his laws." This was the practical design of it all.

Verses to meditate upon today: Psalm 105:37-45.

A THOUGHT TO PONDER
Upon them he showered his favors, that they might rejoice in him as their God and their portion.

SEPTEMBER 17

FOR HE IS GOOD

Praise ye the LORD. O give thanks unto the LORD; for he is good:
for his mercy endureth for ever.
PSALM 106:1

VERSE 1: "Praise ye the LORD." "Hallelujah." This song is for the assembled people, and they are all exhorted to join in praise to Jehovah. It is not meet for a few to praise and the rest to be silent; all should join. If David were present in churches where quartets and choirs carry on all the singing, he would turn to the congregation and say, "Praise ye the LORD." Our meditation dwells upon human sin; but on all occasions and in all occupations it is seasonable and profitable to praise the Lord.

"O give thanks unto the LORD; for he is good." To us needy creatures the goodness of God is the first attribute that excites praise, and that praise takes the form of gratitude. We praise the Lord truly when we "give [him] thanks" for what we have received from his goodness. Let us never be slow to return unto the Lord our praise. To thank him is the least we can do—let us not neglect it.

"For his mercy endureth for ever." Goodness toward sinners assumes the form of "mercy"; "mercy" should therefore be a leading note in our song. Since man ceases not to be sinful, it is a great blessing that Jehovah ceases not to be merciful. From age to age the Lord deals graciously with his church, and to every individual in it he is constant and faithful in his grace, forevermore. In a short space we have here two arguments for praise—"for he is good: for his mercy endureth for ever"—and these two arguments are themselves praises. The very best language of adoration is that which adoringly in the plainest words sets forth the simple truth with regard to our great Lord. No rhetorical flourishes or poetical hyperboles are needed. The bare facts are sublime poetry, and the narration of them with reverence is the essence of adoration.

Verses to meditate upon today: Psalm 106:1-5.

A THOUGHT TO PONDER
Since man ceases not to be sinful, it is a great blessing
that Jehovah ceases not to be merciful.

SEPTEMBER 18

FORGETTING GOD'S LOVE

Our fathers understood not thy wonders in Egypt; they remembered not the multitude of thy mercies; but provoked him at the sea, even at the Red sea.

PSALM 106:7

VERSE 7: "Our fathers understood not thy wonders in Egypt." The Israelites saw the miraculous plagues and ignorantly wondered at them; their design of love, their deep moral and spiritual lessons, and their revelation of the divine power and justice they were unable to perceive. A long sojourn among idolaters had blunted the perceptions of the chosen family, and cruel slavery had ground them down into mental sluggishness. Alas, how many of God's "wonders" are not understood or are misunderstood by us. We fear the sons are no great improvement upon their fathers. We inherit from our fathers much sin and little wisdom; they could only leave us what they themselves possessed. We see from this verse that a want of understanding is no excuse for sin but is itself one count in the indictment against Israel.

"They remembered not the multitude of thy mercies." The sin of the understanding leads to the sin of the memory. What is not understood will soon be forgotten. Men feel little interest in preserving husks; if they know nothing of the inner kernel, they will take no care of the shells. It was an aggravation of Israel's sin that when God's "mercies" were so numerous, they yet were able to forget them all. Surely some of such a multitude of benefits ought to have remained engraven upon their hearts; but if grace does not give us understanding, nature will soon cast out the memory of God's great goodness.

"But provoked him at the sea, even at the Red sea." To fall out at the start was a bad sign. Those who do not begin well can hardly be expected to end well. Israel is not quite out of Egypt, and yet she begins to provoke the Lord by doubting his power to deliver and questioning his faithfulness to his promise. The sea was only called "Red," but their sins were scarlet in reality; it was known as the "sea of weeds," but far worse weeds grew in their hearts.

Verses to meditate upon today: Psalm 106:6-12.

A THOUGHT TO PONDER

If grace does not give us understanding, nature will soon cast out the memory of God's great goodness.

IDOL WORSHIP

They made a calf in Horeb, and worshipped the molten image.
PSALM 106:19

VERSE 19: "They made a calf in Horeb." In the very place where they had solemnly pledged themselves to obey the Lord, they broke the second, if not the first, of his commandments, set up the Egyptian symbol of the ox, and bowed before it. The ox image is here sarcastically called "a calf"; idols are worthy of no respect, and scorn is never more legitimately used than when it is poured upon all attempts to set forth an image of the invisible God. The Israelites were foolish indeed when they thought they saw the slightest divine glory in a bull, nay, in the mere image of a bull. To believe that the image of a bull could be the image of God is great naivete.

"And worshipped the molten image." Before it they paid divine honors and said, "These be thy gods, O Israel." This was sheer madness. After the same fashion ritualists set up their symbols and multiply them exceedingly. Spiritual worship they seem unable to apprehend; their worship is sensuous to the highest degree and appeals to eye, ear, and nose. Oh, the folly of men to block their own way to acceptable worship and to make the path of spiritual religion, which is difficult for our nature, harder still through the stumbling-blocks they cast into it. We have heard the richness of popish paraphernalia much extolled, but an idolatrous image made of gold is not one jot less abominable than it would have been had it been made of dross and dung; the beauty of art cannot conceal the deformity of sin. We are told also of the suggestiveness of their symbols, but what of that when God forbids the use of them? Vain also is it to plead that such worship is hearty. So much the worse. Heartiness in forbidden actions is only an increase of transgression.

Verses to meditate upon today: Psalm 106:13-23.

A THOUGHT TO PONDER
The beauty of art cannot conceal the deformity of sin.

SEPTEMBER 20

UNEQUALLY YOKED

*They joined themselves also unto Baal-peor, and
ate the sacrifices of the dead.*
PSALM 106:28

VERSE 28: "They joined themselves also unto Baal-peor." Ritualism led on to the adoration of false gods. If we choose a false way of worship we shall, ere long, choose to worship a false god. This abomination of the Moabites was an idol in whose worship women gave up their bodies to the most shameless lust. Think of the people of a holy God coming down to this.

"And ate the sacrifices of the dead." Israel joined in the orgies with which the Baalites celebrated their detestable worship, partaking even in their sacrifices as earnest inner-court worshipers, though the gods were but dead idols. Perhaps they assisted in necromantic rites that were intended to open a correspondence with departed spirits, thus endeavoring to break the seal of God's providence and burst into the secret chambers that God has shut up. Those who are weary of seeking the living God have often shown a hankering after dark sciences and have sought after fellowship with demons and spirits. To what strong delusions those are often given who cast off the fear of God! This remark is as much needed now as in days gone by.

VERSE 29: "Thus they provoked him to anger with their inventions: and the plague brake in upon them." Open licentiousness and avowed idolatry were too gross to be winked at. This time the offenses clamored for judgment, and the judgment came at once. Twenty-four thousand persons fell before a sudden and deadly disease that threatened to run through the whole camp. Their new sins brought on them a disease new to their tribes. When men invent sins, God will not be slow to invent punishments. Their vices were a moral pest, and they were visited with a bodily pest. Thus the Lord meets like with its like.

Verses to meditate upon today: Psalm 106:24-31.

A THOUGHT TO PONDER
When men invent sins, God will not be slow to invent punishments.

SEPTEMBER 21

THE WATERS OF STRIFE

They angered him also at the waters of strife, so that it went ill with Moses for their sakes.

PSALM 106:32

VERSE 32: "They angered him also at the waters of strife." Would they never be done? The scene changes, but the sin continues. Earlier they had mutinied about water when prayer would soon have turned the desert into a standing pool, but now they do it again despite their former experience of the divine goodness. This made the sin a double, yea a sevenfold offense and caused the anger of the Lord to be more intense.

"So that it went ill with Moses for their sakes." Moses was at last worn out and began to grow angry with them and utterly hopeless of their ever improving. Can we wonder at this, for he was a man and not God? After forty years bearing with them, the meek man's temper gave way, and he called them rebels and showed unhallowed anger; therefore he was not permitted to enter the land that he desired to inherit. Truly he had a sight of the goodly country from the top of Pisgah, but entrance was denied him, and thus it "went ill" with him. It was their sin that "angered him," but he had to bear the consequences. However clear it may be that others are more guilty than ourselves, we should always remember that this will not shelter us, for every man must bear his own burden.

VERSE 33: "Because they provoked his spirit, so that he spake unadvisedly with his lips." This seems a small sin compared with that of others, but it was the sin of Moses, the Lord's chosen servant, who had seen and known so much of the Lord, and therefore it could not be passed by. He did not speak blasphemously or falsely, but only hastily and without care. But this is a serious fault in a lawgiver, and especially in one who speaks for God. This passage is to our mind one of the most terrifying in the Bible.

Verses to meditate upon today: Psalm 106:32-39.

A THOUGHT TO PONDER

This was the sin of Moses, the Lord's chosen servant, who had seen and known so much of the Lord, and therefore it could not be passed by.

SEPTEMBER 22

GOD'S MERCY

And he remembered for them his covenant, and repented according to the multitude of his mercies.

PSALM 106:45

VERSE 45: "And he remembered for them his covenant." The "covenant" is the sure foundation of mercy, and when the whole fabric of outward grace manifested in the saints lies in ruins, this is the fundamental basis of love that is never moved, and upon it the Lord proceeds to build again a new structure of grace. "Covenant" mercy is as sure as the throne of God.

"And repented according to the multitude of his mercies." He did not carry out the destruction that he had commenced. The psalmist speaks after the manner of men to show that God changed his mind and did not leave his people to their enemies to be utterly cut off, because he saw that "his covenant" would in such a case have been broken. The Lord is so full of grace that he has not only mercy but "mercies," yea, a multitude of them, and these live in the "covenant" and treasure up good for the erring sons of men.

VERSE 46: "He made them also to be pitied of all those that carried them captives." Having the hearts of all men in his hands, he produced compassion even in the heathen. Even as he found Joseph friends in Egypt, so did he raise up sympathizers for his captive servants. In our very worst condition our God has ways and means for allaying the severity of our sorrows. He can find us helpers among those who have been our oppressors, and he will do so if we are indeed his people.

VERSE 47: This is the closing prayer, arranged by prophecy for those who would in future time be captives, and suitable for all who before David's days had been driven from home by the tyranny of the various scatterings by famine and distress that had happened in the age of the judges.

"Save us, O LORD our God." The mention of the covenant encouraged the afflicted to call on the Lord their God.

Verses to meditate upon today: Psalm 106:40-48.

A THOUGHT TO PONDER

God has ways and means for allaying the severity of our sorrows.

SEPTEMBER 23

GOD'S ENDURING LOVE

O give thanks unto the LORD, for he is good: for his mercy endureth for ever.
PSALM 107:1

VERSE 1: "O give thanks unto the LORD, for he is good." This is all we can "give" him, and the least we can "give"; therefore let us diligently render to him our thanksgiving. The psalmist is in earnest in the exhortation, hence the use of the interjection "O" to intensify his words. Let us be at all times thoroughly fervent in the praises of the Lord, both with our lips and with our lives, by thanksgiving and thanks-living. Jehovah, for that is the name here used, is not to be worshiped with groans and cries but with "thanks," "for he is good." And these "thanks" should be heartily rendered, for his is no common goodness; he is "good" by nature and essence and is proven to be "good" in all the acts of his eternity.

Compared with him there is none good, no, not one; but he is essentially, perpetually, superlatively, infinitely good. We are the perpetual partakers of his goodness and therefore ought above all his creatures to magnify his name. Our praise should be increased by the fact that the divine goodness is not a transient thing but in the attribute of "mercy" abides forever the same, "for his mercy endureth for ever." The word "endureth" has been properly supplied by the translators, and yet it somewhat restricts the sense, which will be better seen if we read it, "for his mercy forever." That "mercy" had no beginning and shall never know an end. Our sin required that goodness should display itself to us in the form of "mercy," and it has done so and will do so evermore. Let us not be slack in praising the goodness that thus adapts itself to our fallen nature.

Verse 2: "Let the redeemed of the LORD say so." Whatever others may think or say, "the redeemed" have overwhelming reasons for declaring the goodness of the Lord. Theirs is a special redemption, and for it they ought to render special praise.

Verses to meditate upon today: Psalm 107:1-9.

A THOUGHT TO PONDER
*Let us be at all times thoroughly fervent
in the praises of the Lord, by thanksgiving and thanks-living.*

SEPTEMBER 24

PRAYING IN TIMES OF TROUBLE

Then they cried unto the LORD in their trouble, and
he saved them out of their distresses.

PSALM 107:13

VERSE 13: "Then they cried unto the LORD in their trouble." There was not a prayer till then. While there was any to help below, they would not look above. No cries till their hearts were brought down and their hopes were all dead; "then" they cried, but not before. Many a man offers what he calls prayer when he is in good case and thinks well of himself, but in very deed the only real cry to God is that which is forced out of him by a sense of utter helplessness and misery. We pray best when we are fallen on our faces in painful helplessness.

"And he saved them out of their distresses." Speedily and willingly he sent relief. They waited long before they cried, but he waited not long before he "saved." They had applied everywhere else before they came to him, but when they did address themselves to him, they were welcome at once. He who "saved" men in the open wilderness can also save in the close prison; bolts and bars cannot shut him out, nor long shut in his redeemed ones.

VERSE 14: "He brought them out of darkness and the shadow of death." The Lord in providence fetches out prisoners from their cells and bids them breathe the sweet fresh air again; then he takes off their fetters and gives liberty to their aching limbs. So also he frees men from care and trouble, and especially from the misery and slavery of sin. This he does with his own hand, for in the experience of all the saints it is certified that there is no jail delivery unless by the Judge himself.

"And brake their bands in sunder." He set them free by force, so liberating them that they could not be chained again, for he had broken the manacles to pieces.

Verses to meditate upon today: Psalm 107:10-16.

A THOUGHT TO PONDER

We pray best when we are fallen on our faces in painful helplessness.

SEPTEMBER 25

GOD'S HEALING WORD

He sent his word, and healed them, and delivered them from their destructions.
PSALM 107:20

VERSE 20: "He sent his word and healed them." Man is not "healed" by medicine alone; by the "word" that proceeds out of the mouth of God man is restored from going down to the grave. A "word" will do it; a "word" has done it thousands of times.

"And delivered them from their destructions." They escape though many deadly dangers had surrounded them. The "word" of the Lord has a great delivering power; he has but to speak, and the armies of death flee in an instant. Sin-sick souls should remember the power of "his word" and be devoted to hearing it and meditating upon it.

Spiritually considered, these verses describe a sin-sick soul. Foolish yet aroused to a sense of guilt, it refuses comfort from any and every quarter, and a lethargy of despair utterly paralyzes it. Nothing remains but utter destruction in many forms; the gates of death stand open before it, and it is, in its own apprehension, hurrying in that direction. Then in the bitterness of its grief the soul is driven to cry unto the Lord, and Christ, the eternal Word, comes with healing power in the direst extremity, saving to the uttermost.

VERSE 21: "Oh that men would praise the LORD for his goodness, and for his wonderful works to the children of men." It is incredible that men can be restored from sickness and yet refuse to bless the Lord. It seems impossible that they should forget such great mercy, for we would expect to see both themselves and the friends to whom they are restored uniting in a lifelong act of thanksgiving. Yet when ten are healed it is seldom that more than one returns to give glory to God. Alas, where are the nine? When a spiritual cure is wrought by the great Physician, praise is one of the surest signs of renewed health.

Verses to meditate upon today: Psalm 107:17-22.

A THOUGHT TO PONDER
In the bitterness of its grief the soul is driven to cry unto the Lord, and Christ, the eternal Word, comes with healing power.

SEPTEMBER 26

DIVINE GUIDANCE

*Then are they glad because they be quiet; so he
bringeth them unto their desired haven.*

PSALM 107:30

VERSE 30: "Then are they glad because they be quiet." No one can appreciate this verse unless he has been in a storm at sea [see v. 29]. No music can be sweeter than the rattling of the chain as the shipmen let down the anchor; and no place seems more desirable than the little cove or the wide bay in which the ship rests in peace.

"So he bringeth them unto their desired haven." The rougher the voyage, the more the mariners long for port; and heaven becomes more and more a "desired haven" as our trials multiply. By storms and by favorable breezes, through tempest and fair weather, the great Pilot and Ruler of the sea brings mariners to port and his people to heaven. He must have the glory of the successful voyage of time, and when we are moored in the river of life above, we shall take care that his praises are not forgotten. We would long ago have been wrecked if it had not been for his preserving hand, and our only hope of outliving the storms of the future is based upon his wisdom, faithfulness, and power. Our heavenly "haven" shall ring with shouts of grateful joy once we reach its blessed shore.

VERSE 31: "Oh that men would praise the LORD for his goodness, and for his wonderful works to the children of men!" Let the sea sound forth Jehovah's praises because of his delivering grace. As the sailor touches the shore, let him lift a solemn hymn to heaven, and let others who see him rescued from the jaws of death unite in his thanksgiving.

VERSE 32: "Let them exalt him also in the congregation of the people." Thanks for such mercies should be given in public in the place where men congregate for worship.

Verses to meditate upon today: Psalm 107:23-32.

A THOUGHT TO PONDER

*We would long ago have been wrecked if it had not been for his preserving hand,
and our only hope of outliving the storms of the future is based upon
his wisdom, faithfulness, and power.*

SEPTEMBER 27

POOLS OF WATER IN THE DESERT

*He turneth the wilderness into a standing water, and
dry ground into watersprings.*
PSALM 107:35

VERSE 35: "He turneth the wilderness into a standing water." With another turn of his hand God more than restores that which in judgment he took away. He does his work of mercy on a royal scale, for a deep lake is seen where before there was only a sandy waste. It is not by natural laws, working by some innate force, that this wonder is wrought, but by himself—"he turneth."

"And dry ground into watersprings." Continuance, abundance, and perpetual freshness are all implied in "watersprings," and these are created where all was dry. This wonder of mercy is the precise reversal of the deed of judgment and is wrought by the selfsame hand. Even thus in the church, and in each individual saint, the mercy of the Lord soon works wonderful changes where restoring and renewing grace begin their kind work. Oh, that we might see this verse fulfilled in all around us, and within our own hearts. Then would these words serve us for an exclamation of grateful astonishment and a song of well-deserved praise.

VERSE 36: "And there he maketh the hungry to dwell," where none could dwell before. They will appreciate the change and value his grace. As the barrenness of the land caused their hunger, so will its fertility banish it forever, and they will settle down as a happy and thankful people to bless God for every handful of corn that the land yields to them. None are so ready to return a revenue of praise to God for great mercies as those who have known the lack of them. Hungry souls make sweet music when the Lord fills them with his gracious gifts. Are we hungry? Or are we satisfied with the husks of this poor, swinish world?

Verses to meditate upon today: Psalm 107:33-38.

A THOUGHT TO PONDER
*He does his work of mercy on a royal scale, for a deep lake is seen
where before there was only a sandy waste.*

SEPTEMBER 28

THE NEEDY LIFTED UP

*Yet setteth he the poor on high from affliction, and
maketh him families like a flock.*

PSALM 107:41

VERSES 40-41: In these two verses we see how the Lord at will turns the wheel of providence. Paying no respect to man's imaginary grandeur, he puts princes down and makes them wander in banishment just as they had made their captives wander when they drove them from land to land. At the same time, having ever a tender regard for the "poor" and needy, the Lord delivers the distressed and sets them in a position of comfort and happiness. This is to be seen upon the roll of history again and again, and in spiritual experience we mark its counterpart: The self-sufficient are made to despise themselves and search in vain for help in the wilderness of their nature, while "poor" convicted souls are added to the Lord's family and dwell in safety as the sheep of his fold.

VERSE 42: "The righteous shall see it, and rejoice." Divine providence causes joy to come to God's true people; they see the hand of the Lord in all things and delight to study the ways of his justice and of his grace.

"And all iniquity shall stop her mouth." What can "iniquity" say? God's providence is often so conclusive in its arguments of fact that there is no replying or questioning. It is not long that the impudence of ungodliness can be quiet, but when God's judgments are abroad, it is driven to hold its tongue.

VERSE 43: It is "wise" to "observe" what the Lord does, for he is wonderful in counsel and has given us eyes to see with, and it is foolish to close them when there is most to "observe." But we must "observe" wisely; otherwise we may soon confuse ourselves and others with hasty reflections upon the dealings of the Lord.

Verses to meditate upon today: Psalm 107:39-43.

A THOUGHT TO PONDER

*The Lord delivers the distressed and sets them in
a position of comfort and happiness.*

SEPTEMBER 29

HIGHER THAN THE HEAVENS

For thy mercy is great above the heavens:
and thy truth reacheth unto the clouds.

PSALM 108:4

VERSE 4: "For thy mercy is great above the heavens," and therefore there must be no limit of time, place, or people when that "mercy" is to be extolled. *As "the heavens" arch over the whole earth, and from above "mercy" pours down upon men, so shall you be praised everywhere beneath the sky.* "Mercy" is greater than the mountains, though they pierce the clouds; earth cannot hold it all. It is so vast, so boundless, so exceedingly high that "the heavens" themselves are topped thereby.

"And thy truth reacheth unto the clouds." *As far as we can see, we behold your "truth" and faithfulness, and there is much beyond that lies shrouded in cloud; but we are sure that it is all "mercy," though it be far above and out of our sight. Therefore shall the song be lifted high, and the psalm shall peal forth without restraint in far-resounding music.* Here is ample space for the loudest chorus, and a subject that deserves thunders of praise.

VERSE 5: "Be thou exalted, O God, above the heavens: and thy glory above all the earth." *Let your praise be according to the greatness of your mercy.* Ah, if we were to measure our devotion thus, with what ardor should we sing! The whole earth with its overhanging dome would seem too scant an orchestra, and all the faculties of all mankind too little for the hallelujah. Angels would be called in to aid us, and surely they would come. They will come in that day when the whole "earth" shall be filled with the praises of Jehovah. We long for the time when God shall be universally worshiped and his glory in the Gospel shall be everywhere made known. This is a truly missionary prayer. David had none of the exclusiveness of the modern Jew or the narrow-heartedness of some nominal Christians.

Verses to meditate upon today: Psalm 108:1-5.

A THOUGHT TO PONDER

"Mercy" is greater than the mountains, though they pierce the clouds.

SEPTEMBER 30

GOD HAS SPOKEN

God hath spoken in his holiness; I will rejoice, I will divide Shechem, and mete out the valley of Succoth.

PSALM 108:7

VERSE 7: "God hath spoken in his holiness." Aforetime the Lord had made large promises to David, and these his "holiness" had guaranteed. The divine attributes were pledged to give the son of Jesse great blessings; there was no fear that the covenant God would run back from his plighted word.

"I will rejoice." If God has spoken, we may well be glad. The very fact of a divine revelation is a joy. If the Lord had meant to destroy us, he would not have spoken to us as he has done. But what God has spoken is still further reason for gladness, for he has declared "the sure mercies of David" [Isaiah 55:3] and promised to establish his seed upon his throne and to subdue all his enemies. David greatly rejoiced after the Lord had spoken to him by the mouth of Nathan. He sat before the Lord in a wonder of joy. See 1 Chronicles 17:1-27, and note that in the next chapter David began to act vigorously against his enemies, even as in this Psalm he vows to do.

"I will divide Shechem." Home conquests come first. Foes must be dislodged from Israel's territory, and lands properly settled and managed.

"And mete out the valley of Succoth." On the other side of Jordan as well as on this side, the land must be put in order and secured against all wandering marauders. Some rejoicing leads to inaction, but not that which is grounded upon a lively faith in the promise of God. See how David prays, as if he had the blessing already and could share it among his men. This comes from having sung so heartily unto the Lord his helper.

Verses to meditate upon today: Psalm 108:6-13.

A THOUGHT TO PONDER

Some rejoicing leads to inaction, but not that which is grounded upon a lively faith in the promise of God.

OCTOBER 1

WORDS OF HATRED

They compassed me about also with words of hatred;
and fought against me without a cause.
PSALM 109:3

VERSE 1: "Hold not thy peace." *My enemies speak; may you be pleased to speak too. Break your solemn silence, and silence those who slander me.* This is the cry of a man whose confidence in God is deep and whose communion with him is very close and bold. Note that he only asks the Lord to speak; a word from God is all a believer needs.

"O God of my praise." *You whom my whole soul praises, be pleased to protect my honor and guard my praise.* "My heart is fixed," he said in the former Psalm; "I will sing and give praise" [108:1]. And now he appeals to the God whom he had praised. If we take care of God's honor, he will take care of ours. We may look to him as the guardian of our character if we truly seek his glory. If we live to God's praise, he will in the long run give us praise among men.

VERSE 2: "For the mouth of the wicked and the mouth of the deceitful are opened against me." "Wicked" men must needs say "wicked" things, and these we have reason to dread; but in addition they utter false and "deceitful" things, and these are worst of all. There is no knowing what may come out of mouths that are at once lewd and lying. The misery caused to a good man by slanderous reports no heart can imagine but that which is wounded by them; in all Satan's armory there are no worse weapons than deceitful tongues. To have a reputation, over which we have watched with daily care, suddenly bespattered with the foulest aspersions is painful beyond description. But when wicked and deceitful men get their mouths fully opened, we can hardly expect to escape any more than others.

"They have spoken against me with a lying tongue." Lying tongues cannot lie still.

Verses to meditate upon today: Psalm 109:1-15.

A THOUGHT TO PONDER
Lying tongues cannot lie still.

OCTOBER 2

NEVER A KIND THOUGHT

Because that he remembered not to show mercy, but persecuted the poor and needy man, that he might even slay the broken in heart.

PSALM 109:16

VERSE 16: "Because that he remembered not to show mercy." Because the wicked man did not remember "to show mercy," the Judge of all will have a strong memory of his sins. So little "mercy" had he ever shown that he had forgotten how to do it. He was without common humanity, devoid of compassion, and therefore only worthy to be dealt with after the bare rule of justice.

"But persecuted the poor and needy man." He looked on "poor" men as nuisances upon the earth; he ground their faces, oppressed them in their wages, and treated them as the mire of the streets. Should he not be punished and in his turn laid low? All who know him are indignant at his brutalities and will glory to see him overthrown.

"That he might even slay the broken in heart." He had malice in his heart toward one who was already sufficiently sorrowful, whom it was a superfluity of malignity to attack. Yet no grief excited sympathy in him; no poverty ever moved him to relent. No, he would kill the "broken in heart" and rob their orphans of their inheritance. To him groans were music, and tears were wine, and drops of blood precious rubies. Would any man spare such a monster? Will it not be serving the ends of humanity if we wish him gone to the throne of God to receive his reward? If he will turn and repent, well; but if not, such a tree ought to be felled and cast into the fire. As men kill mad dogs if they can, and justly too, so may we lawfully wish that cruel oppressors of the poor were removed from their place and office and, as an example to others, made to smart for their barbarities.

Verses to meditate upon today: Psalm 109:16-21.

A Thought to Ponder

Because the wicked man did not remember "to show mercy," the Judge of all will have a strong memory of his sins.

OCTOBER 3

A WOUNDED HEART

For I am poor and needy, and my heart is wounded within me.
PSALM 109:22

VERSE 22: "For I am poor and needy." When the psalmist does plead anything about himself, he puts forward not his riches or his merits, but his poverty and his necessities. This is gospel supplication, such as only the Spirit of God can place upon the "heart." This lowliness does not accord with the supposed vengeful spirit of the preceding verses. There must therefore be some interpretation of them that would make them suitable on the lips of a lowly-minded man of God.

"And my heart is wounded within me." The Lord always has a tender regard for the brokenhearted, and such the psalmist had become. The undeserved cruelty, the baseness, the slander of his remorseless enemies had pierced him to the soul, and this sad condition he pleads as a reason for speedy help. It is time for a friend to step in when the adversary cuts so deep. The case has become desperate without divine aid; now, therefore, is the Lord's time.

VERSE 23: "I am gone like the shadow when it declineth." *I am a mere "shadow," a "shadow" at the vanishing point, when it stretches far but is almost lost in the universal gloom of evening that settles over all and so obliterates the shadows cast by the setting sun. Lord, there is next to nothing left of me. Will you not come in before I am quite gone?*

"I am tossed up and down as the locust," which is the captive of the winds and must go up or down as the breeze carries it. The psalmist felt as powerless in his distress as a poor insect, which a child may toss up and down as he pleases. He entreats divine pity because he had been brought to this forlorn and feeble condition by the long persecution that his tender heart had endured. Slander and malice are apt to produce nervous disorders and to lead to pining diseases.

Verses to meditate upon today: Psalm 109:22-25.

A THOUGHT TO PONDER
The Lord always has a tender regard for the brokenhearted.

OCTOBER 4

LORD, HELP ME

Help me, O LORD my God: O save me according to thy mercy.
PSALM 109:26

VERSE 26: "Help me, O LORD my God." Laying hold of Jehovah by the appropriating word "my," the psalmist implores his aid both to help him to bear his heavy load and to enable him to rise superior to it. He has described his own weakness and the strength and fury of his foes, and by these two arguments he urges his appeal with double force. This is a very rich, short, and suitable prayer for believers in any situation of peril, difficulty, or sorrow.

"O save me according to thy mercy." *As your "mercy" is, so let your salvation be.* The measure is a great one, for the "mercy" of God is without bound. When man has no mercy, it is comforting to fall back upon God's "mercy." Justice to the wicked is often "mercy" to the righteous, and because God is merciful he will save his people by overthrowing their adversaries.

VERSE 27: "That they may know that this is thy hand." *My adversaries are dull; let the mercy shown to me be so conspicuous that they shall be forced to see the Lord's agency in it.* Ungodly men will not see God's "hand" in anything if they can help it, and when they see good men delivered into their power, they become more confirmed than ever in their atheism. But in good time God will arise and so effectually punish their malice and rescue the object of their spite that they will be compelled to say like the Egyptian magicians, "This is the finger of God" [Exodus 8:19].

"That thou, LORD, hast done it." There will be no mistaking the author of so thorough a vindication, so complete a turning of the tables.

VERSE 28: "Let them curse, but bless thou," or, "they will curse, and thou wilt bless." Their cursing will then be of such little consequence that it will not matter at all. One blessing from the Lord will take the poison out of ten thousand curses of men.

Verses to meditate upon today: Psalm 109:26-31.

A THOUGHT TO PONDER

One blessing from the Lord will take the poison out of ten thousand curses of men.

OCTOBER 5

THE ORDER OF MELCHIZEDEK

The LORD hath sworn, and will not repent, Thou art a priest for ever after the order of Melchizedek.

PSALM 110:4

VERSE 4: We have now reached the heart of the Psalms, which is also the very center and soul of our faith. Our Lord Jesus is a Priest-King by the ancient oath of Jehovah: He "glorified not himself to be made a high priest" [Hebrews 5:5] but was ordained thereunto from of old and was called of God a high priest "after the order of Melchizedek."

It must be a solemn and a sure matter that leads the Eternal to swear, and with him an oath fixes and settles the decree forever. But in this case, as if to make assurance a thousand times sure, it is added, "and will not repent." It is done, and done forever and ever. Jesus is sworn in to be the priest of his people, and he must abide so even to the end, because his commission is sealed by the unchanging oath of the immutable Jehovah. If his priesthood could be revoked and his authority removed, it would be the end of all hope and life for the people whom he loves. But this sure rock is the basis of our security: The oath of God establishes our glorious Lord both in his priesthood and in his throne. It is the Lord who has constituted him "a priest for ever." He has done it by oath, and that oath is without repentance, is taking effect now, and will stand throughout all ages; hence our security in him is placed beyond all question.

The declaration runs in the present tense as being the only time with the Lord and comprehending all other times. "Thou art"; i.e., "you were and are and are to come, in all ages, a priestly King." The order of Melchizedek's priesthood was the most ancient, the most free from ritual and ceremony, the most natural and simple, and at the same time the most honorable.

The last verses of this Psalm we understand to refer to the future victories of the Priest-King.

Verses to meditate upon today: Psalm 110:1-7.

A THOUGHT TO PONDER
The oath of God establishes our glorious Lord both in his priesthood and in his throne.

OCTOBER 6

GRACIOUS AND COMPASSIONATE

He hath made his wonderful works to be remembered:
the LORD is gracious and full of compassion.
PSALM 111:4

VERSE 4: "He hath made his wonderful works to be remembered." God meant them to remain in the recollection of his people, and they do so partly because they are in themselves memorable, and also because he has taken care to record them by the pen of inspiration and has written them upon the hearts of his people by his Holy Spirit. By the ordinances of the Mosaic law the coming out of Egypt, the sojourn in the wilderness, and other events of Israel's history were constantly brought before the minds of the people, and their children were by such means instructed in the wonders that God had wrought in old time.

Deeds such as God has wrought are not to be admired for an hour and then forgotten; they are meant to be perpetual signs and instructive tokens to all coming generations, and especially are they designed to confirm the faith of his people in the divine love and to make them know that "the LORD is gracious and full of compassion." They need not fear to trust his grace for the future, for they remember it in the past. Grace is as conspicuous as righteousness in the great work of God; yea, a fullness of tender love is seen in all that he has done. He treats his people with great consideration for their weakness and infirmity, having the same pity for them as a father has toward his children. Should we not praise him for this?

A silver thread of loving-kindness runs through the entire fabric of God's work of salvation and providence, and never once is it left out in the whole piece. Let the memories of his saints bear witness to this fact with grateful joy.

Verses to meditate upon today: Psalm 111:1-6.

A THOUGHT TO PONDER

God treats his people with great consideration for their weakness and infirmity,
having the same pity for them as a father has toward his children.

OCTOBER 7

FAITHFUL AND JUST

The works of his hands are verity and judgment; all his commandments are sure.
PSALM 111:7

VERSE 7: "The works of his hands are verity and judgment." Truth and justice are conspicuous in all that Jehovah does. Nothing like artifice or crooked policy can ever be seen in his proceedings; he acts faithfully and righteously toward his people, and with justice and impartiality to all mankind. This should lead us to praise him, since it is of the utmost advantage to us to live under a sovereign whose laws, decrees, acts, and deeds are the essence of truth and justice.

"All his commandments are sure." All that he has appointed or decreed shall surely stand, and his precepts that he has proclaimed shall be found worthy of our obedience, for surely they are founded in justice and are meant for our lasting good. He is no fickle despot, commanding one thing one day and another on another day; rather his commands remain absolutely unaltered, their necessity equally unquestionable, their excellence permanently proven, and their reward eternally secure. Take the word "commandments" to relate either to his decrees or his precepts, and we have in each case an important sense; but it seems more in accordance with the connection to take the first sense and consider the words to refer to the ordinances, appointments, or decrees of the great King.

VERSE 8: "They stand fast for ever and ever." That is to say, God's purposes, commands, and courses of action are eternal. The Lord is not swayed by transient motives or moved by the circumstances of the hour; immutable principles rule in the courts of Jehovah, and he pursues his eternal purposes without the shadow of turning. Our works are too often wood, hay, and stubble, but his doings are gold, silver, and precious stones. We take up a purpose for a while and then exchange it for another, but he is of one mind, and none can turn him. He acts in eternity and for eternity, and hence what he works abides forever.

Verses to meditate upon today: Psalm 111:7-10.

A THOUGHT TO PONDER
God is of one mind, and none can turn him.

OCTOBER 8

PRAISE THE LORD

Praise ye the LORD. Blessed is the man that feareth the LORD, that delighteth greatly in his commandments.

PSALM 112:1

VERSE 1: "Praise ye the LORD." This exhortation is never given too often. The Lord always deserves praise, we ought always to render it, we are frequently forgetful of it, and it is always well to be stirred up to it. This exhortation is addressed to all thoughtful persons who observe the way and manner of life of men who fear the Lord. If there be any virtue, if there be any praise, the Lord should have all the glory of it, for we are his workmanship.

"Blessed is the man that feareth the Lord." According to the last verse of Psalm 111, "the fear of the Lord is the beginning of wisdom." This man, therefore, has begun to be wise, and wisdom has brought him present happiness and has secured him eternal felicity. Jehovah is so great that he is to be feared and reverenced by all who are round about him, and he is at the same time so infinitely good that the fear is sweetened into filial love and becomes a delightful emotion, by no means engendering bondage. There is a slavish fear that is accursed; but godly fear that leads to delight in the service of God is infinitely blessed. Jehovah is to be praised both for inspiring men with godly fear and for the blessedness that they enjoy in consequence thereof.

We ought to bless God for blessing any man, and especially for setting the seal of his approbation upon the godly. His favor toward the God-fearing displays his character and encourages gracious feelings in others; therefore let him be praised.

"That delighteth greatly in his commandments." This man not only studies the divine precepts and endeavors to observe them but rejoices to do so. Holiness is his happiness, devotion is his delight, truth is his treasure. He rejoices in the precepts of godliness; yea, he delights greatly in them.

Verses to meditate upon today: Psalm 112:1-5.

A THOUGHT TO PONDER
The Lord always deserves praise.

OCTOBER 9

A STEADFAST HEART

He shall not be afraid of evil tidings: his heart
is fixed, trusting in the LORD.
PSALM 112:7

VERSE 7: "He shall not be afraid of evil tidings." He shall have no dread that "evil tidings" will come, and he shall not be alarmed when they do come. Rumors and reports he despises; prophecies of evil, vented by fanatical mouths, he ridicules; actual and verified information of loss and distress he bears with equanimity, resigning everything into the hands of God.

"His heart is fixed, trusting in the LORD." He is neither fickle nor cowardly. When he is undecided as to his course, he is still "fixed" in "heart"; he may change his plan, but not the purpose of his soul. His "heart" being "fixed" in solid reliance upon God, a change in his circumstances but slightly affects him. Faith has made him firm and steadfast, and therefore if the worst should come, he will remain quiet and patient, waiting for the salvation of God.

VERSE 8: "His heart is established." His love to God is deep and true; his confidence in God is firm and unmoved; his courage has a firm foundation and is supported by the Omnipotent One. He has become settled by experience and confirmed by years. He is not a rolling stone but a pillar in the house of the Lord.

"He shall not be afraid." He is ready to face any adversary; a holy heart produces a brave face. "Until he see his desire upon his enemies." All through the conflict, even till he seizes the victory, he is devoid of fear. When the battle wavers and the result seems doubtful, he nevertheless believes in God and is a stranger to dismay. Grace makes him desire his enemies' good; though nature leads him to wish to see justice done to his cause, he does not desire for those who injure him anything by way of private revenge.

Verses to meditate upon today: Psalm 112:6-10.

A THOUGHT TO PONDER
He is not a rolling stone but a pillar in the house of the Lord.

OCTOBER 10

FROM THE RISING OF THE SUN

From the rising of the sun unto the going down of the same
the LORD's name is to be praised.

PSALM 113:3

VERSE 3: From early morn till eve the ceaseless hymn should rise unto Jehovah's throne, and from east to west over the whole round earth pure worship should be rendered unto his glory. So ought it to be; and blessed be God, we are not without faith that so it shall be. We trust that ere the world's dread evening comes, the glorious name of the Lord will be proclaimed among all nations, and all people shall call him blessed. At the first proclamation of the Gospel the name of the Lord was glorious throughout the whole earth; shall it not be much more so ere the end? At any rate, this is the desire of our souls. Meanwhile, let us endeavor to sanctify every day with praise to God. At early dawn let us emulate the opening flowers and the singing birds:

> *Chanting every day their lauds,*
> *While the grove their song applauds;*
> *Wake for shame, my sluggish heart,*
> *Wake and gladly sing thy part.*

It is a marvel of mercy that "the sun" should rise on the rebellious sons of men and prepare for the undeserving fruitful seasons and days of pleasantness. Let us for this marvel of goodness praise the Lord of all.

Verse 4: "The LORD is high above all nations." Though the Gentiles knew him not, yet Jehovah was their ruler; their false gods were no gods, and their kings were puppets in his hands. The Lord is high above all the learning, judgment, and imagination of heathen sages and far beyond the pomp and might of the monarchs of the nations. Like the great arch of the firmament, the presence of the Lord spans all the lands where dwell the varied tribes of men, for his providence is universal. This may well excite our confidence and praise.

Verses to meditate upon today: Psalm 113:1-6.

A THOUGHT TO PONDER

The presence of the Lord spans all the lands where dwell the varied tribes of men.

HE RAISES THE POOR

*He raiseth up the poor out of the dust, and lifteth
the needy out of the dunghill.*

PSALM 113:7

VERSE 7: "He raiseth up the poor out of the dust." This is an instance of God's gracious stoop of love; he frequently lifts the lowest of mankind out of their poverty and degradation and places them in positions of power and honor. His good Spirit is continually visiting the downtrodden, giving beauty for ashes to those who are cast down and elevating the hearts of his mourners till they shout for joy. These upliftings of grace are here ascribed directly to the divine hand, and truly those who have experienced them will not doubt the fact that it is the Lord alone who brings his people up from "the dust" of sorrow and death. When no hand but his can help, he interposes, and the work is done. It is worthwhile to be cast down to be so divinely raised from "the dust."

"And lifteth the needy out of the dunghill," whereon they lay like worthless refuse, cast off and cast out, left, as they thought, to rot into destruction and to be everlastingly forgotten. How great a stoop—from the height of God's throne to a "dunghill"! How wonderful that power that occupies itself in lifting up beggars, all befouled with the filthiness in which they lay! For he lifts them "*out of* the dunghill," not disdaining to search them out from amidst the base things of the earth, that he may by this means bring to nought the great ones and pour contempt upon all human glorying. What a "dunghill" was that upon which we lay by nature! What a mass of corruption is our original estate! What a heap of loathsomeness we have accumulated by our sinful lives! What reeking abominations surround us in the society of our fellowmen! We could never have risen out of all this by our own efforts; it was a sepulchre in which we saw corruption and were as dead men.

Verses to meditate upon today: Psalm 113:7-9.

A THOUGHT TO PONDER

When no hand but his can help, he interposes, and the work is done.

OCTOBER 12

THE MOUNTAINS SKIPPED

... ye mountains, that ye skipped like rams; and ye little hills, like lambs?
PSALM 114:6

VERSE 6: What ailed you, that you were thus moved? There is but one reply: The majesty of God made you leap. A gracious mind will chide human nature for its strange insensibility when the sea and the river, the mountains and the hills are all sensitive to the presence of God. Man is endowed with reason and intelligence, and yet he sees unmoved that which the material creation beholds with fear. God has come nearer to us than ever he did to Sinai or to Jordan, for he has assumed our nature, and yet the mass of mankind are neither driven back from their sins, nor moved in the paths of obedience.

VERSE 7: "Tremble, thou earth, at the presence of the Lord, at the presence of the God of Jacob." Or, "from before the Lord, Adonai, the Master and King." Very fitly does the Psalm call upon all nature again to feel a holy awe because its Ruler is still in its midst.

Let the believer feel that God is near, and he will serve the Lord with fear and rejoice with trembling. Awe is not cast out by faith, but rather it becomes deeper and more profound. The Lord is most reverenced where he is most loved.

VERSE 8: "Which turned the rock into a standing water," causing a lake to stand at its foot, making the wilderness a pool. So abundant was the supply of "water" from "the rock" that it remained like "water" in a reservoir.

"The flint into a fountain of waters," which flowed freely in streams, following the tribes in their devious marches. Behold what God can do! It seemed impossible that the flinty "rock" should become "a fountain"; but he speaks, and it is done. Not only do mountains move, but rocks yield rivers when the God of Israel wills that it should be so.

Verses to meditate upon today: Psalm 114:1-8.

A THOUGHT TO PONDER
The majesty of God made you leap.

OCTOBER 13

OUR GOD IS IN HEAVEN

But our God is in the heavens: he hath done whatsoever he hath pleased.
PSALM 115:3

VERSE 3: "But our God is in the heavens"—where he should be, above the reach of mortal sneers, overhearing all the vain jangling of men, but looking down with silent scorn upon the makers of Babel. Supreme above all opposing powers, the Lord reigns upon a throne high and lifted up. Incomprehensible in essence, he rises above the loftiest thoughts of the wise; absolute in will and infinite in power, he is superior to the limitations that belong to earth and time. This God is "our" God, and we are not ashamed to claim him. Albeit he may not work miracles at the beck and call of every vainglorious boaster who may choose to challenge him. Once they bade his Son come down from the cross and they would believe in him; now they would have God overstep the ordinary bounds of his providence and come down from heaven to convince them. But other matters occupy his august mind besides convincing those who willfully shut their eyes to the superabundant evidences of his divine power and Godhead, which are all around them.

If our God be neither seen nor heard and is not to be worshiped under any outward symbol, yet is he nonetheless real and true, for he is where his adversaries can never be—"in the heavens," from whence he stretches forth his scepter and rules with boundless power.

"He hath done whatsoever he hath pleased." Up till this moment his decrees have been fulfilled, and his eternal purposes accomplished. He has not been asleep, nor oblivious of the affairs of men; he has worked, and he has worked effectually. None have been able to thwart, nor even so much as to hinder him. "Whatsoever he hath pleased": However distasteful to his enemies, the Lord has accomplished all his good pleasure without difficulty. Even when his adversaries raved and raged against him, they have been compelled to carry out his designs against their will.

Verses to meditate upon today: Psalm 115:1-8.

A THOUGHT TO PONDER
Supreme above all opposing powers, the Lord reigneth
upon a throne high and lifted up.

OCTOBER 14

FEAR AND TRUST

Ye that fear the LORD, trust in the LORD: he is their help and their shield.
PSALM 115:11

VERSE 11: This verse has the same tenor as the previous one—"Ye that fear the LORD, trust in the LORD." Whether belonging to Israel or the house of Aaron or not, all those who reverence Jehovah are permitted and commanded to confide in him.

"He is their help and their shield." He aids and protects all who worship him in filial fear, no matter what nation they belong to. No doubt these repeated exhortations were rendered necessary by the trying condition in which the children of Israel were found. The sneers of the adversary would assail all the people; they would most bitterly be felt by the priests and ministers, and those who were secret proselytes would groan in secret under the contempt forced upon their religion and their God. All this would be very staggering to faith, and therefore they were bidden again and again and again to trust in Jehovah.

This must have been a very pleasant song to households in Babylon or far away in Persia when they met together in the night to eat the Paschal supper in a land that knew them not, where they wept as they remembered Zion. We seem to hear them repeating the threefold phrase, "Trust in Jehovah" [verses 9-11], men and women and little children singing out their scorn of the dominant idolatry and declaring their adhesion to the one God of Israel. In the same manner, in this day of blasphemy and rebuke it becomes us all to abound in testimonies to the truth of God. The skeptic is loud in his unbelief; let us be equally open in the avowal of our faith.

VERSE 12: "The LORD hath been mindful of us," or "Jehovah has remembered us." His past mercies prove that we are on his heart; and though for the present he may afflict us, yet he does not forget us.

Verses to meditate upon today: Psalm 115:9-13.

A THOUGHT TO PONDER

The skeptic is loud in his unbelief; let us be equally open in the avowal of our faith.

OCTOBER 15

THE HIGHEST HEAVEN

*The heaven, even the heavens, are the LORD's: but the earth
hath he given to the children of men.*

PSALM 115:16

VERSE 16: "The heaven, even the heavens, are the LORD's." There he specially reigns and manifests his greatness and his glory; "but the earth hath he given to the children of men." He has left the world during the present dispensation in a great measure under the power and will of men, so that things are not here below in the same perfect order as the things that are above. It is true the Lord rules over all things by his providence; yet he permits men to break his laws and persecute his people for the time being and to set up their dumb idols in opposition to him.

The free agency that he gave to his creatures necessitated that in some degree he should restrain his power and suffer the children of men to follow their own devices; yet nevertheless, since he has not vacated "heaven," he is still master of "earth" and can at any time gather up all the reins into his own hands.

Perhaps, however, the passage is meant to have another meaning—namely, that God will increase his people because he has given "the earth" to them, and he intends that they shall fill it. Man was constituted originally God's vice-regent over the world, and though as yet we see not all things put under Jesus, we see him exalted on high, and in him "the children of men" shall receive a loftier dominion even on "earth" than as yet they have known. The meek shall inherit "the earth" and shall delight themselves in the abundance of peace, and our Lord Jesus shall reign among his people gloriously.

All this will reflect the exceeding glory of him who reveals himself personally in heaven and in the mystical body of Christ below. The earth belongs to the sons of God, and we are bound to subdue it for our Lord Jesus, for he must reign.

Verses to meditate upon today: Psalm 115:14-18.

A THOUGHT TO PONDER

*The meek shall inherit "the earth" and shall delight themselves in the abundance of
peace, and our Lord Jesus shall reign among his people gloriously.*

I Love the Lord

I love the LORD, because he hath heard my voice and my supplications.
PSALM 116:1

VERSE 1: "I love the LORD." A blessed declaration. Every believer ought to be able to declare without the slightest hesitation, "I love the LORD." This was required under the law but was never produced in the heart of man except by the grace of God and upon gospel principles. It is a great thing to say, "I love the LORD," for the sweetest of all graces and the surest of all evidences of salvation is love. It is great goodness on the part of God that he condescends to be loved by such poor creatures as we are, and it is a sure proof that he has been at work in our heart when we can say, "Thou knowest all things; thou knowest that I love thee" [John 21:17].

"Because he hath heard my voice and my supplications." The psalmist not only knows that he loves God, but he knows why he does so. When love can justify itself with a reason, it is deep, strong, and abiding. They say that love is blind; but when we love God, our affection has its eyes open and can sustain itself with the most rigid logic. We have reason, superabundant reason, for loving the Lord; and so, because in this case principle and passion, reason and emotion go together, they make up an admirable state of mind. David's reason for his love was the love of God in hearing his prayers.

The psalmist had used his "voice" in prayer, and the habit of doing so is exceedingly helpful to devotion. If we can pray aloud without being overheard, it is well to do so. Sometimes, however, when the psalmist had lifted up his "voice," his utterance had been so broken and painful that he scarcely dared to call it prayer. Words failed him, he could only produce a groaning sound, but the Lord heard his moaning "voice."

Verses to meditate upon today: Psalm 116:1-4.

A Thought to Ponder
Every believer ought to be able to declare without the slightest hesitation, "I love the LORD."

OCTOBER 17

SOUL, BE AT REST

Return unto thy rest, O my soul; for the LORD
hath dealt bountifully with thee.
PSALM 116:7

VERSE 7: "Return unto thy rest, O my soul." He calls the "rest" still his own and feels full liberty to "return" to it. What a mercy it is that even if our "soul" has left its "rest" for a while, we can tell it, "It is your rest still." The psalmist had evidently been somewhat disturbed in mind, his troubles had ruffled his spirit; but now with a sense of answered prayer upon him he quiets his "soul." He had rested before, for he knew the blessed repose of faith, and therefore he returns to the God who had been the refuge of his "soul" in former days. Even as a bird flies to its nest, so does his "soul" fly to his God. Whenever a child of God even for a moment loses his peace of mind, he should be concerned to find it again, not by seeking it in the world or in his own experience, but in the Lord alone. When the believer prays, and the Lord inclines his ear, the road to the old "rest" is before him; let him not be slow to follow it.

"For the LORD hath dealt bountifully with thee." You have served a good God and built upon a sure foundation; do not seek to find any other rest, but rather come back to him who in former days has condescended to enrich you by his love. What a text is this, and what an exposition of it is furnished by the biography of every believing man and woman! The Lord has dealt bountifully with us, for he has given us his Son, and in him he has given us all things. He hath sent us his Spirit, and by him he conveys to us all spiritual blessings. God deals with us as God; he lays his fullness open to us, and "of his fulness have all we received, and grace for grace" [John 1:16].

Verses to meditate upon today: Psalm 116:5-11.

A THOUGHT TO PONDER
Whenever a child of God loses his peace of mind, he should
be concerned to find it again, but in the Lord alone.

OCTOBER 18

THE DEATH OF GOD'S SAINTS

Precious in the sight of the LORD is the death of his saints.
PSALM 116:15

VERSE 15: "Precious in the sight of the LORD is the death of his saints." God did not suffer the psalmist to die but delivered his soul from death. This seems to indicate that this song was meant to remind Jewish families of the mercies received by anyone in the household, supposing him to have been seriously sick and to have been restored to health, for the Lord values the lives of his saints and often spares them where others perish. They shall not die prematurely; they shall be immortal till their work is done. And when their time shall come to die, then their deaths shall be "precious." The Lord watches over their dying beds, smooths their pillows, sustains their hearts, and receives their souls.

Those who are redeemed with precious blood are so dear to God that even their deaths are "precious" to him. The deathbeds of saints are very precious to the church, and she often learns much from them. They are very precious to all believers, who delight to treasure up the last words of the departed; but they are most of all "precious" to the Lord Jehovah himself, who views the triumphant deaths of his gracious ones with sacred delight. If we have walked before him in the land of the living, we need not fear to die before him when the hour of our departure is at hand.

VERSE 16: The man of God in paying his vows rededicates himself unto God. The offering that he brings is himself as he cries, *"O LORD, truly I am thy servant,"* rightfully, really, heartily, constantly. *I own that I am yours, for you have delivered and redeemed me.*

"I am thy servant, and the son of thine handmaid," a *"servant"* born in your house, born of a servant and so born a servant, and therefore doubly yours. My mother was "thine handmaid," and I, her son, confess that I am altogether yours by claims arising out of my birth.

Verses to meditate upon today: Psalm 116:12-19.

A THOUGHT TO PONDER
*The Lord watches over their dying beds, smooths their pillows,
sustains their hearts, and receives their souls.*

OCTOBER 19

THE NATIONS

O praise the LORD, all ye nations: praise him, all ye people.
PSALM 117:1

VERSE 1: "O praise the LORD, all ye nations." This is an exhortation to the Gentiles to glorify Jehovah, and a clear proof that the Old Testament spirit differed widely from that narrow and restricted national bigotry with which the Jews of our Lord's day became so inveterately diseased. The "nations" could not be expected to join in the praise of Jehovah unless they were also to be partakers of the benefits that Israel enjoyed; and hence the Psalm was an intimation to Israel that the grace and mercy of their God were not to be confined to one nation, but would in happier days be extended to all the race of man, even as Moses had prophesied when he said, "Rejoice, O ye nations, his people" (Deuteronomy 32:43), for so the Hebrew has it. The "nations" were to be his people. He would call them a people that were not a people, and a beloved that was not beloved. We know and believe that not one tribe of men shall be unrepresented in the universal song that shall ascend unto the Lord of all.

Individuals have already been gathered out of every kindred and people and tongue by the preaching of the Gospel, and these have heartily joined in magnifying the grace that sought them out and brought them to know the Savior. These are but the advance guard of a number that no man can number who will come ere long to worship the all-glorious One.

"Praise him, all ye people." Having done it once, do it again, and do it still more fervently, daily increasing in the reverence and zeal with which you extol the Most High. Praise him not only nationally by your rulers, but popularly in your masses. The multitude of the common folk shall bless the Lord. Inasmuch as the matter is spoken of twice, its certainty is confirmed, and the Gentiles must and shall extol Jehovah—all of them, without exception. Under the gospel dispensation we worship no new god; rather the God of Abraham is our God forever and ever; the God of the whole earth shall he be called.

Verses to meditate upon today: Psalm 117:1-2.

A THOUGHT TO PONDER
Not one tribe of men shall be unrepresented in the universal song that shall ascend unto the Lord of all.

OCTOBER 20

GOD'S LOVE ENDURES FOREVER

Let them now that fear the LORD say, that
his mercy endureth for ever.
PSALM 118:4

VERSE 4: If there are any throughout the world who did not belong to Israel after the flesh but nevertheless had a holy fear and lowly reverence of God, the psalmist calls upon them to unite with him in thanksgiving, and to do it especially on the occasion of his exaltation to the throne. And this is no more than they would cheerfully agree to do, since every good man in the world is benefited when a true servant of God is placed in a position of honor and influence. The prosperity of Israel through the reign of David was a blessing to all who feared Jehovah. A truly God-fearing man will have his eye much upon God's mercy, because he is deeply conscious of his need of it, and because that attribute excites in him a deep feeling of reverential awe. "There is forgiveness with thee, that thou mayest be feared" [Psalm 130:4].

In the three exhortations—to "Israel," to "the house of Aaron," and to "them . . . that fear the Lord" [verses 2-4]—there is a repetition of the exhortation to "say, that his mercy endureth for ever." We are not only to believe but to declare the goodness of God; truth is not to be hushed up but proclaimed. God would have his people act as witnesses and not stand silent in the day when his honor is impugned. Especially is it our joy to speak out to the honor and glory of God in the exaltation of his dear Son.

We should shout hosanna and sing loud hallelujahs when we behold the stone that the builders rejected lifted into its proper place [verse 22].

In each of the three exhortations notice carefully the word "now." There is no time like the present for proclaiming the praises of God.

Verses to meditate upon today: Psalm 118:1-7.

A THOUGHT TO PONDER
There is no time like the present for proclaiming the praises of God.

OCTOBER 21

TAKING REFUGE IN THE LORD

It is better to trust in the LORD than to put confidence in man.
PSALM 118:8

VERSE 8: This is "better" in all ways, for, first of all, it is wiser. God is infinitely more able to help, and more likely to help, than man, and therefore prudence suggests that we put our "confidence" in him above all others. It is also morally "better" to do so, for it is the duty of the creature to trust in the Creator. God has a claim upon his creatures' faith; he deserves to be trusted; and to place our reliance upon another rather than upon him is a direct insult to his faithfulness.

It is also "better" in the sense of safer, since we can never be sure of our ground if we rely upon mortal "man," but we are always secure in the hands of our God. It is "better" in its effect upon ourselves. To trust in man tends to make us mean, crouching, dependent; but confidence in God elevates, produces a sacred quiet of spirit, and sanctifies the soul.

It is, moreover, much better to "trust" in God as far as the result is concerned; for in many cases the human object of our trust fails from want of ability, from want of generosity, from want of affection, or from want of memory. But the Lord, so far from failing, does for us exceeding abundantly above all that we ask or even think. This verse is written out of the experience of many who have first of all had the broken reeds of the creature break under them and have afterwards joyfully found the Lord to be a solid pillar sustaining all their weight.

VERSE 9: "It is better to trust in the LORD than to put confidence in princes." Such should be the noblest of men, chivalrous in character, and true to the core, and yet as a rule princes are not one whit more reliable than the rest of mankind. Princes are but men, and the best of men are poor creatures.

Verses to meditate upon today: Psalm 118:8-12.

A THOUGHT TO PONDER
God is infinitely more able to help, and more likely to help, than man.

OCTOBER 22

THE LORD IS MY STRENGTH

The Lord is my strength and song, and is become my salvation.
PSALM 118:14

VERSE 14: "The LORD is my strength and song," my "strength" while I was in the conflict, my "song" now that it is ended; my "strength" against the strong, and my "song" over their defeat. The psalmist is far from boasting of his own valor; he ascribes his victory to its real source. He has no song concerning his own exploits, but all his praises are unto Jehovah, the Lord whose right hand and holy arm had given him the victory.

"And is become my salvation." The poet-warrior knew that he was saved, and he not only ascribed that "salvation" unto God but declared God himself to be his "salvation." This is an all-comprehending expression, signifying that from beginning to end, in the whole and in the details of it, he owed his deliverance entirely to the Lord. Thus can all the Lord's redeemed say, "Salvation is of the LORD" [Jonah 2:9]. We cannot endure any doctrine that puts the crown upon the wrong head and defrauds the glorious King of his praise. Jehovah has done it all; yea, Christ Jesus *is* all, and therefore in our praises let him alone be extolled. It is a happy circumstance for us when we can praise God as alike our "strength," "song," and "salvation"; for God sometimes gives a secret "strength" to his people, and yet they question their own salvation and cannot therefore sing of it. Many are, no doubt, truly saved, but at times they have so little strength that they are ready to faint, and therefore they cannot sing; when "strength" is imparted and "salvation" is realized, then the "song" is clear and full.

VERSE 15: "The voice of rejoicing and salvation is in the tabernacles of the righteous." They sympathized in the delight of their leader, and they abode in their tents in peace, rejoicing that one had been raised up who, in the name of the Lord, would protect them from their adversaries.

Verses to meditate upon today: Psalm 118:13-18.

A THOUGHT TO PONDER
God sometimes gives a secret "strength" to his people.

OCTOBER 23

I AM THE GATE

This gate of the LORD, into which the righteous shall enter.
PSALM 118:20

VERSE 20: The psalmist loved the house of God so much that he admired the very "gate" thereof and paused beneath its arch to express his affection for it. He loved it because it was the "gate of the LORD"; he loved it because it was the "gate" of righteousness, because so many godly people had already entered it, and because in all future ages such persons will continue to pass through its portals. If the "gate" of the Lord's house on earth is so pleasant to us, how greatly shall we rejoice when we pass that "gate" of pearl that none but the righteous shall ever approach, but through which all the just shall in due time enter to eternal felicity.

The Lord Jesus has passed that way, and he not only set the "gate" wide-open but secured an entrance for all those who are made "righteous" in his righteousness. All "the righteous" must and shall enter there, whoever may oppose them. Under another aspect our Lord is himself that "gate," and through him, as the new and living way, all "the righteous" delight to approach unto the Lord. Whenever we draw near to praise the Lord we must come by this "gate"; acceptable praise never climbs over the wall or enters by any other way, but comes to God in Christ Jesus. As it is written, "No man cometh unto the Father but by me" [John 14:6]. Blessed, forever blessed, be this wondrous "gate" of the person of our Lord.

VERSE 21: Having entered, the champion exclaims, "I will praise thee," for he vividly realizes the divine presence and addresses himself directly to Jehovah, whom his faith sensibly discerns. How well it is in all our songs of praise to let the heart have direct and distinct communion with God himself!

Verses to meditate upon today: Psalm 118:19-24.

A THOUGHT TO PONDER

Our Lord is himself that "gate," and through him, as the new and living way, all "the righteous" delight to approach unto the Lord.

OCTOBER 24

THE NAME OF THE LORD

Blessed be he that cometh in the name of the LORD:
we have blessed you out of the house of the LORD.

PSALM 118:26

VERSE 26: "Blessed is he that cometh in the name of the LORD." The champion had done everything "in the name of the LORD." In that "name" he had routed all his adversaries and had risen to the throne, and in that "name" he had now entered the temple to pay his vows. We know who it is that comes "in the name of the LORD" beyond all others. In the psalmist's days he was The Coming One, and he is still The Coming One, though he has already come. We are ready with our hosannas both for his first and second advent; our inmost souls thankfully adore and bless him and shower upon his head unspeakable joys. "Prayer also shall be made for him continually; and daily shall he be praised" [Psalm 72:15].

For his sake everybody is "blessed" to us who comes "in the name of the LORD." We welcome all such to our hearts and our homes; but chiefly, and beyond all others, we welcome *himself* when he deigns to enter in and sup with us and we with him.

Perhaps this sentence is intended to be the benediction of the priests upon the valiant servant of the Lord, and if so, it is appropriately added, "We have blessed you out of the house of the LORD." The priests, whose business it was to bless the people, in a sevenfold degree "blessed" the people's deliverer, the one chosen out of the people whom the Lord had exalted. All those whose high privilege it is to dwell in the house of the Lord forever, because they are made priests unto God in Christ Jesus, can truly say that they bless the Christ who has made them what they are and placed them where they are.

Verses to meditate upon today: Psalm 118:25-29.

A THOUGHT TO PONDER

We know who it is that comes "in the name of the LORD" beyond all others.

OCTOBER 25

WALKING IN GOD'S WAYS

They also do no iniquity: they walk in his ways.
PSALM 119:3

VERSE 3: "They also do no iniquity." Blessed indeed would those men be of whom this could be asserted without reserve and without explanation. We shall have reached the region of pure blessedness when we altogether cease from sin. Those who follow the Word of God "do no iniquity"; this rule is perfect, and if it be constantly followed, no fault will arise. Life, to the outward observer at any rate, lies much in doing, and he who in his doings never swerves from equity, both toward God and man, has hit upon the way of perfection, and we may be sure that his heart is right. See how a whole heart leads to the avoidance of evil, for the psalmist says, "They . . . that seek him with the whole heart" (verse 2) "do no iniquity."

We fear that no man can claim to be absolutely without sin, and yet we trust there are many who do not designedly, willfully, knowingly, and continuously do anything that is wicked, ungodly, or unjust. Grace keeps the life righteous regarding actions even when the Christian has to bemoan the transgressions of his heart. Judged as men should be judged by their fellows, according to such just rules as men make for men, the true people of God "do no iniquity"; they are honest, upright, and chaste, and touching justice and morality they are blameless. Therefore are they happy.

"They walk in his ways." They attend not only to the great main highway of the law, but to the smaller paths of particular precepts. As they will perpetrate no sin of commission, so do they labor to be free from every sin of omission. It is not enough to them to be blameless—they wish also to be actively righteous. A hermit may escape into solitude, that he may do no iniquity, but a saint lives in society, that he may serve his God by walking in his ways.

Verses to meditate upon today: Psalm 119:1-8.

A THOUGHT TO PONDER
A saint lives in society, that he may serve his God by walking in his ways.

OCTOBER 26

SEEKING GOD WHOLEHEARTEDLY

With my whole heart have I sought thee: O let me not wander from thy commandments.

PSALM 119:10

VERSE 10: "With my whole heart have I sought thee." His "heart" had gone after God himself; he had not only desired to obey his laws, but to commune with his person. This is a royal search and pursuit, and well may it be followed with the "whole heart." The surest mode of cleansing the way of our life is to seek after God himself and to endeavor to abide in fellowship with him. Up to the good hour in which he was speaking to his Lord, the psalmist had been an eager seeker after the Lord, and if faint, he was still pursuing. Had he not sought the Lord he would never have been so anxious to cleanse his way.

It is pleasant to see how the writer's heart turns distinctly and directly to God. He had been considering an important truth in the preceding verse, but here he so powerfully feels the presence of his God that he speaks to him and prays to him as to one who is near. A true heart cannot live long without fellowship with God.

His petition is founded on his life's purpose: He is seeking the Lord, and he prays the Lord to prevent his going astray in or from his search. It is by obedience that we follow after God—hence the prayer, "O let me not wander from thy commandments"; for if we leave the ways of God's appointment, we certainly shall not find the God who appointed them. The more a man's "whole heart" is set upon holiness, the more does he dread falling into sin. He is not so much fearful of deliberate transgression as of inadvertent wandering; he cannot endure a wandering look or a rambling thought that might stray beyond the pale of God's precepts.

Verses to meditate upon today: Psalm 119:9-16.

A THOUGHT TO PONDER

The more a man's "whole heart" is set upon holiness, the more does he dread falling into sin.

OCTOBER 27

OPEN MY EYES

Open thou mine eyes, that I may behold wondrous things out of thy law.
PSALM 119:18

VERSE 18: "Open thou mine eyes." This is a part of the bountiful dealing that he has asked for; no bounty is greater than that which benefits our person, our soul, our mind, and benefits it in so important an organ as the eye. It is far better to have the "eyes" opened than to be placed in the midst of the noblest prospects and remain blind to their beauty.

"That I may behold wondrous things out of thy law." Some men can perceive no wonders in the Gospel, but David felt sure there were glorious things in the "law." He had only half of the Bible, but he prized it more than some men prize the whole. He felt that God had laid up great bounties in his Word, and he begged for power to perceive, appreciate, and enjoy the same. We need not so much that God should give us more benefits as the ability to see what he has given.

The prayer implies a conscious darkness, a dimness of spiritual vision, a powerlessness to remove that defect, and a full assurance that God can remove it. It shows also that the writer knew that there were vast treasures in the Word that he had not yet fully seen, marvels that he had not yet beheld, mysteries that he had scarcely believed. The Scriptures teem with marvels; the Bible is a wonderland; it not only relates miracles, but it is itself a world of wonders. Yet what are these to closed eyes? And what man can open his own eyes since he is born blind? God himself must reveal revelation to each heart. Scripture needs opening, but not one half so much as our "eyes" do; the veil is not on the book, but on our hearts. What perfect precepts, what precious promises, what priceless privileges are neglected by us because we wander among them like blind men among the beauties of nature and they are to us as a landscape shrouded in darkness!

Verses to meditate upon today: Psalm 119:17-24.

A THOUGHT TO PONDER
Scripture needs opening, but not one half so much as our "eyes" do.

OCTOBER 28

WEARY WITH SORROW

My soul melteth for heaviness: strengthen thou me according unto thy word.
PSALM 119:28

VERSE 28: "My soul melteth for heaviness." The psalmist was dissolving away in tears. The solid strength of his constitution was turning to liquid as if melted by the heated furnace of his afflictions. "Heaviness" of heart is a killing thing, and when it abounds, it threatens to turn life into a long death, in which a man seems to drop away in a perpetual drip of grief. Tears are the distillation of the heart; when a man weeps, he wastes away his soul. Some of us know what great "heaviness" means, for we have been brought under its power again and again and often have felt ourselves to be poured out like water and near to being like water spilled upon the ground, never again to be gathered up. There is one good point in this downcast state, for it is better to be melted with grief than to be hardened by impenitence.

"Strengthen thou me according unto thy word." He had found out an ancient promise that the saints shall be strengthened, and here he pleads it. His hope in his state of depression lies not in himself but in his God; if he may be strengthened from on high, he will yet shake off his "heaviness" and rise to joy again. Observe how he pleads the promise of the Word and asks for nothing more than to be dealt with after the recorded manner of the Lord of mercy. Had not Hannah sung, "He shall give strength unto his king, and exalt the horn of his anointed" [1 Samuel 2:10]? God strengthens us by infusing grace through his Word; the Word that creates can certainly sustain. Grace can enable us to bear the constant fret of an abiding sorrow; it can repair the decay caused by the perpetual tear drop and give to the believer the garment of praise for the spirit of "heaviness."

Verses to meditate upon today: Psalm 119:25-32.

A THOUGHT TO PONDER
Grace can enable us to bear the constant fret of an abiding sorrow.

OCTOBER 29

GIVE ME UNDERSTANDING

*Give me understanding, and I shall keep thy law; yea,
I shall observe it with my whole heart.*

PSALM 119:34

VERSE 34: "Give me understanding, and I shall keep thy law." The psalmist not only needs teaching, but the power to learn; he asks to obtain "an understanding." How low has sin brought us, for we even lack the faculty to understand spiritual things and are quite unable to know them till we are endowed with spiritual discernment. Will God in very deed give us "understanding"? This is a miracle of grace. It will, however, never be wrought upon us till we know our need of it; and we shall not even discover that need till God gives us a measure of "understanding" to perceive it.

We are in a state of complicated ruin, from which nothing but manifold grace can deliver us. Those who feel their folly are by the example of the psalmist encouraged to pray for "understanding"; let each man by faith cry, "Give *me* understanding." Others have had it—why may it not come to *me*? It was a gift to them; will not the Lord also freely bestow it upon *me*?

We are not to seek this blessing that we may be famous for wisdom, but that we may be abundant in our love to the "law" of God. He who has "understanding" will learn, remember, treasure up, and obey the commandment of the Lord. The Gospel gives us grace to keep the "law"; the free gift leads us to holy service; there is no way of attaining holiness but by accepting the gift of God. If God gives, we keep; but we never keep the "law" in order to obtain grace. The sure result of regeneration, or the bestowal of "understanding," is a devout reverence for the "law" and a resolute keeping of it in the heart.

Verses to meditate upon today: Psalm 119:33-40.

A THOUGHT TO PONDER

*We are quite unable to know spiritual things till
we are endowed with spiritual discernment.*

OCTOBER 30

GOD'S UNFAILING LOVE

Let thy mercies come also unto me, O LORD,
even thy salvation, according to thy word.
PSALM 119:41

VERSE 41: "Let thy mercies come also unto me, O LORD." The psalmist desires mercy as well as teaching, for he was guilty as well as ignorant. He needed much mercy and varied mercy; hence the request is in the plural. He needed mercy from God rather than from man, and so he asks for "thy mercies." The way sometimes seemed blocked, and therefore he begs that the "mercies" may have their way cleared by God and may "come" to him. He who said, "Let there be light" can also say, "Let there be mercy."

It may be that under a sense of unworthiness the writer feared lest mercy should be given to others and not to himself. He therefore cries in essence, "Bless me, even me also, O my Father."

Lord, your enemies come to me to reproach me. Let your "mercies come" to defend me. Trials and troubles abound, and not a few labors and sufferings approach me. Lord, let your "mercies" in great number enter by the same gate and at the same hour; for are you not the God of my mercy?

"Even thy salvation." This is the sum and crown of all "mercies"—deliverance from all evil, both now and forever. Here is the first mention of salvation in this Psalm, and it is joined with mercy. "By grace are ye saved" [Ephesians 2:8]. Salvation is styled "thy salvation," thus ascribing it wholly to the Lord: "He that is our God is the God of salvation." What a mass of "mercies" are heaped together in the one "salvation" of our Lord Jesus! It includes the "mercies" that spare us before our conversion and lead up to it. Then comes calling mercy, regenerating mercy, converting mercy, justifying mercy, pardoning mercy. Nor can we exclude from complete "salvation" any of those many "mercies" that are needed to conduct the believer safe to glory.

Verses to meditate upon today: Psalm 119:41-48.

A THOUGHT TO PONDER
He who said, "Let there be light" can also say, "Let there be mercy."

OCTOBER 31

COMFORT IN SUFFERING

This is my comfort in my affliction: for thy word hath quickened me.
PSALM 119:50

VERSE 50: He means, "Your word is my comfort," or "the fact that your word has brought quickening to me is my comfort." Or he means that the hope that God's Word had given him was his "comfort," for God had "quickened" him thereby. Whatever may be the exact sense, it is clear that the psalmist had "affliction"—"affliction" peculiar to himself—"my affliction"; that he had comfort in it, comfort specially his own, for he styles it "my comfort"; and that he knew what the "comfort" was and where it came from, for he exclaims, "this is my comfort."

The worldly person clutches his moneybags and says, "This is my comfort"; the spendthrift points to his gaiety and shouts, "This is my comfort"; the drunkard lifts his glass and sings, "This is my comfort." But the man whose hope comes from God feels the giving power of the "word" of the Lord, and he testifies, "This is my comfort." Paul said, "I know whom I have believed" [2 Timothy 2:12]. Comfort is desirable at all times; but "comfort" in "affliction" is like a lamp in a dark place.

Some are unable to find comfort at such times; but it is not so with believers, for their Savior has said to them, "I will not leave you comfortless" [John 14:18]. Some have comfort and no affliction; others have affliction and no comfort. The saints have "comfort" in their "affliction."

The Word frequently comforts us by increasing the force of our inner spirit. "This is my comfort . . . thy word hath quickened me." To quicken the spirit is to cheer the whole man. Often the nearest way to consolation is sanctification and invigoration. If we cannot clear away the fog, we may need to rise to a higher level and so get above it.

Verses to meditate upon today: Psalm 119:49-56.

A THOUGHT TO PONDER
"Comfort" in "affliction" is like a lamp in a dark place.

NOVEMBER 1

SEEKING GOD'S FACE

*I entreated thy favor with my whole heart:
be merciful unto me according to thy word.*
PSALM 119:58

VERSE 58: "I entreated thy favor with my whole heart." A fully assured possession of God does not set aside prayer but rather urges us to it; he who knows God to be his God will seek his face, longing for his presence. Seeking God's presence is the idea conveyed by the marginal reading, "thy face," and this is true to the Hebrew. The presence of God is the highest form of his "favor," and therefore it is the most urgent desire of gracious souls; the light of his countenance gives us a foretaste of heaven. Oh, that we always enjoyed it!

The good man entreated God's smile as one who begged for his life, and the entire strength of his desire went with the entreaty. Such eager pleadings are sure of success; that which comes from our "heart" will certainly go to God's heart. The whole of God's favors are ready for those who seek them with their "whole" hearts.

"Be merciful unto me according to thy word." He has entreated "favor," and the form in which he most needs it is that of mercy, for he is more a sinner than anything else. He asks nothing beyond the promise; he only begs for such mercy as the Word reveals. And what more could he want or wish for? God has revealed such an infinity of mercy in his Word that it would be impossible to conceive of more. See how the psalmist dwells upon "favor" and mercy; he never dreams of merit. He does not demand but entreats, for he feels his own unworthiness. Note how he remains a suppliant, though he knows that he has all things in his God. God is his portion, and yet he begs for a look at God's face. The idea of any other standing before God than that of an undeserving but favored one never entered his head.

Verses to meditate upon today: Psalm 119:57-64.

A THOUGHT TO PONDER
He who knows God to be his God will seek his face, longing for his presence.

NOVEMBER 2

GOING ASTRAY

Before I was afflicted I went astray: but now have I kept thy word.
PSALM 119:67

VERSE 67: "Before I was afflicted I went astray." This was partly, perhaps, through the absence of trial. Often our trials act as a thorny hedge to keep us in the good pasture, but our prosperity is a gap through which we go astray. If any of us remember a time in which we had no trouble, we also probably recollect that then grace was low and temptation was strong.

It may be that some believer cries, "Oh, that it were with me as in those summer days before I was afflicted." Such a sigh is most unwise and arises from a carnal love of ease. The spiritual man who prizes growth in grace will bless God that those dangerous days are over, seeing that if the weather is more stormy it is also more healthy. It is well when the mind is open and candid, as in this instance. Perhaps David would never have known and confessed his own straying if he had not smarted under the rod. Let us join in his humble acknowledgments, for doubtless we have imitated him in his straying. Why is it that a little ease works in us so much disease? Can we never rest without rusting? Never be filled without waxing fat? We never rise in regard to one world without going down in regard to another! What weak creatures we are to be unable to bear a little pleasure! What base hearts are those that turn the abundance of God's goodness into an occasion for sin.

"But now have I kept thy word." Grace is in the heart that profits by its chastening. It is of no use to plow barren soil. When there is no spiritual life, affliction works no spiritual benefit; but where the heart is sound, trouble awakens conscience, wandering is confessed, and the soul becomes again obedient to the command and continues to be so. Whipping will not turn a rebel into a child; but to the true child a touch of the rod is a sure corrective.

Verses to meditate upon today: Psalm 119:65-72.

A THOUGHT TO PONDER
Often our trials act as a thorny hedge to keep us in the good pasture.

NOVEMBER 3

HOPING IN GOD'S WORD

*They that fear thee will be glad when they see me;
because I have hoped in thy word.*

PSALM 119:74

VERSE 74: When a man of God obtains grace for himself, he becomes a blessing to others, especially if that grace has made him a man of sound understanding and holy knowledge. God-fearing men are encouraged when they meet with experienced believers. A hopeful man is a Godsend when things are declining or in danger. When the hopes of one believer are fulfilled, his companions are cheered and established and led to hope also.

It is good for the eyes to see a man whose witness is that the Lord is true; it is one of the joys of saints to converse with their more advanced brethren. The fear of God is not a left-handed grace, as some have called it. It is quite consistent with gladness; for if even the sight of a comrade gladdens the God-fearing, how "glad" must they be in the presence of the Lord himself! We not only meet to share each other's burdens but to partake in each other's joys, and some men contribute largely to the stock of mutual gladness.

Hopeful men bring gladness with them. Despondent spirits spread the infection of depression, and hence few are glad to see them, while those whose hopes are grounded upon God's Word carry sunshine in their faces and are welcomed by their fellows. There are professing believers whose presence scatters sadness, and the godly quietly steal out of their company. May this never be the case with us.

VERSE 75: "I know, O LORD, that thy judgments are right." He who would learn most must be thankful for what he already knows and willing to confess it to the glory of God. The psalmist had been sorely tried, but he had continued to hope in God under his trial, and now he avows his conviction that he had been justly and wisely chastened.

Verses to meditate upon today: Psalm 119:73-80.

A THOUGHT TO PONDER

When a man of God obtains grace for himself, he becomes a blessing to others.

NOVEMBER 4

MY EYES FAIL

Mine eyes fail for thy word, saying, When wilt thou comfort me?
PSALM 119:82

VERSE 82: The psalmist's "eyes" gave out with his eagerly gazing for the kind appearance of the Lord, while his heart in weariness cried out for speedy comfort. To read the Word till the eyes can no longer see is but a small thing compared with watching for the fulfillment of the promise till the inner eyes of expectancy begin to grow dim with hope deferred. We must not set times to God, for this is to limit the Holy One of Israel; yet we may urge our suit with importunity and make fervent inquiry as to why the promise tarries.

David sought no comfort except that which comes from God. His question is, "When wilt thou comfort me?" If help does not come from heaven, it will never come at all. All the good man's hopes look that way; he has not a glance to dart in any other direction. This experience of waiting and fainting is well known by full-grown saints, and it teaches them many precious lessons that they would never learn by any other means.

Among the choice results is this one: The body rises into sympathy with the soul, both heart and flesh cry out for the living God, and even the "eyes" find a tongue, saying, "When wilt thou comfort me?" This is an intense longing that is not satisfied to express itself with the lips but speaks with the "eyes." Eyes can speak eloquently; they sometimes say more than tongues. David says in another place, "The LORD hath heard the voice of my weeping" (Psalm 6:8). Especially are our eyes eloquent when they begin to fail with weariness and woe. A humble eye lifted up to heaven in silent prayer may flash such flame as shall melt the bolts that bar the entrance of vocal prayer, and so heaven shall be taken by storm with the artillery of tears.

Verses to meditate upon today: Psalm 119:81-88.

A THOUGHT TO PONDER
This experience of waiting and fainting is well known by full-grown saints.

NOVEMBER 5

GOD'S ETERNAL WORD

For ever, O LORD, thy word is settled in heaven.
PSALM 119:89

VERSE 89: The strain here is more joyful, for experience has given the sweet singer a comfortable knowledge of the "word" of the Lord, and this makes a glad theme. After tossing about on a sea of trouble, the psalmist here leaps to shore and stands upon a rock. Jehovah's "word" is not fickle or uncertain; it is "settled," determined, fixed, sure, immovable. Man's teachings change so often that there is never time for them to be settled; but the Lord's "word" is from of old the same and will remain unchanged eternally. Some men are never happier than when they are unsettling everything and everybody; but God's mind is not with them.

The power and glory of heaven have confirmed each sentence that the mouth of the Lord has spoken and so confirmed it that to all eternity it must stand the same—"settled in heaven," where nothing can reach it. In the former section David's soul fainted, but here the good man looks out of self and perceives that the Lord faints not, neither is weary, neither is there any failure in his "word."

This verse takes the form of an ascription of praise: The faithfulness and immutability of God are fit themes for holy song, and when we are tired of gazing upon the shifting scene of this life, the thought of the immutable promise fills our mouth with singing. God's purposes, promises, and precepts are all settled in his own mind, and none of them shall be disturbed. Covenant settlements will not be removed, however unsettled the thoughts of men may become; let us therefore settle it in our minds that we will abide in the faith of our Jehovah as long as we have any being.

VERSE 90: "Thy faithfulness is unto all generations." This is an additional glory: God is not only faithful to one man throughout his lifetime, but to his children's children after him.

Verses to meditate upon today: Psalm 119:89-96.

A THOUGHT TO PONDER
The Lord's "word" is from of old the same and will remain unchanged eternally.

NOVEMBER 6

MEDITATING ON GOD'S WORD

I have more understanding than all my teachers:
for thy testimonies are my meditation.
PSALM 119:99

VERSE 99: "I have more understanding than all my teachers." That which the Lord had taught the psalmist had been useful in the camp, and now he finds it equally valuable in the schools. Our "teachers" are not always to be trusted; in fact, we may not follow any of them implicitly, for God holds us to account for our personal judgments. It behooves us then to follow closely the chart of the Word of God, that we may be able to save the vessel even when the pilot errs.

If our "teachers" are in all things sound and safe, they will be glad if we excel them, and they will ever be ready to own that the teaching of the Lord is better than any teaching they can give us. Disciples of Christ who sit at his feet are often better skilled in divine things than doctors of divinity.

"For thy testimonies are my meditation." This is the best mode of acquiring understanding. We may hear the wisest "teachers" and remain fools, but if we meditate upon the sacred Word we must become wise. There is more wisdom in the "testimonies" of the Lord than in all the teachings of men if they were all gathered into one vast library. The one book outweighs all the rest.

David does not hesitate to speak the truth in this place concerning himself, for he is quite innocent of self-consciousness. In speaking of his understanding he means to extol the law and the Lord, and not himself. There is not a grain of boasting in these bold expressions, but only a sincere childlike desire to set forth the excellence of the Lord's Word. He who knows the truths taught in the Bible will be guilty of no egotism if he believes himself to be possessed of more important truth than all the agnostic professors buried and unburied.

Verses to meditate upon today: Psalm 119:97-104.

A THOUGHT TO PONDER
Disciples of Christ who sit at his feet are often better skilled in
divine things than doctors of divinity.

NOVEMBER 7

A LAMP TO MY FEET

*Thy word is a lamp unto my feet, and
a light unto my path.*
PSALM 119:105

VERSE 105: "Thy word is a lamp unto my feet." We are walking through the city of this world, and we are often called to go out into its darkness. Let us never venture there without the light-giving Word, lest we slip with our feet. Each man should use the Word of God personally, practically, and habitually, that he may see his way and see what lies in it. When darkness settles down all around me, the Word of the Lord, like a flaming torch, reveals my way. Having no fixed lamps in eastern towns, in old times each passenger carried a lantern with him, that he might not fall into an open sewer or stumble over the heaps of refuse that defiled the road. This is a true picture of our path through this dark world. We would not know the way or how to walk in it if Scripture, like a blazing torch, did not reveal it.

One of the most practical benefits of Holy Writ is guidance in the acts of daily life. It is not sent to astound us with its brilliance but to guide us by its instruction. It is true that the head needs illumination, but even more the feet need direction, else head and feet may both fall into a ditch. Happy is the man who personally appropriates God's Word and practically uses it as his comfort and counselor, a "lamp" to his own "feet."

"And a light unto my path." It is "a lamp" by night, "a light" by day, and a delight at all times. David guided his own steps by it and also saw the difficulties of his road by its beams. He who walks in darkness is sure, sooner or later, to stumble, while he who walks by the "light" of day, or by the "lamp" of night, stumbles not but keeps his uprightness.

Verses to meditate upon today: Psalm 119:105-112.

A THOUGHT TO PONDER

*Happy is the man who personally appropriates God's Word and practically uses it
as his comfort and counselor, a "lamp" to his own feet.*

NOVEMBER 8

SUSTAINED BY GOD'S PROMISES

Uphold me according unto thy word, that I may live:
and let me not be ashamed of my hope.
PSALM 119:116

VERSE 116: "Uphold me according unto thy word, that I may live." It was so necessary that the Lord should hold up his servant that his servant could not even live without his care. Our soul would die if the Lord did not continually sustain it, and every grace that makes spiritual life to be truly life would decay if he withdrew his upholding hand. It is a sweet comfort that this great necessity of upholding is provided for in the Word, and we do not have to ask for it as for an uncovenanted mercy, but simply to plead for the fulfillment of a promise, saying, "Uphold me according unto thy word." He who has given us eternal life has in that gift secured to us all that is essential thereto, and as gracious upholding is one of the necessary things, we may be sure that we shall have it.

"And let me not be ashamed of my hope." In Psalm 119:114 he had spoken of his hope as founded on the Word, and now he begs for the fulfillment of that Word, that his "hope" might be justified in the sight of all. A man would be ashamed of his hope if it turned out that it was not based upon a sure foundation; but this will never happen in our case. We may be ashamed of our thoughts and our words and our deeds, for they spring from ourselves; but we never shall be "ashamed of [our] hope," for that springs from the Lord our God. Such is the frailty of our nature that unless we are continually upheld by grace, we would fall so foully as to be ashamed of ourselves and ashamed of all those glorious hopes that are otherwise the crown and glory of our life.

Verses to meditate upon today: Psalm 119:113-120.

A THOUGHT TO PONDER
Our soul would die if the Lord did not continually sustain it.

NOVEMBER 9

GIVE ME DISCERNMENT

I am thy servant; give me understanding, that I may know thy testimonies.
PSALM 119:125

VERSE 125: "I am thy servant." This is the third time the psalmist has repeated this title in this one section. He is evidently fond of the name and conceives it to be a very effective plea. We who rejoice that we are sons of God are no less delighted to be his servants. Did not the firstborn Son assume the servant's form and fulfill the servant's labor to the full? What higher honor can the younger brethren desire than to be made like the Heir of all things?

"Give me understanding, that I may know thy testimonies." In the previous verse he sought teaching; but here he goes much further and craves "understanding." Usually if the instructor supplies the teaching, the student finds the understanding; but in our case we are far more dependent and must beg for "understanding" as well as teaching. This the ordinary instructor cannot give, and we are thrice happy that our Divine Tutor can furnish us with it. We are to confess ourselves fools, and then our Lord will make us wise, as well as give us knowledge.

The best "understanding" is that which enables us to render perfect obedience and to exhibit intelligent faith, and it is this that David desires—"understanding, that I may know thy testimonies." Some would rather not know these things; they prefer to be at ease in the dark rather than possess the light that leads to repentance and diligence. The servant of God longs to know in an understanding manner all that the Lord reveals about man and to man; he wishes to be so instructed that he may apprehend and comprehend that which is taught him. A servant should not be ignorant concerning his master or his master's business; he should study the mind, will, purpose, and aim of him whom he serves, for only so can he complete his service.

Verses to meditate upon today: Psalm 119:121-128.

A THOUGHT TO PONDER

We are to confess ourselves fools, and then our Lord will make us wise.

NOVEMBER 10

DIRECT MY FOOTSTEPS

Order my steps in thy word: and let not any iniquity have dominion over me.
PSALM 119:133

VERSE 133: "Order my steps in thy word." This is one of the Lord's customary mercies to his chosen—"He will keep the feet of his saints" [1 Samuel 2:9]. By his grace he enables us to put our feet step by step in the very place that his Word ordains. This prayer seeks a very choice favor—namely, that every distinct act, every step, might be arranged and governed by the will of God. This does not stop short of perfect holiness; neither will the believer's desires be satisfied with anything beneath that blessed consummation.

"And let not any iniquity have dominion over me." This is the negative side of the blessing. We ask to do all that is right and to fall under the power of nothing that is wrong. God is our sovereign, and we would have every thought in subjection to his sway. Believers have no darling sins to which they would be willing to bow. They pant for perfect liberty from the power of evil, and being conscious that they cannot obtain it of themselves, they cry unto God for it.

VERSE 134: "Deliver me from the oppression of man." David had tasted all the bitterness of this great evil. It had made him an exile from his country and banished him from the sanctuary of the Lord; therefore he pleads to be saved from it. It is said that "oppression" makes a wise man mad, and no doubt it has made many a righteous man sinful. "Oppression" is in itself wicked, and it drives men to wickedness. We little know how much of our virtue is due to our liberty; if we had been in bonds under haughty tyrants we might have yielded to them, and instead of being confessors we might now have been apostates. He who taught us to pray, "Lead us not into temptation" will sanction this prayer, which is of much the same tenor, since to be oppressed is to be tempted.

Verses to meditate upon today: Psalm 119:129-136.

A THOUGHT TO PONDER
We ask to do all that is right and to fall under the power of nothing that is wrong.

NOVEMBER 11

Trustworthy Promises

Thy word is very pure: therefore thy servant loveth it.
PSALM 119:140

VERSE 140: "Thy word is very pure." It is truth distilled, holiness in its quintessence. In the Word of God there is no admixture of error or sin. It is "pure" in its sense, "pure" in its language, "pure" in its spirit, "pure" in its influence, and all this to the very highest degree—"very pure." "Therefore thy servant loveth it," which is proof that he himself was pure in heart, for only those who are pure love God's Word because of its purity. The psalmist's heart was knit to the Word because of its glorious holiness and truth. He admired it, delighted in it, sought to practice it, and longed to come under its purifying power.

VERSE 141: "I am small and despised: yet do I not forget thy precepts." That fault of forgetfulness that he condemned in others (Psalm 119:139) could not be charged upon himself. His enemies made no account of him, regarded him as a man without power or ability, and therefore looked down upon him. He appears to accept the situation and humbly take the lowest room, but he carries God's Word with him. How many a man has been driven to do some ill action in order to reply to the contempt of his enemies; to make himself conspicuous he has either spoken or acted in a manner that he could not justify.

The beauty of the psalmist's piety was that it was calm and well-balanced, and as he was not carried away by flattery, so he was not overcome by shame. If seen as "small," he the more jealously attended to the smaller duties; and if "despised," he was the more in earnest to keep the despised commandments of God.

VERSE 142: "Thy righteousness is an everlasting righteousness." Having in a previous verse ascribed righteousness to God, he now goes on to declare that God's "righteousness" is unchanging and endures from age to age.

Verses to meditate upon today: Psalm 119:137-144.

A Thought to Ponder

The psalmist's heart was knit to the Word because of its glorious holiness and truth.

NOVEMBER 12

Calling Out to God

I cried unto thee; save me, and I shall keep thy testimonies.
Psalm 119:146

Verse 146: "I cried unto thee." Again the psalmist mentions that his prayer was unto God alone. The sentence signifies that he prayed vehemently and very often, and that it had become one of the greatest facts of his life that he "cried" unto God.

"Save me." This was his prayer—very short, but very full. He needed saving, and none but the Lord could "save" him. So to him he cried, "Save me from the dangers that surround me, from the enemies that pursue me, from the temptations that beset me, from the sins that accuse me." He did not multiply words, and men never do when they are in downright earnest. He did not multiply objects, and men seldom do when they are intent upon the one thing needful. "Save me" was his one and only prayer.

"And I shall keep thy testimonies." This was his great object in desiring salvation—that he might be able to continue in a blameless life of obedience to God, that he might be able to believe the witness of God and also to become himself a witness for God. It is a great thing when men seek salvation for so high an end. He did not ask to be delivered that he might sin with impunity; his cry was to be delivered from sin itself. He had vowed to keep God's statutes or laws; here he resolves to keep the "testimonies" or doctrines, and so to be sound of head as well as clean of hand. Salvation brings all these good things in its train. David had no idea of a salvation that would allow him to live in sin or abide in error: he knew right well that there is no saving a man while he abides in disobedience and ignorance.

Verse 147: "I prevented [preceded] the dawning of the morning, and cried." He was up before the sun and began his pleadings before the dew began to leave the grass. Whatever is worth doing is worth doing speedily.

Verses to meditate upon today: Psalm 119:145-152

A Thought to Ponder

He did not ask to be delivered that he might sin with impunity;
his cry was to be delivered from sin itself.

NOVEMBER 13

RENEW MY LIFE

Great are thy tender mercies, O LORD: quicken me according to thy judgments.
PSALM 119:156

VERSE 156: This verse is exceedingly like verse 149, and yet it is not vain repetition. There is such a difference in the main idea that the one verse stands distinct from the other. In the first case he mentions his prayer but leaves the method of its accomplishment with the wisdom or judgment of God; here he pleads no prayer of his own but simply the "mercies" of the Lord and begs to be quickened by "judgments" rather than to be left to spiritual lethargy. We may take it for granted that an inspired author is never so short of thought as to be obliged to repeat himself; if we think we have the same idea twice in this Psalm we are misled by our neglect of careful study. Each verse is a distinct pearl. Each blade of grass in this field has its own drop of heavenly dew.

"Great are thy tender mercies, O LORD." Here the psalmist pleads the largeness of God's mercy, the immensity of his "tender" love; yea, he speaks of "mercies"—"mercies" many, "mercies" tender, "mercies" great. And with the glorious Jehovah he makes this a plea for his one leading prayer, the prayer for quickening. Quickening is a great and tender mercy, and it is many "mercies" in one. Shall one so truly good permit his servant to die? Will not one so "tender" breathe new life into him?

"Quicken me according to thy judgments." A measure of awakening comes with the "judgments" of God; they are startling and arousing, and hence the believer's quickening comes thereby. David would have every severe stroke sanctified to his benefit, as well as every "tender" mercy.

The first clause of this verse may run, "Many or manifold are thy compassions, O Jehovah." This he remembers in connection with the "many . . . persecutors" of whom he will speak in the next verse.

Verses to meditate upon today: Psalm 119:153-160.

A THOUGHT TO PONDER
He pleads the "mercies" of the Lord and begs to be quickened by "judgments" rather than to be left to spiritual lethargy.

NOVEMBER 14

SEVEN TIMES A DAY

*Seven times a day do I praise thee, because
of thy righteous judgments.*
PSALM 119:164

VERSE 164: The psalmist labored perfectly to praise his perfect God and therefore fulfilled the perfect number of songs. "Seven" may also indicate frequency. Frequently he lifted up his heart in thanksgiving to God for his divine teachings in the Word and for his divine actions of providence. With his voice he extolled the righteousness of the Judge of all the earth. As often as he thought of God's ways, a song leaped to his lips.

At the sight of the oppressive princes and at the hearing of the abounding falsehood around him, he felt all the more bound to adore and magnify God, who in all things is truth and righteousness. When others rob us of our praise, it should be a caution to us not to fall into the same conduct toward our God, who is so much more worthy of honor. If we praise God when we are persecuted, our music will be all the sweeter to him because of our constancy in suffering. If we keep clear of all lying, our song will be the more acceptable because it comes out of pure lips. If we never flatter men, we shall be in better condition for honoring the Lord. Do we praise God "seven times a day"? Do we praise him once in seven days?

VERSE 165: "Great peace have they which love thy law." What a charming verse is this! It dwells not with those who perfectly keep the "law" (for where can such men be found?) but with those who "love" it, those whose hearts and hands are made to square with its precepts and demands. These men are ever striving, with all their hearts, to walk in obedience to the "law"; and though they are often persecuted they have "peace"—yea, great "peace."

Verses to meditate upon today: Psalm 119:161-168.

A THOUGHT TO PONDER
Do we praise God "seven times a day"? Do we praise him once in seven days?

NOVEMBER 15

OVERFLOWING WITH PRAISE

My lips shall utter praise, when thou hast taught me thy statutes.
PSALM 119:171

VERSE 171: The psalmist will not always be pleading for himself; he will rise above all selfishness and render thanks for the benefit received. He promises to praise God when he has obtained practical instruction in the life of godliness. This is indeed something to praise God for; no blessing is more precious. The best possible praise is that which proceeds from men who honor God not only with their lips but in their lives. We learn the music of heaven in the school of holy living. He whose life honors the Lord is sure to be a man of praise.

David would not only be grateful in silence, but he would express that gratitude in appropriate terms; his "lips" would utter what his life had practiced. Eminent disciples are inclined to speak well of the master who instructed them, and this holy man, when taught the "statutes" of the Lord, promises to give all the glory to him to whom it is due.

VERSE 172: "My tongue shall speak of thy word." When he had finished singing, he began preaching. God's tender mercies are such that they may be either said or sung. When the tongue speaks of God's Word, it has a most fruitful subject; such speaking will be like a tree of life whose leaves shall be for the healing of the people. Men will gather together to listen to such talk, and they will treasure it in their hearts. The worst aspect of us is that for the most part we are full of our own words and speak but little of God's Word. Oh, that we could come to the same resolve as this godly man and say henceforth, "My tongue shall speak of thy word." Then would we break through our sinful silence; we would no more be cowardly and halfhearted but would be true witnesses for Jesus. It is not only of God's works that we are to speak, but of his Word.

Verses to meditate upon today: Psalm 119:169-176.

A THOUGHT TO PONDER

We learn the music of heaven in the school of holy living. He whose life honors the Lord is sure to be a man of praise.

NOVEMBER 16

IN MY DISTRESS

In my distress I cried unto the LORD, and he heard me.
PSALM 120:1

VERSE 1: "In my distress." Slander occasions "distress" of the most grievous kind. Those who have felt the edge of a cruel tongue know assuredly that it is sharper than the sword. Calumny rouses our indignation by a sense of injustice, and yet we find ourselves helpless to fight with the evil or to act in our own defense. We could ward off the strokes of a cutlass, but we have no shield against a liar's tongue. We do not know who was the father of the falsehood, nor where it was born, nor where it has gone, nor how to follow it, nor how to stay its withering influence. We are perplexed and know not which way to turn. Like the plague of flies in Egypt, it baffles opposition, and few can stand before it. Detraction touches us in the most tender point, cuts to the quick, and leaves a venom behind that is difficult to extract.

In all ways it is a sore "distress" to come under the power of "slander, the foulest whelp of sin" [Robert Pollok, *The Course of Time*, book iv, line 725]. Even in such distress we need not hesitate to cry unto the Lord. Silence to man and prayer to God are the best cures for the evil of slander.

"I cried unto the LORD" (or Jehovah). This was the wisest course that the psalmist could follow. It is of little use to appeal to our fellows on the matter of slander, for the more we stir it, the more it spreads. And it is of no avail to appeal to the honor of the slanderers, for they have none, and the most piteous demands for justice will only increase their malevolence and encourage them to issue fresh insults. One might as well plead with panthers and wolves as with black-hearted slanderers. However, when cries to man would be our weakness, cries to God will be our strength. To whom should children cry but to their father?

Verses to meditate upon today: Psalm 120:1-7.

A THOUGHT TO PONDER

Silence to man and prayer to God are the best cures for the evil of slander.

NOVEMBER 17

HELP FROM THE HILLS

I will lift up mine eyes unto the hills, from whence cometh my help.
PSALM 121:1

VERSE 1: It is wise to look to the strong for strength. Dwellers in valleys are subject to many disorders for which there is no cure but a sojourn in the uplands, and it is well when they shake off their lethargy and resolve upon a climb. Down below they are the prey of marauders, and to escape from them the surest method is to fly to the strongholds upon the mountains. Often before the actual ascent the sick and plundered people looked toward "the hills" and longed to be upon their summits.

The holy man who here sings a choice sonnet looked away from the slanderers by whom he was tormented to the Lord, who saw all from his high places and was ready to pour down succor for his injured servant. "Help" comes to saints only from above; they look elsewhere in vain. Let us lift up our eyes with hope, expectancy, desire, and confidence.

Satan will endeavor to keep our eyes upon our sorrows, that we may be disquieted and discouraged. May we firmly resolve that we will look out and look up, for they who lift up their eyes to the eternal "hills" shall soon have their hearts lifted up also. The purposes of God, the divine attributes, the immutable promises, the covenant, ordered in all things and sure, the providence, predestination, and proved faithfulness of the Lord—these are "the hills" to which we must lift up our "eyes," for from these our "help" must come. It must be our resolve that we will not be bandaged and blindfolded but will lift up our "eyes."

VERSE 2: "My help cometh from the LORD, which made heaven and earth." What we need is "help"—powerful, efficient, constant "help." We need a very present "help" in trouble. What a mercy that we have it in our God. Our hope is in Jehovah, for our "help" comes from him.

Verses to meditate upon today: Psalm 121:1-8.

A THOUGHT TO PONDER

"Help" comes to saints only from above; they look elsewhere in vain.

NOVEMBER 18

WITHIN THE GATES

Our feet shall stand within thy gates, O Jerusalem.
PSALM 122:2

VERSE 2: The words imply present and joyous standing within the walls of the city of peace; or perhaps the pilgrims felt so sure of getting there that they anticipated the joy and spoke as if they were already there, though they were as yet only on the road. If we are within the church, we may well triumph in that fact. While "our feet" are "stand[ing]" in "Jerusalem," our lips may well be singing.

Outside the "gates" all is danger, and one day all will be destruction; but within the "gates" all is safety, seclusion, serenity, salvation, and glory. The "gates" are opened that we may pass in, and they are only shut so our enemies may not follow us. The Lord loves the "gates" of Zion, and so do we when we are enclosed within them. What a choice favor it is to be a citizen of the New Jerusalem! Why are *we* so greatly favored? Many feet are running the downward road or kicking against the pricks or held by snares or sliding to an awful fall; but "our feet," through divine grace, are "stand[ing]"—an honorable posture—"within thy gates, O Jerusalem"—an honorable position—and there shall they "stand" forever—an honorable future.

VERSE 3: "Jerusalem is builded as a city that is compact together." David saw in vision the "city" built, no more a waste or a mere collection of tents or a city upon paper, commenced but not completed. God's mercy to the nation of Israel allowed peace and plenty, sufficient for the uprise and perfecting of its capital. That "city" flourished in happy times, even as the church is only built up when all the people of God are prospering. Thanks be to God, "Jerusalem is builded." The Lord by his glorious appearing has built up Zion.

Verses to meditate upon today: Psalm 122:1-9.

A THOUGHT TO PONDER
What a choice favor it is to be a citizen of the New Jerusalem!

I Lift Up My Eyes

Unto thee lift I up mine eyes, O thou that dwellest in the heavens.
PSALM 123:1

VERSE 1: "Unto thee lift I up mine eyes." It is good to have someone to look up to. The psalmist looked so high that he could look no higher. Not to the hills, but to the God of the hills. He believed in a personal God and knew nothing of the modern pantheism that is nothing more than atheism wearing a fig leaf.

The uplifted "eyes" naturally and instinctively represent the state of heart that fixes desire, hope, confidence, and expectation upon the Lord. God is everywhere, and yet it is most natural to think of him as being above us, in that glory-land that lies beyond the skies.

The phrase "O thou that dwellest in the heavens" sets forth the unsophisticated idea of a child of God in distress: "God is in heaven, God resides in one place, and God is evermore the same; therefore I will look to him." When we cannot look to any helper on a level with us, it is greatly wise to look above us; in fact, if we have a thousand helpers, our eyes should still be toward the Lord. The higher the Lord is, the better for our faith since that height represents power, glory, and excellence, and these will be all engaged on our behalf.

We ought to be thankful for spiritual "eyes." The blind men of this world, however much human learning they may possess, cannot behold our God, for in heavenly matters they are devoid of sight. Yet we must use our "eyes" with resolution, for they will not go upward to the Lord of themselves but incline to look downward or inward or anywhere but to the Lord. Let it be our firm resolve that the heavenward glance shall not be lacking. If we cannot see God, at least we will look toward him.

Verses to meditate upon today: Psalm 123:1-4.

A Thought to Ponder

If we have a thousand helpers, our eyes should still be toward the Lord.

NOVEMBER 20

OVERWHELMED

Then the waters had overwhelmed us, the stream had gone over our soul.
PSALM 124:4

VERSE 4: "Then the waters had overwhelmed us." Rising irresistibly, like the Nile, the flood of opposition would soon have rolled over our heads. Across the mighty waste of waters we cast an anxious eye but looked in vain for escape. The motto of a certain royal house is, "Tossed about but not submerged." We would have needed an epitaph rather than an epigram, for we would have been driven by the torrent and would have sunk, never to rise again.

"The stream had gone over our soul." The rushing torrent would have drowned "our soul," our hope, our life. The figures seem to be the steadily rising flood and the hurriedly rushing "stream." Who can stand against two such mighty powers? Everything is destroyed by these unconquerable forces, either by being submerged or swept away. When the world's enmity obtains an outlet, it both rises and rushes; it rages and rolls along and spares nothing. In the great floods of persecution and affliction, who can help but Jehovah? But for him where would we be at this very hour? We have experienced seasons in which the combined forces of earth and hell would have made an end of us had not omnipotent grace interfered for our rescue.

VERSE 5: "Then the proud waters had gone over our soul." The figure here represents the waves as "proud," and so they seem to be when they overleap the bulwarks of a frail bark and threaten every moment to sink her. The opposition of men is usually embittered by a haughty scorn that derides all our godly efforts as mere fanaticism or obstinate ignorance. In all the persecutions of the church a cruel contempt has largely mingled with the oppression, and this is overpowering to the "soul." Had not God been with us, our disdainful enemies would have made nothing of us and dashed over us as a mountain torrent sweeps down the side of a hill, driving everything before it.

Verses to meditate upon today: Psalm 124:1-8.

A THOUGHT TO PONDER
"Tossed about but not submerged."

Mountains Around Jerusalem

As the mountains are round about Jerusalem, so the LORD is round about his people from henceforth even for ever.
PSALM 125:2

VERSE 2: The hill of Zion is a type of the believer's constancy, and the surrounding "mountains" are made emblems of the all-surrounding presence of the Lord. The "mountains" around the holy city, though they do not make a circular wall, are nevertheless set like sentinels to guard her gates. God does not enclose his people within ramparts and bulwarks, making their city to be a prison; but he so orders the arrangements of his providence that his saints are as safe as if they dwelt behind the strongest fortifications. What a double security these two verses [1-2] set before us! First we are established and then entrenched; settled and then sentineled; made like a mount and then protected as if by "mountains." This is no matter of poetry—it is so in fact; and it is no matter of temporary privilege, but it shall be so "for ever."

Date when we please, "from henceforth" Jehovah encircles his people; the protection extends "even for ever." Note that it is not said that Jehovah's power or wisdom defends believers, but he himself is "round about" them; they have his Godhead for their guard. We are here taught that the Lord's people are those who trust him, for they are thus described in the first verse: The line of faith is the line of grace; those who trust in the Lord are chosen of the Lord.

These two verses together prove the eternal safety of the saints: They must abide where God has placed them, and God must forever protect them from all evil. It would be difficult to imagine greater safety than is here set forth.

VERSE 3: "For the rod of the wicked shall not rest upon the lot of the righteous." The people of God are not to expect immunity from trial because the Lord surrounds them, for they may feel the power and persecution of the ungodly. Trouble may come, but it cannot "rest" there. The Lord shall deliver his own (1 Corinthians 10:13).

Verses to meditate upon today: Psalm 125:1-5.

A Thought to Ponder

God so orders the arrangements of his providence that his saints are as safe as if they dwelt behind the strongest fortifications.

NOVEMBER 22

LAUGHTER

Then was our mouth filled with laughter, and our tongue with singing: then said they among the heathen, The LORD hath done great things for them.
PSALM 126:2

VERSE 2: "Then was our mouth filled with laughter, and our tongue with singing." So full were they of joy that they could not contain themselves. They had to express their joy, and yet they could not find expression for it. Irrepressible mirth could do no other than laugh, for speech was far too dull a thing for it. The mercy was so unexpected, so amazing, so singular that they could not do less than laugh; and they laughed much, so that their mouths were full of it, and their hearts too. When at last the "tongue" could move articulately, it could not be content simply to talk, but it must sing, and sing heartily too. Doubtless the former pain added to the zest of the pleasure; the captivity threw a brighter color into the emancipation.

The people remembered this joy flood for years after, and here is the record of it turned into a song. Note the "when" [verse 1] and the "then" [verse 2]. God's when is our then. At the moment when he turns our captivity, the heart turns from its sorrow; when he fills us with grace, we are filled with gratitude. We were "like them that dream" [verse 1], but we both laughed and sang in our sleep. We are wide awake now, and though we can scarcely realize the blessing, yet we rejoice in it exceedingly.

"Then said they among the heathen, The LORD hath done great things for them." "The heathen" heard the songs of Israel, and the better sort among them soon guessed the cause of their joy. Jehovah was known to be their God, and to him the other nations ascribed the emancipation of his people, reckoning it to be no small thing that the Lord had thus done, for those who carried away the nations had never in any other instance restored a people to their ancient dwelling-place.

Verses to meditate upon today: Psalm 126:1-6.

A THOUGHT TO PONDER

The mercy was so unexpected, so amazing, so singular that they could not do less than laugh.

NOVEMBER 23

HOUSE-BUILDING

Except the LORD build the house, they labor in vain that build it: except the LORD keep the city, the watchman waketh but in vain.

PSALM 127:1

VERSE 1: The word "vain" is the keynote here, and we hear it ring out clearly three times [in verses 1-2]. Men desiring to "build" know that they must "labor," and accordingly they put forth all their skill and strength; but let them remember that if Jehovah is not with them, their designs will prove failures.

So was it with the Babel builders; they said, "Go to, let us build us a city, and a tower," and the Lord returned their words, saying, "Go to, let us go down, and there confound their language" [Genesis 11:4, 7]. "In vain" they toiled, for the Lord's face was against them.

When Solomon resolved to build a "house" for the Lord, matters were very different, for all things united under God to aid him in his great undertaking. Even the heathen were at his beck and call, that he might erect a temple for the Lord his God. In the same manner God blessed him in the erection of his own palace, for this verse evidently refers to all sorts of house-building. Without God we are nothing.

Great houses have been erected by ambitious men; but like the baseless fabric of a vision, they have passed away, and scarcely a stone remains to tell where once they stood. The wealthy builder of such a palace, could he revisit it, would be perplexed to find a relic of his former pride; he labored "in vain," for the place of his travail knows not a trace of his handiwork. The like may be said of the builders of castles and abbeys. When the mode of life indicated by these piles ceased to be endurable by the Lord, the massive walls of ancient architects crumbled into ruins, and their toil melted like the froth of vanity. Not only do we now spend our strength for naught without Jehovah, but all who have ever labored apart from him come under the same sentence.

Verses to meditate upon today: Psalm 127:1-5.

A THOUGHT TO PONDER

Without God we are nothing.

THE FEAR OF GOD

Blessed is every one that feareth the LORD; that walketh in his ways.
PSALM 128:1

VERSE 1: "Blessed is every one that feareth the LORD." The last Psalm ended with a blessing, for the word there translated "happy" is the same as that which is here rendered "blessed"; thus the two songs are joined by a catchword. There is also in them a close community of subject. The fear of God is the cornerstone of all blessedness. We must reverence the ever-blessed God before we can be "blessed" ourselves.

Some think that this life is an evil, an infliction, a thing upon which rests a curse, but it is not so; the God-fearing man has a present blessing resting upon him. It is not true that it would be to him "something better not to be." He is happy now, for he is the child of the happy God, the ever-living Jehovah; and he is even here a joint heir with Jesus Christ, whose heritage is not misery but joy.

This is true of every one of the God-fearing of all conditions, in all ages; each one and every one is "blessed." Their blessedness may not always be seen by carnal reason, but it is always a fact, for God himself declares that it is so; and we know that those whom he blesses are "blessed" indeed.

Let us cultivate that holy, filial fear of Jehovah that is the essence of all true religion—the fear of reverence, of dread to offend, of anxiety to please, and of entire submission and obedience. This fear of the Lord is the fit fountain of holy living; we look in vain for holiness apart from it, for none but those who fear the Lord will ever "walk in his ways."

"That walketh in his ways." The religious life, which God declares to be "blessed," must be practical as well as emotional. It is idle to talk of fearing the Lord if we act like those who have no care whether there is a God or not.

Verses to meditate upon today: Psalm 128:1-6.

A THOUGHT TO PONDER
The fear of God is the cornerstone of all blessedness.

NOVEMBER 25

AFFLICTED

Many a time have they afflicted me from my youth, may Israel now say . . .
PSALM 129:1

VERSE 1: In her present hour of trial Israel may remember her former afflictions and speak of them for her comfort, drawing from them the assurance that he who has been with her for so long will not desert her in the end. The song begins abruptly. The poet has been musing, and the fire burns, and therefore he speaks; he cannot help it—he feels that he must speak and therefore "may . . . now say" what he has to say.

The trials of the church have been repeated again and again, times beyond all count. The same afflictions are fulfilled in us as in our fathers. Jacob of old found his days full of trouble, each Israelite was often harassed, and Israel as a whole has proceeded from tribulation to tribulation.

"Many a time," Israel says, because she could not say how many times. She speaks of her assailants as "they" because it would be impossible to write or even to know all their names. They had straitened, harassed, and fought against her from the earliest days of her history—"from my youth"; and they had continued their assaults without ceasing. Persecution is the heirloom of the church and the ensign of the elect.

Israel among the nations was peculiar or distinctive, and this peculiarity brought against her many restless foes who could never be satisfied unless they were warring against the people of God. In Canaan, at the first, the chosen household was often severely tried; in Egypt it was heavily oppressed; in the wilderness it was fiercely assailed; and in the Promised Land it was often surrounded by deadly enemies. Amazingly the "afflicted" nation survived to say, "Many a time have they afflicted me."

The affliction began early—"from my youth," and it continued late. The earliest years of Israel and of the church of God were spent in trial. Babes in grace are cradled in opposition.

Verses to meditate upon today: Psalm 129:1-8.

A THOUGHT TO PONDER
Persecution is the heirloom of the church and the ensign of the elect.

OUT OF THE DEPTHS

Out of the depths have I cried unto thee, O Lord.
PSALM 130:1

VERSE 1: This is the psalmist's statement and plea: He had never ceased to pray even when brought into the lowest state. "The depths" usually silence all they engulf, but they could not close the mouth of this servant of the Lord; on the contrary, it was in the abyss itself that he "cried" unto Jehovah.

Beneath the floods prayer lived and struggled; yea, above the roar of the billows rose the cry of faith. It little matters where we are if we can pray, but prayer is never more real and acceptable than when it rises out of the worst places. Deep places beget deep devotion. Depths of earnestness are stirred by depths of tribulation. Diamonds sparkle most amid the darkness. Prayer *de profundis* [out of the depths] gives to God *gloria in excelsis* [glory in the highest].

The more distressed we are, the more excellent is the faith that trusts bravely in the Lord and therefore appeals to him and to him alone. Good men may be in "the depths" of temporal and spiritual trouble; but good men in such cases look only to their God, and they stir themselves up to be more instant and earnest in prayer than at other times. The depth of their distress moves "the depths" of their being, and from the bottom of their hearts an exceeding great and bitter cry rises unto the one living and true God. David had often been in the deep, and just as often had he pleaded with Jehovah, his God, in whose hand are all deep places. He prayed and remembered that he had prayed, and he pleaded that he had prayed, hoping ere long to receive an answer. It would be dreadful to look back on trouble and feel forced to admit that we did not cry unto the Lord in it; but it is most comforting to know that whatever we did not do or could not do, yet we did pray, even in our worst times.

Verses to meditate upon today: Psalm 130:1-8.

A THOUGHT TO PONDER
Prayer de profundis gives to God gloria in excelsis.

NOVEMBER 27

PRIDE

LORD, my heart is not haughty, nor mine eyes lofty: neither do I exercise myself in great matters, or in things too high for me.

PSALM 131:1

VERSE 1: "LORD, my heart is not haughty." This Psalm is a solitary conversation with the Lord, not a discourse before men. We have a sufficient audience when we speak with the Lord, and we may say to him many things that are not proper for the ears of men. The holy man makes his appeal to Jehovah, who alone knows the "heart." A man should be slow to do this upon just any matter, for the Lord is not to be trifled with; and when anyone ventures on such an appeal he should be sure of his case.

The psalmist begins with his "heart," for that is the center of our nature, and if pride be there it defiles everything, just as mire in the spring causes mud in all the streams. It is a grand thing for a man to know his own heart so as to be able to speak before the Lord about it. It is beyond all things deceitful and desperately wicked. Who can know it unless taught by the Spirit of God?

It is a still greater thing if, upon searching himself thoroughly, a man can solemnly protest unto the Omniscient One that his "heart is not haughty"—that is to say, neither proud in his opinion of himself, contemptuous to others, or self-righteous before the Lord; not boastful of the past, proud of the present, or ambitious for the future.

"Nor mine eyes lofty." What the "heart" desires, the "eyes" look for. Where the desires run, the glances usually follow. This holy man felt that he did not seek after elevated places where he might gratify his self-esteem, neither did he look down upon others as being his inferiors. A proud look the Lord hates, and in this all men are agreed with him; yea, even the proud themselves hate haughtiness in the gestures of others.

Verses to meditate upon today: Psalm 131:1-3.

A THOUGHT TO PONDER

It is a grand thing for a man to know his own heart so as to be able to speak before the Lord about it.

NOVEMBER 28

DAVID'S VOW

. . . how he sware unto the LORD, and vowed unto the mighty God of Jacob.
PSALM 132:2

VERSE 2: Moved by intense devotion, David expressed his resolve in the form of a solemn vow, which was sealed with an oath. The fewer of such vows the better under a dispensation whose great Representative has said, "Swear not at all" [Matthew 5:34]. Perhaps even in this case it would have been wiser to have left the pious resolve in the hands of God in the form of a prayer, for the vow [verses 3-5] was not actually fulfilled as intended, since the Lord forbade David to build him a temple. We had better not swear to do anything before we know the Lord's mind about it, and then we shall not need to swear.

The instance of David's vow shows that vows are allowable, but it does not prove that they are desirable. Probably David went too far in his words, and it is well that the Lord did not hold him to the letter of his bond but accepted the will for the deed and the meaning of his promise instead of the literal sense of it. David imitated Jacob, that great maker of vows at Bethel, and upon him rested the blessing pronounced on Jacob by Isaac, "God Almighty bless thee" (Genesis 28:3), which was remembered by the patriarch Jacob on his deathbed when he spoke of "the mighty God of Jacob" [Genesis 49:24]. God is mighty to hear us and to help us in performing our vow. We should be full of awe at the idea of making any promise to "the mighty God"; to dare to trifle with him would be grievous indeed.

Affliction led both David and Jacob into covenant dealings with the Lord; many vows are made in anguish of soul. We may also remark that if the votive obligations of David are to be remembered by the Lord, much more are the suretyship engagements of the Lord Jesus before the mind of the great God, to whom our soul turns in the hour of our distress.

Verses to meditate upon today: Psalm 132:1-9.

A THOUGHT TO PONDER
We should be full of awe at the idea of making any
promise to "the mighty God."

God's Chosen City

For the LORD hath chosen Zion; he hath desired it for his habitation.
PSALM 132:13

VERSE 13: "For the LORD hath chosen Zion." It was no more than any other Canaanite town till God chose it, David captured it, Solomon built it, and the Lord dwelt in it. So was the church a mere Jebusite stronghold till grace chose it, conquered it, rebuilt it, and dwelt in it. Jehovah has chosen his people, and hence they are his people. He has chosen the church, and hence it is what it is. Thus in the covenant David and Zion, and Christ and his people, go together. David is for Zion, and Zion for David; the interests of Christ and his people are mutual.

"He hath desired it for his habitation." The Lord has spoken; the site of the temple is fixed; the place of the divine manifestation is determined. Indwelling follows upon election and arises out of it. Zion is chosen for a habitation of God.

The desire of God to dwell among the people whom he has chosen for himself is very gracious and yet very natural; his love will not rest apart from those upon whom he has placed it. God desires to abide with those whom he has loved with an everlasting love, and we do not wonder that it should be so, for we also desire the company of our beloved ones. It is a double marvel that the Lord should choose and desire such poor creatures as we are. The indwelling of the Holy Spirit in believers is a wonder of grace parallel to the incarnation of the Son of God. God in the church is the wonder of heaven, the miracle of eternity, the glory of infinite love.

VERSE 14: "This is my rest for ever." Oh, glorious words! It is God himself who here speaks. Think of "rest" for God! A Sabbath for the Eternal and a place of abiding for the Infinite. He calls Zion "my rest." Here his love remains and displays itself with delight.

Verses to meditate upon today: Psalm 132:10-18.

A THOUGHT TO PONDER
*So was the church a mere Jebusite stronghold till grace chose it,
conquered it, rebuilt it, and dwelt in it.*

CHRISTIAN UNITY

Behold, how good and how pleasant it is for brethren to dwell together in unity!
PSALM 133:1

VERSE 1: "Behold." This is a wonder seldom seen, therefore "behold" it. It may be seen, for it is the characteristic of real saints; therefore fail not to inspect it. It is well worthy of admiration; pause and gaze upon it. It will charm you into imitation; therefore note it well. God looks on with approval; therefore consider it with attention.

"How good and how pleasant it is for brethren to dwell together in unity!" No one can tell the exceeding excellence of such a condition; so the psalmist uses the word "how" twice—"Behold how good and how pleasant . . . !" He does not attempt to measure either the "good" or the pleasure but invites us to "behold" it for ourselves.

The combination of the two adjectives "good" and "pleasant" is more remarkable than the conjunction of two stars of the first magnitude; for a thing to be "good" is good, but for it also to be "pleasant" is better. All men love pleasant things, and yet it frequently happens that the pleasure is evil; but here the condition is as "good" as it is "pleasant," and as "pleasant" as it is "good," for the same "how" is set before each qualifying word.

For "brethren" according to the flesh to dwell together is not always wise; for experience teaches that they are better a little apart, and it is shameful for them to dwell together in disunion. They had much better part in peace like Abraham and Lot than dwell together in envy like Joseph's brothers. But when "brethren" can and do "dwell together in unity," then is their communion worthy to be gazed upon and sung of in holy psalmody. Such sights ought often to be seen among those who are near of kin, for they are "brethren" and therefore should be united in heart and aim.

Verses to meditate upon today: Psalm 133:1-3.

A THOUGHT TO PONDER
When "brethren" can and do "dwell together in unity," then is their communion worthy to be sung of in holy psalmody.

DECEMBER 1

BLESS THE LORD

Behold, bless ye the LORD, all ye servants of the LORD, which by night stand in the house of the LORD.

PSALM 134:1

VERSE 1: "Behold." By this call the pilgrims request the attention of the night watch. They shout to them, "Behold!" The retiring pilgrims stir up the holy brotherhood of those who are appointed to keep "the watch of the house of the LORD." Let them look around them upon the holy place and everywhere "behold" reasons for sacred praise. Let them look above them at night and magnify him who made heaven and earth and lighted the one with stars and the other with his love. Let them see to it that their hallelujahs never come to an end. Their departing brethren arouse them with the shrill cry of "Behold! Behold!"—see, take care, be on the watch, diligently mind your work, incessantly adore and bless Jehovah's name.

"Bless ye the LORD." Think well of Jehovah, and speak well of him. Adore him with reverence; draw near to him with love; delight in him with exultation. Be not content with the praise that all his works render to him, but as his saints, see that you "bless" him. He blesses you; therefore be zealous to "bless" him.

The word "bless" is the characteristic word of this Psalm. The first two verses stir us up to "bless" Jehovah, and in the last verse Jehovah's blessing is invoked upon the people. Oh, to abound in blessing! May *blessed* and *blessing* be the two words that describe our lives. Let others flatter their fellows or bless their stars or praise themselves; as for us, we will "bless" Jehovah, from whom all blessings flow.

"All ye servants of the LORD." It is your office to "bless" him; take care that you lead the way therein. Servants should speak well of their masters. Not one of you should serve God out of compulsion, but all should "bless" him while you serve him; yea, "bless" him for permitting you to serve him, fitting you to serve him, and accepting your service.

Verses to meditate upon today: Psalm 134:1-3.

A THOUGHT TO PONDER

Think well of Jehovah, and speak well of him.

DECEMBER 2

GOD'S SPECIAL TREASURE

Ye that stand in the house of the LORD, in the courts of the house of our God.
PSALM 135:2

VERSE 2: You are highly favored; you are the servants of the palace, nearest to the Father of the heavenly family, privileged to find your home in his "house"; therefore you must, beyond all others, abound in thanksgiving.

You "stand" or abide in the temple; you are constant occupants of its various "courts"; and therefore from you is expected unceasing praise. Should not ministers be commended for celebrating the praises of Jehovah? Should not church officers and church members excel all others in the excellent duty of adoration? Should not all of every degree who wait even in his outer "courts" unite in his worship? Ought not the least and feeblest of his people to proclaim his praises, in company with those who live nearest to him? Is it not a proper thing to remind them of their obligations? Is not the psalmist wise when he does so in this case and in many others?

Those who can call Jehovah "our God" are highly blessed and therefore should abound in the work of blessing him. Perhaps these are the sweetest words in these first two verses. This God is "our God" forever and ever. "Our God" signifies communion in possession, assurance of possession, delight in possession. Oh, the unutterable joy of calling God our own!

VERSE 3: "Praise the LORD." Do it again; continue to do it; do it better and more heartily; do it in growing numbers; do it at once. There are good reasons for praising the Lord, and among the first is this—"for the LORD is good." He is so "good" that there is none good in the same sense or degree. He is so "good" that all good is found in him, flows from him, and is rewarded by him. The word *God* is brief for *good*; and truly God is the essence of goodness. Should not his goodness be well spoken of? Yea, with our best thoughts and words and hymns let us glorify his name.

Verses to meditate upon today: Psalm 135:1-7.

A THOUGHT TO PONDER

You are highly favored, nearest to the Father of the heavenly family.

DECEMBER 3

EGYPT

Who smote the firstborn of Egypt, both of man and beast.
PSALM 135:8

VERSE 8: Herein the Lord is to be praised, for this deadly smiting was an act of justice against "Egypt" and of love to Israel. But what a blow it was! All "the firstborn" slain in a moment! How this must have horrified the nation and cowed the boldest enemies of Israel! Beasts because of their relationship to man as domestic animals are in many ways made to suffer with him. The "firstborn" of beasts must die as well as the "firstborn" of their owners, for the blow was meant to astound and overwhelm, and it accomplished its purpose. The firstborn of God had been sorely smitten, and they were set free by the Lord's meting out to their oppressors the like treatment.

VERSE 9: "Who sent tokens and wonders into the midst of thee, O Egypt, upon Pharaoh, and upon all his servants." The Lord is still seen by the psalmist as sending judgments upon rebellious men; he keeps before us the personal action of God, "who sent tokens," etc. The more distinctly God is seen, the better.

Even in plagues he is to be seen, as truly as in mercies. The plagues were not only terrible "wonders" that astounded men, but forcible "tokens" or signs by which they were instructed. No doubt the plagues were aimed at the various deities of the Egyptians and were a grand exposure of their impotence; each one had its own special significance. The judgments of the Lord were no side blows; they struck the nation at the heart—he sent his bolts "into the midst of thee, O Egypt." These marvels happened in the center of the proud and exclusive nation of Egypt, which thought itself far superior to other lands; many of these plagues touched the nation in points upon which it prided itself.

The psalmist addresses that haughty nation, saying, "O Egypt," as though reminding it of the lessons it had been taught by the Lord's right hand.

Verses to meditate upon today: Psalm 135:8-14.

A THOUGHT TO PONDER

No doubt the plagues were aimed at the various deities of the Egyptians and were a grand exposure of their impotence.

DECEMBER 4

IDOLS OF GOLD AND SILVER

The idols of the heathen are silver and gold, the work of men's hands.
PSALM 135:15

VERSE 15: Idols' essential material is dead metal; their attributes are but the qualities of senseless substances, and whatever form and fashion they exhibit they derive from the skill and labor of those who worship them. It is the height of insanity to worship metallic manufactures. Though "silver and gold" are useful to us when we rightly employ them, there is nothing about them that can entitle them to reverence and worship.

If we did not know the sorrowful fact to be indisputable, it would seem to be impossible that intelligent beings could bow down before substances that they must themselves refine from ore and fashion into form. One would think it less absurd to worship one's own hands than to adore that which those hands have made. What great works can these mock deities perform for man when they are themselves the works of man? "Idols" are fitter to be played with, like dolls by babes, than to be adored by grown-up men. Hands are better used in breaking than in making objects that can be put to such an idiotic use. Yet "the heathen" love their abominable deities better than "silver and gold"; it would be well if we could say that some professed believers in the Lord had as much love for him.

VERSE 16: "They have mouths," for their makers fashioned them like themselves. An opening is made where the mouth should be, and yet it is no mouth, for they eat not, and "they speak not." They cannot communicate with their worshipers; they are as mute as death. Jehovah speaks, and it is done; but these images utter never a word. Surely, if they could speak, they would rebuke their worshipers. Is not their silence a still more powerful rebuke? When our philosophical teachers deny that God has made any verbal revelation of himself, they also confess that their god is dumb.

Verses to meditate upon today: Psalm 135:15-21.

A THOUGHT TO PONDER
It is the height of insanity to worship metallic manufactures.

DECEMBER 5

ENDURING MERCY

O give thanks unto the LORD; for he is good: for his mercy endureth for ever.
PSALM 136:1

VERSE 1: "O give thanks unto the LORD." This exhortation is intensely earnest: The psalmist pleads with the Lord's people with an "O," three times repeated [verses 1-3]. "Thanks" are the least that we can offer, and these we ought freely to "give." The inspired writer calls us to praise Jehovah for all his goodness to us and for all the greatness of his power in blessing his chosen. We thank our parents—let us praise our heavenly Father; we are grateful to our benefactors—let us give thanks unto the Giver of all good.

"For he is good." Essentially he is goodness itself. Practically, all that he does is "good"; relatively, he is "good" to his creatures. Let us thank him that we have seen, proved, and tasted that "he is good." He is "good" beyond all others. Indeed, he alone is "good" in the highest sense; he is the source of good, the good of all good, the sustainer of good, the perfecter of good, and the rewarder of good. For this he deserves the constant gratitude of his people.

"For his mercy endureth for ever." We shall have this repeated in every verse of this song, but not once too often. It is the sweetest stanza that a man can sing. What joy that there is "mercy," "mercy" with Jehovah, "mercy" enduring forever. We are ever needing it, trying it, praying for it, receiving it; therefore let us forever sing of it.

When all else is changing within and around,
In God and his mercy no change can be found.

VERSE 2: "O give thanks unto the God of gods." If there be powers in heaven or on earth worthy of the name of "gods," he is "the God" of them. From him their dominion comes; their authority is derived from him, and their very existence is dependent upon his will.

Verses to meditate upon today: Psalm 136:1-9.

A THOUGHT TO PONDER
We are ever needing mercy, trying it, praying for it, receiving it;
therefore let us forever sing of it.

DECEMBER 6

WITH A STRONG HAND

With a strong hand, and with a stretched out arm:
for his mercy endureth for ever.
PSALM 136:12

VERSE 12: "With a strong hand, and with a stretched out arm." Not only the matter but the manner of the Lord's mighty acts should be the cause of our praise. We ought to bless the Lord for adverbs as well as adjectives. In the Exodus the great power and glory of Jehovah were seen. He dashed in pieces the enemy with his right "hand." He led forth his people in no common or clandestine manner. "He brought them forth also with silver and gold: and there was not one feeble person among all their tribes" [Psalm 105:37]. Egypt was glad when they departed.

God worked with great display of force and with exceeding majesty; he "stretched out" his "arm" like a workman intent on his labor; he lifted up his "hand" as one who is not ashamed to be seen. Even thus was it in the deliverance of each one of us from the thralldom of sin: "according to the working of his mighty power, which he wrought in Christ, when he raised him from the dead, and set him at his own right hand in the heavenly places" [Ephesians 1:20].

"For his mercy endureth for ever"; therefore his power is put forth for the rescue of his own. If one plague will not set them free, there shall be ten. But free they shall all be at the appointed hour; not one Israelite shall remain under Pharaoh's power. God will not only use his "hand" but his "arm"; his extraordinary power shall be put to work sooner than his purpose of mercy shall fail.

VERSE 13: "To him which divided the Red sea into parts." He made a road across the sea bottom, causing the divided waters to stand like walls on either side. Men deny miracles; but granted that there is a God, they become easy to believe. Since I must be an atheist to logically reject miracles, I prefer the far smaller difficulty of believing in the infinite power of God.

Verses to meditate upon today: Psalm 136:10-21.

A THOUGHT TO PONDER

In the Exodus the great power and glory of Jehovah were seen.

DECEMBER 7

REDEEMED

And hath redeemed us from our enemies: for his mercy endureth for ever.
PSALM 136:24

VERSE 24: "And hath redeemed us from our enemies." Israel's "enemies" brought the people low; but the Lord intervened and turned the tables by a great redemption. This expression implies that they had become like slaves and were not set free without price and power, for they needed to be "redeemed." In our case the redemption that is in Christ Jesus is an eminent reason for giving thanks unto the Lord. Sin is our enemy, and we are "redeemed" from it by the atoning blood; Satan is our enemy, and we are "redeemed" from him by the Redeemer's power; the world is our enemy, and we are "redeemed" from it by the Holy Spirit. We are ransomed—let us enjoy our liberty; Christ has wrought our redemption—let us praise his name.

"For his mercy endureth for ever." Even to redemption by the death of God's Son did divine "mercy" stretch itself. What more can be desired? What more can be imagined? Many waters could not quench love, neither could the floods drown it.

VERSE 25: "Who giveth food to all flesh." Common providence, which cares for all living things, deserves our most devout thanks. If we think of heavenly "food," by which all saints are supplied, our praises rise to a still greater height; meanwhile the universal goodness of God in feeding all his creatures is as worthy of praise as his special favors to the elect nation. Because the Lord feeds all life, therefore we expect him to take special care of his own family.

"For his mercy endureth for ever." Reaching downward even to beasts and reptiles, this is, indeed, a boundless "mercy" that knows no limit because of the shabbiness of its object.

VERSE 26: "O give thanks unto the God of heaven." This title is full of honor. The Lord is "God" in the highest realms and among celestial beings. His throne is set in glory, above all, out of reach of foes, in the place of universal oversight.

Verses to meditate upon today: Psalm 136:22-26.

A THOUGHT TO PONDER

The redemption that is in Christ Jesus is an eminent reason for giving thanks unto the Lord.

DECEMBER 8

BY THE RIVERS OF BABYLON

By the rivers of Babylon, there we sat down, yea, we wept, when we remembered Zion.
PSALM 137:1

VERSE 1: "By the rivers of Babylon, there we sat down." Watercourses were abundant in Babylon, wherein were not only natural streams but artificial canals; it was a place of broad rivers and streams. Glad to be away from the noisy streets, the captives sought the riverside, where the flow of the waters seemed to be in sympathy with their tears. It was some slight comfort to be out of the crowd and to have a little breathing room, and therefore they "sat down," as if to rest a while and solace themselves in their sorrow. In little groups they "sat down" and made common lamentation, mingling their memories and their tears.

The "rivers" were well enough, but, alas, they were "the rivers of *Babylon*," and the ground whereon the sons of Israel sat was foreign soil, and therefore they "wept." Those who came to interrupt their quiet were citizens of the destroying city, and their company was not desired. Everything reminded Israel of her banishment from the holy city, her servitude beneath the shadow of the temple of Bel, her helplessness under a cruel enemy; and therefore her sons and daughters "sat down" in sorrow.

"Yea, we wept, when we remembered Zion." Nothing else could have subdued their brave spirits; but the remembrance of the temple of their God, the palace of their king, and the center of their national life quite broke them down. Destruction had swept down all their delights, and therefore they "wept." The strong men "wept"; the sweet singers "wept." They did not weep when they remembered the cruelties of "Babylon"; the memory of fierce oppression dried their tears and made their hearts burn with wrath. But when the beloved city of their solemnities came into their minds, they could not refrain from floods of tears. Even thus do true believers mourn when they see the church despoiled and find themselves unable to succor her. We could bear anything better than this.

Verses to meditate upon today: Psalm 137:1-9.

A THOUGHT TO PONDER

The ground whereon the sons of Israel sat was foreign soil, and therefore they "wept."

DECEMBER 9

I WILL WORSHIP

I will worship toward thy holy temple, and praise thy name for thy loving-kindness and for thy truth: for thou hast magnified thy word above all thy name.

PSALM 138:2

VERSE 2: "I will worship toward thy holy temple," or the place of God's dwelling, where the ark abode. He would "worship" God in God's own way. The Lord had ordained a center of unity, a place of sacrifice, a house of his indwelling; and David accepted the way of worship enjoined by revelation. Even so, the true-hearted believer of these days must not fall into the will-worship of superstition or the wild worship of skepticism but must reverently worship as the Lord himself prescribes. The idol gods had their temples; but David averts his glance from them and looks earnestly to the spot chosen by the Lord for his own sanctuary. We are not only to adore the true God, but to do so in his own appointed way. The Jew looked to the "temple"; we are to look to Jesus, the living temple of the Godhead.

"And praise thy name for thy loving-kindness and for thy truth." Praise would be the main part of David's worship, the "name" or character of God the great object of his song, and the special point of his praise the grace and "truth" that shone so conspicuously in that "name." The person of Jesus is the temple of the Godhead, and therein we behold the glory of the Father, "full of grace and truth" [John 1:14].

It is upon these two points that the "name" of Jehovah is at this time assailed—his grace and his "truth." He is said to be too stern, too terrible, and therefore modern thought displaces the God of Abraham, Isaac, and Jacob and sets up an effeminate deity of its own making. As for us, we firmly believe that God is love and that in the summing up of all things it will be seen that hell itself is not inconsistent with the beneficence of Jehovah but is indeed a necessary part of his moral government now that sin has intruded into the universe.

Verses to meditate upon today: Psalm 138:1-8.

A THOUGHT TO PONDER

We are not only to adore the true God, but to do so in his own appointed way.

SUCH KNOWLEDGE

Such knowledge is too wonderful for me; it is high, I cannot attain unto it.
PSALM 139:6

VERSE 6: "Such knowledge is too wonderful for me." I cannot grasp the omniscience of God. I can hardly endure to think of it. The theme overwhelms me. I am amazed and astounded at it. "Such knowledge" not only surpasses my comprehension but even my imagination.

"It is high, I cannot attain unto it." Mount as I may, this truth is too lofty for my mind. It seems to be always above me, even when I soar into the loftiest regions of spiritual thought. Is it not so with every attribute of God? Can we attain to any idea of his power, his wisdom, his holiness? Our mind has no line with which to measure the Infinite. Do we therefore question? Say, rather, that we therefore believe and adore. We are not surprised that the Most Glorious God should in his knowledge be "high" above all the knowledge to which we can attain. It must of necessity be so since we are such poor, limited beings; even when we stand on tiptoe we cannot reach to the lowest step of the throne of the Eternal.

VERSE 7: Here omnipresence is the theme, a truth to which omniscience naturally leads.

"Whither shall I go from thy Spirit?" Not that the psalmist wished to go away from God or to avoid the power of the divine life; but he asks this question to set forth the fact that no one can escape from the all-pervading being and observation of the Great Invisible Spirit. Observe how the writer makes the matter personal to himself: "Whither shall *I* go?" It would be well if we all thus applied truth to our own cases. It would be wise for each one to say, "The Spirit of the Lord is ever around *me:* Jehovah is omnipresent *to me.*"

"Or whither shall I flee from thy presence?" Go from him or "flee" from him we cannot; neither by patient travel nor by hasty flight can we withdraw from the all-surrounding Deity.

Verses to meditate upon today: Psalm 139:1-10.

A THOUGHT TO PONDER
Even when we stand on tiptoe we cannot reach to the lowest step of the throne of the Eternal.

DECEMBER 11

THE NIGHT WILL BE LIGHT

*Yea, the darkness hideth not from thee; but the night shineth as the day:
the darkness and the light are both alike to thee.*

PSALM 139:12

VERSE 12: "Yea"; of a surety, beyond all denial. "The darkness hideth not from thee." It veils nothing; it is not the medium of concealment in any degree whatever. It hides from men but not from God.

"But the night shineth as the day." It is but another form of "day." It shines, revealing all; it "shineth as the day," just as clearly and distinctly manifesting all that is done.

"The darkness and the light are both alike to thee." This sentence seems to sum up all that went before and most emphatically puts the negative upon the faintest idea of hiding under the cover of "night." Men cling to this notion because it is easier and less expensive to hide under "darkness" than to journey to remote places; and therefore this foolish thought is here beaten to pieces by statements that in their varied forms effectually batter it.

Yet the ungodly are still duped by their groveling notions of God and inquire, "How does God know?" They must fancy that he is as limited in his powers of observation as they are, and yet if they would but consider for a moment, they would conclude that he who could not see in the dark could not be God, and he who is not present everywhere could not be the Almighty Creator. Assuredly God is in all places at all times, and nothing can by any possibility be kept from his all-observing, all-comprehending mind.

The Great Spirit comprehends within himself all time and space, and yet he is infinitely greater than these and all else that he has made.

VERSE 13: "For thou hast possessed my reins." *You are the owner of my inmost parts and passions—not the indweller and observer only, but the acknowledged Lord and possessor of my most secret self.*

Verses to meditate upon today: Psalm 139:11-16.

A THOUGHT TO PONDER

*God is in all places at all times, and nothing can be kept from his
all-observing, all-comprehending mind.*

DECEMBER 12

GOD'S THOUGHTS

How precious also are thy thoughts unto me, O God! How great is the sum of them!
PSALM 139:17

VERSE 17: "How precious also are thy thoughts unto me, O God!" The psalmist is not alarmed at the fact that God knows all about him; on the contrary, he is comforted, and even feels himself to be enriched, as with a chest of precious jewels. That God should think upon him is the believer's treasure and pleasure. He cries, "How costly, how valued are your thoughts, how dear to me is your perpetual attention!" He thinks upon God's thoughts with delight; the more of them, the better is he pleased. It is a joy worth worlds that the Lord should think upon us who are so poor and needy; it is a joy that fills our whole nature to think upon God, returning love for love, thought for thought after our poor fashion.

When we remember that God thought upon us from eternity, continues to think upon us every moment, and will think of us when time shall be no more, we may well exclaim, "How great is the sum of them!"

Thoughts such as are natural to the Creator, the Preserver, the Redeemer, the Father, the Friend are evermore flowing from the heart of the Lord. Thoughts of our pardon, renewal, upholding, supplying, educating, perfecting, and a thousand more marvels perpetually well up in the mind of the Most High. It should fill us with adoring wonder and reverent surprise that the infinite mind of God should turn so many "thoughts" toward us who are so insignificant and so unworthy! What a contrast is all this to the notion of those who deny the existence of a personal, conscious God! Imagine a world without a thinking, personal God! Conceive of a grim providence of machinery, a fatherhood of law! Such philosophy is hard and cold. As well might a man pillow his head upon a razor's edge as to seek rest in such a fancy.

Verses to meditate upon today: Psalm 139:17-24.

A THOUGHT TO PONDER

It should fill us with adoring wonder and reverent surprise that the infinite mind of God should turn so many "thoughts" toward us who are so insignificant and so unworthy!

DECEMBER 13

KEEP ME

Keep me, O LORD, from the hands of the wicked; preserve me from the violent man; who have purposed to overthrow my goings.
PSALM 140:4

VERSE 4: "Keep me, O LORD, from the hands of the wicked." To fall into their hands would be a calamity indeed. David in his most pitiable plight chose to fall into the hand of a chastising God rather than to be left in the power of men. No creature among the wild beasts of the wood is so terrible an enemy to man as man himself when guided by evil and impelled by violence.

The Lord by providence and grace can keep us out of the power of "the wicked." He alone can do this, for neither our own watchfulness nor the faithfulness of friends can secure us against the serpentine assaults of the foe. We have need to be preserved from the smooth as well as the rough hands of the ungodly, for their flatteries may harm us as much as their slanders. The hands of their example may pollute us and so do us more harm than the hands of their oppression. Jehovah must be our keeper, or evil hands will do what evil hearts have imagined and evil lips have threatened.

"Preserve me from the violent man." His intense passion makes him terribly dangerous. He will strike in any way, use any weapon, smite from any quarter. He is so furious that he is reckless of his own life if he can accomplish his detestable design. *Lord, preserve us by your omnipotence when men attack us with their violence.* This prayer is a wise and suitable one.

"Who have purposed to overthrow my goings." They resolve to turn the good man from his resolve; they would defeat his designs, injure his integrity, and blast his character. Their own goings are "wicked," and therefore they hate those of the righteous, seeing they are a standing rebuke to them.

Verses to meditate upon today: Psalm 140:1-8.

A THOUGHT TO PONDER
Jehovah must be our keeper, or evil hands will do what evil hearts have imagined and evil lips have threatened.

DECEMBER 14

SURROUNDED BY ENEMIES

As for the head of those that compass me about, let the mischief of their own lips cover them.
PSALM 140:9

VERSE 9: To the Lord who had covered the psalmist's head amid the din of arms, David appeals against his foes, that their heads may be covered in quite another sense—covered with the reward of their own malice. David's foes were so many that they hemmed him in, encircling him as hunters do their prey. It is little wonder that he turns to the Lord in his dire need.

The poet represents his adversaries as so united as to have but one "head," for there is often a unanimity among evil spirits that makes them the more strong and terrible for their vile purposes. The *lex talionis*, or law of retaliation, often brings down upon violent men the evil that they planned and spoke of for others; their arrows fall upon themselves. When a man's lips vent curses, they will probably, like chickens, come home to roost. A stone hurled upward into the air is apt to fall upon the thrower's head.

David's words may be read as a prophecy; but in this verse there is no need to do so in order to soften their tone. It is so just that the mischief that men plot and the slander that they speak should recoil upon themselves that every righteous man must desire it. He who does not desire it may wish to be considered humane and Christlike, but the chances are that he has a sneaking agreement with the wicked or is deficient in a manly sense of right and wrong.

When evil men fall into pits that they have dug for the innocent, we believe that even the angels are glad. Certainly the most gentle and tender philanthropists, however much they pity the sufferers, must also approve the justice that makes them suffer. We suspect that some of our excessively soft-spoken critics only need to be put into David's place, and they would become a vast deal more bitter than he ever was.

Verses to meditate upon today: Psalm 140:9-13.

A THOUGHT TO PONDER
When a man's lips vent curses, they will probably, like chickens, come home to roost.

DECEMBER 15

THE WAY HE SPEAKS

Set a watch, O LORD, before my mouth; keep the door of my lips.
PSALM 141:3

VERSE 3: "Set a watch, O LORD, before my mouth." That "mouth" had been used in prayer; it would be a pity if it should ever be defiled with untruth or pride or wrath. Yet so it will become unless carefully watched, for these intruders are ever lurking about the "door." David feels that even with all his own watchfulness he may be surprised into sin, and so he begs the Lord himself to "keep" him. When Jehovah sets the "watch," the city is well guarded; when the Lord becomes the guard of our "mouth," the whole man is well garrisoned.

"Keep the door of my lips." God has made our "lips" the "door" of the "mouth," but we cannot keep that "door" by ourselves; therefore do we entreat the Lord to take the rule of it. Oh, that the Lord would both open and shut our "lips," for we can do neither the one nor the other aright if left to ourselves. In times of persecution by ungodly men we are peculiarly liable to speak hastily or evasively, and therefore we should be specially anxious to be preserved in that direction from every form of sin. How condescending is the Lord! We are ennobled by being doorkeepers for him, and yet he deigns to be a doorkeeper for us.

Verse 4: "Incline not my heart to any evil thing." This is equivalent to the petition, "Lead us not into temptation." Oh, that nothing may arise in providence that would excite our desires in a wrong direction. The psalmist is here concerned about his "heart." He who holds the "heart" is lord of the man; but if the tongue and the "heart" are under God's care, all is safe. Let us pray that he may never leave us to our own inclinations or we shall soon decline from the right.

"To practise wicked works with men that work iniquity." The way the "heart" inclines, the life soon tends; evil things desired bring forth wicked things practiced.

Verses to meditate upon today: Psalm 141:1-10.

A THOUGHT TO PONDER

*We cannot keep the "door" by ourselves; therefore do we
entreat the Lord to take the rule of it.*

DECEMBER 16

COMPLAINING IN PRAYER

I poured out my complaint before him; I showed before him my trouble.
PSALM 142:2

VERSE 2: "I poured out my complaint before him." The psalmist's inward meditation filled his soul; the bitter water rose up to the brim. What was to be done? He must pour out the wormwood and the gall; he could not keep it in. He lets it run away as best it can, so his heart may be emptied of the fermenting mixture.

But he took care *where* he outpoured his "complaint," lest he should do mischief or receive an ill return. If he poured it out before man, he might only receive contempt from the proud, hard-heartedness from the careless, or pretended sympathy from the false; and therefore he resolved upon an outpouring before God alone, since *he* would pity and relieve. The word is probably not "complaint"; but even if it be so, we may learn from this text that our complaint must never be of a kind that we dare not bring before God. We may complain *to* God, but not *of* God. When we complain, it should not be before men, but before God alone.

"I showed before him my trouble." He exhibited his griefs to one who could assuage them; he did not fall into the mistaken plan of so many who publish their sorrows to those who cannot help them. This verse is parallel with the first. David first pours out his "complaint," letting it flow forth in a natural, spontaneous manner, and then afterwards he makes a more elaborate show of his affliction. As in a former section (Psalm 141:1-10), he began with crying and went on to "make . . . supplication" [142:1]. Praying men pray better as they proceed.

Note that we do not show our trouble before the Lord that *he* may see *it*, but that *we* may see *him*. It is for our relief and not for his information that we make plain statements concerning our woes.

Verses to meditate upon today: Psalm 142:1-7.

A THOUGHT TO PONDER
We do not show our trouble before the Lord that he may see it, but that we may see him.

DECEMBER 17

HEAR MY PRAYER

Hear my prayer, O LORD, give ear to my supplications: in thy faithfulness answer me, and in thy righteousness.

PSALM 143:1

VERSE 1: "Hear my prayer, O LORD, give ear to my supplications." In the preceding psalm David began by declaring that he had "cried unto the LORD"; here he begs to be favorably regarded by Jehovah, the living God. He knew that Jehovah hears prayer, and therefore he entreated him to hear his "supplications," however feeble and broken they might be.

In two forms he implores the one blessing of gracious audience: "hear" and "give ear." Gracious men are so eager to be heard in "prayer" that they double their entreaties for that boon. The psalmist desires to be heard and to be considered; hence he cries, "hear," and then "give ear." Our case is difficult, and we plead for special attention.

Here it is probable that David wished his suit against his adversaries to be heard by the righteous Judge, confident that if he had a hearing in the matter whereof he was slanderously accused, he would be triumphantly acquitted. Observe that he offered so much pleading that his life became one continual "prayer"; but that petitioning was so varied in form that it broke out in many "supplications."

"In thy faithfulness answer me, and in thy righteousness." Saints desire to be answered as well as heard; they long to find the Lord faithful to his promise and righteous in defending the cause of justice. It is a happy thing when we dare appeal even to "righteousness" for our deliverance; and this we can do upon gospel principles, for "if we confess our sins, he is faithful and just to forgive us our sins" [1 John 1:9]. With God's "faithfulness" and "righteousness" at our side, we are guarded on the right hand and on the left. Requests that do not appeal to either of these attributes it would not be for the glory of God to hear, for they must contain desires for things not promised and unrighteous.

Verses to meditate upon today: Psalm 143:1-6.

A THOUGHT TO PONDER

Saints long to find the Lord faithful to his promise and righteous in defending the cause of justice.

TEACH ME

*Teach me to do thy will; for thou art my God: thy Spirit is good;
lead me into the land of uprightness.*
PSALM 143:10

VERSE 10: "Teach me to do thy will." How childlike—"teach me." How practical—"Teach me to do." How undivided in obedience—"to do thy will." *To do all of it, let it be what it may.* This is the best form of instruction, for its source is God, its object is holiness, its spirit is that of hearty loyalty. The man is hidden in the Lord and spends his peaceful life in learning the will of his Preserver. A heart cannot long be desolate that is thus docile.

"For thou art my God." *Who else can teach me as you can? Who else will care to do it but my God? You have given me yourself; you will surely give me purity of teaching. If I have you, may I not ask to have your perfect mind?* When the heart can sincerely call Jehovah "my God," the understanding is ready to learn from him, the will is prepared to obey him, the whole man is eager to please him.

"Thy Spirit is good." God is all spirit and all "good." His essence is goodness, kindness, holiness; it is his nature to do good, and what greater good can he do to us than to hear such a prayer as that which follows—"Lead me into the land of uprightness." David desires to be among the godly, in a land of another sort from that which had cast him out. He sighed for the upland meadows of grace, the tablelands of peace, the fertile plains of communion. He could not reach them by himself; he must be led there. God, who is "good," can best conduct us to the goodly land. There is no inheritance like a portion in the land of promise, the land of precept, the land of perfectness. He who teaches us must put us into reins and must guide and conduct us to his own dwelling place in the country of holiness.

Verses to meditate upon today: Psalm 143:7-12.

A THOUGHT TO PONDER
*When the heart can sincerely call Jehovah "my God,"
the understanding is ready to learn from him, the will is prepared to obey him,
the whole man is eager to please him.*

DECEMBER 19

THE LORD MY STRENGTH

*Blessed be the LORD my strength, which teacheth
my hands to war, and my fingers to fight.*

PSALM 144:1

VERSE 1: "Blessed be the LORD my strength." The psalmist cannot delay the utterance of his gratitude; he bursts at once into a loud note of praise. His best word is given to his best friend—"Blessed be Jehovah." When the heart is in a right state it must praise God—it cannot be restrained; its utterances leap forth as waters forcing their way from a living spring. With all his strength David blesses the God of his "strength." We ought not to receive so great a boon as "strength" to resist evil, to defend truth, and to conquer error without knowing who gave it to us and rendering to him the glory of it. Not only does Jehovah give "strength" to his saints, but he *is* their "strength." The "strength" is made theirs because God is theirs. God is full of power, and he becomes the power of those who trust him. In him our great "strength" lies, and to him be blessings more than we are able to utter.

"Which teacheth my hands to war, and my fingers to fight." The psalmist in the second part of the verse sets forth the Lord as teacher in the arts of war. If we have "strength," we are not much the better unless we have skill also. Untrained force is often an injury to the man who possesses it, and it even becomes a danger to those who are round about him; therefore the psalmist blesses the Lord as much for teaching as for "strength." Let us also bless Jehovah if he has in anything made us efficient. The instruction mentioned was very practical; it was not so much of the brain as of the "hands" and "fingers," for these were the members most needful for conflict.

Verses to meditate upon today: Psalm 144:1-8.

A THOUGHT TO PONDER

With all his strength David blesses the God of his "strength."

A New Song

*I will sing a new song unto thee, O God: upon a psaltery and
an instrument of ten strings will I sing praises unto thee.*
PSALM 144:9

VERSE 9: "I will sing a new song unto thee, O God." Weary of the false, I will adore the true. Fired with fresh enthusiasm, my gratitude shall make a new channel for itself. I will "sing" as others have done, but it shall be "a new song," such as no others have sung. That "song" shall be all and altogether for my God. I will extol none but the Lord, from whom my deliverance has come.

"Upon a psaltery and an instrument of ten strings will I sing praises unto thee." The psalmist's hand should aid his tongue, not as in the case of the wicked, cooperating in deceit; rather his hand should unite with his mouth in truthful praise.

David intended to tune his best instruments as well as to use his best vocal music. The best is all too poor for so great a God, and therefore we must not fall short of our utmost. He meant to use many instruments of music, that by all means he might express his great joy in God. The Old Testament dispensation abounded in types and figures and outward ritual, and therefore music dropped naturally into its place in the worldly sanctuary; but after all, it can do no more than represent praise and assist our expression of it. The real praise is in the heart; the true music is that of the soul.

When music drowns the voice, and artistic skill takes a higher place than hearty singing, it is time that instruments were banished from public worship; but when they are subordinate to the song, as here, it is not for us to prohibit them or condemn those who use them, though we ourselves greatly prefer to do without them, since it seems to us that the utmost simplicity of praise is far more congruous with the spirit of the Gospel than is the pomp of organs.

Verses to meditate upon today: Psalm 144:9-15.

A THOUGHT TO PONDER
The real praise is in the heart; the true music is that of the soul.

DECEMBER 21

EVERY DAY

Every day will I bless thee; and I will praise thy name for ever and ever.
PSALM 145:2

VERSE 2: "Every day will I bless thee." Whatever the character of the day, or of my circumstances and conditions during that day, I will continue to glorify God. If we consider the matter, we will see abundant cause each day for rendering special blessing unto the Lord. All before the day, all in the day, all following the day should constrain us to magnify our God "every day," all the year round. Our love to God is not a matter of holy days; "every day" is alike holy to holy men.

David here comes closer to God than when he said, "I will bless thy name." It is now, "I will bless *thee*." This is the center and kernel of true devotion; we not only admire the Lord's words and works, but himself. Without realizing the personality of God, praise is well nigh impossible; you cannot extol an abstraction.

"And I will praise thy name for ever and ever." He said he would "bless" that name, and now he vows to "praise" it; he will extol the Lord in every sense and way. Eternal worship shall not be without its variations; it will never become monotonous. Heavenly music is not harping upon one string; all strings shall be tuned to one praise.

Observe the personal pronouns here. Four times he says, "I will." Praise is not to be discharged by proxy; there must be your very self in it or there is nothing in it.

VERSE 3: "Great is the LORD, and greatly to be praised." Worship should be somewhat like its object—great praise for a great God. There is no part of Jehovah's greatness that is not worthy of great praise. In some beings greatness is but vastness of evil; in him it is magnificence of goodness. Praise may be said to be great when the song contains great matter, when the hearts producing it are intensely fervent, and when large numbers unite in the grand acclaim.

Verses to meditate upon today: Psalm 145:1-7.

A THOUGHT TO PONDER

Our love to God is not a matter of holy days; "every day" is alike holy to holy men.

DECEMBER 22

THE LORD IS GRACIOUS

The LORD is gracious, and full of compassion; slow to anger, and of great mercy.
PSALM 145:8

VERSE 8: "The LORD is gracious." Was it not in such terms that the Lord revealed himself to Moses? Is not this Jehovah's glory? To all living men he is "gracious," or full of goodness and generosity. He treats creatures with kindness, his subjects with consideration, and his saints with favor. His words and ways, his promises and his gifts, his plans and his postures all manifest his grace or free favor. There is nothing suspicious, hypocritical, morose, tyrannical, or unapproachable in Jehovah; he is condescending and kind.

"And full of compassion." To the suffering, the weak, the despondent, he is very pitiful. He feels for them, and he feels with them—heartily and in a practical manner. Of this pity he is full; so he has "compassion" freely, constantly, deeply, divinely, and effectually—in fullness in a sense not known among men, and this fullness is fragrant sympathy for human misery. If the Lord be "full of compassion," there is in him no forgetfulness or harshness, and none should suspect him of either.

What an ocean of "compassion" there must be since the infinite God is "slow to anger." Even those who refuse his grace share in his long-suffering. When men do not repent but, on the contrary, go from bad to worse, he is "slow" to let his wrath flame forth against them, greatly patient and anxious that the sinner may live. "Charity [love] suffereth long, and is kind" [1 Corinthians 13:4] and "God is love" [1 John 4:8]

"And of great mercy." This is his attitude toward the guilty. When men at last repent, they find pardon awaiting them. Great is their sin, and "great" is God's "mercy"; they need great help, and they have it, though they deserve it not, for he is good to the greatly guilty.

Verses to meditate upon today: Psalm 145:8-13.

A THOUGHT TO PONDER
God treats creatures with kindness, his subjects with
consideration, and his saints with favor.

DECEMBER 23

THE FALLEN UPHELD

The LORD upholdeth all that fall, and raiseth up all those that be bowed down.
PSALM 145:14

VERSE 14: "The LORD upholdeth all that fall." Read this verse in connection with the preceding and admire the unexpected contrast: He who reigns in glorious majesty yet condescends to lift up and hold up those who are apt to "fall." The form of the verb shows that he is always doing this; he is Jehovah upholding. His choice of the fallen, and the falling, as the subjects of his gracious help is specially to be noted.

The fallen of our race, especially fallen women, are shunned by us, and it is peculiar tenderness on the Lord's part that such he looks upon, even those who are at once the chief of sinners and the least regarded of mankind. The falling ones among us are too apt to be pushed down by the strong; their timidity and dependence make them the victims of the proud and domineering. To them also the Lord gives his upholding help. The Lord loves to reverse things—he puts down the lofty and lifts up the lowly.

"And raiseth up all those that be bowed down." Here is another deed of condescension. Many are despondent and cannot lift up their heads in courage or their hearts with comfort; but these he cheers. Some are bent with their daily load, and these he strengthens. Jesus loosed a daughter of Abraham whom Satan had so bound that she was "bowed down" and could by no means lift up herself. In this he proved himself to be the true Son of the Highest. Think of the Infinite bowing to lift up the bowed and stooping to be leaned upon by those who are ready to fall. The two "alls" should not be overlooked; the Lord has a kindly heart toward the whole company of the afflicted.

VERSE 15: "The eyes of all wait upon thee." *They have learned to look to you; it has become their nature to turn to you for all they want.*

Verses to meditate upon today: Psalm 145:14-21.

A THOUGHT TO PONDER
Some are bent with their daily load, and these the Lord strengthens.

DECEMBER 24

WHILE I LIVE

*While I live will I praise the LORD: I will sing praises
unto my God while I have any being.*

PSALM 146:2

VERSE 2: "While I live will I praise the LORD." I shall not live here forever. This mortal life will find a *finis* in death; but while it lasts I will laud the Lord my God. I cannot tell how long or short my life may be; but every hour of it shall be given to the praises of my God. While I live I'll love, and while I breathe I'll bless. It is but for a while, and I will not while that time away in idleness but will consecrate it to that same service that shall occupy eternity. As our life is the gift of God's mercy, it should be used for his glory.

"I will sing praises unto my God while I have any being." When I am no longer a being on earth, I hope to have a higher being in heaven, and there I will not only praise but "*sing* praises." Here I have to sigh and praise, but there I shall only "sing" and praise. "While I have any being" will be a great while, but the whole of it shall be filled up with adoration; for the glorious Jehovah is my God—my own God by covenant and by blood relationship in Christ Jesus. I have no being apart from my God; therefore I will not attempt to enjoy my "being" otherwise than by singing to his honor.

Twice the psalmist says "I will" or "will I." Here first thoughts and second thoughts are alike good. We cannot be too firm in a holy resolve to praise God, for it is the chief end of our living and "being" that we should glorify God and enjoy him forever.

VERSE 3: "Put not your trust in princes." If David is the author, this warning comes from a prince. In any case it comes from the Spirit of the living God. Men are always far too apt to depend upon the great ones of earth and to forget the Great One above.

Verses to meditate upon today: Psalm 146:1-4.

A THOUGHT TO PONDER

*This mortal life will find a finis in death; but while
it lasts I will laud the Lord my God.*

DECEMBER 25

OPENING BLIND EYES

The LORD openeth the eyes of the blind: the LORD raiseth them that are bowed down: the LORD loveth the righteous.
PSALM 146:8

VERSE 8: "The LORD openeth the eyes of the blind." Jesus did this very frequently and hereby proved himself to be Jehovah. He who made the eye can open it, and when he does so, it is to his glory. How often is the mental eye closed in moral night! And who can remove this dreary effect of the Fall but the Almighty God? This miracle of grace he has performed in myriads of cases, and it is in each case a theme for loftiest praise.

"The LORD raiseth them that are bowed down." This also Jesus did literally, thus doing the work peculiar to God. Jehovah consoles the bereaved, cheers the defeated, solaces the despondent, comforts the despairing. Let those who are "bowed" to the ground appeal to him, and he will speedily raise them up.

"The LORD loveth the righteous." He gives to them the love of peace, communion, and reward. Bad kings love the licentious, but Jehovah makes the upright to be his favored ones. This is greatly to his glory. Let those who enjoy the inestimable privilege of his love magnify his name with enthusiastic delight. Loved ones, you must never be absent from his choir! You must never pause from the praise of him whose infinite love has made you what you are.

VERSE 9: "The LORD preserveth the strangers." Many monarchs hunted aliens down or transported them from place to place or left them as outlaws unworthy of the rights of man. But Jehovah made special laws for their shelter within his domain. In this country [England] the stranger was, a little while ago, looked upon as a vagabond, a kind of wild beast to be avoided, if not to be assaulted; and even to this day there are prejudices against foreigners that are contrary to our holy religion. Our God and King is never distant to any of his creatures, and if any are left in a solitary and forlorn condition, he has a special eye to their preservation.

Verses to meditate upon today: Psalm 146:5-10.

A THOUGHT TO PONDER
How often is the mental eye closed in moral night!
And who can remove this dreary effect of the Fall but the Almighty God?

BUILDING JERUSALEM

The LORD doth build up Jerusalem: he gathereth together the outcasts of Israel.

PSALM 147:2

VERSE 2: "The LORD doth build up Jerusalem." God appears both in the material and spiritual world as a Builder and Maker, and therein he is to be praised. His grace, wisdom, and power are all seen in the formation and establishment of the chosen seat of his worship—once a city with material walls, but now a church composed of spiritual stones. The Jews rejoiced in the uprising of their capital from its ruins, and we triumph in the growth of the church from among a godless world.

"He gathereth together the outcasts of Israel," and thus he repairs the waste places and causes the former desolations to be inhabited.

This sentence may relate to Nehemiah and those who returned with him; but there is no reason why it should not with equal fitness be referred to David, who, with his friends, was once an outcast but ere long became the means of building up Jerusalem.

In any case the psalmist ascribes to Jehovah all the blessings enjoyed; the restoration of the city and the restoration of the banished he equally traces to the divine hand. How clearly these ancient believers saw the Lord present, working among them and for them! Spiritually we see the hand of God in the edification of the church and in the ingathering of sinners. What are men under conviction of sin but outcasts from God, from holiness, from heaven, and even from hope? Who could gather them from their dispersions and make citizens of them in Christ Jesus save the Lord our God? This deed of love and power he is constantly performing. Therefore let the song begin at Jerusalem our home, and let every living stone in the spiritual city echo the strain; for it is the Lord who has brought again his banished ones and builded them together in Zion.

Verses to meditate upon today: Psalm 147:1-9.

A THOUGHT TO PONDER

What are men under conviction of sin but outcasts from God?
Who could make citizens of them in Christ Jesus save the Lord our God?

DECEMBER 27

IN FEAR AND IN HOPE

The LORD taketh pleasure in them that fear him, in those that hope in his mercy.
PSALM 147:11

VERSE 11: While the bodily powers give no pleasure to God, spiritual qualities are his delight. He cares most for those emotions that center in himself: The fear that he approves is "fear [of] *him*," and the hope that he accepts is "hope *in his mercy*."

It is a striking thought that God is not only at peace with some kinds of men but even finds solace and joy in their company. Oh, the matchless condescension of the Lord, that he in his greatness should take pleasure in the insignificant creatures of his hand. Who are these favored men in whom Jehovah "taketh pleasure"? Some of them are the least in his family, who have never risen beyond hoping and fearing. Others of them are more fully developed, but still they exhibit a blended character composed of "fear" and "hope." They "fear" God with holy awe and filial reverence, and they also "hope" for forgiveness and blessedness because of the divine "mercy."

As a father takes pleasure in his own children, so does the Lord solace himself in his own beloved ones, whose marks of new birth are "fear" and "hope." They "fear," for they are sinners; they "hope," for God is merciful. They "fear" him, for he is great; they "hope" in him, for he is good. Their "fear" sobers their "hope"; their "hope" brightens their "fear." God takes pleasure in them, both in their trembling and in their rejoicing.

Is there not rich cause for praise in this special feature of the divine character? After all, it is a poor nature that is delighted with brute force; it is a diviner thing to take pleasure in the holy character of those around us. As men may be known by the nature of the things that give them pleasure, so is the Lord known by the blessed fact that he "taketh pleasure" in the righteous, even though that righteousness is as yet in its initial stage of "fear" and "hope."

Verses to meditate upon today: Psalm 147:10-14.

A THOUGHT TO PONDER

They "fear," for they are sinners; they "hope," for God is merciful.

December 28

Snow Like Wool

He giveth snow like wool: he scattereth the hoar frost like ashes.
Psalm 147:16

Verse 16: Here follow instances of the power of God upon the elements. "He giveth snow like wool." As a gift he scatters the "snow," which falls in flakes like fleecy "wool." "Snow" falls softly, covers universally, and clothes warmly, even as "wool" covers the sheep. The most evident resemblance lies in the whiteness of the two substances; but many other likenesses can be seen by the observant eye. It is wise to see God in winter and in distress as well as in summer and prosperity. He who one day feeds us with the finest of the wheat at another time robes us in "snow"; he is the same God in each case, and each form of his operation bestows a gift on men.

"He scattereth the hoar frost like ashes." Here again the psalmist sees God directly and personally at work. As "ashes" powder the earth when men are burning up the foul herbage, and as when men cast "ashes" into the air they cause a singular sort of whiteness in the places where they fall, so also does the "frost." Moreover, excessive cold burns as effectually as great heat, and hence there is an inner as well as an outer likeness between "hoar frost" and "ashes." Let us praise the Lord who condescends to give wings to each flake of "snow." Ours is no absent or inactive deity; he works all things and is everywhere at home.

Verse 17: "He casteth forth his ice like morsels." Such are the crumbs of hail that he "casteth forth," or the crusts of ice that he creates upon the waters. These morsels are "*his* ice," and "he" casts them abroad. The two expressions indicate a very real presence of God in the phenomena of nature.

Verses to meditate upon today: Psalm 147:15-20.

A Thought to Ponder
Ours is no absent or inactive deity; he works all
things and is everywhere at home.

DECEMBER 29

HEAVENS OF HEAVENS

*Praise him, ye heavens of heavens, and ye waters
that be above the heavens.*
PSALM 148:4

VERSE 4: "Praise him, ye heavens of heavens." By "heavens" are meant those most heavenly abodes where the most choice spirits dwell. As with the highest of the highest, the best of the best are to praise the Lord. If we could climb as much above the "heavens" as the "heavens" are above the earth, we could still cry out to all around us, "Praise ye the Lord." There can be none so great and high as to be above praising Jehovah.

"And ye waters that be above the heavens." Let the clouds roll up volumes of adoration. Let the sea above roar, and the fullness thereof, at the presence of Jehovah, the God of Israel. There is a mystery about these supposed reservoirs of water; but let them be what they may, and as they may, they shall give glory to the Lord our God. Let the most unknown and perplexing phenomena take up their parts in the universal praise.

VERSE 5: "Let them praise the name of the LORD: for he commanded, and they were created." The Maker should have honor from his works—they should tell forth *his* praise; and thus they should praise his "name," meaning his character. The name of Jehovah is written legibly upon his works, so that his power, wisdom, goodness, and other attributes are therein made manifest to thoughtful men, and thus his "name" is praised. The highest praise of God is to declare what he is. We can invent nothing that would magnify the Lord; we can never extol him better than by repeating his "name" or describing his character. The Lord is to be extolled as creating all things that exist and as doing so by the simple agency of his word.

Verses to meditate upon today: Psalm 148:1-14.

A THOUGHT TO PONDER
*The Maker should have honor from his works—
they should tell forth his praise.*

DECEMBER 30

THE JOYFUL SAINTS

*Let the saints be joyful in glory:
let them sing aloud upon their beds.*
PSALM 149:5

VERSE 5: "Let the saints be joyful in glory." God has honored them and put a rare "glory" upon them; therefore let them exult therein. Shall those to whom God is their "glory" be cast down and troubled? Nay, let their joy proclaim their honorable estate.

"Let them sing aloud upon their beds." Their exultation should express itself in shouts and songs, for it is not a feeling of which they have any need to be ashamed. That which is so fully justified by fact may well be loudly proclaimed. Even in their quietest moments let them burst into song; when no one hears them, let them "sing aloud" unto God. If confined by sickness, let them rejoice in God. In the night watches let them not lie awake and weep, but like nightingales let them charm the midnight hours. Their shouts are not now for the battlefield, but for the places of their rest: They can peacefully lie down and enjoy the victory with which the Lord has beautified them. Faith wins and sings the victory. What a blessing—to have our "beds" made into thrones, and our times of quietness turned into triumphs!

VERSE 6: "Let the high praises of God be in their mouth, and a two-edged sword in their hand." It seems they are not always on their beds but are ready for deeds of prowess. When called to fight, the meek are very hard to overcome; they are just as steady in conflict as they are steadfast in patience. Besides, their way of fighting is of an extraordinary sort, for they sing to God but keep their swords in their hands. They can do two things at a time; if they do not wield the trowel and the sword, at least they sing and strike.

Verses to meditate upon today: Psalm 149:1-9.

A THOUGHT TO PONDER
Shall those to whom God is their "glory" be cast down and troubled?

DECEMBER 31

EXCELLENT GREATNESS

Praise him for his mighty acts: praise him according to his excellent greatness.
PSALM 150:2

VERSE 2: "Praise him for his mighty acts." Here is a reason for praise. In these deeds of power we see the Lord himself. These doings of his omnipotence are always on behalf of truth and righteousness. His works of creation, providence, and redemption all call for praise; they are "his . . . acts," and his "acts" of might; therefore let him be praised for them.

"Praise him according to his excellent greatness." His being is unlimited, and his praise should correspond therewith. He possesses a multitude or a plenitude of "greatness," and therefore he should be greatly praised. There is nothing little about God, and there is nothing great apart from him. If we were always careful to make our worship fit and appropriate for our great Lord, how much better would we sing! How much more reverently would we adore! Such excellent deeds would have excellent praise.

VERSE 3: "Praise him with the sound of the trumpet." With the loudest, clearest note, call the people together. Make all men to know that we are not ashamed to worship. Summon them with unmistakable sound to bow before their God. The sound of "the trumpet" is associated with the grandest and most solemn events, such as the giving of the law, the proclamation of Jubilee, the coronation of Jewish kings, and the raging of war. It is to be thought of in reference to the coming of our Lord in his second advent and the raising of the dead. If we cannot give voice to this martial instrument, at least let our praise be as decided and bold as if we could give a blast upon the horn. Let us never sound a "trumpet" before us to our own honor, but reserve all our trumpeting for God's glory. When the people have been gathered by the blast of "the trumpet," they then proceed to "praise him with the psaltery and harp." Stringed instruments are to be used as well as those that are rendered vocal by wind. Pleasant notes are to be consecrated as well as more startling sounds.

Verses to meditate upon today: Psalm 150:1-6.

A THOUGHT TO PONDER
There is nothing little about God, and there is nothing great apart from him.

Scripture Index

Genesis
11:4, 7	Nov. 23
15	Sept. 13
26:2-5	Sept. 13
28:3	Nov. 28
28:10-15	Sept. 13
32:29	Sept. 13
49:24	Nov. 28

Exodus
8:19	Oct. 4

Deuteronomy
32:43	Oct. 19
33:2	May 28

1 Samuel
2:9	Nov. 10
2:10	Oct. 28

1 Chronicles
17:1-27	Sept. 30

Nehemiah
9:6	Jan. 13

Job
9:8-9	Jan. 13
38:4	Sept. 7

Psalms
1:1	Jan. 1
1:2	Jan. 1
1:3	Jan. 1
2:1-3	Jan. 2
2:4	Jan. 2
2:5	Jan. 2
2:6	Jan. 2
2:10	Jan. 3
2:11	Jan. 3
2:12	Jan. 3
3:3	Jan. 4
3:4	Jan. 4
4:1	Jan. 5
5:3	Jan. 6
5:7	Jan. 6
5:8	Jan. 7
5:9	Jan. 7
6:2	Jan. 8
6:8	Nov. 4
6:9	Jan. 9
6:10	Jan. 9
7:1	Jan. 10
7:2	Jan. 10
7:11	Jan. 11
7:12	Jan. 11
7:13	Jan. 11
7:14	Jan. 12
7:15	Jan. 12
8:1	Jan. 13
9:1	Jan. 14
9:9	Jan. 15
9:10	Jan. 15
9:13	Jan. 16
9:14	Jan. 16
10:1	Jan. 17
10:15	Jan. 18
10:16-18	Jan. 18
11:4	Jan. 19
12:7	Jan. 20
12:8	Jan. 20
13:1	Jan. 21
14:1	Jan. 22
15:1	Jan. 23
16:7	Jan. 24
16:9	Jan. 25
16:10	Jan. 25
17:8	Jan. 26
17:9	Jan. 26
17:14	Jan. 27
17:15	Jan. 27
18:2	Jan. 28
18:4	Jan. 29

18:16	Jan. 30	30:2	Feb. 28
18:17	Jan. 30	30:11	Feb. 29
18:18	Jan. 30	30:12	Feb. 29
18:19	Jan. 30	31:2	Mar. 1
18:30	Jan. 31	31:3	Mar. 1
18:31	Jan. 31	31:11	Mar. 2
18:46	Feb. 1	31:19	Mar. 3
18:47	Feb. 1	32:7	Mar. 4
19:1	Feb. 2	32:8	Mar. 5
19:7	Feb. 3	32:9	Mar. 5
19:7-9	Feb. 3	33:2	Mar. 6
20:4	Feb. 4	33:3	Mar. 6
20:5	Feb. 4	33:6	Mar. 7
20:7	Feb. 5	33:7	Mar. 7
21:2	Feb. 6	33:12	Mar. 8
21:9	Feb. 7	33:13	Mar. 8
22:1	Feb. 8	34:5	Mar. 9
22:7	Feb. 9	34:6	Mar. 9
22:8	Feb. 9	34:8	Mar. 10
22:17	Feb. 10	34:9	Mar. 10
22:18	Feb. 10	34:18	Mar. 11
22:23	Feb. 11	34:19	Mar. 11
22:24	Feb. 11	35:9	Mar. 12
22:26	Feb. 12	35:10	Mar. 12
22:27	Feb. 12	35:20	Mar. 13
23:1	Feb. 13	35:21	Mar. 13
23:2	Feb. 14	35:26	Mar. 14
23:3	Feb. 15	35:27	Mar. 14
23:4	Feb. 16	36:5	Mar. 15
23:5	Feb. 17	36:6	Mar. 15
23:6	Feb. 17	37:3	Mar. 16
24:1	Feb. 18	37:4	Mar. 16
25:1	Feb. 19	37:7	Mar. 17
25:4	Feb. 19	37:8	Mar. 17
25:15	Feb. 20	37:19	Mar. 18
25:16	Feb. 21	37:20	Mar. 18
25:17	Feb. 21	37:27	Mar. 19
26:2	Feb. 22	37:28	Mar. 19
26:3	Feb. 22	38:4	Mar. 20
26:10	Feb. 23	38:5	Mar. 20
26:11	Feb. 23	38:9	Mar. 21
26:12	Feb. 23	38:10	Mar. 21
27:1	Feb. 24	38:18	Mar. 22
27:4	Feb. 24	38:19	Mar. 22
27:8	Feb. 25	39:4	Mar. 23
27:9	Feb. 25	39:12	Mar. 24
28:8	Feb. 26	40	June 7
28:9	Feb. 26	40:2	Mar. 25
29:9	Feb. 27	40:8	Mar. 26

40:9	Mar. 26	51:15	Apr. 24
40:13	Mar. 27	51:16	Apr. 24
40:14	Mar. 27	52:1	Apr. 25
41:3	Mar. 28	52:2	Apr. 25
41:10	Mar. 29	52:8	Apr. 26
41:11	Mar. 29	52:9	Apr. 26
42:2	Mar. 30	53:1	Apr. 27
42:5	Mar. 31	54	June 1
43:3	Apr. 1	54:4	Apr. 28
44:3	Apr. 2	54:5	Apr. 28
44:4	Apr. 3	55:4	Apr. 29
44:5	Apr. 3	55:5	Apr. 29
44:17	Apr. 4	55:13	Apr. 30
44:18	Apr. 4	55:14	Apr. 30
44:20	Apr. 5	55:16	May 1
44:21	Apr. 5	55:17	May 1
44:22	Apr. 5	55:22	May 2
45:1	Apr. 6	55:23	May 2
45:6	Apr. 7	56:3	May 3
45:7	Apr. 7	56:11	May 4
45:15	Apr. 8	56:12	May 4
45:16	Apr. 8	56:13	May 4
46:1	Jan. 17; Apr. 9	57:3	May 5
46:7	Apr. 10	57:4	May 5
46:8	Apr. 10	57:9	May 6
47:1	Apr. 11	57:10	May 6
47:7	Apr. 12	57:11	May 6
47:8	Apr. 12	58:1	May 7
48:1	Apr. 13	58:2	May 7
48:9	Apr. 14	58:10	May 8
48:10	Apr. 14	58:11	May 8
49:3	Apr. 15	59:5	May 9
49:4	Apr. 15	59:9	May 10
49:7	Apr. 16	59:10	May 10
49:8	Apr. 16	59:16	May 11
49:9	Apr. 16	59:17	May 11
49:15	Apr. 17	60:5	May 12
49:16	Apr. 17	60:7	May 13
50:1	Apr. 18	60:8	May 13
50:2	Apr. 18	61:2	May 14
50:3	Apr. 18	62:2	May 15
50:7	Apr. 19	62:3	May 15
50:7-15	Apr. 19	62:5	May 16
50:16	Apr. 20	63:1	May 17
50:22	Apr. 21	63:8	May 18
50:23	Apr. 21	63:9	May 18
51:2	Apr. 22	64:9	May 19
51:11	Apr. 23	64:10	May 19
51:12	Apr. 23	65:3	May 20

65:4	May 20	73:17	June 16
65:9	May 21	73:18	June 16
66:5	May 22; May 24	73:23	June 17
66:6	May 22	73:24	June 17
66:9	May 23	74:2	June 18
66:10	May 23	75:7	June 19
66:16	May 24	75:8	June 19
67:2	May 25	76:2	June 20
67:3	May 25	76:3	June 20
68:6	May 26	76:4	June 20
68:9	May 27	76:7	June 21
68:10	May 27	76:8	June 21
68:17	May 28	77:1-20	Aug. 9
68:25	May 29	77:3	June 22
68:26	May 29	77:8	June 23
68:28	May 30	77:9	June 23
68:29	May 30	77:12	June 24
68:34	May 31	77:13	June 24
68:35	May 26; May 31	77:16	June 25
69:1	June 1	77:17	June 25
69:6	June 2	77:18	June 25
69:15	June 3	78:1	June 26
69:16	June 3	78:2	June 26
69:20	June 4	78:6	June 27
69:21	June 4	78:7	June 27
69:22	June 5	78:8	June 27
69:23	June 5	78:12	June 28
69:29	June 6; June 7	78:13	June 28
69:30	June 6	78:14	June 28
70	June 7	78:17	June 29
70:4	June 7	78:23	June 30
70:5	June 7	78:24	June 30
71:3	June 8	78:35	July 1
71:4	June 8	78:36	July 1
71:5	June 8	78:40	July 2
71:15	June 9	78:41	July 2
71:19	June 10	78:53	July 3
71:20	June 10	78:54	July 3
72:6	June 11	78:56	July 4
72:12	June 12	78:57	July 4
72:13	June 12	78:68	July 5
72:15	Oct. 24	78:69	July 5
72:17	June 13	78:70	July 5
72:18-19	June 13	79:1	July 6
72:20	June 13	79:3	July 6
73:2	June 14	79:5	July 7
73:3	June 14	79:6	July 7
73:8	June 15	79:7	July 7
73:9	June 15	80:3	July 8

Scripture Index

80:4	July 8	89:14	Aug. 5
80:7	July 9	89:15	Aug. 5
80:8	July 9	89:26	Aug. 6
80:9	July 9	89:27	Aug. 6
80:14	July 10	89:35	Aug. 7
80:15	July 10	89:36	Aug. 7
80:17	July 11	89:38	Aug. 8
80:18	July 11	89:39	Aug. 8
81:1	July 12	89:50	Aug. 9
81:6	July 13	90:4	Aug. 10
81:7	July 13	90:5	Aug. 10
81:12	July 14	90:8	Aug. 11
81:13	July 14	90:14	Aug. 12
81:14	July 14	91:1	Aug. 13
82:1	July 15	91:11	Aug. 14
83:1	July 16	91:14	Aug. 15
83:2	July 16	91:15	Aug. 15
83:3	July 16	92:4	Aug. 16
83:5	July 17	92:5	Aug. 16
83:6	July 17	92:12	Aug. 17
83:7	July 17	92:13	Aug. 17
83:16	July 18	93:2	Aug. 18
83:17	July 18	93:3	Aug. 18
83:18	July 18	94:4	Aug. 19
84:1	July 19	94:12	Aug. 20
84:2	July 19	94:17	Aug. 21
84:3	July 20	94:18	Aug. 21
84:5	July 21	95:1	Aug. 23
84:6	July 21	95:2	Aug. 22
84:10	July 22	95:6	Aug. 23
85:2	July 23	95:7	Aug. 23
85:3	July 23	96:3	Aug. 24
85:10	July 24	96:9	Aug. 25
86:2	July 25	96:10	Aug. 25
86:9	July 26	97:2	Aug. 26
86:10	July 26	98:3	Aug. 27
86:11	July 27	98:4	Aug. 27
87:1	July 28	99:1	Aug. 28
88:1	July 29	99:5	Aug. 28
88:6	July 30	100:3	Aug. 29
88:11	July 31	101:2	Aug. 30
88:12	July 31	102:2	Aug. 31
88:15	Aug. 1	102:6	Sept. 5
89:1	Aug. 2	102:12	Sept. 1
89:5	Aug. 3	102:13	Sept. 1
89:6	Aug. 3	102:19	Sept. 2
89:11	Aug. 4	102:20	Sept. 2
89:12	Aug. 4	102:27	Sept. 3
89:13	Aug. 4	102:28	Sept. 3

103:3	Sept. 4	107:41	Sept. 28
103:5	Sept. 5	107:42	Sept. 28
103:15	Sept. 6	107:43	Sept. 28
103:17	Sept. 6	108:1	Oct. 1
104:1	Sept. 7	108:4	Sept. 29
104:4	Sept. 7	108:5	Sept. 29
104:5	Sept. 7	108:7	Sept. 30
104:14	Sept. 8	109:1	Oct. 1
104:15	Sept. 8	109:2	Oct. 1
104:24	Sept. 9	109:3	Oct. 1
104:28	Sept. 10	109:16	Oct. 2
104:29	Sept. 10	109:22	Oct. 3
104:34	Sept. 11	109:23	Oct. 3
104:35	Sept. 11	109:26	Oct. 4
105:4	Sept. 12	109:27	Oct. 4
105:5	Sept. 12	109:28	Oct. 4
105:9	Sept. 13	110:4	Oct. 5
105:10	Sept. 13	111:4	Oct. 6
105:17	Sept. 14	111:7	Oct. 7
105:26	Sept. 15	111:8	Oct. 7
105:27	Sept. 15	112:1	Oct. 8
105:37	Dec. 6	112:7	Oct. 9
105:42	Sept. 16	112:8	Oct. 9
105:43	Sept. 16	113:3	Oct. 10
105:44	Sept. 16	113:4	Oct. 10
105:45	Sept. 16	113:7	Oct. 11
106:1	Sept. 17	114:6	Oct. 12
106:7	Sept. 18	114:7	Oct. 12
106:19	Sept. 19	114:8	Oct. 12
106:28	Sept. 20	115:3	Oct. 13
106:29	Sept. 20	115:9-11	Oct. 14
106:32	Sept. 21	115:11	Oct. 14
106:33	Sept. 21	115:12	Oct. 14
106:45	Sept. 22	115:16	Oct. 15
106:46	Sept. 22	116:1	Oct. 16
106:47	Sept. 22	116:7	Oct. 17
107:1	Sept. 23	116:15	Oct. 18
107:2	Sept. 23	116:16	Oct. 18
107:13	Sept. 24	117:1	Oct. 19
107:14	Sept. 24	118:2-4	Oct. 20
107:20	Sept. 25	118:4	Oct. 20
107:21	Sept. 25	118:8	Oct. 21
107:29	Sept. 26	118:9	Oct. 21
107:30	Sept. 26	118:14	Oct. 22
107:31	Sept. 26	118:15	Oct. 22
107:32	Sept. 26	118:20	Oct. 23
107:35	Sept. 27	118:21	Oct. 23
107:36	Sept. 27	118:22	Oct. 20
107:40-41	Sept. 28	118:26	Oct. 24

119:2	Oct. 25	129:1	Nov. 25
119:3	Oct. 25	130:1	Nov. 26
119:10	Oct. 26	130:4	Oct. 20
119:18	Oct. 27	131:1	Nov. 27
119:28	Oct. 28	132:2	Nov. 28
119:34	Oct. 29	132:3-5	Nov. 28
119:41	Oct. 30	132:13	Nov. 29
119:50	Oct. 31	132:14	Nov. 29
119:58	Nov. 1	133:1	Nov. 30
119:67	Nov. 2	134:1	Dec. 1
119:74	Nov. 3	135:2	Dec. 2
119:75	Nov. 3	135:3	Dec. 2
119:82	Nov. 4	135:8	Dec. 3
119:89	Nov. 5	135:9	Dec. 3
119:90	Nov. 5	135:15	Dec. 4
119:99	Nov. 6	135:16	Dec. 4
119:105	Nov. 7	136:1	Dec. 5
119:114	Nov. 8	136:1-3	Dec. 5
119:116	Nov. 8	136:2	Dec. 5
119:125	Nov. 9	136:12	Dec. 6
119:133	Nov. 10	136:13	Dec. 6
119:134	Nov. 10	136:24	Dec. 7
119:139	Nov. 11	136:25	Dec. 7
119:140	Nov. 11	136:26	Dec. 7
119:141	Nov. 11	137:1	Dec. 8
119:142	Nov. 11	138:2	Dec. 9
119:146	Nov. 12	139:6	Dec. 10
119:147	Nov. 12	139:7	Dec. 10
119:156	Nov. 13	139:12	Dec. 11
119:164	Nov. 14	139:13	Dec. 11
119:165	Nov. 14	139:17	Dec. 12
119:171	Nov. 15	140:4	Dec. 13
119:172	Nov. 15	140:9	Dec. 14
120:1	Nov. 16	141:1-10	Dec. 16
121:1	Nov. 17	141:3	Dec. 15
121:2	Nov. 17	141:4	Dec. 15
122:2	Nov. 18	142:1	Dec. 16
122:3	Nov. 18	142:2	Dec. 16
123:1	Nov. 19	143:1	Dec. 17
124:4	Nov. 20	143:10	Dec. 18
124:5	Nov. 20	144:1	Dec. 19
125:1-2	Nov. 21	144:9	Dec. 20
125:2	Nov. 21	145:2	Dec. 21
125:3	Nov. 21	145:3	Dec. 21
126:1	Nov. 22	145:8	Dec. 22
126:2	Nov. 22	145:14	Dec. 23
127:1	Nov. 23	145:15	Dec. 23
127:1-2	Nov. 23	146:2	Dec. 24
128:1	Nov. 24	146:3	Dec. 24

146:8	Dec. 25
146:9	Dec. 25
147:2	Dec. 26
147:11	Dec. 27
147:16	Dec. 28
147:17	Dec. 28
148:4	Dec. 29
148:5	Dec. 29
149:5	Dec. 30
149:6	Dec. 30
150:2	Dec. 31
150:3	Dec. 31

Proverbs
25:2	Aug. 26

Song of Solomon
2:16	Aug. 23

Isaiah
11:2-3	Jan. 24
33:24	Sept. 4
49:14-16	Jan. 21
55:3	May 24; Sept. 30
65:22	Aug. 17

Jonah
2:9	Oct. 22

Matthew
5:34	Nov. 28
15:13	Jan. 1

John
1:3	Mar. 7
1:14	Dec. 9
1:16	Oct. 17
7:16	Jan. 24
8:28	Jan. 24
12:49-50	Jan. 24
14:6	Oct. 23
14:18	Oct. 31
21:17	Oct. 16

Acts
27:41	Jan. 17

Romans
8:29	Aug. 6
8:31	Feb. 24
10:17	June 27

1 Corinthians
10:13	Nov. 21
13:4	Dec. 22

Ephesians
1:20	Dec. 6
2:8	Oct. 30
3:14	Aug. 3

2 Timothy
2:12	Oct. 31

Hebrews
1:7	Sept. 7
5:5	Oct. 5
5:7	June 1
12:22	May 28

1 Peter
1:6	Jan. 17

1 John
1:5	Aug. 11
1:9	Dec. 17
4:8	Dec. 22

Revelation
14:3	Aug. 3